MOREHEAD
ON
BIDDING

ALBERT H. MOREHEAD'S CLASSIC BOOK
REVISED AND MODERNIZED BY

RICHARD L. FREY

SIMON AND SCHUSTER
New York

Published by Simon and Schuster
Rockefeller Center, 630 Fifth Avenue
New York, New York 10020

SBN-671-21699-6

Library of Congress Catalog Card Number: 73-21053

Designed by Irving Perkins

Manufactured in the United States of America
Printed by Mahony & Roese, Inc.
Bound by American Book-Stratford Press, Inc.

1 2 3 4 5 6 7 8 9 10

ACKNOWLEDGMENTS

The author gratefully acknowledges assistance received, from time to time, from George L. Bard, Sam Fry, Jr., Paul J. C. Friedlander, Alphonse Moyse, Jr. Alfred Sheinwold, Alan Truscott, and Waldemar von Zedtwitz.

—A.H.M.

ACKNOWLEDGMENTS

CONTENTS

PART II / BIDDING CONVENTIONS

PART III / THE PROCESS OF CARD VALUATION

PART IV / THE THEORY AND STRATEGY OF BIDDING

INTRODUCTION

ALBERT H. MOREHEAD remains the best bridge writer of the long era of contract bridge. I have known them all since the days of Ely Culbertson, whose gifted pen was often guided—if not actually wielded—by Al Morehead, frequently as editor and sometimes as ghost. None could equal his ability to sit down at a typewriter and swiftly, smoothly, and seemingly effortlessly produce a deadline story flawlessly analyzed, witty, clear, and a pleasure to read. He thought in sentences and paragraphs that required no editing and typed them with a two-fingered dexterity so fast and so errorless that it could scarcely be matched by a touch-typist hammering the keyboard with all ten digits flying. I soon discovered that it was hopeless to try to beat him to the waiting teletypists. *The New York Times,* whose bridge reporter and editor he was for more than a quarter century, always got their story first.

So much for his professional skills. These alone would be sufficient to commend to any bridge player reading everything he ever wrote. But what Morehead dared, and in this book did, was to translate the way a bridge expert *thinks* so that the nonexpert could understand and hope to emulate the process.

Regardless of the system they profess, all true experts think along similar lines. Any system, as you know, is merely an attempt to codify this process into rules that may guide the less practiced player toward mechanical approximation of the expert's answer a fair percentage of the time. Most other writers were content to drill their readers in the ways of a system; to explain how the *system* handles the situation. Al Morehead had faith in the power of his readers to understand why experts handle the situation as they do; he gave them the means to produce the right bid in almost every situation.

In this book. Morehead took the ceiling off how much a thoughtful player could learn; he opened the way for you to approximate the expert's skill by understanding the processes that

13

led to the formulation of the "rules" that serve as a bidding guide —but only a general one at best.

In the few years that have passed since Morehead undertook this task, systems may have changed but the processes of expert valuation have not; virtually everything first presented here remains as true today. The task of updating the book was thus doubly enjoyable; it gave me the incentive to read it again, and I found that most revisions were of tense, not of sense.

Some of the conventions in vogue have been altered. A few— indeed a very few—new ideas that have been introduced have been widely accepted. Wherever there has been a change in expert practice or expert preference, the fact has been duly noted. The new conventions have been added; the new ideas are explained. In readying this portion of the book, I have been greatly assisted by Amalya L. Kearse, a brilliant new talent both in the play and in the exposition of the game.

Miss Kearse, a partner in the prestigious law firm of Hughes, Hubbard, and Reed, is a specialist in antitrust and corporate litigation. She has been setting records in two fields: the second woman and the first black to become a partner in a major Wall Street law firm and, the part you won't find in her listing among *Who's Who in American Women,* a bridge partner with an extraordinary accomplishment to her credit in two bridge organizations. She became an almost "instant" Life Master when she won the first three events in which she ever played in the American Bridge Association, in 1972. But she had already set a record by winning a major national championship of the American Contract Bridge League in 1971, and in 1972 she became the first black player ever to hold two major national titles. When she finished her part of the work on this book she said: "I wish I had known Albert Morehead. His book is unique."

Al Morehead, too, was unique. I considered him my best friend, but many others shared that feeling. I had the joy of collaborating with him in many literary ventures for more than twenty years. I always regretted having no part in the original writing of this greatest of bridge books; now I am happy to have made some small contribution to it.

But the book remains almost entirely the work of Albert H.

Morehead. Not only does it blaze a new trail toward your becoming a better player; it provides a rare treat for every bridge
reader.

RICHARD L. FREY

1973

FOREWORD

THIS BOOK is a series of documented essays on aspects of contract bridge bidding as practiced by the principal experts.

Originally I wrote many of these essays for my bridge column in *The New York Times*. They were not intended for republication and did not necessarily form a logical sequence. But I expanded them, shuffled them, rearranged them, and made them fit into the plan of a book that is a connected whole.

Much of what appears in the following pages was written specifically for this book and has never been published before.

I was gratified to find, when I had completed the process of new writing and rearrangement of old material, that the book does constitute a treatise on bidding and yet has not ceased to be a collection of independent essays, each of which can be read without reference to the others.

This is primarily a book on bidding, but there are so many bridge hands in it that the technique of card-playing arises every few pages.

Generally the bidding is approached from the standpoint of the rubber-bridge player, but in most cases the advice given is equally valid for rubber and duplicate bridge and when I speak specifically of duplicate-bridge tactics I always say so.

Parts III and IV discuss subjects that have seldom been touched upon in bridge books and Part III, I believe, is unique.

ALBERT H. MOREHEAD

New York
1964

PART I

STANDARD AMERICAN
BIDDING—
EXPERT STYLE

1

POINT-COUNT VALUATION

BIDDING BEGINS with hand valuation. Perhaps the most surprising development of bridge in the 1950s and 1960s was that expert players in all countries, after more than twenty-five years of disagreement on methods of valuation, almost unanimously adopted the method called the "4,3,2,1 point count."

This means (not that anyone really needs to be told) that each ace in one's hand is counted as 4 points, each king 3, each queen 2, each jack 1.

The following would be called a 10-point hand.

♠ 1062   ♡ J73   ◇ Q84   ♣ AK95

This also is the classic "average hand," for it is the hand—varying only by suits—that every player at the table would hold if one dealt out a new pack of cards without shuffling it.

Since the 4,3,2,1 point count has achieved almost universal acceptance, it will be used in this book to describe the relative strength of each hand cited.

However, the 4,3,2,1 point count as it is presented in bridge books differs in one essential particular from the 4,3,2,1 point count as it is used by experts. To explain the difference one must delve briefly into the history of the bridge science.

ORIGIN AND RISE OF POINT-COUNT BIDDING

In their efforts to educate the average bridge player by substituting rule for reason, bridge authorities have used many different kinds of formula for estimating the strength of a hand.

There have been tables of quick tricks, honor tricks, high-card tricks, primary and secondary tricks. There have been point counts in which the numerical values assigned to the honors have been 7,5,3,2,1 (the "Robertson Rule"), 6,4,3,2,1 (the Reith or New England count), 1½,1,½ (the Winslow count), 3,2,1,½ (the Four Aces count), and the presently popular 4,3,2,1 (the "pitch count"* or Work count, or, as it is now called, the Goren count).

Since no method is entirely accurate, theoretically it matters little which is used. The true process of hand valuation is not simple; it will be the subject of an entire section of this book in later pages. From the standpoint of the bridge teacher and writer, the important thing is that the average player be able to understand and willing to use a particular method.

The 4,3,2,1 count that is now dominant dates back to 1915 or before, and was espoused by some of the most respectable authorities during the 1920s and thereafter, but it never achieved mass acceptance until Charles Goren adopted it in 1949.

The 4,3,2,1 count and other point-count schedules missed out in their earliest years because they were devised only to count the high-card content of a hand. Experts know that every bridge hand's value depends on its distribution as much as on its high cards. If only the original 4,3,2,1 count of high cards were applied, the following hands might seem equivalent:

	1.		2.	
	♠	K Q J	♠	K Q J 10 7 6
	♡	K Q J	♡	K Q J 10 7 6
	◊	7 6 5 3	◊	5
	♣	7 6 5	♣	———

Each hand is worth 12 points in high cards, but No. 1 can hardly be expected to win more than four or five tricks while No. 2 is almost sure to win ten tricks with either spades or hearts as trumps. Such a difference is too great to be tolerated in any method of valuation.

The differential between high-card values and distributional values was reconciled in 1948 when a Toronto insurance actuary named William Anderson, who happened also to be a bridge enthusiast, devised a schedule for equating high-card values with distributional values.

* Because, in the game of auction pitch, these are the respective values of the top honors when won in tricks.

To the high-card points in each hand he proposed that there be added:

> 1 point for each doubleton
> 2 points for each singleton
> 3 points for each void suit

Mr. Anderson offered this method first to the late Ely Culbertson, who at the time had the best-known name among bridge authorities, but Mr. Culbertson was wedded to the honor-trick system of valuation and he turned Mr. Anderson down.

Next Mr. Anderson offered his discovery to Mr. Goren and Mr. Goren proved his manifest destiny by not only accepting the Anderson point-count approach but revising all his books accordingly and basing their future on point-count bidding. No venture in bridge history has ever paid off better.

However, Mr. Goren made several essential modifications that have served further to equate high-card and distributional points.

Going back to the hands shown above, if No. 2 receives the addition of 3 points for the club void and 2 points for the singleton diamond, it will count 17 as against 12 for hand No. 1.

But this still does not suffice to differentiate between a hand that may win only four tricks and a hand that will win ten tricks.

By deducting a point for the "flat" (4-3-3-3) distribution of hand No. 1; another point because the honors in No. 1 are not accompanied by small cards; and a third point because the hand is aceless, these being general principles advocated by Mr. Goren,* one may reduce the value of hand No. 1 to 9 points and move much closer to a count that will express the relative values in the two hands.

QUICK TRICKS

The point-count method has never been all-sufficient, especially when one is measuring requirements for opening bids. When a player makes an opening bid, his partner must be able to rely on

---

* Mr. Goren has now eliminated the deduction of a point for 4-3-3-3 distribution.

POINT-COUNT VALUATION

Before bidding, count the number of points in your hand. High-card points control no-trump bidding; both high-card and distributional points are counted when you bid a suit.

THE NO-TRUMP POINT COUNT

Ace	4	Queen	2
King	3	Jack	1

ADD 1 point if you hold all four aces.
DEDUCT 1 point for an aceless hand, or for king singleton or Q-J doubleton.
These are the only points counted for no-trump opening bids.

POINT COUNT FOR OPENING SUIT BIDS

I. COUNT OF HIGH-CARD POINTS

Same as at no-trump: 4,3,2,1,

(Including 1-point addition for four aces and deduction for an aceless hand, king alone, or Q-J alone.) Also,
ADD 1 point for 100 honors in a suit and 2 points for 150 honors.

II. COUNT OF DISTRIBUTIONAL POINTS

To your high-card point total,

When bidding your own suit, add:
1 point for each doubleton
2 points for each singleton
3 points for each void

For raising partner's suit, add:
1 point for each doubleton
3 points for each singleton
5 points for each void

The extra points for short suits when raising may be added only if you have adequate trump support.
DEDUCT 1 point if you have only three-card trump support, no matter how high (or low) the cards.
DEDUCT 1 point if you have 4-3-3-3 distribution.

The count of a hand is calculated by adding together its high-card and distributional points.

QUICK TRICKS

IF YOU HAVE	COUNT
A-K in the same suit	2 quick tricks
A-Q in the same suit	1½ quick tricks
Ace K-Q in the same suit K-x and K-x	1 quick trick
K-x Q-J-x	½ quick trick

him for some defensive tricks—called quick tricks—and every authority has had to accompany his table of point-count values with a listing of quick tricks. However many points his hand may have, one may not make an opening bid without at least two quick tricks.

The following hand has 13 points, counting 10 in high cards, 2 for the singleton, and 1 for the doubleton; but according to the book rules one should not make an opening bid of one spade on it because it does not have two quick tricks.

♠ Q 10 9 x x x   ♡ K x   ◇ A J x x   ♣ x

The novice and the haphazard bridge player have found the point-count rules useful and even indispensable. Until a person becomes proficient at card playing he does not appreciate distributional values. The point-count method forces him to reckon on his distribution as well as his high cards. Competent authorities have said that the average player bids twice as well today as he did before the 4,3,2,1 method was popularized, and this may even be an understatement.

The honor-trick approach that was used before is too vague to represent the true strength of a hand.

1. ♠ A K x x	2. ♠ A K x x x	3. ♠ A K x x x x
♡ A K x x	♡ A K x x x	♡ A K x x x
◇ A x x	◇ A x	◇ A
♣ x x	♣ x	♣ x

By honor-trick calculation, these three hands are the same. Each has 5 honor tricks. The unthinking player, having been told that 5 honor tricks are required for a forcing two-bid, used to bid two spades indiscriminately on the three hands. The point-count method, adding distributional values to the 18 high-card points in each of the hands, shows No. 1 to have only 19 points—far from enough for a two-bid; No. 2 to have 21 points—not quite enough; and No. 3 to have 22 points—just enough. Therefore the average player will content himself with a one-bid on No. 1 or No. 2 but will make a two-bid on No. 3. This concurs with what the expert would decide to do, but by a different process.

WHERE THE EXPERT APPROACH DIFFERS

As I said before, experts throughout the world have adopted the 4,3,2,1 count—but for high cards only. They have not adopted the distributional count for doubletons, singletons, and voids. They trust to experience and intuition to measure the distributional value of a hand.

When the casual player says "I had 14 points" he has included the distributional points, perhaps a couple of points for a singleton or for two doubletons. When the expert says "I had 14 points" he means he had 14 high-card points. Any distributional values will be mentioned in a qualifying phrase; for example, "I had 14 points and a seven-card suit," or "I had 14 points and good distribution."

The expert also frequently describes his high-card points as "good" points or "bad" points, depending on a number of factors. When he says "I had a good 16," he may mean that his high cards were located in his long suits rather than his short suits, or that they consisted primarily of aces and kings rather than queens and jacks, or that his high cards were bunched within suits rather than scattered, or that his hand was rich in tens and nines. Strictly construed, the expert's method does not conform exactly to any published method; and it should not, because the published methods are not designed for experts.

The expert's appraisal of his values is based on his experience in card playing. His method is more accurate than the point-count method—that is what makes him an expert—but until the casual player achieves similar proficiency in card playing he can do no better than stick to the point-count rules.

For example, most experts would scrap the "rules" and bid one spade on the first hand shown on page 25, but they would not do so if the 10-9 of spades were replaced by two lower spades, or if the high cards were more scattered, or concentrated in the short suits, e.g.:

♠ 10 9 x x x x   ♡ K J   ◇ A x x x   ♣ Q

2

THE OPENING BID

Since contract bridge was first played in 1925, nearly every bid has changed in meaning, but there has been least change in the standards for opening bids.

There have been noticeable trends among the leading players. Around 1930, very light opening bids were fashionable. Then, as increasing numbers of players learned to make trap passes early and come in later with penalty doubles, the trend was to greater conservatism in opening bids. This caused doubling to become less frequent, whereupon bids became lighter again.

In the 1960s, the majority of players arrived at the middle of the road. They now open most hands in which they have 13 or 14 points and a few hands in which they have only 12 points but have a strong major suit. They are flanked by two groups of extremists. One of these groups is called the "open on anything" school. To this group the following hand is an obligatory opening bid (usually one club):

♠ 10 7 6 3   ♡ A 7   ◇ Q J 3   ♣ K J 7 6

At the other extreme we have the followers of the Roth-Stone system, whose watchword is that an opening bid must be "sound" (which means "strong"). Not only would this group pass the hand shown above, it would pass the following hand:

♠ A Q 6 4 2   ♡ A 6 5   ◇ Q 7 4   ♣ 7 4

The middle-of-the-roaders would pass the first of the two hands shown above, partly because it has only 11 points in high cards and partly because it does not have 2 quick tricks; they would bid one spade on the other hand, not necessarily because it has 12 points (remember, they do not count the distributional point accorded by the doubleton) but because it has a rebiddable suit and 2½ quick tricks and the suit is a major suit and is the best suit, spades, and the hand as a whole has 12 points—it all adds up.

To the majority of the experts, quick tricks are very important and especially aces are important. Experience has shown that declarer's side is usually at a disadvantage if it does not have at least two of the four aces. Therefore, an aceless hand is not bid unless it is fairly far above average and has a good suit also. Consider the two following hands, one of which was previously cited:

1.	♠ A Q 6 4 2	2.	♠ K Q 9 6 3
	♡ A 6 5		♡ K J 7
	◇ Q 7 4		◇ Q J 9 7
	♣ 7 4		♣ 6

As mentioned above, most experts will bid one spade on hand No. 1. Most experts will pass originally on hand No. 2. Hand No. 2 seems likely to produce at least one trick more in the play than hand No. 1. By standard valuation methods the two hands are equivalent, each having 12 points in high cards and 13 points net after all distributional additions and subtractions are made. But possession of at least one ace in a borderline hand is essential and possession of two aces in such a hand is always sufficient to sway the decision from a pass to a bid.

The trick-taking power of a hand is none the less important, and between two hands of equivalent high-card content the line is often finally drawn on the basis of "intermediates":

1.	♠ 8 7	2.	♠ 8 7
	♡ K Q 8 4		♡ K Q 8 4
	◇ A Q 5		◇ A Q 5
	♣ Q 8 4 3		♣ Q 10 4 3

These two hands were prepared as a test. Each has 13 points in high cards, which places it on the borderline between biddable and unbiddable hands, by usual expert standards. Each hand has 14 points, counting the spade doubleton, and 2½ quick tricks, and therefore is an obligatory opening bid by the Goren and similar standards based on the point-count method of valuation. The extreme light bidders would not dream of passing either hand, and the Roth-Stone "sound" bidders would not dream of bidding either hand.

Hand No. 1 was offered to ten highly ranked players with the question: "Would you bid this hand as dealer?" Seven of them would not.

Hand No. 2 was offered to ten different but equally high-ranking players with the same question, and nine of the ten would bid it.

None of the twenty experts to whom the hand was offered can be placed in either extremist group. The two hands differ only in that No. 2 has the club ten instead of the club eight. This may be some indication of how important a couple of spots can be.

THE FIVE-CARD MAJOR

Even more than between the light bidders and the sound bidders, there is a cleavage between those who will open the bidding in a four-card major suit and those who will not open the bidding in a major suit unless it has at least five cards.

The doctrine of the five-card major suit goes far back in bridge history. Geoffrey Mott-Smith was the first to advance it and he made virtually a religion of it. In a 1927 book he proposed bidding first in a five-card major ahead of any longer minor suit—presumably, even an eight-card minor suit—and he proposed the principle that an opening bid in a major suit would always guarantee at least a five-card suit and an opening bid in a minor suit would deny a five-card major.

At the other end of the seesaw sit a vast majority of the expert players, in addition to nearly all the lesser players, who would rather bid one club than one spade on the following hand:

♠ A J 10 6 3   ♡ 7 2   ◊ 8   ♣ A K 7 5 2

The object in bidding one club on this hand is to keep the bidding low as long as possible. It is to be expected that partner's response to the one-club bid will be one diamond or one heart.

The opening bidder can then bid one spade and show both his suits at the lowest possible level.

However, a player would also have bid one club and rebid one spade on the following hand:

♠ A J 10 6   ♡ 7 2   ◇ 8 3   ♣ A K 7 5 2

Then how is his partner to know when he has a five-card major suit?

There is a large and strong segment of America's best tournament- and rubber-bridge players today that never open the bidding in a major suit without a five-card or longer suit. The principal systems in which this is established policy are the Roth-Stone and Kaplan-Sheinwold systems.

It is true that often it is comforting for a player to know his partner's major suit is at least five cards long. Packing this extra information into the opening bid may give the opening bidder a chance to show something extra when otherwise he would be showing that his suit is rebiddable (if it is) and the responding player may raise with three trumps and occasionally with a high doubleton such as Q-x or even J-x without waiting for a rebid of the suit. Nevertheless the majority of the very high-ranking players in all countries, and especially those whose careers go back thirty-five years or more, have continued to make opening bids on four-card major suits.

Howard Schenken, who undoubtedly has more votes than any other person as the best bridge player of all time, summed up the disadvantages of the five-card major suit requirement in an interview published in *The Bridge World* in November, 1960.

Mr. Schenken mentioned the fact that if you may not bid a four-card major suit, often you must open in a weak minor suit. This makes it easier for your opponents to overcall, because your left-hand opponent may be able to overcall at the one-level when he would not be strong enough to overcall at the two-level. The bidding may be so high when it comes around to you again that you never get a chance to show your four-card major. And (quoting Mr. Schenken) "you lose the advantage of having your best suit led against opposing contracts."

In choosing the suit to bid on any borderline hand there are two factors to be kept in mind. First, the hand must provide a safe rebid if partner bids a new suit, for such a response will be forcing. (See §3, page 37.) But if either of two suits will answer the first purpose, then a suit headed by an ace or king is usually preferred to a suit headed by no better card than a queen.

Bridge instruction books provide rules of guidance in choice of suits, but the rules have exceptions. Consider again the hand cited above:

♠ 87   ♡ KQ84   ◇ AQ5   ♣ Q1043

This is a one-club bid according to the books; by bidding clubs one keeps to the lowest possible level and permits partner to respond at the one-level. Yet several of the experts queried on the hand would open with one heart. The top cards in the heart suit make it a better suit to show, provided there is no embarrassing rebid problem to fear. If, to a one-heart bid, partner responds one spade it will be possible to rebid one no-trump; and if he responds two clubs or two diamonds, the trump support is good enough to permit a raise in partner's suit.

REQUIREMENTS FOR OPENING BIDS

Every authority has joined in the statement that with 14 points one must open the bidding; with 13 points one should usually open the bidding; with 12 points there are occasional hands that because of their long suits and solidity are acceptable opening bids.

Here again, however, experts and average players (or the teachers of the average players) are likely to be talking two different languages.

♠ KQ1063   ♡ AQ754   ◇ 82   ♣ 5

The expert calls this an 11-point hand with good distribution and a major-suit two-suiter, and he bids it although it has only 11 points. The instruction books call it a 14-point hand, since they count 2 points for the singleton and one for the doubleton, and as a 14-point hand it is a compulsory bid. The two methods come to the same thing in this case and in most other cases.

1. ♠ A 6 5   2. ♠ K 6 5
    ♡ K 7 5 3   ♡ A Q 10 7
    ◊ K 8 4   ◊ K 4 3
    ♣ A 9 2   ♣ J 7 2

Hand No. 1 contains 14 high-card points and so conforms to the requirements cited by most authorities. Probably most of the authorities would bid a club on it since there is no genuinely biddable suit and it is agreed that it is better to bid a three-card minor suit than a very weak four-card major suit.

The vast majority of the expert players in all countries would open also on hand No. 2, which has 13 points, although the "sound" bidders would never dream of opening on such a hand, and conservatives such as Mr. Goren consider it doubtful, or borderline, or optional. Most players would open this hand one heart, although some, because they prefer not to bid four-card majors, might bid one club. The rapidly increasing number of players who use the weak opening no-trump bid would bid one no-trump, which is patently the best bid to show the nature of the hand.*

Hands that count only to 12 points including distributional values are seldom opened unless the hand in question contains a six-card major suit. Unless an expert is wedded to a fairly rigid system, he will usually open one heart on the following hand:

♠ 6 3   ♡ A Q J 10 7 6   ◊ K 6 5   ♣ 7 2

He will pass with:

♠ 10 8 6 5 3 2   ♡ 5 3   ◊ A Q J   ♣ K 7

In this case also one may see the expert's reluctance to bid on a suit without the top cards when he has a hand of only moderate strength. The opponents are likely to play the hand, and in such a case he hesitates to bid a suit he does not want his partner to lead.

_____

* The trend ebbed sharply as popularity of Kaplan-Sheinwold ebbed, then resurged when the Precision Club system advocated an "intermediate" 13-15-point no-trump. This eliminated the risky 11-12-point no-trump opening and reinforced AHM's designation of the weaker no-trump as "patently the best bid."

WHO'S GOT THE SPADES?

I will have more to say—much more—in a later section on the function of the spade suit in hand valuation, but here it will suffice to mention briefly the part that the spade suit plays in determining a player's choice between a bid and a pass.

In the earlier positions, first and second hands, the decision to bid is seldom controlled by the suits that one holds. There are two opposing factors and they balance each other. When a player has strength in the major suits, he has an advantage over his opponents and this gives him an incentive to open the bidding. When a player's strength is chiefly in the minor suits, he may be at a disadvantage but it is important to him to get his bid in lest he be shut out later—perhaps by reason of the opponents' higher-ranking suits.

The following minor-suit hand is opened by many of the experts, as dealer or second hand:

♠ 6 2 ♡ J 6 3 ◇ K Q 9 ♣ A J 10 5 4

The hand is substandard in high cards, but the holder of it would be embarrassed if one opponent bid a spade and the other raised to two spades. Partner may hold:

♠ 7 3 ♡ A Q 9 7 4 2 ◇ 10 8 5 3 ♣ 6

He could not safely overcall a spade bid with two hearts, especially if vulnerable, but the opponents could make two or three spades against him while he might make four hearts if permitted to play there and could beat four spades if his opponents venture so far.

Transpose the spade and diamond holdings, or even the spade and heart holdings, and more experts will pass than will bid. They will not be so afraid of being shut out by an opposing spade suit.

When third hand, a player may often open the bidding on a substandard hand. He does this on the assumption that fourth hand is bound to have enough to bid anyway, and he may as well get the first blow in, both to interfere with the opponents' bidding and to inform his partner as to a good suit to lead. This latter factor being an essential one, a player does not make a weak third-hand opening bid unless his suit is a strong one, such as K-Q-10-x-x or A-J-10-x-x, something he wants his partner to open.

If there seems to be a good chance that the hand will be passed out, a player does not open the bidding third hand on a substandard hand (10 or 11 points) unless his strength is largely in the major suits. Fourth hand, after three passes, does not open the bidding on less than 14 points unless he has some strength in spades.

	1.		2.	
	♠ K 6 3		♠ 7 2	
	♡ 9 5		♡ 9 5	
	◇ A 7 4		◇ A 8 7 4	
	♣ K Q 10 8 2		♣ A Q J 6 5	

The same expert player bid one club, fourth hand, on hand No. 1 and passed, fourth hand, on hand No. 2. Each hand counts 13 points including distributional values. Hand No. 1 was accepted because it could support spades. Hand No. 2 was rejected because even if partner had spades or hearts there would be no support for him and if the opponents had those suits there would be no defense against them.

A player might fear to open the following hand in fourth position, because his bid might unleash whatever major-suit forces the opponents might have:

♠ 8 2   ♡ 5   ◇ K Q 10 6 3   ♣ A Q 7 5 4

(And if partner has the major suits, the combined hands will be a misfit.)

There was a time when this hand would have been opened in first or second position, to avoid being shut out of the bidding. General adoption of the "unusual no-trump" (see page 190) has converted the hand to an automatic first- or second-hand pass, because its holder can show its nature better by passing originally and making a no-trump overcall later, promising a minor-suit two-suiter. The hand is still an acceptable third-hand one-diamond bid, but some good players make it a practice to pass it in any position and await developments.

The following deal, in the bidding of the South hand, was

widely cited as a case of deviation from the rules, but when one considers it more deliberately it seems instead to represent a high degree of adherence to the unpublished "rules" that are actually followed by expert players. In any case the bidding of the South hand merits respectful attention because the holder of the hand, Morrie Elis, has been the winner of many of the most important titles in American tournament bridge and is highly reputed in rubber bridge.

NORTH
♠ 9 8 5 4
♡ A K
◇ Q 3
♣ 10 9 7 6 2

WEST
♠ Q J
♡ Q 8 6 4
◇ 10 8 6 2
♣ K J 8

EAST
♠ A K 6
♡ J 10 9
◇ J 9 7 4
♣ Q 5 3

SOUTH
♠ 10 7 3 2
♡ 7 5 3 2
◇ A K 5
♣ A 4

West was the dealer. Both sides were vulnerable. The bidding was:

WEST	NORTH	EAST	SOUTH
Pass	Pass	Pass	1 ♠
Pass	3 ♠	Pass	Pass
Pass			

The fact that Mr. Elis opened the bidding, fourth hand, on a hand that counts only 12 points including the club doubleton (11 points by the expert standard to which Mr. Elis adheres) can be attributed largely to the fact that he had the major suits and was not worried for fear he would open the way to a game or unchallengeable part-score by his opponents. The fact that he bid one spade in a conventionally unbiddable suit, rather than the one-club or one-diamond opening bid advocated in the majority of bridge books, can be attributed to his knowledge of the preëmptive effect of the spade suit. To overcall his spade bid, either of his opponents would have to bid two, and an overcall at the two-level when vulnerable requires a strong hand—usually, a hand strong enough for an opening bid. Since neither opponent had made an opening bid, Mr. Elis knew that a two-level overcall by either of them was unlikely.

North's jump raise to three spades would have been forcing if he had not passed originally, but after an original pass a player may bid a suit or make a jump raise or a jump no-trump bid without its being forcing. Mr. Elis had planned to pass any response his partner made, so he passed the three-spade response.

West opened the deuce of diamonds and the three was played from dummy. East put up the jack and South won with the diamond ace. South then led the four of clubs.

West took this trick with the jack of clubs and shifted to the queen of spades. When this won the trick he continued with the jack of spades and East cashed the ace and king.

Another diamond lead, this time by East, was won by the queen in dummy. South put himself in with the ace of clubs, led to the king of hearts, and trumped a club. This made dummy's hand high. Since the defenders got only three trump tricks and one club trick, the three-spade contract was made.

The contract can be made in at least one other way by putting up the diamond queen on the first trick, cashing all the high cards in the red suits, and ruffing two hearts in dummy, the last of them with the ♠ 8.

3

RESPONSES AND THEIR EFFECT
ON OTHER BIDS

THE BIDDING practices that were current some twenty-five to thirty-five years ago, and are still expressed in most bridge instruction books, have changed radically in at least three departments of the game: the choice of suits for an opening bid; the strength required for certain responses; and the strength required for certain rebids.

This is not a matter of accidental coincidence. Nearly any change in one aspect of bridge bidding can necessitate changes in several others.

Within three or four years of the birth of contract bridge—meaning by 1930 or before—bridge experts had unanimously adopted the principle of "keeping the bidding open light." It is not the principle that has changed but the application of it. The bidding is still kept open "light"; the responding hand does not pass his partner's opening bid more than once in twenty times. But the different types of response have become more rigidly conventionalized.

There was a time, in the earliest years of contract bridge, when the player might pass his partner's opening one-spade bid on the following hand:

♠ 63   ♡ Q 8 2   ◇ J 7 5 4   ♣ K 7 6 3

Once the principle of keeping the bidding open was established, such a hand became an obligatory one no-trump response, and it would have remained a one no-trump response even if the jack of diamonds had been reduced to the ten or even to a lower diamond. In other words, an opening bid is seldom passed if the responder has 5 high-card points or more. Sometimes, for tactical purposes—as when the responding hand is not vulnerable and does not wish to reveal his weakness to his vulnerable opponents lest they enter the bidding and reach a game—a player might then have responded one no-trump on considerably less than 5 high-card points—and might still do so.

But on the following hand a player in responding to his partner's spade opening would then have bid two hearts, rather than suppress his major suit:

♠ 6 ♡ K Q J 5 4 ◇ J 7 5 4 ♣ 7 6 3

And on the following hand the response would have been two diamonds, it having been thought at that time that one must not distort the picture of his distribution for the mere purpose of showing weakness.

♠ 6 3 ♡ Q 8 5 2 ◇ K J 10 7 5 2 ♣ 6

Today the response on each of the three hands shown would be one no-trump.*

The principle that the experts ultimately adopted in responding, as previously they had done in rebidding, is this: It is more important to show first the general strength of the hand than to show the location of the strength or the distribution of the hand. When one bid may be made to serve two or all three of these purposes, it is of course the preferred bid. When there is a choice, it should be made in favor of the bid that best shows how strong the hand is.

The validity of this approach will be discussed at greater length in later sections of this book. For the time being it suffices to note the fact that it exists and is generally accepted.

THE STEP SYSTEM

The controlling factor in bidding has come to be "the step system." One diamond is one step higher than one club; one heart is two steps higher than one club; and so forth.

---

* It should be noted here, for the record, that in the early 1930s S. Garton Churchill, a Brooklyn expert who has since won several of the most important national championships, advocated almost exactly the same principle in responding that has been generally adopted today; but in those times his was a voice crying in the wilderness and the best players rejected and even scoffed at the ideas that they were later to embrace so enthusiastically— twenty years later.

In 1935, in a book that represented the most enlightened bridge opinion of those times, the Four Aces cited the following hand as a one no-trump response to a one-club bid:

♠ K x x   ♡ K x x   ◇ x x x x   ♣ x x x

Today the one no-trump response to a one-club bid has virtually ceased to exist—unless the responding hand is strong enough to justify a response four steps higher. Experts almost without exception would respond with a bid of one diamond on this hand.

The decision to keep the bidding open on a very weak hand depends largely on having a suit in which a one-over-one response can be made. Most experts prefer not to show a major suit weaker than Q-x-x-x or at worst J-10-x-x; but if their partner's bid is one club, and they can respond one diamond, almost any suit will do, even a three-card suit. So a one-club bid would probably receive a response of one diamond on the following hand:

♠ 9 6 5 3   ♡ 8 6 4 2   ◇ K 4 3   ♣ Q 7

This response gives partner an opportunity to rebid at a low and therefore safe level if he has a four-card major suit. At the same time, by bidding, the responder escapes the danger of revealing the weakness of his hand to the opponents.

But quite a few players might elect to pass if partner opened with one diamond. The spade and heart suits are too weak to bid safely. The hand as a whole is too weak for a raise to two diamonds. If partner is permitted to play at one diamond, the contract cannot be unsafe. If the opponents enter the bidding, the hand has some defensive strength—either by trump length in one of the major suits, an honor in the club suit, or a fit with partner's diamond suit—against any contract they might undertake.

If partner's opening bid were one spade or one heart, the majority of the experts would consider this hand worth a raise to two of his suit.

Some players would prefer to respond one no-trump originally and show support or preference for his suit later, if the opportunity should arise, because they would rather show the general weakness of the hand first by the one no-trump response. These, however, are chiefly the players who use a one no-trump response to a major-suit opening as a forcing bid (page 181); so they will surely have the double opportunity of showing weakness first and trump support later. The only exception would be when the opponents enter the bidding and shut them out.

The one no-trump response to one club, which above was said virtually to have ceased to exist, under the application of the step system must show a reasonable amount of strength because it is four steps higher than one club. It cannot show a very strong hand because a one no-trump response never does, but it does show about an average hand, which is the top level of the range permitted for the one no-trump response, and usually it shows a hand that the responder would like to play at no-trump if that is to be the contract. The following hand might be a one no-trump response to one club:

♠ K 10 2   ♡ 7 6 4 3   ◇ A J 7   ♣ J 10 4

This is a fairly good hand, counting only 9 points in high cards but as good as most 10-point hands because of the two tens. The hearts are too weak to bid—at least, they are too weak for most American experts to bid, although some American experts and many British experts consider any four-card suit biddable in responding, however weak it may be. The club strength just misses being desirable for a raise to two clubs. A one-diamond response misrepresents the general nature of the hand. And at no-trump, this player does wish the lead to come up to him, since spades or diamonds may be opened.

On any weak hand a player usually chooses the response that will conserve steps. With

♠ A J 6 4   ♡ 5 3   ◇ Q 6 4 3   ♣ Q 7 4

one diamond, not one spade, is bid in response to partner's opening one-club bid. The partner may now rebid one heart, whereupon one spade may be bid and all suits shown at the lowest possible level.

Undoubtedly the greatest effect of the step system has been on the two-over-one response, which is the response in a lower-ranking suit—for example, a two-diamond response to an opening one-heart bid.

This response always skips at least one step, and also increases the contract from seven tricks to eight. Among nearly all experts in nearly all countries, it has come to be a strength-showing bid that must at least approach the strength required for an opening bid. In some systems the two-over-one response not only forces a rebid by the opening hand but guarantees a rebid by the responding hand and nearly always results in a game's being reached.

The instruction books cite 10 points (some, 11 points) as the minimum for the two-over-one response, but there are many hands with 10 or 11 points and eminently biddable suits that these experts do not consider strong enough for the two-over-one response. An expert recently held the following hand facing his partner's opening one-spade bid:

♠ 8 6   ♡ 7 5 4   ◇ Q J 7   ♣ A K 7 6 3

He responded one no-trump. He did not consider the hand strong enough for two clubs.

THE REVERSE BID

Among several outstanding cases in which the new standards for responses have affected bidding practices, there are two bids— the reverse bid and the two no-trump rebid—that once were considered invariably strong and no longer are; and at least one bid, the preference bid, that once was considered invariably weak and no longer is.

It is just as well that the reverse bid has been redefined in many cases, because it always mystified the bridge student. The student considers it one of the conventions of bridge, such as the convention that makes an opening two-bid a strength-showing or game-forcing bid. Reverse bids actually never were that. The experts' logical interpretation of a bidding sequence caused such bids to be, and to be read as, strong. For example,

South	West	North	East
1 ◇	Pass	1 ♠	Pass
2 ♡	Pass		

South's two-heart rebid is a reverse bid—it reverses the order of the suits since the natural thing with two suits is to bid the higher-ranking first. When South bids two hearts he risks finding North with a hand like this:

♠ Q 9 8 6 4   ♡ 7 3   ◇ A 7 2   ♣ 7 6 3

North's spades are too weak to rebid, North does not have enough club protection to bid two no-trump safely, certainly North cannot pass two hearts when he has a low doubleton and South may have a four-card suit, and so North shows preference for diamonds by returning to three diamonds. Now, South had to anticipate the fact that North might have such a problem, so by bidding two hearts South announced sufficient strength to play at a contract of three diamonds with very little support from North. A hand that can undertake a contract for nine tricks with so little support must be a strong hand. Ergo, the reverse bid of two hearts shows a strong hand.

Such is still the case when the response is a one-over-one bid or one no-trump. But in this bidding sequence, there is not necessarily any such implication:

SOUTH	WEST	NORTH	EAST
1 ◇	Pass	2 ♣	Pass
2 ♡			

North's two-club bid has shown substantial strength, so North-South are unquestionably safe in undertaking a contract at the three-level. Therefore many partnerships have agreed that South's rebid of two hearts does not necessarily show great strength. He may have only a fair hand and be bidding on the basis of the support he can rely upon receiving from his partner.

A rebid of two no-trump by the opening hand was once used invariably to show considerable strength, even if it was not a jump bid. Consider the two following hands:

	1.		2.	
♠	8 7		♠	K Q 8 4
♡	K Q 8 4		♡	8 7
◇	A Q 5		◇	A Q 5
♣	Q 10 4 3		♣	Q 10 4 3

Hand No. 1 was previously cited as a borderline opening bid. Most of the experts who bid such a hand preferred to open it one heart (unless they were playing some system in which one heart would be unsystemic). The one-heart bid is superior because it locates the strength of the hand. The bidder cannot be embarrassed for a rebid, because he can bid one no-trump over a spade response and can raise a two-diamond or two-club response. On hand No. 2, the policy used to be to bid one club, even though an opening club lead by partner would be less desirable. The reason was that the bidder could not stand a two-heart response. He would be too weak for a two no-trump rebid. Today many experts take the view that one spade may be bid safely because over a two-heart response the hand is strong enough for a two no-trump rebid. In this case also the bidder is venturing two no-trump on the basis of the strength known to be in his partner's hand. Without such strength his partner would not have made the two-over-one response of two hearts.

As for the preference bid, which used to be a denial of strength, in some cases it has become almost a strength-showing bid. The following bidding sequence is typical:

SOUTH	WEST	NORTH	EAST
1 ♠	Pass	2 ♣	Pass
2 ♦	Pass	2 ♠	Pass

At one time North's return to two spades would have been noncommittal at best, and the likelihood would have been that South would now pass. Today, since North's hand had to be so strong for the two-club response, South will very likely bid again—unless he has a minimum. North's bidding shows that he was too strong for a simple raise to two spades on his first turn. He may have the kind of hand that is jocularly called a "two-and-a-half spade bid," not quite strong enough for a jump raise to three spades, which would be forcing to game, but too good for a single raise. Such a hand might be the following:

♠ K753   ♡ 95   ♦ J63   ♣ AK62

If this hand had the king of diamonds instead of the jack, it would be a double raise, a better three-spade response than two-club response. As it is, North shows the hand best by temporizing with a two-club response and then showing spade support. But

North must not jump to three spades over two diamonds, as he once would have. Since the two-club bid has already shown strength, a jump to three spades would be forcing and also would tend to indicate a stronger hand than even a jump raise to three spades would have shown on the first turn.

THE TWO NO-TRUMP REBID, MODERN STYLE

The following deal was bid according to today's style. Also it developed into one of those situations in play that bridge players like to talk about.

NORTH
- ♠ A 9
- ♡ 8 6 2
- ◇ K 6 2
- ♣ A Q 10 6 4

WEST
- ♠ Q J 6 4
- ♡ K J 7 4 3
- ◇ 9 4 3
- ♣ 5

EAST
- ♠ 10 8 5
- ♡ Q 10 9
- ◇ Q J 7
- ♣ J 9 8 7

SOUTH
- ♠ K 7 3 2
- ♡ A 5
- ◇ A 10 8 5
- ♣ K 3 2

South dealt, both sides were vulnerable, and the bidding was:

SOUTH	WEST	NORTH	EAST
1 ◇	Pass	2 ♣	Pass
2 N.T.	Pass	3 N.T.	Pass
Pass	Pass		

By the standards that controlled bidding from the late '30s into the early '50s, South would not have been strong enough for a rebid of two no-trump. Probably he would have opened the bidding with one club so as not to let himself be in an embarrassing position if his partner responded two clubs to one diamond.

No embarrassment is felt now. Because South knew his partner was strong, and because South had to rebid and had a no-trump type of hand, he simply bid two no-trump. Over an old-style two no-trump rebid, which would have shown considerable strength, North might then have probed for a slam. By modern bidding, North could content himself with a simple raise to three no-trump because he had already shown his strength by his two-club response.

In one way, the modern style has made the bidding more natural by permitting South to rebid two no-trump. If South had to bid three clubs, North would have to take a chance on three no-trump without positive knowledge that his side had a heart stopper.

West opened the four of hearts and East played the queen. South let East hold this trick and took his ace of hearts when East led back the ten.

South cashed his club king and then led a low club to dummy's queen. This revealed the fact that East had a club stopper. South could run only eight tricks—two spades, the heart already won, two diamonds, and three clubs—without letting East into the lead. By letting East take his club jack, South could establish dummy's last club as his ninth trick; but unfortunately (for South) as soon as East got in with a club, the defenders could run three more heart tricks and defeat the contract.

South found the solution by a time-honored play that all players can profit from knowing. He led the eight of hearts from dummy to permit the defenders to run their three established hearts first.

On the eight of hearts East played the nine, South discarded a spade, and West won with the jack. West cashed the king of hearts, dummy discarded a diamond, East a spade, and South a diamond.

But if West led his last heart, he would squeeze his partner. And if West led anything but his last heart, he would never get in again to take the last heart. South could give up a club trick to

East, establishing dummy's other club as his ninth trick, and the defenders still would get only four tricks.

West did not happen to note the possible consequences of his lead of the last heart, or the fact that he was helpless; he did lead the last heart. A club was thrown from dummy and another spade was thrown by East. South also threw a spade.

West led the queen of spades and South took the ace and king. On the second of these, East had to discard either a diamond or a club. A club discard would make dummy's fourth club good, and a diamond discard would make South's ten of diamonds good. East chose to throw the diamond, and South ran off the remaining tricks with the king, ace, and ten of diamonds and the ace of clubs.

AN OLD STORY IN NEW FORM

The following deal typifies a situation that is quite old and has nothing to do with the modern relaxation of "reverse bid" standards; but the new definition of those standards may save many players from going wrong on such hands, when usually they did before.

NORTH
♠ K 8 5 3
♡ A J 10 9 7
◇ A J 8
♣ 3

WEST
♠ 10
♡ K 8 2
◇ 9 4 3
♣ A K J 9 5 2

EAST
♠ J 9 7 6
♡ Q 6 4
◇ 10 6 2
♣ 10 6 4

SOUTH
♠ A Q 4 2
♡ 5 3
◇ K Q 7 5
♣ Q 8 7

South dealt, neither side was vulnerable, and the bidding was:

SOUTH	WEST	NORTH	EAST
1 ◇	2 ♣	2 ♡	Pass
2 ♠	Pass	4 N.T.	Pass
5 ◇	Pass	6 ♠	Pass
Pass	Pass		

Against six spades West opened the king of clubs, then shifted to a diamond.

Because the spades did not break, South had to lose a spade trick to East and also South had to lose a heart trick to East's queen. The slam was down two, but even if the spades had broken 3-2 as expected it would have been a hopeless contract, losing at least one club and one heart.

North, supporting his Blackwood bid of four no-trump and his later insistence on a slam, argued, "But you reversed; I thought you had a strong hand."

Logically, under the step system, South's two-spade bid was not a strength-showing bid for the simple reason that it was the lowest bid he could possibly make. North's hand had to be strong when he bid two hearts. South had no choice but to rebid, because North's response was forcing, and it would be highly artificial if a system prevented South from showing his spade suit at this point, when he could show it so cheaply.

What the North player should remember before making such a bid as two hearts in that bidding situation is this: South has bid one diamond prepared to rebid safely over any response by North. Over one heart by North, South could bid one spade and keep the bidding low; but when North bid two hearts, he created a situation that South could not have anticipated. Therefore North's hand has to be a strong one. North did have this strength, and he went wrong only in misinterpreting the strength shown by South's rebid.

As for South's choice of one diamond as an opening bid, this was a proper and economical choice because in high cards the diamond and spade suits were about the same and South would about as soon have one led as the other. But if South's diamonds had been very weak and his spades considerably stronger than the diamonds, South might have bid one spade to "show his strength" (see page 31).

EFFECT OF THE STEP SYSTEM ON WEAK ONE-OVER-ONE RESPONSES

When a response may be made by bidding the suit that is exactly one step higher, a very weak hand is sometimes bid:

♠ 853   ♡ Q J 7 4 2   ◇ 974   ♣ 10 6

On this hand an expert responded one heart to his partner's opening one-diamond bid. But with this hand—exactly the same cards in different suits—

♠ Q J 7 4 2   ♡ 853   ◇ 106   ♣ 974

he would undoubtedly pass his partner's opening one-club bid, for to respond one spade would force him to skip two steps.

When it is necessary to "skip a step" in responding, the hand should usually contain at least a king and a queen, or two queens and a jack, or an ace and a jack. It must also, of course, have a suit for the one-over-one response.

Since the one-over-one response is forcing, it may range from the weak hand shown above up to a very strong hand with as many as 18 points. With 19 points or more, the responder should usually make some jump response that is forcing to game, because a 19-point hand will so often produce a slam even opposite a bare minimum bid (and may often produce a game opposite even a psychic bid, not that good players bid many psychics today).

Paradoxically, when a player makes one of these weak one-over-one responses, he worries more that his partner will be very strong than that his partner will be weak. If his partner is weak, the opponents will probably enter the bidding and the opening side will be out of trouble.

The following deal resulted in a contract calculated to produce shivers of fear in almost any bridge player, but because the declarer recognized one of the elementary aspects of bridge technique the ending was a happy one.

NORTH
♠ Q 7 6
♡ 9 4 2
◇ Q 8 7 5 3
♣ 9 3

WEST
♠ J 4
♡ J 10 8 5
◇ J 10 9
♣ K 6 4 2

EAST
♠ A 10 9 5 2
♡ K 6 3
◇ K 4 2
♣ J 7

SOUTH
♠ K 8 3
♡ A Q 7
◇ A 6
♣ A Q 10 8 5

South dealt, with both sides vulnerable. The bidding:

SOUTH	WEST	NORTH	EAST
1 ♣	Pass	1 ◇	Pass
2 N.T.	Pass	Pass	Pass

North shuddered as he passed two no-trump. He could take only cold comfort from the fact that any rescuing bid would make matters worse.

West opened the heart jack, East played the six, and South took the queen.

There is little point to trying for a finesse in clubs with no sure entry to dummy, so South next led the club ace.

Then South led the club queen, hoping to drop a doubleton jack. This was his only correct play; the queen should always be led in such cases. It could not have helped him to play for, and find, a doubleton king of clubs, for he would still have to lose a trick to the guarded jack.

South was fortunate; the jack of clubs dropped under the queen. South won a heart continuation, cashed three clubs, and later got a spade and a diamond, making his contract.

4

THE OPENING TWO-BID

NEARLY EVERY system employs some special opening bid to show an unusually powerful hand, a hand that will produce game by itself or with the most meager support—including unbiddable support—from partner, and a hand that gives high hopes of a slam if partner has anything better than that.

The earliest such bid to be introduced was the two-bid in a suit, which is variously called the forcing two-bid, the forcing two, the strong two, the two-demand, and the two-command. By this system, any opening bid of two in a suit shows a hand of the greatest power, forces partner to respond, and forces both players then to keep on bidding until game has been reached. Among rubber-bridge players probably 90 percent of the average players and nearly half of the expert players use forcing two-bids. Among tournament players probably fewer than one quarter of all players use the forcing two.

Most experts who do not use every opening two-bid as a game-forcing bid use instead an opening one-club bid (see page 243) or two-club bid as an artificial strength-showing bid. Some of those who follow the two-club system use other two-bids as weak, preëmptive bids; some use the other two-bids as strength-showing but not forcing bids. Some who use the two-club bids prefer ace-showing responses (with *three* diamonds to show the diamond ace), some prefer responses showing aces and kings ("controls"), and some prefer natural responses, with the two-diamond response always showing a weak hand.

For the purposes of this discussion it does not make any difference which of these systems is used. The forcing two-bid as used by some players and the forcing artificial two-club bid as used by others are almost always equivalent. That is, a hand on which a member of the former school would open two spades is a hand on which a member of the latter school would open two clubs and show his spade suit later.

Whichever kind of original forcing bid he uses, the expert uses it sparingly. He does not necessarily make a two-bid when he has 22 or more points; he does not necessarily make a two-bid when he has a sure game in his own hand.

Either of the following hands would be an opening two-spade bid for the average player, but there are some experts (believe it or not) who would bid only one spade on hand No. 1, and nearly every expert would content himself with a bid of one spade on hand No. 2:

	1.		2.	
♠	A K Q 8 4		♠	A Q 10 9 6 3
♡	A K 10 6 5		♡	K Q 10 5
◇	A 7		◇	A K
♣	3		♣	4

The advantage of the one-bid is that partner's response means something. When partner makes an unforced response to a one-bid, he shows definite values. When he makes a forced response to a two-bid, he shows nothing that the two-bidder can count on.

The advantage—not the only one—of the two-bid is that game may still be reached when partner is too weak to respond to a one-bid and the opponents are too weak to overcall.

The two-bid does not make it more difficult to reach a slam; nor, admittedly, does it facilitate reaching a slam except in rare cases when a one-bid would be passed out and not even a game would be reached.

The purpose of the forcing two-bid should be not to facilitate reaching a slam, but to guard against missing a game. Not the strength of the two-bidder's hand, but the probable strength of the other three hands, determines the advisability of opening with a two-bid. The following hand promises a sure game, but is merely a one-spade bid:

♠ K Q J 10 6 5   ♡ A K Q J 8   ◇ 5 3   ♣ ———

Over a one-spade bid, someone—partner or opponent—will surely be strong enough to bid, so the chance to reach game will not be lost.

When the opening hand is "missing" six of the top cards (aces, kings, and queens) it is likely that the bidding will be kept open. If partner has two such cards, he will probably be able to make some response; if partner is weaker than that, one of the opponents will probably be able to reopen the bidding. But when the opening hand has all but four or five of the aces, kings, and queens, he is in danger of being dropped in a one-bid. The following hand, with all but four of the top cards, is generally opened with a two-spade bid:

♠ A K Q 7 5   ♡ A Q J 6   ◇ A Q 5   ♣ K

The king of clubs, being singleton, is unlikely to contribute to the trick-taking power of the hand but its presence in the hand affects the ability of other players to keep the bidding open.

In choosing between a one-bid and a two-bid, the number of "controls" is also important. An expert seldom bids two on a hand that has two quick losing tricks in any suit, and almost never bids two when he has three small cards in one suit.

♠ A K Q J 8 5   ♡ A K Q 6 2   ◇ 7 6   ♣ ———

In an expert game this hand was opened with a bid of only one spade. The holder feared that if he bid two, his partner might take him to a slam with ♣ A K and nothing in diamonds and the slam might be lost.

There is a distinct change from the days when experts felt some loss of face in opening with a two-bid. They seemed, they thought, to be insulting their partners' boldness in keeping the bidding open. The late P. Hal Sims, who had the largest expert following of the early 1930s and who was captain of a team called the Four Horsemen, which for about two years won all the principal team championships, rather famously bid only one heart on the following hand:

♠ A K 8 3   ♡ A K Q 5 4   ◇ A K Q 10   ♣ ———

The Sims system included an opening, game-forcing two-bid on a hand that had "a sure game"; but perhaps Mr. Sims did not feel that this hand would surely take ten tricks with hearts as trumps. The hand might conceivably have lost two spade tricks, two heart tricks, and one diamond trick.

Mr. Sims came out reasonably well on the hand, because over his one-heart bid his left-hand opponent made a preëmptive club bid, which kept the bidding open for him. Eventually he got to six hearts and made it, and that was the normal contract on the hand. Nevertheless, his refusal to make a two-bid on such a hand was a reminder of an incident reported by Col. Frank Cook, who conducted a humorous column in a bridge magazine of the 1920s.

According to Colonel Cook, a reader sent in this question:

"I held the ace of spades five times, the ace of hearts four times, and the ace of diamonds four times, with no club in my hand. What should I have bid?"

Colonel Cook shut his eyes and visualized the correspondent's hand:

♠ A A A A A   ♡ A A A A   ◇ A A A A   ♣ ———

"I would pass," the colonel replied. "Against the players I know, I wouldn't dare bid," he continued somberly, "unless I had a club in my hand."

An indication of the extent to which the expert's demand for assured trick-taking power has been reduced may be found in the fact that William Grieve, an American international player and one of the highest-ranking experts, opened with a two-club bid on the following hand in 1961:

♠ A J 6   ♡ A 8   ◇ J 10   ♣ A K Q J 5 4

This hand misses seven of the top cards and is unlikely to be passed out if the bidding is opened with one club. Mr. Grieve's bid of two clubs becomes more significant ·in the light of this knowledge. The expert player of the preceding generation thought first of withholding information from his opponents; the expert player of this generation thinks first of giving information to his partner.

USE OF TWO-BID TO AVOID LATER OVERBIDDING

There is a recognized advantage to making a forcing bid (that is, a two-bid or two-club bid) on a hand that is powerful in top tricks but doubtful in playing strength. Paradoxically, by starting with a slight overbid one may avoid more dangerous overbidding later. For example:

NORTH
♠ Q 10 6 5
♡ 8
♢ J 10 6 3
♣ K J 7 2

WEST
♠ 8 4 3
♡ 10 4 3 2
♢ Q 8 4 2
♣ A 8

EAST
♠ J
♡ K J 9 7 5
♢ 7 5
♣ Q 10 9 5 4

SOUTH
♠ A K 9 7 2
♡ A Q 6
♢ A K 9
♣ 6 3

South dealt. Many experts would not consider South's hand strong enough for more than a one-bid. South did make a one-bid on it, and the record shows what happened:

SOUTH	WEST	NORTH	EAST
1 ♠	Pass	2 ♠	Pass
3 ♢	Pass	4 ♠	Pass
4 N.T.	Pass	5 ♣	Pass
5 ♠	Pass	Pass	Pass

Unfortunately, five spades went down. West opened a heart, but the free finesse did South no good. After drawing trumps, he went after the diamonds and West was in with the queen. West led his low club and South guessed wrong, putting in the jack. The defenders got two club tricks.

The two-club bid (or any two-bid) does actually avoid such tragedies. Having shown his full strength on his first bid, a player does not feel required to make further slam tries later. He stops at four spades—and makes it.

BIDS OF TWO AND THREE NO-TRUMP

It used to be said, truly, that two no-trump was the expert's favorite strength-showing bid. The opening bid of two no-trump shows a very strong hand and will rarely be passed if partner has a smattering of strength. But it is a reasonably safe bid because partner is not required to carry on to game if he is weak, it facilitates slam bidding because partner can expect a fit with any suit he has when his distribution is unbalanced, and it guarantees enough high-card strength so that partner can carry on to a slam on his own responsibility if he has a fairly good hand with a fairly good suit.

Only in rare cases does the expert make a forcing two-bid on a four-card suit (though he will if necessary) because such hands usually justify a two no-trump bid, which is preferred:

♠ A 6   ♡ A K 6 3   ◇ A K 5 2   ♣ K Q 10

This hand was opened with a two no-trump bid, although, with its 6 quick tricks, it might appear a better two-heart bid to the average player. The bid of two no-trump is also preferred to a two-bid on hands with a strong five- or six-card minor, and strength in every suit, like this one:

♠ A K 8   ♡ K Q 4   ◇ K Q J 10 4   ♣ A 5

Finally, there is the hand that does not quite fit the requirements for a forcing two-bid or for a two no-trump bid, and which is yet so strong that a one-bid may be passed out:

♠ A K Q 8   ♡ 6 3   ◇ A K J 2   ♣ A Q 4

With only a four-card suit and with no control in hearts, the expert hesitates to bid two spades; with no stopper in hearts he will not bid two no-trump. So—though no such expedient is countenanced in any popular bidding system—he usually opens with one club. This is the lowest possible bid, and therefore the easiest bid for his opponents to overcall or for his partner to find a response to. If some other player does bid, the holder of the powerful hand will make some forcing bid on the next round.

Those experts who use the opening two-club bid as the only game-forcing bid, however, find less difficulty in dealing with strong hands because they would bid two clubs on any one of these hands, after which they would rebid in a suit if the two-club bid is a genuine two-bid as might be made by the two-demand bidders but would rebid two or three no-trump if the hand is such that the two-demand bidders would open it with a strong no-trump bid.

The South hand in the following deal was once a classic three no-trump opening (25 to 27 points) and still is so listed in most of the bridge books (and may be so bid by some experts). However, the trend has been away from the three no-trump bid on such hands. The bid is expressive and accurate, and in this particular deal it did no harm, but psychologically the opening three no-trump bid on such a strong hand has proved hard for the responder to handle. With a weak-looking hand that includes perhaps a five-card suit to the king-jack and an outside queen, the responder should appreciate the fact that a slam is probable and should be bid, but it is hardly human nature to make a slam try on such a hand.

In this deal, of course, the problem was just the opposite. North had so much less than should be expected that South had to use an obscure playing device even to make his contract.

NORTH
♠ 3 2
♡ 10 7
♢ 8 6 5 3
♣ Q 10 9 4 3

WEST
♠ Q 10 7
♡ 8 5 4 2
♢ J 9 7 4
♣ 7 6

EAST
♠ J 8 6 5
♡ Q J 9
♢ K 10 2
♣ K 8 2

SOUTH
♠ A K 9 4
♡ A K 6 3
♢ A Q
♣ A J 5

South dealt, with North-South vulnerable. The bidding:

SOUTH	WEST	NORTH	EAST
3 N.T.	Pass	Pass	Pass

The deuce of hearts was opened by West, dummy's ten was played on the bare but unavailing chance that West might have led from the Q-J, and East's jack forced South's ace.

To inexperienced players, it might seem that South's only chance to make his contract would be to find a doubleton king of clubs in the hand of either opponent (or, of course, a singleton king of clubs).

However, South used a different method of play and made his contract despite his failure to find the king of clubs doubleton.

After winning the ace of hearts, South led the jack of clubs and overtook with the queen of clubs in dummy.

If East had won this trick with the king, South would have had at least nine sure tricks, so East played low.

The nine of clubs was next led from dummy and East had no choice but to play low again, so South finessed by playing his five of clubs and the nine won.

This left the lead still in dummy, and the three of diamonds was led. South finessed the queen, which won, and ran off the remainder of his nine tricks with the aces of diamonds and clubs, the king of hearts, and the A-K of spades.

South was lucky, but the play of the club suit is still worth studying as an example of how one may win three tricks in such a suit even when he cannot reach dummy for a finesse.

5

FORCING RESPONSES AND REBIDS

In 1929, when the game of contract bridge was very new, a woman in Cleveland, Ohio, attended a lecture by one of the most reputable authorities.* She was a serious student and she was equipped with an open notebook and a sharp pencil for recording the lecturer's pearls of bridge wisdom.

The whole idea of forcing bids was new then, too, and the lecturer devoted his time to explaining such bids—opening two-bids, jump bids, one-over-one bids, cue-bids. While he talked, the serious woman in his audience busily plied pencil on notebook.

On his way out of the hall the lecturer curiously side-glanced the woman's notebook. The page was covered with doodling except for two words, her sole notes on the lecture. The two words were "Never pass."

Yet the bids that the lecturer wished to have treated as forcing then would not have represented 10 percent of the bids that are treated as forcing today.

Waggishly, S. Garton Churchill said in 1961 that his next book would be on the subject of "nonforcing bids" and would have five hundred pages. "All the pages," he added thoughtfully, "will be blank."

By the ultrarefined bidding system used by the leading American players today, it is almost as hard to pass as that woman thought it was in 1929. Forcing bids no longer need be two-bids or jump bids—in fact, jump bids are considered somewhat unsporting, perhaps because they make matters easier for the partner. Almost any suit-bid is likely to be a forcing bid, and some simple bids turn out unexpectedly to be forcing to game.

* Ely Culbertson.

FORCING BIDS THAT ARE NOT JUMP BIDS

Forcing bids were an American invention and perhaps for that reason American players have always used many forcing bids while Europeans, using fewer, have won the world championship from American teams year after year.

As early as 1927 Culbertson proposed that opening two-bids and "jump shifts" be forcing bids, and it was twenty years before anyone disputed this theory; even today, such bids are almost universally treated as forcing.

It was also Culbertson who (in 1929) proposed the first forcing bid that was not a jump bid—the bid that came to be called the one-over-one.

For example:

SOUTH	WEST	NORTH	EAST
1 ◇	Pass	1 ♡	Pass

The one-heart bid is a one-over-one and is forcing—South must bid again. The bid is still so interpreted by nearly every player in the world, good or bad.

Before a year had passed—sometime before the end of 1930—Culbertson had abandoned this theory, concluding that it was unsound. But his original argument had been too convincing. American experts had taken up the one-over-one principle and nothing that has happened or that has been said since has persuaded them to abandon it. Even Culbertson was forced to backtrack, five years later, and call the one-heart response forcing, because all the good players were treating it as forcing.

The fact is that the forcing one-over-one response is unsound. If South in the bidding sequence given above cannot pass one heart, he cannot open the bidding on quite so weak hands as he might bid if he were permitted to pass at the one-level. It is not harmful to permit South to pass one heart, because he will seldom do so when he has a sufficiently sound hand to make a game contract a good possibility. By passing one heart, South may often lure his opponents into overcalls at which they can be profitably doubled. And if North is unwilling to have South pass in any circumstances, he always has the right to bid two hearts, rather than one heart, over the opening diamond bid. The prospect that South might pass one heart will prevent East from making trap passes, because East cannot be wholly confident of having another chance.

Perhaps once in a hundred deals a proper pass of partner's one-over-one response will cost a game, but an unusual combination of circumstances is required: The responder must be strong, the fit must be very good, the opener's left-hand opponent must be very weak or very discerning, sufficiently so to suspect that his opponents have stopped short of a makable game. The principle that a suit response (one- or two-over-one) may be passed also opens up some trapping opportunities to the opening bidder.

The extension of the one-over-one principle—the idea that a new suit-bid at the one-level even by opener should be forcing—lasted only a few years and then was generally abandoned.

For example:

SOUTH	WEST	NORTH	EAST
1 ◇	Pass	1 ♡	Pass
1 ♠	Pass		

At one time the idea was that South's one-spade rebid was forcing and North must bid again, but this gave way to the principle that if North was allowed to pass the one-diamond bid, he might now pass the one-spade rebid. In fact, the one-spade rebid has become quite a discouraging rebid, because of the present practice of bidding originally on such hands as this:

♠ A J 5 3   ♠ 9 5   ◇ A 7 4   ♣ K 10 5 4

It is customary to open with one club on this hand, because partner's response will probably be one diamond or one heart and a weak-sounding rebid of one spade may then be made. If the one-spade rebid were forcing, it would be dangerous to open the bidding on such hands.

SUIT OVER SUIT

Nevertheless the "suit-over-suit" principle, proposed as early as 1932 and rejected by most experts at that time, soon came to be a tenet of the American bridge religion and is generally followed today. By 1935 it was firmly established in American practice that any new-suit response to an opening bid was forcing for one round, whether the response was at the one-level or the two-level. In the following sequence:

SOUTH	WEST	NORTH	EAST
1 ♡	Pass	2 ♣	Pass

South had to bid again over two clubs and if he couldn't conveniently bid over two clubs the conclusion was that he shouldn't have opened the bidding in the first place.

After that it did not take long to arrive at a system whereby the suit-over-suit principle, rejected in 1932, became an effective part of every popular system—as it still is. By this definition, when partner's last bid was in a suit, one may force him by bidding in a new (that is, previously unbid) suit.

The new-suit bid is not forcing when partner's previous bid was one no-trump, unless responder has reversed:

SOUTH	WEST	NORTH	EAST
1 ♢	Pass	1 ♡	Pass
1 N.T.	Pass	2 ♣	

North's two-club bid, though "a rebid in a new suit made by the responding hand," is not played as forcing. North may have a weak hand, but has bid two clubs because he has unbalanced distribution that would make it dangerous to play in no-trump. For example:

♠ 7   ♡ K 8 7 5 3   ♢ 8 4   ♣ K J 6 4 2

But if North had rebid two spades over one no-trump, his bid would be a reverse and would be forcing.

By the usual definition as published in the most popular bridge books, a new-suit rebid is forcing only when made by the responding hand. In the following sequence:

SOUTH	WEST	NORTH	EAST
1 ♡	Pass	1 ♠	Pass
2 ♣	Pass	2 ◊	Pass

South's rebid of two clubs is not forcing because South is the opening hand, but North's rebid of two diamonds is forcing because North is the responding hand. Also because most experts today play "fourth suit forcing."

Nevertheless, a new-suit rebid by the opening hand often shows so much additional strength that a responding hand seldom dares pass it, even though he knows it can occasionally be made on a fairly weak hand. The following hand is a good example:

♠ Q   ♡ A K J 5 3   ◊ A K Q 2   ♣ Q J 4

Several experts opened with one heart; their partners responded one spade; and they contented themselves with a rebid of two diamonds. True, the majority of experts consulted preferred a jump rebid of two no-trump, but the fact that even a few were willing to bid two diamonds shows how strong such a bid has become. Only one (Howard Schenken) felt it necessary to jump to three diamonds—or felt that the hand was strong enough for this bid.

Yet it is hard to conceive a hand on which partner might have responded one spade and opposite which this hand would not produce a good play for game. North might pass two diamonds, holding

♠ K 8 7 3   ♡ 4 2   ◊ J 8 5   ♣ K 9 6 3

The combined hands should play at three no-trump and seldom will fail to make their game.

If partner had been able to respond two clubs, game at some contract would have been sure and a slam would have been probable—note the hand previously shown on page 41, when a player was unwilling to respond two clubs on five clubs to the A-K and a Q-J on the side—and yet over a two-club response nearly all of the best players would rebid only two diamonds, not three diamonds or three no-trump. When such is the bidding practice, clearly the two-diamond rebid must be considered forcing or many games may be missed.

When a player's rebid is three of a suit, or a "reverse" bid, it is likely to be so strong that the partner almost never dares pass it.

SOUTH	WEST	NORTH	EAST
1 ♡	Pass	2 ◊	Pass
3 ♣			
or 2 ♠			

It makes little difference whether or not South's rebid—either three clubs or two spades—is called "forcing." North will not pass it; because, having responded two diamonds in the first place, North probably has at least 11 points.

The suit-over-suit situation ceases to be practically forcing only when the first response may have been made on a very weak hand:

SOUTH	WEST	NORTH	EAST
1 ♣	Pass	1 ♠	Pass
2 ♡			

Now North, if he has about one trick or less, and no great support for hearts, may pass. With anything more he should bid again:

♠ K J 7 5 4   ♡ 10 6 4 3   ◊ 5 4   ♣ 9 8

On this hand North should raise to three hearts. North would pass a hand like this:

♠ A 8 7 4 3   ♡ J 8 5   ◊ 10 8 5 4   ♣ 8

THE NEW FORCING BIDS

To summarize, the following have all become forcing bids in American practice, either because they are defined as forcing or because they may be so strong that it is not safe to pass them:

Any bid in a new suit by the responding hand, except over one no-trump.

Any rebid of two in a new suit by the opening hand, if the response was at the two-level.

Any new-suit rebid at the three-level by the opening hand.

Going even further, a reverse bid or a three-level rebid in a new suit by the responding hand is treated as forcing to game. Except among players of a few systems, jump bids also are forcing and show even stronger hands, but there is a decreasing tendency to bid them, since one may force without jumping. In the following deal, it never occurred to either partner that he should make a jump bid.

NORTH
♠ A K 6 5
♡ A Q 8 7
◊ J 8 5 3
♣ 4

WEST
♠ J 9 8 2
♡ 6 5 2
◊ Q 10 9 2
♣ Q 8

EAST
♠ Q 10 4 3
♡ J 9 4
◊ 6
♣ K J 9 7 2

SOUTH
♠ 7
♡ K 10 3
◊ A K 7 4
♣ A 10 6 5 3

North dealt, with neither side vulnerable. The bidding:

NORTH	EAST	SOUTH	WEST
1 ♠	Pass	2 ♣	Pass
2 ♡	Pass	3 ◊	Pass
4 ◊	Pass	4 ♡	Pass
5 ◊	Pass	6 ◊	Pass
Pass	Pass		

Observe that South, who could be absolutely sure of making game, made a nonjump rebid of three diamonds with no fear that it would be passed.

South's bid of four hearts, which the average player might have passed, is a slam try when read in all of its subtle implications. If South was simply interested in reaching game at hearts, he could have raised to three hearts immediately instead of bidding three diamonds. North now tentatively accepted the slam try by going beyond the four-heart bid that he might have passed, and at the same time by his five-diamond bid he showed that he had four-diamond support and not simply a high-card fit with the suit. South took the final plunge when he bid six, a contract that was not wholly safe but that provided a good enough play to be an acceptable gamble.

West opened the six of hearts. Dummy played low, East played the jack, and South won with the king. South then led the king and ace of diamonds, for if the outstanding diamonds were 3-2 he could establish dummy's hand. But the diamonds did not break.

South could now get twelve tricks only if West held exactly two clubs and exactly three hearts, so he played for this distribution. He took the heart ten and led a heart to the queen. Then he cashed the ace and king of spades and ruffed a spade in his hand. Then he cashed the club ace, ruffed a club with the diamond eight in dummy, and ruffed the last spade in his hand.

When South finally led a club from his hand, West could do nothing to prevent dummy's diamond jack from winning the twelfth trick for South.

SOME FORCING FALLACIES

From the fact that I have described all the nonjump forcing bids in this section, it should not be inferred that I believe them best. The best European players, to put it baldly, think that American experts are crazy to attach such subtle nuances to so many of their bids and to keep their partners under such unremitting pressure to decide whether a particular suit-bid is strong or weak. Many of these Europeans are saddened by the thought that players with such great talent as many of the Americans should waste their card-playing skill at inferior contracts reached by inept bidding. The Europeans jump twice as often, and pass nonjump bids twice as often, and reach the best contract much more often.

There are, it is true, some European players who have conventionalized the new-suit forcing idea in the "fourth-suit forcing" convention, which will be discussed later in this book; but they are a minority and few of them are among the most successful European players.

The current American methods made it virtually impossible for North-South to reach their only makable contract in the following deal:

NORTH
♠ A J 7 3
♡ 8
◇ 6 2
♣ A Q 10 8 7 3

WEST
♠ 9 4
♡ Q 9 6 5
◇ A 8 3
♣ K 9 5 4

EAST
♠ Q 10 8 2
♡ 10 3
◇ K Q 9 4
♣ J 6 2

SOUTH
♠ K 6 5
♡ A K J 7 4 2
◇ J 10 7 5
♣ ———

South dealt. Both sides were vulnerable. The bidding:

SOUTH	WEST	NORTH	EAST
1 ♡	Pass	2 ♣	Pass
2 ♡	Pass	2 ♠	Pass
2 N.T.	Pass	3 ♣	Pass
3 ♠	Pass	3 N.T.	Pass
Pass	Pass		

West opened the nine of spades, an intelligent lead based on West's conclusion that South could not be very strong in spades or he would have raised immediately; North could not be very strong in spades or he would have bid four spades instead of three no-trump; and the lead of any of the other three suits might cost a trick.

South put up the spade ace in dummy, led dummy's heart, and finessed his jack. This was an all-out attempt to make the contract. If East had held Q-x-x in hearts, South would have been almost sure to win nine tricks; with any favorable division of the opponents' hearts, South would have gone down no more than one trick.

But the hearts did not break. West won the first heart trick and led a spade, South winning. South cashed two high hearts and led a third heart for West to win with the nine.

East had discarded a diamond and a club. After taking his nine of hearts, West led a low diamond and East took the queen and king, cashed the spade queen, and led a spade. Dummy won the spade jack and club ace, but West then had the club king and diamond ace, and South was down three, 300 points.

North could have made a two-spade contract, but by today's bidding practices there was no way for North-South to stop there. North had only a choice of evils. If he passed two hearts, South would go down. If he bid two spades, the one contract his side could make, the bidding could not stop there because a "reverse bid by the responder" is forcing.

North should, of course, have passed three spades. The North-South hands were obviously a misfit since neither partner could support the other's suit. All bridge authorities advise passing as soon as possible when a misfit is suspected.

THE NO-TRUMP EXCEPTIONS

At almost any stage, a bid of one no-trump breaks the chain of forcing bids and a new-suit bid over it is not forcing.

One such example was shown on page 61:

SOUTH	WEST	NORTH	EAST
1 ♡	Pass	1 ♠	Pass
1 N.T.	Pass	2 ♣	Pass

Here two clubs is not forcing. Similarly:

SOUTH	WEST	NORTH	EAST
1 ♡	Pass	1 N.T.	Pass
2 ◇	Pass		

Here North feels little pressure to bid again. Unless North was exceptionally strong for his one no-trump response, he will either pass two diamonds or show preference by returning to two hearts. South would not bid two diamonds, in that sequence, on such a hand as the following:

♠ Q 6   ♡ A Q 10 5 4   ◇ A K J 4   ♣ Q 5

This hand is not strong enough for a jump to three diamonds, and a simple two-diamond rebid would not reflect the strength of the hand, so South would bid two no-trump. Because two no-trump is a dangerous contract, a raise of one no-trump to two is regularly read as a fairly strong bid. South's two-diamond bid over North's one no-trump response is more likely to show such a hand as this:

♠ 6   ♡ A Q 10 5 4   ◇ K Q 8 6 3   ♣ Q 5

When one no-trump is an opening bid, rather than a response or a rebid, it still cancels the normal forcing or encouraging implications of a suit response.

SOUTH	WEST	NORTH	EAST
1 N.T.	Pass	2 ♠	Pass

Although many systems have made North's two-spade response forcing, and no other interpretation has proved palatable to the average player, almost no expert plays the bid that way. The two-spade bid denies the strength required to raise to two no-trump and also it denies enough strength to try for a major-suit game.

Even if South is playing "strong no-trumps," he is expected to pass two spades and usually does.

This implication is even stronger when the response is a "free bid" over an intervening overcall:

SOUTH	WEST	NORTH	EAST
1 N.T.	2 ♡	3 ♣	Pass
		or 2 ♠	

Regardless of the level at which North's bid is made, if it is not a jump bid it denies hope of game and while it does not forbid a rebid by South, it discourages one. South usually will and should pass. If North had a strong hand he could jump in his suit, or he could bid two no-trump (even without a heart stopper, which he can assume in South's hand), or with some heart strength he could double.

Note that it is only the bid of *one* no-trump that creates these nonforcing new-suit bids. A suit-bid over two no-trump, whether or not it is a new suit, is almost always treated as forcing.

SOUTH	WEST	NORTH	EAST
1 ♡	Pass	2 ◇	Pass
2 N.T.	Pass	3 ♡	
	or 3 ♣	
	or 3 ♠	} *all forcing*
	or even 3 ◇	

Only the last of these bids, the three-diamond rebid, requires much comment. There was a time when this rebid of three diamonds was classed as a "sign-off" and South was not only urged to pass, he was virtually required to pass. But that was before custom required that North show so much strength by his initial two-diamond response. Now three diamonds cannot be a weak bid because North has already guaranteed considerable strength by bidding two diamonds. The three-diamond bid should be a sign-off, but it isn't.

PREFERENCE BIDS IN THE 1970s

Another erstwhile sign-off bid that has changed character, with far-reaching ramifications, is the preference bid.

In the following bidding sequence, North's two-spade bid was once an invitation to pass but now is made with considerable hope that South will bid again:

SOUTH	WEST	NORTH	EAST
1 ♠	Pass	2 ♣	Pass
2 ◊	Pass	2 ♠	

No bid by North can sound weak when North has already said, by his earlier two-club response, that his hand is strong.

When the first response has promised no great strength, a preference bid is still weak; it can be and often is passed:

SOUTH	WEST	NORTH	EAST
1 ♡	Pass	1 ♠	Pass
		or 1 N.T.	
2 ◊	Pass	2 ♡	

The logical meaning of North's two-heart bid is this: North probably lacked either the heart support or the general strength to raise to two hearts in the first place; therefore North's return to hearts promises no more than the original one-spade or one no-trump response, which could have been made on a very weak hand. The only additional information given by the preference bid of two hearts is that North likes hearts better than diamonds. North may have such a hand as

♠ 10 8 7 6 3   ♡ J 5   ◊ 6   ♣ A 7 6 4 3

He cannot reasonably pass two diamonds and he is too weak for a two-spade bid (strength-showing) or a three-club or two no-trump bid (forcing). He must bid two hearts.

South appreciates this fact and will pass two hearts unless his hand is exceptionally strong and his two-diamond bid was an underbid.

But if the two-heart preference bid is to be used as a warning and pass-inviting bid, it is similarly reasonable to expect a jump by North to three hearts to promise only a good, not an overwhelming hand. Holding this:

♠ A K J 5   ♡ J 7 3   ◊ 6 3   ♣ 7 6 4 2

North could hardly respond anything but one spade to one heart. The one-spade bid shows the location of his strength and does not give an exaggerated picture of his heart support, as an immediate raise to two hearts might. But when South has rebid two diamonds, how can North merely bid two hearts on this hand and let his partner think it may be as weak as the previous hand?

The solution, once considered old-fashioned but now regaining acceptance among good players, is for North to bid three hearts over two diamonds. Logically the jump to three hearts shows more than the hopeless hand but less than enough to force—if North wished to force he would also be able to jump to *four* hearts. South should be permitted to pass a jump to three hearts with a hand like this:

♠ 7 3   ♡ A 9 8 4 2   ◊ A K 8 4   ♣ J 9

The combined North-South hands will probably make three hearts but are unlikely to make game. South's principle should be that he will pass the preference raise to three hearts if he would have passed an immediate raise to two hearts. The intervening one-spade response merely took advantage of an opportunity to give additional information.

In the 1950s the tendency was for nearly all players to reject the Culbertsonian rule that jump rebids by the responder were not forcing. In recent years, however, matters have come almost full circle. For example, a 1967 *Bridge World* poll of approximately 125 leading experts and thousands of readers revealed a preference for treating responder's jump rebids as *non*forcing, except when in a new suit or in the opener's minor suit.

But even the jump rebid in opener's minor could often be put to better use if it were nonforcing. The delicate problems are emphasized in duplicate bridge and arose in the next deal.

NORTH
♠ Q 10 8 5
♡ Q
◇ A 7
♣ A 8 6 4 3 2

WEST
♠ K 9 4 3
♡ A 9 8 2
◇ 9 8 5 4
♣ J

EAST
♠ A J
♡ J 7 6 4
◇ K 10 6 3 2
♣ 10 5

SOUTH
♠ 7 6 2
♡ K 10 5 3
◇ Q J
♣ K Q 9 7

North dealt. East-West were vulnerable. The bidding:

NORTH	EAST	SOUTH	WEST
1 ♣	Pass	1 ♡	Pass
1 ♠	Pass	1 N.T.	Pass
Pass	Pass		

In a rubber-bridge game North would have rebid two clubs over one no-trump. But this deal occurred in a duplicate-bridge game, in which it is better to make a no-trump contract than the same number of tricks in a suit contract, and North passed the one no-trump bid to take advantage of the higher trick score at no-trump.

The fact remains that North probably could have made game at no-trump. East's normal opening would have been the three of diamonds, giving North two diamond tricks. North would have led a heart, and could not have been prevented from winning a heart trick. With six club tricks, two diamonds, and one heart, North would have had the nine tricks he needed.

South, playing at one no-trump, did not even make his contract. West opened the four of diamonds, dummy's seven was played, and East won with the king. East returned a low diamond to dummy's ace. South could have run his six clubs, but instead he tried to sneak an extra trick by leading the queen of hearts. West won, East took three more diamonds, and then East cashed the spade ace and led to West's spade king for the setting trick.

South played badly. He should have cashed all his clubs assuring himself of seven tricks and his contract. Always in duplicate bridge and usually at rubber bridge, it is wisest to play for a sure plus score when there is a question as to whether or not the contract can be made.

But the fact that North-South missed a probable game, if North had played the hand, is attributable to the limitation placed on South by the forcing nature of jump bids. South did not want to bid two clubs over North's one spade, because two clubs is a very weak bid that might be passed, leaving North-South in a low-scoring club contract. South was afraid to jump to three clubs because three clubs would have been a forcing bid and South was not strong enough to force North to bid again.

In the actual circumstances, the three-club bid would have told North that he could probably win six club tricks at no-trump. Unfortunately, South did not know that North held a six-card club suit; North might have held only four clubs or even three. North did not know his six clubs were all trick winners; South might have held only one or two valueless clubs.

Logically, South should have been able to bid three clubs merely to show that his hand had more strength than he would need to bid two clubs. He could have risked a jump to three clubs if North had been free to pass a weak or ill-fitting hand. However, when nearly any bid of any kind is forcing, one can hardly expect partner to pass a jump bid.

6

AN APPROACH TO THE JUMP SHIFT

IN THE formative years of contract bridge bidding systems there
were "jumpers" and there were "minimum bidders." In responding to an opening bid such as one heart the jumpers would jump
to two spades or three clubs on merely a strong, game-going
hand; the minimum bidders would respond only one spade or
two clubs on such a hand, reserving the jump response for probable slam hands.

The argument revolved about such cases as the following:

WEST	EAST
♠ 9 6	♠ A J 10 6 5
♡ A J 10 6 5	♡ K 2
◇ A K 3	◇ 7 4
♣ 10 5 2	♣ A K J 2

West deals and opens with one heart. North passes. What
should East respond?

"One spade!" cried the minimum bidders. "Two spades!"
shouted the jump bidders.

The minimum bidders maintained that the one-over-one saved
a round of bidding. Their argument was plausible. Look, they
said:

WEST	EAST
1 ♡	1 ♠

Doesn't this save a round of bidding as against

WEST	EAST
1 ♡	2 ♠ ?

Culbertson neatly exploded this fallacy by carrying the bidding
one round further:

74

WEST	EAST
1 ♡	1 ♠
1 N.T.	3 ♣

comes to the same thing as

WEST	EAST
1 ♡	2 ♠
2 N.T.	3 ♣

since even the minimum bidder could not dare bid only two clubs on the second round, whereupon the same level would be reached.

What with one example and another, the warring camps managed to win arguments back and forth. All of this proved only one thing: that you can make up an example to support any side of a bridge dispute.

Now the war is over. All is quiet on the bridge front. In the United States, at least, there are no longer conflicting schools. The erstwhile minimum bidders decreased their requirements slightly. The erstwhile jump bidders slightly increased theirs. There is not even a good reason to debate the subject any longer, because a jump forcing takeout so seldom occurs: No one often has a good enough hand to make it.

Meanwhile European players continue to make jump responses on all hands that seem likely to go game and when they do so they usually disgrace their American opponents who are minimum bidders according to our national custom.

From the meetings between United States and European teams in international competition in the 1960s, most of which ended disastrously for the Americans, it is possible to pick out at least five cases in which European use of the more liberal jump response resulted in a serious loss to the Americans,* and in these

---

* There might have been six such cases, but on one occasion Terence Reese dropped a card on the floor and the card happened to be the ace of hearts. Not noticing that he had dropped the card, but having still a very strong hand, he forced to game. When he put down his dummy his partner, Boris Schapiro, said in a total monotone, "What a remarkable hand. Only twelve cards." The missing ace of hearts was then found and restored to the hand. As a result, the British pair missed a slam; but they still made a profit. The American players, although seeing all their cards, bid the slam in the wrong suit and went down.

matches no case occurred in which American use of the minimum response can be held to have given them an advantage over the Europeans.

HOW A STRONG RESPONDING HAND IS BID

Just as taxi drivers adhere to the policy of always getting as far ahead as possible, even if they land behind a stalled moving van, American bridge experts always make the lowest possible bid, so long as it is forcing.

In one respect it is unfortunate that peace in the bridge battle came so soon. The conflicting sides stumbled around in their arguments without ever figuring out exactly when the one-over-one is to be preferred, and when the forcing takeout. If they had kept on arguing, someone might have reached the proper solution.

Both sides were wrong in the original argument and both sides, if there still are two sides, continue to be wrong. A hand can be too strong for a jump response, just as it can be too weak.

The decision has very little to do with the apparent strength of the hand, given a certain minimum. It is not necessary to have support for partner's suit. It is not necessary to have a solid suit of your own. A hand with 20 high-card points and good support for partner may be just right for a one-over-one, whereas a hand weak in playing strength and containing no more than 15 or 16 high-card points may be a good forcing takeout.

Few if any experts, holding either of the following hands, would make a jump response to partner's opening bid of one heart:

	1.		2.	
♠	A K 8 4 3	♠	7 6 4	
♡	Q 5	♡	A 7 6	
♢	A 7 5	♢	A K 9 5 2	
♣	A 8 2	♣	A 7	

The standard responses would be one spade on No. 1, two diamonds on No. 2. Yet experience indicates that a jump to two spades will work out better on No. 1 and a jump to three diamonds will work out better on No. 2.

The same players who consider the hands above far too weak for jump responses would consider the following hands strong enough:

3. ♠ Q J 9 7 5   4.   ♠ 7 5
    ♡ A K   ♡ A 6
    ◇ A J 10 3 2   ◇ A K Q 10 5 3
    ♣ A   ♣ A J 4

The standard response to partner's one-heart bid is two spades on No. 3, three diamonds on No. 4. One spade and two diamonds, respectively, should produce better results.

The choice of responses should usually be governed by the answer to one question: Which partner will make the final decision as to the contract? This decision is usually made by the hand that is "solid"—has great trick-winning strength.

For example, Nos. 1 and 2 above have almost no trick-winning strength beyond their high cards. They are full of "holes." Nos. 3 and 4 are each about four tricks better.

Consider hands 1 and 3 if partner did not open the bidding and if partner has an almost worthless hand containing nothing but four spades to the ten. Opposite such a hand, No. 1 is likely to win only six or seven tricks; No. 3 is a three-to-one shot to make game.

And consider Nos. 2 and 4 if partner has an almost worthless hand including nothing of value except the king of hearts. No. 2 can barely make a part-score contract and will be hard put to win the contract from the opponents in the auction. No. 4 is odds-on to make game at no-trump if spades are not led.

WHEN TO UNDERBID

Let us consider the hand designated above as No. 3, a beautiful hand—beautiful in more ways than one, as will be shown.

♠ Q J 9 7 5   ♡ A K   ◇ A J 10 3 2   ♣ A

Partner opens with one heart. What should be the response? There are 19 points. A blank A-K of partner's suit may not be the strongest support one would ask for, but you can be assured it's no misfit. By what rules wouldn't one make a jump two-spade response on this hand?

It isn't a matter of rules, though. The best bid in bridge is the bid that will work out best. On a hand like this a forcing takeout will seldom work out as well as one-over-one. And when you go into the reasons why this is so, you discover the entire basis on which to make your choice between a jump and a nonjump suit response.

Suppose your response is one spade, as recommended in the preceding paragraph. What happens then is:

NORTH	SOUTH
1 ♡	1 ♠
3 ♠	

Now South knows that North has a powerful hand and that a grand slam is virtually sure. North has given a jump raise in spades—and has given it over a minimum one-over-one response that might have been made on a hand as weak as

♠ Q J x x   ♡ x x   ◇ K x x   ♣ x x x x

If North could take the responsibility for a contract of three-odd opposite so weak a hand, and could urge a game contract if South's hand is any stronger, North must be very strong. Furthermore, North probably has ♠ A K x x. Since North bid the hearts first, despite having so much in spades, he must have five hearts or more. Needing more strength than this for his double raise, North undoubtedly has at least the king in one minor suit and the king or a singleton in the other. Even if North has a small doubleton in diamonds, South can expect to get enough discards in hearts and clubs to ditch his entire string of diamond losers. This is an unusual case in which South can go to seven spades over the three-spade bid and have about a ten-to-one chance of making it.

What would have happened if South had made the less imaginative response of two spades over one heart? Every later bid would have lost some meaning; the following bidding would have been meaningless:

NORTH	SOUTH
1 ♡	2 ♠
3 ♠	

North might readily have raised to three spades on a hand like the following; three spades would be his best bid:

♠ A 8 6 2   ♡ Q 10 9 5 3   ◊ Q 5   ♣ K Q

Since his partner has forced to game, he is simply confirming the spade suit. South cannot tell whether North has such a hand, or whether he has three-card spade support, A-K-x, which would make the grand slam a reasonable gamble. On the supporting hand shown above, even the small slam—though the bidding of a small slam on South's hand was a foregone conclusion as soon as North opened the bidding—even a small slam might in some circumstances fail to make.

The only way South can find out with any confidence is by letting North make a free, rather than a forced, rebid.

Thus is revealed the great advantage of the one-over-one response: It makes partner's rebids far more informative, because those rebids must be made with due allowance for the possible weakness of the one-over-one response.

Does this mean that the one-over-one response is invariably superior to the immediate game force? It most emphatically does not. In fact, the jump response is not used by Americans nearly as often as it should be. But the jump response should be made on a different type of hand from the one-over-one, and with a different object. The difference may be roughly stated in this way:

The one-over-one response is superior when the responder expects to have to make the final decision himself. This occurs, usually, when his hand has great playing strength and very few "holes" (required key cards) in it, and when general information as to his partner's strength will be all he needs.

The game-forcing jump response is superior when the responder, despite his high-card strength, is missing so many key cards that he can hardly hope to find out about all of them in the course of a normal bidding sequence. In such cases it is best for the responder to make the jump response, revealing his abnormal high-card holding immediately. Given this information, his partner may be able to guide the combined hands into the best contract.

Most bridge players, including American experts, do exactly the opposite of what is right. They make the game-forcing jump response only on hands that are strong in playing strength; they make minimum responses (or occasionally jump no-trump responses) on hands that have little to recommend them except their high-card content. They demand strong support for partner's suit, or a solid suit of their own, before they will make the jump response. To partner's one-club bid they will respond two diamonds, when it should be one diamond, on the following hand:

♠ A   ♡ K 6 2   ◇ A K Q J 7 5   ♣ 7 5 4

and they will bid one diamond, when they should bid two, on this:

♠ 7 4 2   ♡ A K J   ◇ A K 6 5 2   ♣ 8 6

The question to ask oneself, when having a concentration of high cards but not a great deal of dependable playing strength, is this: "Considering my partner's opening bid, am I willing to stop short of game?" If the answer is No, then the jump response should be made.

JUMP RESPONSES IN LOWER-RANKING SUITS

Exactly the same considerations prevail when the choice is between a nonjump response at the two-level and a game-forcing jump to the three-level—that is, the question of whether to bid two or three diamonds over partner's one-spade bid. If you bid two diamonds, you will find out more about partner's hand. If you bid three diamonds, you will tell him more about yours.

This is a good three-heart response to partner's one-spade bid:

♠ A x x ♡ A K x x x ◇ x x x ♣ A x

You are not going to stop short of game; but where do you go from there? If you bid only two hearts and partner rebids two spades, you can make no safe bid that will tell partner you have four tricks in top cards; yet this may be all he needs to know if he has something like

♠ K Q x x x x ♡ Q x ◇ A x ♣ x x x

On such a hand partner will never make a slam try unless you invite him to strongly and at once; yet you are not strong enough to make a slam try that would risk passing the game level, for if partner has

♠ K Q 10 x x ♡ x x ◇ A Q x ♣ Q 10 x

you don't want to be any further along than four spades when the bidding ends.

The three-heart bid solves the problem beautifully. You bid it and then relax. You can content yourself with absolute minimum rebids thereafter: If there is any chance of a slam, partner can bid it himself. After all, he knows what you have—and you couldn't very well have less.

Another case of the hand with many holes in it:

♠ A Q x x ♡ Q x ◇ A Q x x ♣ A x x

Partner bids one heart; this is a good two-spade response. Unless the circumstances are exceptional (in which case any response should work) you will not have time to find out if your partnership has a good trump suit and if your partner's hand will plug the many holes in yours. The two-spade response lets your partner do the deciding. Again, you couldn't have less.

THE DANGER IN THE MINIMUM RESPONSE

The great danger when one makes a minimum response on a hand with four top tricks in it, but little else, is that he will always thereafter be doubtful that he has adequately shown his slam-going assets, so he will try to make up later for his earlier underbidding and he may find himself at a contract that has passed game but is not quite a slam—undertaking a risk out of all proportion to the possible gain.

NORTH
♠ A 8 3
♡ A K 7 5 4
♢ 7 6 2
♣ A 5

WEST
♠ J 5 4
♡ 10 2
♢ Q 9 4 3
♣ K Q 9 2

EAST
♠ 7 2
♡ J 9 8 3
♢ K 10 8
♣ 10 7 4 3

SOUTH
♠ K Q 10 9 6
♡ Q 6
♢ A J 5
♣ J 8 6

South dealt. Neither side was vulnerable. The bidding:

SOUTH	WEST	NORTH	EAST
1 ♠	Pass	2 ♡	Pass
2 ♠	Pass	3 ♣	Pass
3 ♡	Pass	3 ♠	Pass
4 ♠	Pass	5 ♠	Pass
Pass	Pass		

West opened the club king. Dummy won, then South cashed the queen and king of spades and the queen and king of hearts. South tried to trump a low heart, but West overtrumped with the spade jack.

West led a diamond and East's king fell to South's ace. Unable at this point to lead a club and establish a club ruff in dummy— for West would cash the diamond queen and defeat the contract —South led to dummy's spade ace, discarded two clubs on dummy's hearts, and led a diamond. He lost two diamond tricks and was down one.

Granted that South played badly and could have made his five-spade contract in several different ways, there was no good reason for him to be at five spades in the first place. Five in a major suit is a futile contract, with nothing to gain and everything to lose.

Most bridge players do misplay hands occasionally. Why must they also be saddled with bad contracts?

Too often a player with a hand such as North's, having reached game, becomes fearful that he has not adequately shown his many high cards, carries on beyond game, and arrives at the unprofitable five-bid. An immediate jump response would relieve North of this fear. The bidding might go:

SOUTH	WEST	NORTH	EAST
1 ♠	Pass	3 ♡	Pass
3 ♠	Pass	4 ♠	Pass

Now South, with his minimum, might pass. Give him only a slightly stronger hand—for example, a six-card spade suit—and he would surely bid six, for North could not possibly have less for his jump response; and with a six-card spade suit in the South hand, the slam would be a virtual laydown.

BAD PLAY, WORSE BIDDING

Another tragedy for the minimum bidders occurred in the following deal, and this time there might have been a double solution.

NORTH
♠ A Q 7 2
♡ 4 3
◊ A 7 6
♣ A K 9 4

WEST
♠ J 10 9 8
♡ K J 9 2
◊ 10 3
♣ 10 6 3

EAST
♠ 6 4 3
♡ 8 6
◊ Q 9 5 4
♣ Q J 8 7

SOUTH
♠ K 5
♡ A Q 10 7 5
◊ K J 8 2
♣ 5 2

South dealt. Neither side was vulnerable. The bidding was:

SOUTH	WEST	NORTH	EAST
1 ♡	Pass	1 ♠	Pass
2 ◊	Pass	3 ♣	Pass
3 N.T.	Pass	4 N.T.	Pass
Pass	Pass		

Here again, North simply could not believe that he had shown as strong a hand as he had, so in an effort to repair the damage he got beyond game. Double-dummy, South could have made ten tricks at no-trump. But there is no excuse for having to play four no-trump double-dummy when six is hopeless and three would be enough for the game.

West opened the jack of spades and South won it with the king, led a diamond to dummy's ace, and finessed the ten of hearts, losing to the jack.

West led another spade and dummy won. Another heart finesse was tried and it lost. A third spade lead knocked dummy's last stopper. South discarded a diamond from his hand.

South now had a problem. If the hearts had broken 3-3, he

could have made his contract by taking the king of diamonds and running the hearts. South decided against this and took a diamond finesse against East's queen, the finesse winning; but South still did not have ten tricks. He wound up with three spades, one heart, three diamonds, and two clubs—down one on a game-going hand.

The great fault was not in South's play but in North's one-spade response. North might have made one of two better bids. He might have responded three no-trump, which would have shown accurately the number of points he held but would not have indicated that they were all in top cards. When a player's points mount up so high and are concentrated in aces and other quick-trick combinations, three no-trump is not a good response because it is so easy for partner to pass.

North's other recourse would be the proper one, an immediate jump to two spades—after which North could relax and make minimum bids. The bidding then would have gone as follows:

SOUTH	WEST	NORTH	EAST
1 ♡	Pass	2 ♠	Pass
3 ♢ or	Pass	3 N.T.	Pass
2 N.T.			
Pass	Pass		

Without a show of heart or diamond support from North, South would be unlikely ever to make a slam try; and North would have no reason to make a further slam try, having shown all he had by his first response. The three no-trump contract that would have resulted, no matter which member of the North-South partnership played it, would have been both logical and foolproof.

GOOD BIDDING, BETTER PLAY

Back now to the beautiful hand mentioned earlier, for the entire play of that hand should be given. It had a point that many a famous player fell down on.

NORTH
♠ A K 8 3
♡ Q 10 9 6 5 2
◇ 6
♣ K Q

WEST
♠ 6
♡ J 8 7 4
◇ Q 9 5
♣ J 10 9 8 3

EAST
♠ 10 4 2
♡ 3
◇ K 8 7 4
♣ 7 6 5 4 2

SOUTH
♠ Q J 9 7 5
♡ A K
◇ A J 10 3 2
♣ A

West dealt, with neither side vulnerable. The bidding:

WEST	NORTH	EAST	SOUTH
Pass	1 ♡	Pass	1 ♠
Pass	3 ♠	Pass	7 ♠ *
Pass	Pass	Pass	

West opened the jack of clubs and South won with the ace. South then laid down the jack of spades. So far, declarer plus the various people who later essayed to make the contract all played the same.

The question concerns South's next lead. Declarer didn't do right. He led the five of spades to dummy's king. Then, suddenly realizing that if the hearts did not break 3-2 he would not have enough entries to dummy to establish the heart suit and get back to run it, he tried to cash the ace and king of hearts. East ruffed the second round of hearts and declarer was down one. It didn't matter, anyway: South might just as well have gone down on the fifth trick as on a later one. Once he took the second round of spades he had thrown away the grand slam.

* If using the grand slam force, South should bid five no-trump.

South was a good player, and his downfall should be attributed to carelessness in the face of an apparent abundance of wealth rather than to inability to figure out the proper line of play. After he took his licking, he showed the declarer's and dummy's hands to several of his expert friends, and only about half of them played so as to make the contract.

Yet the proper play is quite obvious when you stop to consider. If the hearts break no worse than 4-1, it is perfectly safe to cash a high heart. A 5-0 heart break is too remote a possibility to guard against. Therefore the ace of hearts should be cashed at trick three.

Having got this round of hearts through, South proceeds to take a second round of trumps, leading to the king. When the trumps do not break, he makes his contract absolutely safe by leading the king of clubs and discarding his king of hearts. Now he ruffs a low heart with the queen of spades, not caring whether the suit breaks or not; draws the last trump with a lead to dummy's spade ace, and ruffs another low heart with his last trump. Dummy is left with an established heart suit and the eight of trumps for entry. Thirteen tricks are in.

7

PREËMPTIVE OR SHUT-OUT BIDS

A BRIDGE AUTHORITY named P. Hal Sims, who had the largest following among advanced bridge players throughout the United States for two or three years—especially 1932 and 1933—did not believe in ever making a high shut-out bid.

In this doctrine Sims was alone among bridge authorities, before and since. Every other authority advocates using the opening suit-bids of three and four to shut out the opponents, on hands that are weak defensively but have long trump suits. In no other department of the game has there ever been such unanimity among the experts.

Sims was wrong, the other authorities are right. Even though certain countermeasures have been developed against preëmptive bids, the preëmptive bid must be effective because there is no way for the opponents to recapture those lost rounds of bidding, in which they might have exchanged information to guide them to their best contract.

NORTH
♠ Q 10 5 3
♡ Q J 9 3
♢ J 9 8 7
♣ A

WEST
♠ A 9 7 4 2
♡ A K 10 8 6
♢ K 6
♣ 9

EAST
♠ K 8 6
♡ 7 5
♢ A Q 4 3 2
♣ 8 6 5

SOUTH
♠ J
♡ 4 2
♢ 10 5
♣ K Q J 10 7 4 3 2

Suppose South, not vulnerable, makes an opening bid of four clubs. West may suspect that his side can make four-odd in whichever major suit East can best support. For West to show both his suits, however, would require two bids. This would necessitate a contract of five-odd, which might go down. For West to attempt, by guessing, to select the best suit would be equally dangerous. Finally, there is the danger that East can support neither suit, and that North can double and severely penalize any overcall. West may find in these circumstances that it is safer merely to double South's four-club bid; if East passes, East-West collect a penalty of 300 points minus 100 honors—poor pay for the spade game they could have reached and made if South had passed.

STANDARDS FOR PREËMPTIVE BIDS

In stating the requirements for preëmptive bids, the authorities show almost as complete unanimity as they do in accepting the principle.

One requirement is that the hand contain no more than 10 points in high cards.

The other requirement is that the hand be able to win within two tricks of the contract if vulnerable and within three tricks if not vulnerable, so that it will not go down more than 500 points (the approximate value of an opposing game) even if partner cannot add a trick.

Both of these rules are more honored in the breach than the observance. The experts may agree on pronouncing them but at the card table they do not often follow them.

Always, in setting the maximum of 10 high-card points, an outside jack and often a queen is disregarded. The following hand is an opening four-spade bid for anybody:

♠ A K Q J 8 6 3 2   ♡ 5   ◇ 6 5   ♣ J 4

If the jack were counted the hand would have 11 points, but the jack is treated no differently from a small card.

The theory of the 500-point limit, often called the Rule of Two and Three, is so plausible that perhaps it is no wonder the experts have all espoused it. But it is only plausible, not logical.

The 500-point rule applies, of course, only to bids that are made more or less blindly—that is, with no reasonable way of estimating the number of tricks the respective sides can win. After the bidding has progressed somewhat, no "rule" controls sacrifice bidding, except the scoring table.

South	West	North	East
1 ♠	2 ◇	2 ♡	3 ◇
3 ♡			

At this point West has enough information to estimate, or at least to make an intelligent guess, as to how many points, if any, he should sacrifice to keep North-South from playing the hand. If in West's opinion North-South can make three hearts but not four, West will not deliberately go down more than 100 points. If West believes North-South can make a game, he will gladly go down 300 points at diamonds, and may risk as many as 500 points. But in any case he is measuring known risk against known gain.

But when the dealer picks up a hand like this:

♠ J   ♡ 4 2   ◇ 10 5   ♣ K Q J 10 7 4 3 2

(the South hand in the deal shown above) he has no real knowledge of where he wants the bidding to end up. Maybe the opponents can make game, but maybe if unmolested they will get in trouble. Maybe partner has a powerhouse and will be hindered by an opening preëmptive bid. The possibilities both of gain and of loss are countless. It is necessary to choose the call that over a period of time will work out to South's advantage more often than not.

The true criterion of a preëmptive bid is the same as for any call—bid, pass, or double. If over an infinite number of deals a certain call produces a better result than any other call, it is a good bid. If it produces an inferior result, then it is a bad bid.

Take the previous hand, with eight clubs to the K-Q-J and nothing else. We say that the hand will win only seven tricks and may go down three at a four-club bid. The rule, then, will permit you to open with four clubs if you are not vulnerable, when your maximum loss is 500. If you are vulnerable, you are too weak for a four-club bid, at which you might be down 800.

But it is never the extent of your possible loss that really counts; it is the likelihood of your loss, balanced against the extent and the likelihood of your gain.

A bid that may go down 1,400 points is not *ipso facto* a bad bid; what matters is how that bid will come out in the long run.

Most experts will open four clubs on the South hand with the eight-card club suit, vulnerable or not, and they will do it even if they do not have the 100 honors to come off their score.

NEW PRINCIPLES FOR PREËMPTIVE BIDDING

For those who wish to cast off their shackles and range anywhere from a Rule of 1 and 2 on down to a Rule of 4 and 5, there are some basic principles to be observed.

First principle: The harder the bid to overcall, the stronger the hand should be.

When you make a shut-out bid, it is quite obvious to your opponents that you do not want them to bid. They will react in a human manner and try to bid anyway. In a close choice between a bid and a penalty double, they will tend to favor the bid. If unable to bid and having a close choice between a pass and a penalty double, they will tend to double so as not to be shut out altogether.

If your preëmpt is four clubs, they are twice as likely to find a bid as if your preëmpt were four hearts, and even more likely to find a bid than if your preëmpt were four spades.

A four-spade bid must be strong because it is the most likely to be doubled, and because the double of four spades is clearly for penalties, while the double of a lower preëmpt is generally takeout or optional (see page 205).

Second principle: Every defensive trick in your hand decreases the advisability of a shut-out bid. You might even say that every defensive trick calls for an extra playing trick, though that would be an oversimplification.

With this hand:

♠ Q J 9 8 7 5 4 3 2   ♡ 6   ◇ 9   ♣ 4 3

you have only seven winners, but not a prayer of a defensive trick; a vulnerable four-spade bid is justified. Add a defensive trick:

♠ A Q J 9 8 7 5 4   ♡ 6   ◇ 9 3   ♣ 4 3

and you have better than seven winners, but four spades stands to gain much less. One trick in partner's hand will probably stop an adverse slam, and if he has his fair proportion of the strength you may be able to stop a game. This is a good nonvulnerable four-bid but a doubtful vulnerable one. You'll never be shut out of the bidding on such a hand, anyway.

Finally:

♠ J 9 8 7 5 4 3 2   ♡ 6   ◇ A K   ♣ 4 3

On this hand, with eight tricks, a four-spade bid would be "safe" in theory, but why bid it? You have some defense; you have some help for partner if he has a long suit, too. A four-spade bid would shut out your partner as well as your opponents, and if he has a good hand with a singleton in spades and perhaps A-K-Q-J-x-x in hearts, your side may make four hearts when you couldn't make four spades.

Therefore a corollary to this principle is that a shut-out bid is best when you have nothing that will help partner if he plays the hand at his own suit.

Third principle: Vulnerability controls not only the number of points you will lose if doubled but also the probability that you will be doubled. If you are vulnerable and the opponents are not, they would rather double your preëmptive bid than overcall it; therefore any preëmpt you make should be on the assumption that you will play the hand doubled. If you are not vulnerable and your opponents are, they will prefer to bid if possible and you will have a good chance to escape even if you run into one of those cases when they could double and beat you a million— if only they knew.

MORE DISREGARDED RULES

Nearly all the books advise one to avoid making a preëmptive bid when holding four cards of a major suit outside the trump suit.

The idea is that the preëmpt may shut partner out with four or five cards of that suit, causing your side to miss a game.

The principle is logical but frequently an expert will feel that the chance of such a major-suit game is sufficiently remote to be disregarded. If a preëmptive bid is indicated in the bidding situation, the chance of missing a game is just one more hazard to accept along with the principal hazard, which is that the bid will go down more than you wish it to.

Such bugaboos are especially disregarded when a preëmptive bid is used as a trap, which often occurs in third or fourth positions after partner has passed and the chance for a slam is known to be remote or nonexistent.

In the following deal a high-ranking expert made the third-hand bid of four hearts. In almost every respect this hand violates the rules for preëmptive bids, which of course is the principal reason he selected the bid. Such offbeat tactics are like bluffs in poker—they are and should be used sparingly.

NORTH
- ♠ J 10 5 4
- ♡ Q J 6
- ◇ J
- ♣ A 10 7 3 2

WEST
- ♠ K 9 2
- ♡ 7 2
- ◇ A Q 10 8
- ♣ Q 8 6 4

EAST
- ♠ A Q
- ♡ 5 3
- ◇ K 9 7 5 4 3
- ♣ J 9 5

SOUTH
- ♠ 8 7 6 3
- ♡ A K 10 9 8 4
- ◇ 6 2
- ♣ K

North dealt and both sides were vulnerable. The bidding was:

NORTH	EAST	SOUTH	WEST
Pass	Pass	4 ♡	Pass
Pass	Pass		

When West opened a low club, South was given an opportunity to make an unusual throw-in play.

The king of clubs won the first trick, and then South led the eight of hearts to dummy's jack and trumped a low club with the king of hearts. The nine of hearts was led to dummy's queen.

Now South played the ace of clubs and discarded not a spade but a diamond, though he could have trumped his second diamond in dummy after giving up the one trick he had to lose in that suit.

South trumped the seven of clubs, which made the ten of clubs in dummy good.

Finally South executed his throw-in by leading the diamond.

Whichever opponent won the diamond trick, after taking two spade tricks the defenders would have to lead another diamond, giving South a ruff and discard for one of his spades, while his last spade would go off on the ten of clubs. Only one diamond and two spade tricks were lost and the contract was made.

This line of play makes the contract if either defender has a singleton spade honor or two spade honors doubleton, and may make the contract even if the spade suit is not blocked but is misplayed. This can easily happen. For example, if West held K-Q-2 of spades he might neglect to start by leading the deuce.

8

OVERCALLS AND DOUBLES

BRIDGE AUTHORITIES almost without exception counsel against overcalling opponents' opening bids. It (almost) never pays, they say.

Yet in a strong game the bidding is usually hotly contested, and if experts followed their own advice strictly it could not be, for they would too seldom get in the bidding. So what they mean, in advising against overcalls, is to advise against the average player's habit of making an overcall at the two-level on a hand like this:

♠ 96   ♡ A J 4   ◇ A K 8 7 5   ♣ 9 4 3

To bid two diamonds over an opponent's one-spade bid on such a hand is suicidal in a strong game. Even if two diamonds can be made there is little to be gained, while the two-diamond contract is very likely to be doubled and defeated at least three tricks—500 points even if not vulnerable.

High cards mean far less than playing strength in deciding whether or not to overcall, except in the case of a no-trump overcall. How much playing strength is required depends on whether the player is vulnerable or not vulnerable, and whether he can overcall with a one-bid or would have to bid two.

The expert overcalls quite freely when he need bid only one to do so. There are three reasons why a one-bid may be made on considerably less strength than a two-bid:

1] The danger of being doubled is far less. An overcall at the level of one is seldom doubled. An overcall at the level of two is almost always doubled if the opponents can easily defeat it.

2] It is possible for partner to rescue, if a one-bid is doubled and partner has a fairly good suit; it is usually dangerous for partner to rescue a doubled two-bid, for he is almost sure to be doubled.

3] There is little to gain by overcalling at the two-level. The very fact that a bid of two is required means that the opponents have the higher-ranking suit. If the strength is evenly divided, the overcalling side will surely be outbid.

Therefore, despite the "Rule of Two and Three," a vulnerable overcall at two means the bidder expects to win eight tricks. Only with bad breaks or a very bad dummy will he win fewer.

♠ 6   ♡ K J 10   ◇ A Q 10 9 8 3   ♣ J 4 3

This hand is an acceptable overcall of two diamonds over an opponent's one-spade bid, whether vulnerable or not. Remove the ten, nine and eight of diamonds and replace them with three smaller diamonds and the expert would pass if vulnerable, but would still bid two diamonds if not vulnerable. Even if vulnerable, he would bid one diamond over an opponent's one-club bid.

The hand shown offers some incentive for overcalling: It has a six-card suit, and if partner has the diamond king and most of the high cards unaccounted for, there may be a game in no-trump. It has strength in hearts, and if partner can bid hearts there may even be a heart game to be made. Put the side strength in clubs instead of hearts and many experts would pass one spade, there being too little to gain from overcalling, and danger of a two-trick penalty if doubled.

A hand with most of its strength in high cards is usually passed, unless it is strong enough for a takeout double.

♠ 10 6 3   ♡ K 3   ◇ A K J 5   ♣ A 6 3 2

Over an opposing bid of one spade or one heart, most experts are likely to pass this hand. It is dangerous to double, since the hand does not have sufficient strength in spades or hearts to support a weak response. Over an opposing bid of one club most experts would bid one diamond.

The reason for a pass when holding high-card strength but no long suit is that no game contract is likely to be made, while the opponents can probably be defeated if they overbid. This does not apply to a typical no-trump hand, however.

♠ A Q 6   ♡ Q 7   ◇ K Q 10 4   ♣ K J 7 6

This hand is a typical one no-trump overcall of an opponent's opening one-spade bid, whether vulnerable or not. Note that the hand is short in hearts. This fact is characteristic of the no-trump overcall. With heart length, a player should double. This principle paved the way for the "unusual no-trump," a bidding convention described later in this book.

Especially when not vulnerable against vulnerable opponents, a weak overcall at any level may be made on freak distribution, without any high-card strength to speak of. When vulnerable, an overcall is seldom made without about two tricks, although exceptionally it may be.

1. ♠ 8
    ♡ 9
    ◇ Q J 10 7
    ♣ K J 9 8 7 5 3

2. ♠ 10 9 7 6 5 3
    ♡ A Q J 6 5
    ◇ 8
    ♣ 2

Hand No. 1 justifies a nonvulnerable overcall of two clubs over an opponent's opening bid, but would be passed if vulnerable, although it is almost sure to win seven tricks at clubs. (Three clubs, not vulnerable, might be bid by some who treat it as a weak bid.) Hand No. 2 would justify a one-spade overcall of an opponent's bid whether vulnerable or not, because of its distribution.

When the two-level overcall can be made in hearts rather than a minor suit, a slightly greater chance is taken, even when vulnerable, because a game may more easily be produced. Even so, no more than half the experts would have overcalled on West's hand in the following deal; the remainder would have passed.

NORTH
♠ J 8 7 4
♡ 6 5 3
◇ J 3 2
♣ J 10 7

WEST
♠ 9
♡ K Q J 7 4
◇ K Q 10 8
♣ 6 3 2

EAST
♠ K 6 5
♡ 10 9 2
◇ A 9 6 5 4
♣ K Q

SOUTH
♠ A Q 10 3 2
♡ A 8
◇ 7
♣ A 9 8 5 4

South dealt, with both sides vulnerable. The bidding:

SOUTH	WEST	NORTH	EAST
1 ♠	2 ♡	Pass	2 N.T.
3 ♣	Pass	Pass	3 ♡
Pass	4 ♡	Pass	Pass
Double	Pass	4 ♠	Double
Pass	Pass	Pass	

Nearly every expert would make a one-heart overcall on West's hand, if South's opening bid had been one club.

The four-spade contract could have gone down, but the defenders fell into a losing defense. West opened the king of diamonds and continued with the queen. South trumped and then cashed the ace of spades. Then South led the ten of spades and played dummy's jack on it, trying to force entry to dummy either on this round or on the next one.

East took his king of spades, and now could have assured the defeat of the contract by switching to hearts. But East saw no reason to discontinue the diamond leads, which were forcing out all of South's trumps, so he led the ace of diamonds.

South trumped with the spade queen; led his low spade to

dummy's eight; and led the club jack from dummy. East had to cover and South won with the club ace. Then South gave up a club trick to East's king and had the remaining tricks, since he could discard two of dummy's hearts while running the clubs. He made four spades doubled; East-West could have made their four hearts.

THE QUESTION OF JUMP OVERCALLS

"Question" is the right word to apply. In the matter of jump overcalls there are two schools among the experts, and they are apparently irreconcilable. One group uses single jump overcalls as weak, shut-out bids; the other group uses them as strong bids.

But there is no question as to which is the larger group today. Among players of the very highest rank, those who prefer weak jump overcalls outnumber by four or five to one those who prefer strong jump overcalls.

By a jump overcall is meant a bid of one trick more than necessary over an opponent's opening bid. It occurs in such a situation as this:

SOUTH	WEST	NORTH	EAST
1 ♡	2 ♠		
	or 3 ♢		

West's bid in either instance is a jump overcall. The term is not applied to "double jump overcalls." If West had bid three spades, or four diamonds, there would be universal agreement that his bid was preëmptive—a weak bid, asking partner to pass.

Among most of those who use the single jump overcall as a weak bid, the bid is a very weak one indeed. Either of the following hands would be typical:

♠ Q J 9 6 5 3   ♡ 6 3   ♢ J 10 5 2   ♣ 7

or

♠ Q J 9 6 5 4   ♡ 6 3   ♢ K 8 7   ♣ 7 5

If not vulnerable, a player might make a jump overcall of two spades on either of these hands over an opposing one-heart or one-club bid. A vulnerable two-spade overcall would be exactly one trick stronger—a spade suit of K-Q-J-x-x-x instead of Q-J-9-x-x-x.

Almost always, the partner of the weak jump bidder will pass; when he raises, his purpose usually is to carry the preëmptive principle further and shut out the opponents; and when he bids no-trump he usually has about 15 high-card points, chiefly in aces and kings, including a sure stopper in the opposing suit and a high honor in his partner's suit. On this bidding:

SOUTH	WEST	NORTH	EAST
1 ♡	2 ♠	Pass	

East would pass the nonvulnerable two-spade jump overcall with a hand as strong as this:

♠ A 7   ♡ K 5 2   ◇ A Q 6 4   ♣ J 8 4 2

East probably would risk two no-trump over a vulnerable two-spade overcall, but since many experts use two no-trump as the only forcing response to the weak jump overcall, and no-trump is not a safe game contract on this hand (because of the danger of a club opening and a heart return), East might prefer simply to bid four spades. Four spades would also be the bid on the following hand:

♠ 10 8 7 2   ♡ 9 8 4   ◇ 7   ♣ Q 9 8 6 2

Here the bid is a shut-out and an anticipated sacrifice bid, not only expecting but hoping for a double because the opponents may be able to make a slam and can surely make a game.

The minority group argues that a single jump overcall is not high enough to be an effective shut-out bid. The majority retorts that since one seldom holds a powerful hand over an opponent's opening bid, the single jump overcall is wasted if used as a strong bid.

THE CASE FOR THE STRONG JUMP OVERCALL

An advantage for the strength-showing jump overcall is found especially when the overcaller holds a two-suited hand with the top cards in both suits and at least one of the suits a major. Such a two-suiter often produces game if partner fits the major suit, but it can be very dangerous at a high level if partner cannot support either suit. Examples are:

1] South bids one diamond and West, second hand holds:

♠ A K 10 5 4   ♡ A Q J 7 5   ◊ 6   ♣ 3 2

If West doubles, East's response will probably be two clubs. West must then bid two spades and risk having the bidding dropped (though East may have support for hearts); or bid *three* spades, which forces East to bid again even though East may have no support for either major suit.

The jump overcall shows one of the two suits and gives the proper impression of strength at the same time; it asks for a light raise, yet retains the advantage of being able to pass short of game if partner has a blank.

2] South bids one diamond and West holds:

♠ A Q 10 9 6 5 3   ♡ 6   ◊ A K 5   ♣ 3 2

Many players would jump to four spades on this hand, but four spades might go down when two or three spades could be made —and could not be outbid by the opponents.

Players who use weak jump overcalls would probably double one diamond; but over a two-club or one-heart response from East, West would face the same dilemma as in Case 1: Play safe and risk missing game at one or two spades, or be bold and risk going down at three or four spades?

If West finds his partner with a doubleton diamond plus any three spades, or two fairly good spades (J x or K-x), game should be bid. If East has a singleton spade and a weak hand, West wishes to stop as soon as possible. The strong jump overcall, inviting a response on the barest kind of support but permitting a pass on a Yarborough or misfit, solves the problem of such hands.

A jump overcall in a minor suit, such as three clubs over an opponent's one-spade bid, is also useful as a strength-showing bid but invites a three no-trump response, not a raise.

Therefore the minor-suit jump overcall, when used to show

strength, indicates a long and probably solid suit with some high cards outside—in all, enough to run seven or eight tricks at no-trump. A "strong jump overcaller" would bid three clubs over an opposing one-spade bid on this hand:

♠ 6 2   ♡ Q 8   ◇ K J   ♣ A K Q J 7 4 2

His partner would be expected to bid three no-trump with 8 to 10 points including a sure stopper in the opposing suit, for example with this hand:

♠ Q J 7   ♡ A 7 6 5 2   ◇ 10 9 3   ♣ 8 5

The contract would not be without risk, but anyone would wish to be there.

A strong jump overcall in a major suit can be raised with 5 or 6 points and some fit with partner's suit. Either of the following hands would justify raising a strong two-spade overcall to three:

<table>
<tr><td>1.</td><td>♠ 8 6 4</td><td>2.</td><td>♠ 8 6 4</td></tr>
<tr><td></td><td>♡ K 7 5 2</td><td></td><td>♡ 6</td></tr>
<tr><td></td><td>◇ 8 3</td><td></td><td>◇ 9 8 5 3</td></tr>
<tr><td></td><td>♣ Q J 7 6</td><td></td><td>♣ K 7 6 4 2</td></tr>
</table>

THE CASE FOR THE WEAK JUMP OVERCALL

As observed above, those who prefer the weak jump overcall use as one of their primary arguments the fact that there are few opportunities to use the strong jump overcall.

This argument is irrefutable. There are indeed few cases when one player is strong enough to open the bidding and the next player has a hand of not only the type but also the strength to make a strong jump overcall.

The weak-jump-overcall adherents argue also that their bids often shut out the bidding side. The partner of the opening bidder, if he has a fair hand, may still not have enough to bid over such an overcall as two spades. The opening bidder, unable to rely upon his partner for anything after such a sequence as

South	West	North	East
1 ◇	2 ♠	Pass	Pass

—for North may have passed a weak hand, and East a strong hand—will be risking much if he makes a doubtful rebid.

The best defense against the weak jump overcall is the "sputnik," or Roth-Stone double, described on page 174; and it is a curious anomaly of bridge experts' thinking that the players most enthusiastic about the weak jump overcall are usually the very players who espouse the "negative" double that defeats it.

THE QUICK RAISE

Those who do use the weak jump overcall and do not wish to miss some fortuitous no-trump games must cultivate the quick raise of a minor-suit overcall made at the two-level.

The following is not an unusual bidding sequence—

South	West	North	East
1 ♠	2 ♣	Pass	3 ♣

—but East's club raise was unusual on the hand he held:

♠ 76   ♡ A J 7 5 2   ◇ Q 8 5 4   ♣ K 6

Only the East player who raised to three clubs found his side eventually in a no-trump game contract that could be made. West held:

♠ K 5   ♡ 9 4 3   ◇ A 6   ♣ A Q J 7 5 2

Without the raise, West could not have dared bid three no-trump, being vulnerable. A pass by East would have closed the bidding; a three-heart bid by East would have been raised to four hearts by West, and four hearts would have been an inferior contract. As the cards lay, it could not have been made, while three no-trump could not be defeated.

TAKEOUT DOUBLES AND RESPONSES

Probably the most widely practiced bidding convention in contract bridge has been the takeout double. It was originally developed in auction bridge about sixty years ago,* for the same purpose it serves in contract bridge: to show a strong hand after an opponent has opened the bidding, and to force partner to bid his best suit in response.

Rebels against the multiplicity of bidding conventions in contract bridge have frequently proposed that all conventional bids be barred; but these rebels have made one exception: the takeout double.

The typical hand for a takeout double is strong in all three of the suits not bid by the opponent; but the expert as often uses a double merely to advertise a strong hand, even though the strength may be nearly all in one suit.

If an opponent opened with one heart, many experts would double with either of these hands:

1.	♠ A J 5 3	2.	♠ A Q J 5 3 2
	♡ 8		♡ 8 2
	◇ K J 6 2		◇ A Q 5
	♣ A Q 7 4		♣ 7 4

The average player, who would double with hand No. 1, would scarcely think of doubling with hand No. 2; he would overcall

---

* The origin of the takeout double is disputed and can never be determined because all the disputants are dead. Bryant McCampbell claimed the invention as of 1912 and called it (in his 1915 book) the McCampbell double. Charles L. Patton claimed it and called it the Patton double. Originally the double was used only over an opening bid of one no-trump, which became the only case in which it is no longer treated as calling for a takeout. Wilbur Whitehead may have adapted it first to suit-bids. Ely Culbertson gave the takeout double its present name, but it seemed for many years that players could not be diverted from the names "informatory double" and "negative double"; only the present generation of bridge players has adopted "takeout double." Sidney Lenz wished to introduce a new call in bridge, the "challenge," to serve as a takeout double and leave the double always for business. Mr. Lenz was influenced by the fact that auction bridge players often considered it discreditably sharp to pass a double of one no-trump for penalties.

with one spade, or perhaps with two spades. But to most experts, an overcall at the one-level is strictly limited in strength; since it is often made on a weak hand, it can never be made on a strong hand, for that would make the bid ambiguous.* Since the expert is more concerned with showing the extent of his strength than with showing its location, he doubles first to show strength and bids his suit later, after he has told his partner to expect a strong hand.

In recent years, however, the takeout double itself has tended to become somewhat vague in describing the doubler's strength. This is because the double, though it is a strength-showing call, is often safer than a mere overcall, which is supposed to be far weaker.

A good player would shudder at the thought of overcalling an opposing spade bid on the following hand:

♠ 5 3   ♡ K Q 8 6 4   ◇ A 10 7   ♣ K 9 8

At two hearts he might be doubled for penalties, and he would have no escape. The overcall, therefore, would risk a loss of 500 points or more, and for what compensating gain? Probably no more than a part-score, when an opponent has an opening bid.

Nevertheless it is desirable to enter the bidding when it is safely possible, and by doubling on the above hand a player can enter the bidding with reasonable safety. His partner may be weak but may still have a fairly long diamond or club suit. Whereas a two-heart overcall makes everything depend on finding partner with support in hearts, the takeout double leaves the way open to safety if partner has length in any of three suits. Nor does it necessarily preclude showing the five-card heart suit later if partner bids strongly.

It is advantageous to get into the bidding, if it can be done without undue risk, even when the opening bidder's side seems sure to play the hand. Information given by a defensive bid, including a double, may guide partner's defense and produce the winning trick. Undue caution cost the contract in this deal:

* An important school of experts treats even an overcall at the one-level as a strong bid, since a weak jump overcall would be made on a weaker hand; but even to this school the simple overcall, though strong, is strictly limited. It does not have such a wide range as the double has.

NORTH
♠ 9 3
♡ A Q J 4
◇ Q 10 7 6
♣ K 10 5

WEST
♠ 10 8 7 6 2
♡ 9 3 2
◇ 8 4
♣ 9 8 3

EAST
♠ A K 5 4
♡ K 10 8 6
◇ 3
♣ J 7 6 2

SOUTH
♠ Q J
♡ 7 5
◇ A K J 9 5 2
♣ A Q 4

South dealt and East-West were vulnerable. The bidding:

SOUTH	WEST	NORTH	EAST
1 ◇	Pass	1 ♡	Pass
3 ◇	Pass	5 ◇	Pass
Pass	Pass		

East may not have had a good takeout double, when vulnerable, of an opposing nonvulnerable bid. Game is seldom bid or made in a minor suit; East had much strength in the major suits; and a successful no-trump game by North-South seemed to depend on their having long and solid diamonds, which was not more than an even chance if that.

But when East passed, as in the bidding shown above, South made his game because West, forced to guess an opening lead, chose the nine of clubs.

South won the first trick with his club queen, drew the opposing diamonds in two rounds, and cashed the other two top clubs. Then South led spades.

Only East could win a spade trick, and after taking his two high spades East could not lead so as to get another trick. A heart lead would be into a finesse. A spade or club lead would give South a ruff and discard. One way or the other, South would win his eleven tricks.

If East had doubled one heart, proclaiming spade strength, West would probably have opened a spade. East could have taken his high spades, exited with a diamond, and kept the heart king safe for the setting trick.

The responses to partner's takeout double are reasonably well standardized in the bidding systems, and the principles governing the responses are sound enough in theory. The partner must respond in his best suit, even if he holds a bust. To his partner's double of one heart, he must bid one spade on a hand like this:

♠ 7 6 3 2   ♡ 9 5 4   ◇ J 9 2   ♣ Q 8 5

Since a one-spade response may be made on so weak a hand, it would seem unreasonable to make the same one-spade response on a hand like the following:

♠ K Q 10 4   ♡ 9 5 4   ◇ A 9 2   ♣ 8 5 3

Therefore, the recommended response on such a hand is a jump to two spades.

Nevertheless, it seems to go against the grain to make jump bids on hands that look so weak, and in nearly any game, including very strong ones, it is more customary to respond only one spade. When—and if—the chance to rebid comes, which it usually does, the responder will take pains to make a strength-showing bid. For example, if the doubler now bids one no-trump, the responder will raise not to two no-trump but to three.

THE CUE-BID RESPONSE

There is, finally, the cue-bid response to a takeout double. Once almost unheard of, this response has become very common in recent years. A typical situation is:

SOUTH	WEST	NORTH	EAST
1 ◇	Double	Pass	2 ◇

By his bid in the opposing suit, East may mean any of several things: He may have the ace, or a void, in that suit, and be showing that he can control it. Or he may be strong in the other suits, and ask the doubler to bid no-trump if he can stop diamonds. Or he may simply be showing strength, to find out the doubler's best suit, thereafter to rebid in no-trump if that suit does not fit his hand. He may even have a genuine playable holding in the opposing suit. The one message that the cue-bid response invariably carries is a forcing one. The doubler must rebid.

One thing the responder should always remember is that the doubler has shown considerable strength, and that even a moderate number of high cards in the responding hand are quite likely to produce a slam.

NORTH
♠ A Q 10 9 4
♡ 9 7 4
♢ A 6 3
♣ K 5

WEST
♠ 5
♡ 10 6 2
♢ Q 10 9 4 2
♣ J 9 8 4

EAST
♠ 8 7 2
♡ A K Q J 8 5
♢ 7
♣ Q 6 3

SOUTH
♠ K J 6 3
♡ 3
♢ K J 8 5
♣ A 10 7 2

East dealt, with North-South vulnerable; the bidding:

EAST	SOUTH	WEST	NORTH
1 ♡	Double	Pass	2 ♡
Pass	2 ♠	Pass	3 ♢
Pass	4 ♢	Pass	5 ♠
Pass	6 ♠	Pass	Pass
Pass			

When North bid diamonds at his second turn, South assumed that his partner had a real diamond suit. North's next bid, the jump to five spades, made it clear that he had been interested in playing in spades all the time. Hence his diamond bid was manifestly a cue-bid, showing the ace of diamonds.

South reflected that he had made no strength-showing bid after North's cue-bid of two hearts—since his spade bid and the diamond raise had been forced. Since North was able to go to five spades, South's singleton heart seemed enough to warrant risking the slam.

West opened the two of hearts and East took it with the jack and continued the suit. South ruffed the second heart with a high trump, led a trump to dummy, again ruffed a heart high, and then drew trumps, discarding a low diamond on the third round of trumps.

Declarer next cashed the high clubs and ruffed a club, hoping to drop the queen and jack. By this time East had played six black cards. Since East was marked with a long heart suit, there was room in his hand for at most two diamonds. The diamond finesse, otherwise the simplest play for the slam, was therefore foredoomed to failure.

A squeeze, however, was successful. Dummy's last trump was led. South discarded another diamond and West could not find a good discard. If West discarded the jack of clubs, South would win a trick with the club ten. And if West discarded down to only two diamonds, the top diamonds would clear the suit, establishing dummy's six of diamonds.

THE CUE-BID OVERCALL—HOW IT HAS CHANGED

The term "cue-bid" has several meanings in bridge, but the original sense is still used: a bid in a suit previously bid by an opponent, as in the following bidding.

SOUTH	WEST	NORTH	EAST
1 ♡	2 ♡ !		

In the original sense, West's two-heart bid (1) is a super-[takeout]-double, requiring East to show his best suit; (2) asserts that West has first-round control in hearts, either the ace or a void; (3) is forcing to game; (4) promises either strong support for whatever suit East bids or a solid suit in West's hand that requires no support.

The traditional two-heart bid over one heart, as shown above, would be made on a hand equivalent to one of the following:

<table>
<tr><td>1.</td><td>♠ A Q J 6</td><td>2.</td><td>♠ K 10 5 4</td></tr>
<tr><td></td><td>♡ A</td><td></td><td>♡ ———</td></tr>
<tr><td></td><td>◊ K J 10 8 5</td><td></td><td>◊ A K Q J 8 6 3</td></tr>
<tr><td></td><td>♣ A K 5</td><td></td><td>♣ A Q</td></tr>
</table>

An expert might still bid two hearts on either of these hands (if once in a blue moon he were lucky enough to hold it), because it would be the most convenient or at least the surest way to make a forcing bid and defer the decision on what to do next. However, no longer does any expert *demand* such great strength, and some experts have changed the requirement diametrically, using the cue-bid overcall as a weak takeout double.

The original requirement, as illustrated by the hands shown above, might be described as 21 or more points, including distributional points, for a void in the opposing suit is as desirable as the ace. A void indicates that an essential part of the opening bidder's high-card strength is in his own suit. This fact increases the likelihood that the cue-bidder's partner will have a high card or two in the other suits.

If the hand is strong enough, there may be a singleton in the opposing suit instead of a void or the ace; and a loser or two in the opposing suit, accompanying the ace, is equally acceptable. Any of the following hands would fit the classic requirements for a two-heart overcall of an opposing one-heart bid.

<table>
<tr><td>1.</td><td>♠ A K Q 6</td><td>2.</td><td>♠ A Q J 10 8</td><td>3.</td><td>♠ A K Q J 9 7</td></tr>
<tr><td></td><td>♡ 5</td><td></td><td>♡ A 6</td><td></td><td>♡ A 3 2</td></tr>
<tr><td></td><td>◊ K Q J 9</td><td></td><td>◊ A K J 6</td><td></td><td>◊ K Q 6</td></tr>
<tr><td></td><td>♣ A K 10 5</td><td></td><td>♣ K 4</td><td></td><td>♣ 4</td></tr>
</table>

Given a void in the opposing suit, however, an expert is likely to shade the high-card requirement considerably. The two-heart over-call would be made on the following hand:

♠ A Q 10 6 3   ♡ ——————   ◇ K J 10 5   ♣ A J 8 6

This would be a classic hand for a takeout double, but the holder of the hand is afraid to double one heart because his partner might pass for penalties. *It is almost impossible to support a penalty double of a low opposing contract with a void in the trump suit.* Even the holding of a single trump can make a difference of several tricks, for then the trump suit can be led, and a penalty pass of a doubled one-bid usually demands a trump opening.

The principal effect of this downgrading of the cue-bid overcall is that *the cue-bid overcall is no longer treated as forcing to game.* Either the cue-bidder or his partner is free to pass later if he detects a misfit or the absence of game-going strength in the combined hands.

Nevertheless the cue-bid invites optimism in responding. Any expert would bid four spades on the South hand in the following deal, once North made his cue-bid.

NORTH
♠ K 9 5 4
♡ ——
◇ A K Q J 8 6 3
♣ K J

WEST
♠ A
♡ A K J 6 5 4
◇ 9 7
♣ Q 10 3 2

EAST
♠ J 8 3
♡ Q 10 8 7 3
◇ 10 5
♣ A 9 7

SOUTH
♠ Q 10 7 6 2
♡ 9 2
◇ 4 2
♣ 8 6 5 4

West dealt, with North-South vulnerable. The bidding:

WEST	NORTH	EAST	SOUTH
1 ♡	2 ♡	4 ♡	4 ♠
Pass	Pass	Pass	

South's spade suit could have been even weaker—say, J-x-x-x-x, or even 9-x-x-x-x with an outside queen, as in clubs—and South would still have come in freely at four spades. A five-card spade suit is a precious asset when partner has made a cue-bid.

West knew he could not be hurt at five hearts and was optimistic when he passed in the hope of beating four spades. He was very lucky to beat it.

South started well in the play but made a fatal lapse later.

The king of hearts was opened and was trumped in dummy, East playing the encouraging ten.

The five of spades was then led, East put on the three, and South made a good guess by playing the ten. This drew out West's ace and West continued hearts, leading the six.

Dummy trumped with the spade nine, after which the spade king was cashed. Obviously South hoped to fell both of the outstanding trumps, and if he could have done so he would have won all the rest of the tricks. But spades did not break and East was left with the jack.

Now South began to run dummy's diamonds. On the third high diamond lead from dummy East trumped with the spade jack and South overtrumped with his queen.

All would still have been well for South if he had played the clubs correctly. The four of clubs was the lead and West played the three. A finesse of the jack would have brought forth East's act, leaving the king as an entry to dummy. The club ace would have been the defenders' last trick.

But South, overhastily placing the club ace in West's hand because of West's opening bid, put up dummy's club king. Now dummy was dead and the defenders could take four club tricks.

After taking his club ace, East led the seven to West's queen. West did not make the mistake of cashing his club ten for the setting trick. South had no more diamonds, so any club in South's hand would have to be lost sooner or later. West led the ace of hearts.

South trumped and led the club eight. West played the deuce, for if South held the club nine he could not escape losing it. East got his club nine, South had to trump another heart lead, and West's ten of clubs won the last trick. Down two.

A premature lead of the club ten by West would have cost the trick that was won by East's nine.

South made his mistake and lost the game and rubber when he ruffed the second heart lead with the nine of spades. He should have unblocked the trump suit by ruffing with the spade king.

This would have cost a trump trick, for East would have been left with a J-8 tenace over dummy's nine, but it would have made the contract 100 percent sure. The spade nine would have been led to South's queen and a low spade would have given East his trump **trick** immediately. Then East could have done no better than to take his ace of clubs, the defenders' third and last trick. Unless East took the club ace at once he could never get it and South would have made not only the game but an overtrick.

WEAK CUE-BIDS, MICHAELS AND OTHERS

However wide the range of hands to which it has been applied, the cue-bid overcall has nearly always been used as a bid similar to the takeout double but *stronger*.

There is some sentiment in favor of making the cue-bid overcall *weaker* than the takeout double. The founder of this school was the late Michael Michaels of Miami, Florida.

Mr. Michaels used the cue-bid much as the "unusual no-trump" (described later) is used: To force one response from partner, but at the same time warn him of limited strength. Any further bidding he does is on his own.

Over an opponent's one-diamond bid, Mr. Michaels bid two diamonds on any of the following hands (his examples):

1.	♠ J x x x x	2.	♠ Q J 9 x x	3.	♠ K Q x x
	♡ A K J x		♡ J 9 x x x		♡ A x x x
	◇ x		◇ K x		◇ x x
	♣ x x x		♣ x		♣ x x x

The point range is 6 to 11 points in high cards. The argument for this use of the cue-bid is twofold: (1) the ultrapowerful cue-bid is largely wasted because appropriate hands so seldom occur, and (2) a bid is needed for hands on which an overcall would be unsafe but a tentative contract in a suit that fits is usually safe.

Of course the hand must be stronger when the cue-bidder is vulnerable (on No. 3 above, two diamonds would be bid only if not vulnerable against vulnerable opponents) and the Michaels cue-bids were devised chiefly for tournament play in which it is important to sacrifice even when the gain will be only a few points (neither No. 1 nor No. 3 above would justify the two-diamond cue-bid at rubber bridge).

The cue-bidder's partner, in the Michaels system, takes charge. If he makes a minimum response in his longest suit, the cue-bidder simply passes. If the partner is strong, he responds with a cue-bid:

SOUTH	WEST	NORTH	EAST
1 ◊	2 ◊	Pass	3 ◊

East holds, for example,

♠ K x x x x   ♡ A x   ◊ A Q x   ♣ x x x

Mr. Michaels went whole hog and made his cue-bids apply to major suits as well as minor suits. Over an opposing one-spade bid one might bid two spades on:

♠ x	♠ x
♡ K x x x x	♡ K Q 9 x x
◊ A 9 x x x	◊ A J 10 x x
♣ x x	♣ x x
Not vulnerable,	*Vulnerable or not,*
opponents vulnerable	*especially against*
	vulnerable opponents

Some use the minor-suit cue-bid on any two-suiter. When partner's response is not in one of the two suits, the cue-bidder rebids in the cheaper of the two suits. Suppose a spade-diamond two-suiter when the bidding goes

SOUTH	WEST	NORTH	EAST
1 ♣	2 ♣	Pass	2 ♡
Pass			

West would bid two spades, which is lower than three diamonds. East may bid three diamonds if he cannot safely pass two spades. But with a heart-diamond two-suiter, when the bidding goes

SOUTH	WEST	NORTH	EAST
1 ♠	2 ♠	Pass	3 ♣
Pass			

West would bid three diamonds, leaving East free to pass if his diamonds are better than his hearts, but telling East to bid three hearts if he prefers hearts.

In any event, if the cue-bidder takes out his partner's response into a different suit he is not showing strength. He is denying support for his partner's suit and showing a two-suiter in the other suits.

Mr. Michaels' idea still has a following, but few of his followers have adopted his idea *in toto*. By the majority of those who use them, the Michaels cue-bids are used only to overcall opening bids in the minor suits. Major-suit cue-bids show much stronger hands.

Finally there are those who use cue-bid overcalls (especially in the minor suits) to show genuine long suits. The prevalence of forcing club systems and opening minor-suit bids on three-card suits has made these genuine overcalls in the opponent's suit useful in some cases.

Over an opposing one-club bid, two clubs might be bid by this school on such a hand as:

♠ K 6   ♡ 7   ◊ Q 8 4   ♣ A Q J 9 8 5 4

When one has this hand, it makes little difference whether or not the original club bidder had a genuine suit.

Would-be users of the genuine-suit overcall should be warned, however, to bid on the assumption that there is a biddable suit out against them, and not on mere suspicion. A suit such as A-Q-10-x-x will not do.

9

DOUBLING FOR PENALTIES

IF THERE is one "greatest difference" between the strong bridge game and the average bridge game, it is in the use and frequency of penalty doubles. In the average game, moderate overbidding is seldom punished. The average player almost never doubles a low contract, seldom doubles anything on a weak-looking hand, but is apt to double a high contract on "general principles." In the expert game, unsound overbidding seldom goes unpunished, low contracts are doubled more often than high ones, and many a double is made on a hand that seems weak, in terms of high-card points at least.

Perhaps these differences are attributable to the expert's habit of considering a double first, before he thinks of bidding; and to the average player's tendency to keep on bidding as long as he can, and to double only when he can no longer bid.

Ely Culbertson proposed certain basic situations in which a player should consider a double before he determines to bid. Briefly, these are: (1) when your side has superior cards, and the opponents outbid you; (2) when your partner's opening bid is overcalled by an opponent; (3) when the ·opponents seem to stumble into a gambling contract and you have a fair hand.

Seldom does any player neglect the first opportunity.

The second of these situations—when an opponent has over-called—has received much attention from bridge writers yet is still overlooked by most players. In a typical case, both sides are vulnerable; South deals and bids one spade, West bids two clubs, and North holds

♠ 7 ♡ A K 8 5 4 ◇ J 9 4 3 ♣ Q 6 5

This hand is a proper double of two clubs. The expert would hardly consider anything but the double. The average player would bid two hearts without even thinking of the double.

Yet the two-heart bid can hardly pay, unless by chance South has excellent support for hearts; for North has no support for spades, and a no-trump game seems out of the question with clubs so insecurely stopped. If North-South can make at most a part-score (which seems likely) it will be worth less than 200 points to them. The opposing two-club contract should go down at least one trick (200 points) and may easily go down 500 even if West has a fairly good hand. North should win two heart tricks and a club trick, and may pick up an extra trick by trumping spades; South has bid and can probably win three tricks.

Less often analyzed in bridge literature, and more often overlooked in the casual bridge game, is the opportunity to double the opponents' gambling contracts. Said Culbertson, "The biggest invisible losses come when the opponents are defeated 150 points not vulnerable, or 300 points vulnerable, while doubling would have increased these scores to 500 and 800 points, respectively."

The British expert the late S. J. Simon, in his book *Why You Lose at Bridge,* did give proper attention to these situations. In a rather startling but entirely convincing example, he proposed bidding like this:

NORTH	EAST	SOUTH	WEST
1 ♣	Pass	1 ♡	Pass
2 ♣	Pass	2 N.T.	Pass
3 N.T.	Pass	Pass	

Then he supposed that West held either of these hands:

1.	♠ A 10 x	2.	♠ 10 x x
	♡ K Q 10		♡ K Q 10
	◇ A K J x x		◇ A K J x x
	♣ K x		♣ x x

If he must double three no-trump on either of these hands, he said, he would far rather have hand No. 2. Hand No. 1 is too strong; partner must have a totally worthless hand and North must have a six- or seven-card club suit lying over the king. The clubs will be run, West will be squeezed, and the contract will be made. When West holds the weaker hand, there is a good chance that East will have a high club or spade with which he can get the lead to play through South's queen of diamonds, and the contract goes down.

The moral implied by Mr. Simon is that the defensive strength must be divided between the two defenders' hands; and that the crux of doubling is in the diagnosis that these two hands together have enough strength to defeat the contract. For example:

SOUTH	WEST	NORTH	EAST
1 ♡	Pass	1 ♠	Pass
1 N.T.	Pass	2 ◇	Pass
2 ♡	Pass	2 ♠	Pass
2 N.T.	Pass	3 ◇	Pass
3 N.T.			

West held ♠ 4 3 ♡ K J 7 4 ◇ J 10 9 3 ♣ K Q 6—and West doubled. Obviously, North had only spades and diamonds, and could not support hearts even after they had been rebid, so West's heart holding must be good for two tricks. South could not have risked three no-trump, in the face of North's refusal to raise, without A-J-10 in clubs; but West was sitting over this strength. South had refused to support spades, so East must hold a comfortable amount of spade strength, which would be properly placed over the dummy. South's first rebid, which was only one no-trump, showed that he could not have a very strong hand; therefore, East must have a high card or two. It all added up to a strong probability that North-South could not win nine tricks at no-trump.

The complete deal was as follows:

NORTH
♠ A 8 6 5 2
♡ 3
◇ K Q 7 6 4
♣ 7 5

WEST
♠ 4 3
♡ K J 7 4
◇ J 10 9 3
♣ K Q 6

EAST
♠ K 10 9 7
♡ 10 9 5
◇ A
♣ 9 8 4 3 2

SOUTH
♠ Q J
♡ A Q 8 6 2
◇ 8 5 2
♣ A J 10

Everyone passed West's double of three no-trump, and West opened the four of spades. Dummy's deuce was played, and East won with the king. East returned the ten of hearts.

South guessed (because of the double) that West held the heart king and a finesse would not work; and, also because of the double, he saw a good chance that West held the diamond ace. So South put up the ace of hearts, led a small diamond, and put up the queen when West played the three.

East took his diamond ace and led the nine of hearts, which the queen covered and West won with the king. Now West led the jack of diamonds, which was allowed to hold, and the ten of diamonds, which dummy's king won.

South was in trouble, and could not escape. He led a spade to his queen, then led the deuce of hearts, hoping the jack would fall; but West took the seven and cashed the nine of diamonds. On this, South had to let a heart go, so West cashed the jack of hearts and still had to get a club trick. South was down four, and though he was not vulnerable it was a clear gain of 700 points to East-West—500 points more than they would have had if West had not doubled.

The North-South bidding was indefensible, but that is just the point: The big profits come of not letting the opponents get away with indefensible bidding.

THE DOUBLE DILEMMA

Nevertheless, the phase of bridge most likely to produce ambivalent neuroses in bridge players is that of penalty doubles.

Any experienced rubber bridge player knows that one cannot win without doubling the opponents when they overbid. Against this indisputable fact there is the contrary fact that a double often gives the declarer information that permits him to save a trick or even to make a contract he could not have made if he had not been doubled.

The following deal, from a game in a New York club, proved to be a lesson to the player who doubled unwisely.

NORTH
♠ A Q 4
♡ 6 4
◇ A K Q 10 6
♣ 7 4 2

WEST
♠ K 10 9 3
♡ A 7 2
◇ 7 3
♣ K Q 9 8

EAST
♠ 2
♡ 10 9 8 5 3
◇ 8 5 4
♣ 10 6 5 3

SOUTH
♠ J 8 7 6 5
♡ K Q J
◇ J 9 2
♣ A J

Both sides were vulnerable. The bidding was:

NORTH	EAST	SOUTH	WEST
1 ◇	Pass	1 ♠	Pass
2 ♠	Pass	4 ♠	Double
Pass	Pass	Pass	

West opened the king of clubs and South took it with his ace. South saw one club trick to lose, and a second trick to lose to the ace of hearts, and a probable losing trick in spades.

If West had not doubled, South's play would have been quite simple. He might have made the percentage play of the spade ace, surrendering his best chance of getting an overtrick if a spade finesse won but guarding against a singleton king of spades in the East hand; or he might have made the usual play of leading a small spade from his hand and finessing dummy's queen on the first round.

Whichever of these two plays South selected, he would have gone down. West would have been left with two trump tricks, plus the heart ace and club queen. But South was forewarned by West's double and figured West for a four-card trump holding, at least K-10-3-2 and perhaps (as was the actual case) K-10-9-x.

In either case, South had an advantage by leading the jack of spades from his hand on the first trump trick. South did lead the jack and West could not play so as to get more than one spade trick.

West covered the jack of spades with his king and dummy's ace won the trick. South reëntered his hand by leading the six of diamonds from dummy and taking it with the nine in his hand.

Then South led the eight of spades and West tried to save himself by playing the three, but South played the four from dummy and the eight won the trick. Dummy's queen drew another round of trumps, leaving West with only one trump trick, the ten.

If West had covered the eight of spades he still would have had only one trump trick, for dummy's queen would have taken the trick, another spade lead would have forced out West's ten, and South would have had the high spades to draw West's last trump, which was the lowly three.

West's double cost his side 890 points, the difference between the 790 South scored by making four spades and the 100 East-West would have scored if West had kept quiet.

In the following deal a similarly overoptimistic double was even more costly because a slam was involved.

NORTH
♠ 9 8 4 3
♡ A 10 2
◊ A Q 10 5
♣ 9 7

WEST
♠ K Q 10 6
♡ K J 8 6
◊ J 4 2
♣ 5 4

EAST
♠ 5
♡ Q 9 7 5 4
◊ 9 8 6 3
♣ J 6 3

SOUTH
♠ A J 7 2
♡ 3
◊ K 7
♣ A K Q 10 8 2

North-South were vulnerable. The bidding was:

SOUTH	WEST	NORTH	EAST
1 ♣	Pass	1 ◊	Pass
1 ♠	Pass	3 ♠	Pass
4 N.T.	Pass	5 ♡	Pass
6 ♠	Double	Pass	Pass
6 N.T.	Double	Pass	Pass
Pass			

West's first double drove his opponents from a contract they could not make, six spades, to a contract they could not fail to make.

Although West opened the six of hearts, his best lead, nothing could have affected the result because South had twelve sure tricks when the jack of diamonds dropped on the third round of that suit.

South used proper technique when he ducked the first heart trick, which was won by East's queen. East returned his singleton spade and South won with the ace. This spade return by East made it necessary for South simply to run off his six clubs, stripping dummy down to the blank ace of hearts and four diamonds, and then cash the king, queen, and ace of diamonds, hoping the jack would drop. It did, and South made six no-trump.

RESOLVING THE DILEMMA

The dilemma—to double or not to double—is solved in this way:

If intelligent opponents have bid to a high contract under their own power, by standard bidding methods, it is unwise to double unless one has in his own hand enough sure tricks to defeat the contract—and to defeat also any other contract to which the opponents may retreat.

If the opponents' bidding indicates that they have a misfit and are groping for some safe contract—as when one opponent bids two of the four suits and the other opponent bids the other two suits—a gambling double may be justified; but against strong players there is no assurance that such bidding has revealed a misfit.

If the opponents apparently have the weaker cards and have out-bid a game or higher contract that one's side can almost surely make, it is essential to double. Once in the proverbial blue moon the opponents will have freak hands and will make their intended sacrifice contract, but this does not happen often enough to affect one's doubling habits.

PART II

BIDDING CONVENTIONS

1

WHAT IS A CONVENTION?

THE NATURAL meaning of any bid is that the bidder is prepared to play at the contract named. When a player bids two spades, the natural meaning of the bid is that the player wishes spades to be trumps and expects to win at least eight tricks.

If a bid carries any additional meaning that can be fully understood only by agreement between partners, in bridge terminology it is a convention.

A conventional bid may be either natural or artificial. The opening two-spade bid used as a game-forcing bid is conventional because it demands a response from partner—something not implicit in the bid itself—but it also is natural because the two-spade bidder does have a spade suit and a hand strong enough to make the contract he undertakes. A one-club bid used to show a certain number of high-card points, without any representation as to the bidder's club suit, is artificial as well as conventional. The bidder may not be prepared to play at a club contract.

In 1951 I wrote, "The expert player dislikes artificial bids, views them with suspicion, and is slow to adopt them. He considers them theoretically unsound, because they give too much information to the enemy. He considers them dangerous, because his partner may forget what they mean. . . ."

Twenty years later, almost exactly the opposite is true. Most of the world's bridge experts have joyously espoused the principle of artificial bidding and vie with one another in devising the newest and fanciest bidding conventions.

ETHICAL AND PRACTICAL CONSIDERATIONS

A convention is a signal. The idea of signals is controversial in bridge ethics, and there are still players—especially in England—

who cling to the doctrine of Admiral Burney, one of the ancients, who wrote in 1821 that signals "impinge on the integrity of the game." Even the most hidebound proponents of natural bidding use some conventions, for example forcing bids and the takeout double, but they agree with the rank and file of players when they oppose the unrestricted use of bidding conventions.

To the serious bridge player and especially to the minority who play tournament bridge, there is no current topic of greater moment. Italian teams, which use many special conventions, have won the world championship fourteen times.*

A multiplicity of conventions may increase a bridge player's effectiveness but it can be self-defeating. Literally hundreds of fancy bids have been proposed and new ones appear every week or month. If casual players began to use more than a few of these, it would become impossible to sit down in a bridge club or at a bridge party with three comparative strangers and play an enjoyable game. Furthermore, there would be so many partnership misunderstandings that the standard of play would go down.

A most unenviable job falls to directors of the American Contract Bridge League and to tournament and club committees. They have the power and duty to decide what conventions may and may not be used. However they decide, there is always turmoil. Should they rule in favor of the experts, who like conventions? Or is their duty to the rank and file, who, if given full democratic control, would bar most of the conventions and all psychic bids?

Nearly all authorities agree that such restrictions would hurt the game, by reducing the element of skill. So the committees thread their way gingerly between the conflicting points of view, yielding to majority pressure enough to bar the fanciest bidding conventions but being paternalistic enough to admit some that are unpopular but that seem good for the game.

Inevitably, the committees commit some errors of judgment and some abuses of power. During an Eastern States tournament in New York City some years ago, the tournament committee barred

---

* After the Italian Blue Team temporarily retired in 1969, the Americans won the next two world championships. It is interesting to note that each of these American teams had two pairs that used quite complicated systems or sets of conventions.

use of the "weak," or limited, double raise of an opening spade or heart bid—a feature of the Acol system that is popular in England but was rarely played in the United States.* It came up on the following deal:

NORTH
♠ 10 8 6 5 2
♡ 9 4
◇ A K 8 3
♣ 8 2

WEST
♠ K 9
♡ Q 7 3
◇ Q J 10 5 2
♣ J 5 4

EAST
♠ J 4
♡ A 8 6 2
◇ 9
♣ K Q 9 7 6 3

SOUTH
♠ A Q 7 3
♡ K J 10 5
◇ 7 6 4
♣ A 10

South was dealer. Neither side was vulnerable. The bidding was:

SOUTH	WEST	NORTH	EAST
1 ♠	Pass	3 ♠	Pass
Pass	Pass		

North's bid was the limited double raise. Under the standard American system a jump to three spades by North would show a stronger hand (by perhaps a king) and would be forcing to game. The majority of bridge players have learned this standard system and to them North's three-spade bid seems odd and "conventional." Yet North's hand is somewhat too strong for a simple raise to two spades and the alternative, which is to respond two

* Among expert tournament players, limit jump raises have recently achieved a high degree of acceptance.

diamonds and suppress the strong spade support, is artificial and unnatural.

The fact is that the laws of contract bridge do not permit a committee to bar a bid such as North's three-spade response. A bridge player cannot be forbidden to bid what he thinks he can make. Committees often misunderstand this and rule against a natural bid simply because it is unfamiliar, while an artificial bid is permitted on the grounds that "everybody understands it"; and such rulings are popular.

Incidentally, the deal shown above did not result in a protest and the committee at the Eastern States tournament soon rescinded its ruling. The three-spade bid was very successful because South lost one trick in each suit and made exactly his contract.

Usually the problem of deciding which conventions to admit, and which to exclude, is attended by so many complexities and delicacies and conflicting interests that no committee can be expected to judge wisely at all times. Both philosophically and practically, the bidding and playing conventions of bridge are the major issue of the game, and they are likely to continue to be so.

The American Contract Bridge League divides all conventions of bidding and play into five classes: Class A consists of conventions that must be allowed in all A.C.B.L. events and duplicate clubs. Classes B, C, and D consist of conventions that must be allowed in tournaments of certain levels and that are recommended to be allowed at certain other levels; included in Class D are the Roman and Neapolitan ("Blue Team") systems, which for years were barred nationally. In addition, a Class E exists to give the tournament director discretion to allow any other convention or system.

THE BASIC CONVENTIONS

Even those who dislike conventional bidding recognize certain situations in which some understanding between partners is desirable.

The opening forcing bid, such as the two-bid, and the takeout double cover two of these situations. The cue-bid showing control of an opposing suit is a third convention universally recognized. Other situations, and the principal solutions, are:

To locate aces for a slam bid. (Blackwood or similar convention.)

To find a major-suit fit after a no-trump opening. (Stayman convention.)

To overcall no-trump bids safely. (Landy and similar conventions.)

To show a two-suited hand for defensive purposes. (Unusual no-trump.)

If these were the only situations covered by conventional bids, the casual player would still complain. The degree of his complaint in present circumstances may be measured by the fact that there are literally hundreds of other bidding conventions to cover bidding situations that are rare or obscure. Only the ones most generally used will be discussed in this part of the book; others will be summarized in Chapter 18 of Part II.

POLICY IN AMERICAN TOURNAMENTS

The American Contract Bridge League requires each pair in a tournament to fill out and display a card that shows its opponents what conventions it will use, for bridge ethics forbid the use of a convention without informing the opponents.

The actual information on the card is condensed in an esoteric bridge shorthand, some of which may be paraphrased in the following questions:

1] What is your strong forcing opening bid?

2] What is the range of each of your no-trump openings?

3] What are the responses to your no-trump bids? (Usually the use of the Stayman convention is assumed, but there are several variations.)

4] How frequently do you open the bidding with a four-card major suit? Often? Seldom? Never? Does it vary according to your position in the auction? What length do your minor-suit openings promise?

5] What kind of two-bids do you use? Weak? Intermediate? Strong? What are your forcing and conventional responses?

6] What are your agreements on competitive auctions? Do you use the unusual no-trump? Negative doubles? Are single jump overcalls weak, intermediate, or strong?

7] What slam bidding conventions do you use? Do you use a variation of four no-trump?

8] What are your defensive card play agreements? Do you use special leads or special signals?

The significance of this list is both positive and negative. It reveals that some of the best players use strong no-trump openings (15 to 18 points) and some use weak (12 to 14 points); that most use the Stayman convention in one form or another; that a sizable portion of bridge players use weak two-bids and artificial, forcing, opening two-club bids; that there is a difference of opinion on the use of no-trump overcalls, jump overcalls, and the bidding of four-card major suits.

Most of all, the card reveals that there is only one artificial bidding convention in the United States that has achieved sufficient universality to require no mention except to require a listing of variants from it. It is the Blackwood slam convention.

2

THE BLACKWOOD CONVENTION

In 1943 I wrote a series of articles for *The New York Times* on expert bidding practices. I consulted the twenty-six highest-ranking Eastern players on their slam methods and only one of them had a good word to say for the Blackwood convention.

Today virtually every expert uses Blackwood, and as for the rank and file of bridge players, they have always doted on it. The Blackwood convention has achieved a worldwide following exceeded only by that of the takeout double.

The takeout double dates from 1915 and its authorship* has been widely disputed. This is not an unusual state of affairs in bidding conventions. Several of the most popular of them have been independently worked out by different players in different parts of the world.

The authorship of the Blackwood convention has never been in doubt. Easley Blackwood of Indianapolis, Indiana, solely invented it in 1933 and first published it in 1934. He endured several years in which his convention was either ignored or scorned, and then he saw it rapidly capture favor throughout the world. Innumerable variations, some of them quite complicated, have been built on the original Blackwood principle.

The Blackwood principle is simple. When a player wishes to know how many aces his partner has, he bids four no-trump. His partner must respond five clubs with no ace, five diamonds with one ace, five hearts with two aces, five spades with three aces. Originally a response of five no-trump was used to show all four aces, but later Mr. Blackwood adopted the clever device of using the five-club response to show either no ace or all four aces. This is a workable solution, because it should always be clear from

* See note on page 104.

the previous bidding whether a player may have an aceless hand. *

A later bid of five no-trump, by the player who first bid four no-trump, demands king-showing on the same step system of responses: six clubs to show no king, six diamonds for one king, six hearts for two kings, six spades for three kings, six no-trump for all four kings. Here the six-club response cannot be given a double meaning.

The king-showing extension of the Blackwood convention can be of value only in grand slam bidding and the big value of the five no-trump bid is to show that the partnership has all the aces so that if responder has a long solid suit he can jump to a grand slam without showing his kings.

The popularity of Mr. Blackwood's slam method is due largely to its simplicity, but there is nothing very simple about the experts' application of it. "We use Blackwood," they explain, "when the bidding makes it obvious that four no-trump means Blackwood and not something else." Unfortunately, what is obvious to an expert may not be obvious to the average player. On occasion it may not even be very obvious to the expert's partner, and the wrong contract is reached.

A slam usually results from the combination of two strong hands, but there are two distinct types of strong hand:

WEST	EAST
♠ A J x	♠ x
♡ A x	♡ K Q x x x x x
◇ A x x x	◇ K Q x x
♣ A Q x x	♣ x

* It should be clear, assuming that both partners are playing the same system. However, in the 1971 world championship, a French pair playing together for the first time found the five-club response anything but clear. The bidding started

SOUTH	NORTH
1 ♣	1 ◇
1 ♡	3 ♡

North intended his three-heart bid as a mere invitation, but South thought it was strong and forcing. Therefore, when South (looking at his own aceless hand) heard North's five-club response to Blackwood, he assumed North had four aces when in fact he had none. When the partnership reached seven hearts holding no aces, one of the opponents found a double . . .

West's hand is strong because it has a lot of quick tricks, but alone it could guarantee no contract whatsoever. Opposite a Yarborough it might conceivably win only four tricks.

East's hand is strong enough because it will win a lot of tricks with hearts trumps, but its ability to make a game or a slam depends on how many aces West holds.

It is difficult, in the opening bids and responses, to differentiate between a hand that has its strength primarily in high cards and a hand that has little in high cards but much in playing strength. Since the essential requirement for any slam is the ability to win twelve or more tricks, it is better for the hand with the playing strength (such as East's above) to become the master hand in slam bidding. This is the hand whose four no-trump must be construed as Blackwood; this is the hand that should make the decision.

With the West-East hands shown above, it is patently unproductive for West to use a Blackwood four no-trump bid. West, having all four aces, knows what his partner's response will be: five clubs. West still will have no useful information on which to base a slam decision.

Even if West, seeing all four aces in his own hand, could elicit a response telling him that East had all four kings, West still could not confidently bid a slam. East could have such a hand as

♠ K x   ♡ K J x x x   ◇ K x x   ♣ K x x

—and there might be little or no play for twelve tricks.

It is entirely different when, on the hand previously shown, East is permitted to bid four no-trump and find out about his partner's aces. The bidding might go:

WEST	EAST
1 ♣	1 ♡
2 N.T.	3 ◇
4 ◇	4 N.T.
5 ♣	

The five-club bid shows all four aces. Holding 1-7-4-1 distribution, East can bid seven hearts with this information. A 3-2 diamond break will give him his contract easily and even against a 4-1 diamond break he has several plays for the grand slam, making the prospect better than the two-to-one chance to win that is the rule-of-thumb requirement for grand slam bids.

The best application of the Blackwood convention therefore requires that the player whose hand has good high-card strength but lots of "holes" in it refrain from bidding four no-trump himself and also bid so as to make it easy for his partner to bid four no-trump. Then if his partner has an appropriate hand for the Blackwood bid, the way to a slam will be eased.

The bidding usually makes it clear when a hand has a solid, trick-winning pattern and needs only information about high cards. For example:

NORTH
♠ Q J 7 6 2
♡ A 6 4 3
◇ A 10
♣ 7 5

WEST
♠ 10 8 5 4
♡ ————
◇ 8 6 5 3
♣ Q J 9 3 2

EAST
♠ K 9 3
♡ J 10 8 7
◇ 9 2
♣ K 10 6 4

SOUTH
♠ A
♡ K Q 9 5 2
◇ K Q J 7 4
♣ A 8

South dealt, with neither side vulnerable. The bidding:

SOUTH	WEST	NORTH	EAST
1 ♡	Pass	1 ♠	Pass
3 ◇	Pass	4 ♡	Pass
4 N.T.	Pass	5 ♡	Pass
7 ♡	Pass	Pass	Pass

South's four no-trump bid had to be a slam try; he would have had no other reason to disturb a good game contract. And he could not be trying to give information by bidding four no-trump, since he had the two-suiter and the strong trump suit and would have to make the final decision. Therefore his four no-trump had to be Blackwood, and North responded accordingly.

The grand slam was easy to bid. North had shown eight cards, at least, in spades and hearts, by bidding the former and giving a jump raise in the latter. He could have no more than five cards in diamonds and clubs, and South's diamond suit and club ace were more than enough to take care of those. North had shown the other two aces by his five-heart response.

The hand required some judgment in playing. West opened the queen of clubs and South won. Since South's technique was good, he first got the ace of spades out of the way, then led a low heart to dummy's ace.

This is the standard method of handling a suit of nine combined trumps with K-Q-9 opposite the ace (or the equivalent such as A-Q-9 opposite the king). The single honor must be played first, to retain a finessing position in case the outstanding trumps break 4-0.

The 4-0 break seldom occurs, but this time South was unlucky enough to get it. Now he had to plan so that he could lead hearts twice through East, so as to pick up the jack and ten, and also get rid of the losing club either from his own hand or from dummy.

There were two ways in which South might get a club discard and still have enough entries to finesse trumps twice through East.

South could play for East to have the spade king, and also to have two diamonds. The queen of spades would be led from dummy, and if East held the king and covered, South would trump. Then South would lead a low diamond to dummy's ace, discard his club on the spade jack, lead a heart, and capture East's heart ten with the queen. Another low diamond lead would put dummy in again with the diamond ten, and a final heart lead from dummy would give South an indicated finesse and the remaining tricks.

Or South could play for East to have at least three diamonds. In this case, after winning the heart ace South would immediately lead a heart through East, overtaking the heart ten with the queen. Three high diamonds would be cashed, dummy's club being discarded on the third. If East followed to this third diamond, South would trump his club in dummy and take a final heart finesse.

The odds were against the success of either plan, but they were the only two available and South had to try one of them. Luckily for South, he chose to play East for the spade king and that line of play succeeded where the other would have failed. Some elaborate mathematical calculations are required to determine which line of play had the better chance, and one cannot perform such calculations in the middle of a bridge hand. A priori the finesse (50%) is a better chance than the 3-3 break (35%).

But since the 4-0 trump break will not occur once in ten times, the grand slam contract was an excellent one.

WHEN BLACKWOOD IS NOT "OBVIOUS"

Mr. Blackwood originally established two principles for his slam convention:

1] Provided either partner has previously bid any suit, a bid of four no-trump is always conventional, calling for ace-showing responses.

2] The player who bids four no-trump takes complete charge of the bidding. His partner must respond as directed and can make no decision as to the final contract.

Neither principle is wholly accepted by expert players, for reasons that may be rooted in the psychology of the bridge expert, who wishes to make his own interpretation of bids and to retain freedom of action in all circumstances.

When four no-trump is bid as a direct raise of partner's no-trump bid, nearly all experts treat it as a natural bid and not as Blackwood, even if a suit has been bid previously.

SOUTH	WEST	NORTH	EAST
1 ◇	Pass	1 ♠	Pass
2 N.T.	Pass	4 N.T.	

North is deemed to have a balanced hand, also of the no-trump type, that makes a slam seem possible but that does not permit a spade rebid, a diamond raise, or the showing of a second suit. Such a hand might be:

♠ K Q 9 5   ♡ A J 6   ◇ J 7   ♣ 10 8 7 3

South is not expected to show aces in response. South may decide to go on to a slam if his rebid was based on many trick-winners in a long diamond suit plus outside controls, such a hand as

♠ 10 4   ♡ K 10   ◇ A K Q 9 6 5   ♣ A Q 3

A more subtle exception is the use of four no-trump to show second-round control of some doubtful suit. The following deal is an example:

NORTH
♠ A Q 8 6
♡ A J 7 4
◇ K 3
♣ J 5 2

WEST	EAST
♠ 10 4 2	♠ J 9 5 3
♡ K 6 3 2	♡ Q 9 8
◇ 9 7 5 4	◇ A J 10 8 6
♣ 10 3	♣ 7

SOUTH
♠ K 7
♡ 10 5
◇ Q 2
♣ A K Q 9 8 6 4

North dealt, with neither side vulnerable. The bidding:

NORTH	EAST	SOUTH	WEST
1 ♠	Pass	2 ♣	Pass
2 ♡	Pass	4 ♣	Pass
4 N.T.	Pass	6 ♣	Pass
Pass	Pass		

North's four no-trump was a bid to show some strength in diamonds. This is a natural, not an artificial meaning. North had shown strength in two suits, South in a third, and to bid no-trump North had to have something in the fourth.

Such a bid is almost invariably made with a suit headed by the king, which supplies second-round control if the opening lead must come up to it but may be trapped, giving the opponents two immediate tricks to defeat the slam, if the opening lead can be made through it.

South bid six clubs because with the queen of diamonds opposite the king it did not matter if a diamond were opened through North's hand. With smaller diamonds, South would have had to bid six no-trump to make a slam contract safe, or forgo a slam by passing or bidding five clubs. The club slam was safe; a different placement of defenders' cards would have beaten six no-trump.

North had not indicated a solid suit by jumping, and South had not raised either of North's suits, so there was no reason to think North might have a hand that needed only aces to reach twelve tricks and a slam. In the absence of such evidence, North's four no-trump was not read as a Blackwood bid.

BLACKWOOD AND VOID SUITS

The original Blackwood convention was often criticized because it shut out information about void suits, which can be even more valuable than aces. Mr. Blackwood devised a solution to this problem, as shown in the following deal:

NORTH
♠ ———
♡ K J 8 6 3
◇ A 9 4 2
♣ K 10 6 3

WEST
♠ Q J 10 9 5 3
♡ 4
◇ J 8
♣ Q 9 8 2

EAST
♠ A 6 4 2
♡ 10
◇ 10 7 5 3
♣ J 7 5 4

SOUTH
♠ K 8 7
♡ A Q 9 7 5 2
◇ K Q 6
♣ A

Neither side was vulnerable. The bidding:

SOUTH	WEST	NORTH	EAST
1 ♡	1 ♠	3 ♡	3 ♠
4 N.T.	Pass	6 ◇	Pass
7 ♡	Pass	Pass	Pass

North's response to the Blackwood four no-trump bid is his natural response, but one level higher, to show that in addition to his ace or aces, he has a void. In this case a response of five diamonds would show one ace; therefore a response of six diamonds shows one ace plus a void. South can assume that the void is in spades, on the basis of the East-West bidding. So South, assuming that North has very strong heart support (because of his jump raise) and one ace (on the basis of his six-diamond bid) and a void in spades, can bid seven hearts.

Another Blackwood void-showing variation is used by adherents of the Kaplan-Sheinwold system.

The situation arises only when you have agreed on a trump suit, your partner bids a Blackwood four no-trump, and you have at least one ace and a void suit.

With such a hand you jump to six in the void suit if that suit is lower than the agreed suit. If the void suit is higher you jump to six in the agreed suit.

That is, if the agreed suit is hearts you may jump to six clubs or six diamonds to show a void in clubs or diamonds, respectively, plus one ace, but you would have to jump to six hearts, not to six spades, to show a void in spades.

The opportunity for use of this convention arose when the following deal was played:

NORTH
♠ A J 3 2
♡ J 10 9 7 5
◇ ———
♣ Q J 10 4

WEST
♠ Q 8 6 5
♡ 8
◇ K J 9 5 3
♣ 9 6 3

EAST
♠ K 10 7 4
♡ 4 3
◇ A 10 7 6 4 2
♣ 7

SOUTH
♠ 9
♡ A K Q 6 2
◇ Q 8
♣ A K 8 5 2

South dealt. Both sides were vulnerable. The bidding:

SOUTH	WEST	NORTH	EAST
1 ♡	Pass	3 ♡ *	Pass
4 N.T.	Pass	6 ◇	Pass
7 ♡	Pass	Pass	Pass

The six-diamond response, being a jump above the normal level of responses to the Blackwood four no-trump bid, showed that North held one ace plus a void in diamonds. This made it a good gamble for South to bid a grand slam.

But grand slam opportunities are rare at best and even rarer are

* This deal occurred before the Kaplan-Sheinwold system incorporated, as it now does, the principle that a double raise is a limited bid and may be passed and that an immediate response of three no-trump is equivalent to a game-forcing double raise.

cases in which a bidding convention will assure a player of thirteen tricks once he bids the grand slam.

ROMAN BLACKWOOD

There is increasing adoption of the variation of Blackwood used in the Roman Club system (one of the systems used by the Italian players who have won the world championship so often). Their original responses to the Blackwood four no-trump were as follows:

5 ♣ shows no ace or three aces
5 ◇ shows one ace or four aces
5 ♡ shows two aces, both red or both black or both major or both minor
5 ♠ shows two aces different both in color and in suit status (spades and diamonds, or hearts and clubs)

As for the five-club and five-diamond responses, the previous bidding should always show which holding the responding hand may have.

The responses to show two aces often give information that is of great value in fixing the contract. This was a tournament hand:

NORTH
♠ Q 10 7 5
♡ A
◇ J 10 8 7 3
♣ A 5 4

WEST
♠ 9 4 3
♡ 10 9 7 5
◇ A 2
♣ Q 10 6 3

EAST
♠ 6
♡ 8 4 3 2
◇ 9 6 4
♣ J 9 8 7 2

SOUTH
♠ A K J 8 2
♡ K Q J 6
◇ K Q 5
♣ K

South dealt. The bidding was:

SOUTH	WEST	NORTH	EAST
1 ♠	Pass	3 ♠	Pass
4 N.T.	Pass	5 ♠	Pass
6 N.T.	Pass	Pass	Pass

North's five-spade response promised two aces different in color (so they could not be the two red aces) and different in suit status (so they could not be the two minors, clubs and diamonds). Seeing his own ace of spades, South knew that partner must hold the aces of hearts and clubs. Had there been any danger North lacked the ace of clubs, South would have to settle for a safe six-spade contract. Having placed the ace of clubs in North's hand, South was able to bid six no-trump, beating the pairs that played at six spades.

Strangely enough, the Romans themselves could not so easily profit from such a result because European duplicate bridge has eliminated the artificiality that makes six no-trump (990 or 1,440 points) beat six spades or hearts (980 or 1,430). Nevertheless, six no-trump is the superior contract because it precludes a first-round ruff.

It may be noted that on the deal shown a response of five clubs or diamonds could not have been ambiguous. For his jump raise North had to have at least one ace. Since South had an ace, North could not have all four. Therefore if North had responded five clubs, South would have known he had three aces and would have bid seven. If North had responded five diamonds, South would have known he had only one ace and would have signed off at five spades.

Only five hearts, showing two matching aces, would have been ambiguous. From South's point of view these might have been the red aces (diamonds and hearts) or the minor-suit aces (diamonds and clubs). With the club ace possibly missing, South would have had to settle for a safe six-spade contract.

Roman Blackwood is most useful on a hand such as the deal shown, when the four no-trump bidder has one ace, the responder has two unmatched aces, and the partnership can find out which ace is missing. However, the Italians have modified their responses to Roman Blackwood, probably because this ideal situation occurs relatively infrequently.

The new schedule leaves the five-club and five-diamond responses as before, showing no or three aces and one or four aces, respectively. Now, however, a five-heart response shows any two aces with no extra values, considering the previous bidding, and a five-spade response shows any two aces with extra values.

OTHER VARIATIONS—KEY CARD, GERBER

Hard upon the introduction of the Blackwood convention there came a spate of variations—the San Francisco version, the Smith version, and countless others.

Nearly all of these were efforts to combine information about aces and kings in one response. The responder counted 2 points for each ace and 1 point for each king (or some similar schedule) and responded to four no-trump in such a way as to show how many points he held.

A few of these variations are still used, but not widely. They failed because they did not have the magnificent simplicity of the original Blackwood convention and some of the variations were inferior to basic Blackwood in another respect: Too often it is not clear whether a response shows one ace or two kings, and it is aces a slam-going bidder must know about. A king can be finessed, an ace cannot be.

The simplest king-showing variation, called Key Card Blackwood, treats the king of the agreed-upon trump suit as the equivalent of an ace in responding to four no-trump. The rationale is that if the partnership is missing one ace and the king of the trump suit, slam is likely to be significantly worse than a 50 percent proposition.

The responses to Key Card Blackwood are the same as to ordinary Blackwood, except that there are in effect five "aces" and the response of five diamonds shows either one or five.

The chief disadvantage of Key Card Blackwood is this: When it is not absolutely clear which suit has been agreed upon as trumps, the partner of the four no-trump bidder may not be sure which is the "key" king. For example:

WEST	EAST
1 ◇	1 ♠
3 ♣	3 ◇
3 ♠	4 ◇
4 N.T.	

If East has the king of one of the suits bid and supported by his side he may not know whether to show it. Key Card disasters occur when the responder counts the wrong king and the partnership reaches a slam with too few aces.

The variation that has the most widespread following does not use four no-trump as the ace-asking bid. It was devised in 1937 by John Gerber of Houston, and the bid that asks for aces is four clubs.

The Gerber four-club bid is treated as conventional in about the same general circumstances as the Blackwood four no-trump bid: There must have been signs of strength; a suit must have been agreed upon; and the four-club bid cannot logically be genuine.

In response to four clubs Gerber, aces are shown by the step system on the Blackwood principle, but of course much lower: four diamonds to show no aces, four hearts with one ace, four spades with two aces, four no-trump with three aces, five clubs with all four aces. (Many make the four-diamond response serve the dual purpose of showing either no ace or all four aces, as is done with the five-club response to a Blackwood four no-trump.)

King-showing also is part of the full Gerber convention and the design is still to keep the bidding as low as possible. If the four-club bidder, upon receiving his response, bids the next-higher denomination he asks for kings and the bidding begins again by the step system:

SOUTH	NORTH
1 ♠	3 ♠
4 ♣ (aces?)	4 ◇ (no ace)
4 ♡ (kings?)	5 ♣ (two kings)

Four hearts, the next step higher than North's response, was king-asking; a response of four spades by North would have shown no king, four no-trump one king, hence five clubs two kings.

The agreed trump suit is omitted from the steps in king-asking:

SOUTH	NORTH	
1 ♠	3 ♠	
4 ♣	4 ♡	*(one ace)*
4 N.T.	5 ◇	*(one king)*

If South had bid four spades over four hearts he would not have been asking for kings, although four spades was the next step higher, because spades were the agreed trump suit. Four spades would have been a sign-off, abandoning hope of a slam, and North would have been required to pass.

The agreed trump suit is not omitted in responding to four clubs (or to the king-asking bid that may follow it). Though hearts be the agreed suit, the response to show one ace is still four hearts.

Nearly all experts in the United States and many abroad use the Gerber convention, but not as it is described above.

In general they use it only after an opening bid of one or two no-trump, or a jump response or rebid of two no-trump, and when the four-club bid is made by the partner of the no-trump bidder, not by the no-trump bidder himself. For king-asking they use a five-club bid.

Some treat the four-club bid as Gerber only when it is a direct response to the opening no-trump bid; some, only when it is either a direct response or a jump bid:

SOUTH	NORTH	SOUTH	NORTH	
1 N.T.	4 ♣ *(Gerber)*	1 N.T.	2 ♣	*(Stayman)*
		2 ♠	4 ♣	*(Gerber)*

"Gerber over no-trump" was used in the following deal, at duplicate bridge, with an unusual purpose and with unusual effect.

NORTH
♠ A Q J 10 7 6 3
♡ 7
◇ 6 2
♣ J 7 6

WEST   EAST
♠ 5   ♠ 9 4 2
♡ K 8 5 4 3   ♡ J 10 9
◇ K Q J 5   ◇ 9 7 3
♣ 10 8 2   ♣ A Q 5 4

SOUTH
♠ K 8
♡ A Q 6 2
◇ A 10 8 4
♣ K 9 3

North dealt. Both sides were vulnerable. The bidding was:

NORTH	EAST	SOUTH	WEST
Pass	Pass	1 N.T.	Pass
4 ♣	Pass	4 ♠	Pass
Pass	Pass		

The four-club bid was a Gerber bid and the four-spade response showed two aces; but in this case North's use of the Gerber convention was not the usual slam try. The North hand can hardly produce a slam opposite a no-trump hand, which is limited to 18 high-card points at most. North intended to pass if South showed three aces, since four no-trump is a more lucrative contract than four spades; to bid four spades if South showed one ace; and to pass if South showed two aces. (Under strict rules of the Gerber convention, a four-spade rebid by North would then have called for king-showing; but North-South were not using the king-showing extension of the Gerber convention.)

Neither were North-South using transfer bids (page 184); if they had been, North might have bid four hearts.

The score at four spades was a top because the declarer, Mrs.

Rixi Markus of England, played the hand very skillfully. She described her play in her bridge column in *The Guardian:*

"West led the king of diamonds and my first instinct was to take this trick, enter dummy, finesse the heart, get rid of my diamond loser, and then hope to be lucky with the club situation. Fortunately I thought again and decided to let West hold the diamond trick and then took West's queen of diamonds with the ace. East played the seven of diamonds. I led the ten of diamonds, West covered with the jack, I trumped in dummy with the ten of spades, East dropped the nine of diamonds, and my eight became a certain winner. I then played three rounds of spades, discarding one heart, returned to my hand with the ace of hearts, discarded a club on my eight of diamonds, ruffed a heart in dummy, and finally made the king of clubs as my eleventh trick. Plus 650 was a top score, as at most tables North played four spades and after East had led the jack of hearts only ten tricks could be made for a score of plus 620. An uncovenanted triumph for 'Gerber' or 'transfer.' "

Gerber devised his convention to keep the bidding low even while making a slam try. With spades the agreed suit, a player may ask for aces via the four-club bid and if he receives a weaker response than he hoped for, such as four diamonds, four hearts, or even four spades, he can stop without passing the game level. Blackwood gets one to the five-level willy-nilly, and there is nothing more dismaying then reaching five voluntarily, stopping there, and going down one. It is such a waste of good cards.

Nevertheless, very few experts use Gerber when the bidding has been opened in a suit. They use Blackwood. They are unwilling to relinquish the use of four clubs as a cue-bid or as an occasional genuine suit-showing bid.

One Blackwood variation which can be used to conduct a low-level slam investigation when the bidding is opened in a suit is called Baby Blackwood. Customarily Baby Blackwood is a bid of three no-trump after responder has made a strong raise of his partner's one-of-a-suit opening:

West	East
1 ♠	3 ♠
3 N.T.	

An alternative method is to treat an immediate two no-trump response to one of a suit as Baby Blackwood. With this agreement two no-trump would ask for aces, and subsequent bids of three, four, and five no-trump, respectively, can be used to ask for kings, queens, and jacks.

WHEN THE OPPONENTS INTERFERE

Sometimes when the partnership is trying to find out whether or not to bid a slam the opponents try to muddy the waters by bidding over four no-trump or over Gerber. For example:

SOUTH	WEST	NORTH	EAST
1 ♡	2 ♠ (*weak*)	4 N.T.	5 ♠

After this intervention by East, how should South show his aces?

Several methods have been devised to deal with this situation, each recognizing that the intervention puts at responder's disposal two additional calls: the double and the pass. The simplest solution is to double with no aces, pass with one ace (D = 0; P = 1; therefore mnemonically "DOPI"); bid the cheapest suit with two aces, and so on "up the line."

Another possibility is to double with an even number of aces (0, 2, or 4) and to pass with an odd number (1 or 3). This has the advantages of saving room and allowing the partnership to elect to defend even when the Blackwood responder has two aces.

The drawback of the latter method is that the responses are somewhat ambiguous, and if expert players of international caliber can err in judging whether a response shows no aces or four, it must be expected that error will often occur in deducing whether partner has no aces or two.

3

THE STAYMAN CONVENTION

NEXT TO the Blackwood slam convention, the bidding convention most used by American players is probably the Stayman convention, which is a response of two clubs to the opening bid of one no-trump.

The basic purpose of this convention, which was devised independently by players in several different countries, is to reach game in a major suit rather than in no-trump when a player opens with one no-trump and his partner has a hand like this:

♠ K J x x   ♡ K x x x   ◊ x x   ♣ K x x

Opposite an opening no-trump bid of the usual strength, as such bids are reckoned today, consisting of 16 or 17 points, this responding hand gives promise of game. But if the opening no-trump bidder happens to have only moderate strength in diamonds but does have a four-card suit in either spades or hearts, the combined hands are more likely to produce game in the best-fitting major suit than at no-trump.

The responding hand bids two clubs as a signal to his partner to show a four-card major suit if he has one, whereupon the partnership may reach game at a contract of four in that major suit and if so will have their best chance of making their contract. If he does not have a four-card major suit, his rebid must be two diamonds.

ORIGIN OF THE CONVENTION

In 1945, Samuel M. Stayman of New York and his then regular partner, George Rapée, experimented with this bidding device, found it effective, and adopted it for regular use. Mr. Stayman wrote an article about it, which was published in *Bridge World* magazine in the United States and was translated and published in the bridge magazines of several other countries. Bridge players throughout the world liked this convention and by 1948 it was in general use. (It is doubtful if any other bidding convention had ever won favor so fast.) Those who adopted the bid called it the Stayman convention.

Having thus had international fame thrust upon him, Mr. Stayman engaged in a continuing and exhaustive study of the convention that bore his name and he has become the unchallenged authority on it.

FORCING AND NONFORCING STAYMAN

The possible variations of the Stayman convention are all but innumerable, but expert players group them in two main classes which they call "forcing Stayman" and "nonforcing Stayman."

Neither is a wholly descriptive name. In the Stayman convention the response of two clubs is always forcing, since the player who bid two clubs may have only a singleton or even a void in clubs, and his partner, the original no-trump bidder, cannot pass and leave him to play the hand there. Therefore the no-trump bidder must rebid at least once. The forcing or nonforcing aspect of the convention depends upon whether the no-trump bidder is required to bid a third time.

The typical bidding situation might be as follows:

South	West	North	East
1 N.T.	Pass	2 ♣	Pass
2 ♦	Pass	2 ♠	Pass

If South is permitted to pass the two-spade rebid, he is playing nonforcing Stayman. If he must bid again, he is playing forcing Stayman.

Mr. Stayman prefers the rule that the two-club response is forcing at least to the level of two no-trump. In the bidding situation just given, South's weakest rebid would therefore be two no-trump, which North might pass; or South might raise spades to three, and now North might pass if sure the combined hands will not produce game.

Forcing Stayman—even when the opener must continue only to the level of two no-trump—has the effect of restricting the number of hands on which the responding hand can make the two-club response. This may enhance partnership discipline but it would deter East from responding two clubs in the following case:

WEST	EAST
♠ A J 5	♠ K 9 3 2
♡ J 9 3	♡ 10 8 7 5 4
◊ A J 5	◊ 10 9 6
♣ K Q 7 6	♣ 5

These hands would be unlikely to make one no-trump but will usually make two hearts. They were bid, with wholly nonforcing Stayman, as follows:

WEST	EAST
1 N.T.	2 ♣
2 ◊	2 ♡
Pass	

East made two hearts. If West had bid two spades over the two-club response, East would have passed and the contract would have been the best available, for of course West would have had a four-card spade suit.

But if the bidding had to reach two no-trump or higher after a two-diamond rebid, East could not have used the two-club response—or at least would have had nothing to gain by using it, for it would have become necessary to reach a contract too high to be made.

It is implicit in the Stayman convention that a direct response of two spades or two hearts (or also, as most persons play, two diamonds) shows a one-suited hand so weak that game is impossible and the no-trump bidder must pass. A two-spade response to one no-trump might be made on the following hand:

♠ J 8 6 5 3 2   ♡ 10 6   ◊ 8 2   ♣ J 8 4

From the weakness of this hand it is apparent that the efficacy of the bid depends on partner's passing it automatically. Two spades is a better contract than one no-trump, but three spades, which may be doubled, is no better than one no-trump undoubled and may be much worse.

The wholly nonforcing Stayman that permits a player to try

two clubs and then bid two hearts with virtual assurance that two hearts will be passed, as East did in the example shown earlier, serves the same purpose.

SHOWING A FIVE-CARD MAJOR

When a player responds two clubs, receives a two-diamond rebid, and then bids one of the major suits, he promises at least a five-card suit. He would have no reason to rebid in a four-card major, for he already knows (from the two-diamond rebid) that his partner cannot have good four-card major support for him.

The use of nonforcing Stayman does not necessarily shut off a game when the responder makes a nonjump rebid in a (five-card or longer) major suit. With a maximum for his no-trump, the opening hand may try again.

NORTH
♠ Q 7 5
♡ A Q 5
◇ K 6 3
♣ A K 7 4

WEST
♠ A 2
♡ J 9 4
◇ J 9 5 2
♣ 10 8 6 3

EAST
♠ 8 4 3
♡ K 10 8 6 3
◇ A 10
♣ Q J 2

SOUTH
♠ K J 10 9 6
♡ 7 2
◇ Q 8 7 4
♣ 9 5

North dealt. North-South were vulnerable. The bidding:

NORTH	EAST	SOUTH	WEST
1 N.T.	Pass	2 ♣	Pass
2 ◇	Pass	2 ♠	Pass
3 ♠	Pass	4 ♠	Pass
Pass	Pass		

South's two-spade bid showed a five-card suit. Having adequate support for a five-card spade suit and almost the strongest possible hand on which one may bid one no-trump, North raised to invite a game and South accepted.

With a weaker hand North would have passed two spades; and South would have passed North's raise to three spades if he had held less than his 6 points, while he would have made a jump rebid to three spades instead of bidding only two spades if he had held 8 or 9 points in high cards with his good five-card major.

As it was, the game contract was touch-and-go. If South's technique had been poorer, or his choice of plays less fortunate, or his adversaries more accurate in their defense, he would have gone down.

The three of clubs was opened and dummy's king won. South planned to amass ten tricks by trumping two clubs and a heart in his hand, plus his top cards, two other trump tricks, and a diamond trick. This was a good plan, but it depended on winning the heart finesse.

The first lead from dummy was the three of diamonds, for a side trick must be established and won quickly in any cross-ruff or dummy-reversal hand.

East played the diamond ten and South's queen of diamonds won. South led to the club king and trumped a club with the nine of spades. Then South led the ten of spades.

West put up his spade ace and led the last club. East discarded a heart and South trumped with the king.

Sure that East would have discarded a low diamond if he had held one, South led the seven of diamonds and ducked it in dummy, a play called the "obligatory finesse." East's ace had to take the trick.

With only hearts and spades left, East led the four of spades. South played the six and dummy won with the seven.

The king of diamonds was led from dummy and East could not resist the opportunity to trump it, but this was only the defenders' third trick and now East was stuck with the lead. He had to lead a heart, giving dummy two heart tricks, South a heart ruff with the spade jack, and dummy the last trick with the spade queen.

If East had refused to trump the king of diamonds, or if West had led a heart through dummy instead of the safer lead of the ten of clubs, South would have gone down, but these facts do not make South's contract a bad one. The game is always worth a gamble.

FORCING REBIDS AFTER THE STAYMAN CONVENTION

Facing a one no-trump opening, most tournament players nowadays use an immediate response of three clubs or three diamonds as either a preëmptive bid, or a bid showing a semisolid six-card suit and inviting the opener to bid three no-trump with a fit plus three probable outside winners. As a ramification of these treatments, a rebid of three clubs or three diamonds by the Stayman two-club bidder is forcing to game. The bid suggests the possibility of a minor-suit game or slam, but does not rule out a major-suit contract (and indeed may be a mild slam try in the major suit bid by opener). An unusual game-probing Stayman sequence came up in the following deal:

NORTH
♠ K Q 6
♡ Q 10 4
♢ Q 9 6 5 3
♣ 9 2

WEST
♠ 8 4
♡ A 7 2
♢ 10 8 4
♣ Q 10 7 4 3

EAST
♠ 9 7 3 2
♡ 9 6 5
♢ A 2
♣ K J 8 5

SOUTH
♠ A J 10 5
♡ K J 8 3
♢ K J 7
♣ A 6

South dealt. Neither side was vulnerable. The bidding was:

SOUTH	WEST	NORTH	EAST
1 N.T.	Pass	2 ♣	Pass
2 ♠	Pass	3 ◇	Pass
3 ♡	Pass	3 ♠	Pass
4 ♠	Pass	Pass	Pass

North's two-club response was the conventional Stayman bid, asking South to show a four-card major if he had one. South, having two four-card major suits, rebid in the higher-ranking one, spades—the more convenient first rebid, even when the heart suit is somewhat stronger.

North's three-diamond bid simply asked South to bid again. South had a four-card heart suit and bid it. North showed that he preferred spades and South went on to four spades because the three-diamond rebid by North was forcing to game and South's clubs were not good enough for a three no-trump bid.

North's hand was atypical for the two-club response, but there was sound reasoning behind it. He had just enough high-card strength to give hope for a game. If South had proved not to hold any four-card major, North would have taken a chance on a three no-trump contract because in that case South would probably be long in clubs and could stop North's one weak suit. When South proved to have four cards in at least one of the majors and high-card strength in the other, North feared that clubs were insufficiently stopped for a game at no-trump. He preferred to try for game in a major suit in which he had only three-card support.

Obviously three no-trump would have been a hopeless contract, because West would have opened a club and South's only club stopper would have been knocked out while he still had to give up the lead in diamonds and hearts to develop his tricks.

This deal, which as it happens Mr. Stayman played, developed a very delicate series of choices in the play at four spades. Even if given a 3-3 spade break, South cannot be sure of making his contract and is almost sure not to make it against perfect defense.

One opponent must have a doubleton in hearts or in diamonds, or both, and if South leads those suits before he draws trumps, by skillfully holding up their aces the opponents can force a situation in which they must win their two red aces, a ruff in one of these suits, and the club trick established on the opening lead, for a total of at least four tricks, defeating the contract.

Mr. Stayman discerned the fact that the key to the hand is not a 3-3 break in trumps but a 3-3 break in hearts, plus the chance that one opponent holds a doubleton ace of diamonds (or, always a possibility, the chance that one opponent will take his ace of hearts or diamonds too soon).

On West's opening lead of the four of clubs, East played the king and South won with the ace. South led a heart to the queen in dummy and it was allowed to win. A low heart was led from dummy to South's jack, and West still let it win, which was his best defense. It was important now for South to lead a third round of hearts and get the ace out. While the possibility remained for East to trump a third round of diamonds, a sure entry in West's hand would destroy any plan South might have.

West's actual lead at this point was another club, which made South's job easy, but the best defense by West would have been to lead a diamond. If East had taken his ace it would have established South's suit and three tricks would have been the most the defenders could take, so East had to duck the diamond trick and hope he could clear the diamonds while West still had a club entry. Now, upon East's ducking the diamond, South would have to lead his losing club immediately, to shut off West's entry. West could lead another diamond, or a trump, or even another club, but he could no longer beat the contract. South would win the return, lead a diamond to knock out East's ace, win the next lead, draw all of East's trumps, and have only high cards in his own hand. It is such a hand as to baffle almost any declarer.

TWO-WAY STAYMAN

The most prevalent variation of the Stayman convention is called "two-way Stayman" or "double-barreled Stayman," which means that a two-club response to one no-trump asks for a four-card major but shows a weak hand, not enough for game, while a two-diamond response to one no-trump also asks for a four-card major but shows a strong responding hand and is forcing to game.

The main advantage of two-way Stayman is that after the forcing two-diamond response the possibility of slam can be explored at the three-level because the partnership is already committed to game. There are, however, disadvantages.

In addition to giving the opponents perhaps too much information, this use of the two-diamond response shuts off the weak two-diamond response to get out of a dangerous no-trump contract, but proponents of extended Stayman contend that this is unimportant.

If the responder has a hand such as

♠ 65   ♡ 73   ◇ J 9 7 6 5 3   ♣ 8 5 2

he bids two clubs and passes his partner's two-diamond rebid or bids three diamonds over a spade or heart rebid. Three diamonds as the responder's rebid is not forcing when extended Stayman is used. In fact, it demands a pass, if only because the earlier two-club response warned of weakness.

The fact remains that the responding hand has pushed himself up to three diamonds on a hand he might have played at two diamonds. It is bad enough when one is pushed up by his opponents.

ASKING FOR STOPPERS

A different use for the two-diamond response is to ask the opener about his stoppers in the major suits. When this modification of the Stayman convention is used, the two-diamond bidder generally has a hand containing a singleton or a void, and has no interest in locating a four-card major in opener's hand. A typical hand would be

♠ Q 5 3   ♡ 7   ◇ Q J 4   ♣ A K 7 5 3 2

The two-diamond bid is forcing to game and asks the no-trump opener to bid two of whichever major suit he has stopped (no worse than Q-4-3-2 or Q-10-2), or to bid two no-trump if he has both majors stopped. If opener shows a stopper in responder's short suit, responder can bid three no-trump. If the opener's rebid reveals weakness in responder's short suit the partnership can explore other game—or slam—possibilities at the three-level.

4

THE WEAK TWO-BID

The "weak two-bid" is a bid used throughout the world, although its adherents are not very numerous, percentage-wise. Only expert and advanced players use it; the average player is reluctant to make a high bid on a weak hand.

The object of the weak two-bid is to interfere with the opponents' bidding. Opening three- and four-bids are universally used as shut-out bids, of course, but they have two disadvantages. First, hands of the proper type for such bids are rare. Second, so high a bid will shut out partner as well as opponents.

The weak two-bid has neither of these disadvantages. Ideally it is made on a hand with a fairly strong six-card suit and a total high-card strength of about a trick and a half, and such hands are frequently encountered. An example, for a two-heart bid, might be:

♠ 83   ♡ Q J 10 8 7 4   ◇ A 7 6   ♣ 6 5

Provided the bid is never made on a hand materially stronger or weaker than this, partner's bidding is not affected, because he is given quite precise information. Necessarily, the opponents have this information too, but they will still find it dangerous and therefore difficult to enter the bidding at so high a level. For example, the following case from a rubber-bridge game:

NORTH
♠ A 7 5 2
♡ Q 7 6
◇ A 8 7 6
♣ 10 4

WEST
♠ K Q 9 4
♡ 9
◇ J 9 3
♣ K Q 9 5 2

EAST
♠ J 10 8 3
♡ A 4 2
◇ Q 2
♣ A J 7 3

SOUTH
♠ 6
♡ K J 10 8 5 3
◇ K 10 5 4
♣ 8 6

South dealt, with East-West vulnerable. The bidding:

SOUTH	WEST	NORTH	EAST
2 ♡	Pass	3 ♡	Pass
Pass	Pass		

North's raise to three hearts was intended to make it even more difficult for the opponents to enter the bidding—North would have bid two no-trump or perhaps a new suit if he had wanted to invite game. North's bid had the desired preëmptive effect, for West did not feel strong enough to bid over two hearts, nor East over three, since they were vulnerable.

As a result South made three hearts easily, losing one heart trick, one diamond, and two clubs. West could as easily have made three spades, and might have made four if the defense were not very careful.

The weak two-bid applies only to bids of two spades, two hearts, and two diamonds. The opening bid of two clubs is reserved as an artificial forcing bid, which will be discussed later in this chapter.

The weak two-bid was introduced by Howard Schenken and

incorporated in the system of his team, the Four Aces, about thirty years ago. Harold Vanderbilt's original club system, the first contract bridge system, had incorporated a weak two-bid but it had so wide a range that it resulted in the occasional loss of a game. The Schenken development put the weak two-bid in a straitjacket and greatly increased its effectiveness.

Despite Mr. Schenken's great prestige among bridge experts, many qualified bridge theorists dislike the weak two-bid. They admit it is hard to play against when used by good players, but they add that "anything is hard to play against when used by good players." They indict the weak two-bid principally on the ground that it seldom keeps the opponents out of game.

This may be true enough but it does not mean the weak two-bid is ineffective. The great value of the bid is (as in the deal shown above) when the strength is fairly well divided and either side can make a part-score. On game-going hands the opponents may get into the bidding without too much trouble; on part-score hands they do not dare.

Furthermore, the weak two-bid does occasionally keep the opponents out of a game. It did in this deal:

NORTH
♠ J 6
♡ K Q 8 6 4
◇ Q J 6
♣ 10 9 3

WEST
♠ Q 8 2
♡ 10 3
◇ A K 10 9 3
♣ K J 5

EAST
♠ A 4
♡ A J 7 5
◇ 7 2
♣ Q 8 7 4 2

SOUTH
♠ K 10 9 7 5 3
♡ 9 2
◇ 8 5 4
♣ A 6

Again East-West were vulnerable, North-South were not,
North dealt, and the bidding went:

NORTH	EAST	SOUTH	WEST
Pass	Pass	2 ♠	Pass
3 ♠	Pass	Pass	Pass

North's raise was a shut-out bid in its own right. Many of those
who use the weak two-bid give a single raise on the sort of hand
with which they would raise a one-bid (except that less trump
support is needed, because the opener is known to have a six-card
suit).

In this case West was not strong enough to risk a bid of three
diamonds. East might have summoned up enough courage to bid
if North had passed, but the three-spade level was too much for
him. North's raise was known to be preëmptive, but South, bidding third hand, might have been trapping with a good hand.

A double of three spades would have given East-West a fair
score, because South was down three, but South got bad breaks.
West opened the king of diamonds and continued with the ace
and a small one. East trumped, cashed his ace of spades, and led
a club. South had a club, a heart, and another trump to lose.

The loss of 150 points was of course a big profit for North-
South, because their opponents had an easy game at no-trump. At
worst they would win four club tricks, two spades, two diamonds,
and a heart.

How could East-West get into the bidding and reach their
game? The only answer is that in expert play they usually do, by
intuition or inspiration or whatever unusual quality it is that
experts have. Since most bridge players are not so gifted, the
weak two-bid is likely to be a most effective tool when used by
the best players against weaker players. In fact, opponents of the
weak two-bid have called it an intentional "sucker-killing" device.

The average player would be wise to use the weak two-bid only
on classic hands such as are shown above. He should confine
himself to six-card suits, and not make the weak two-bid (as Mr.
Schenken himself has been known to do) on a hand like this:

♠ 6   ♡ K Q 10 7 4   ◇ K J 8 3   ♣ 7 5 2

Perhaps the principal pitfall to avoid is bidding two hearts on this kind of hand:

♠ 9 6 5 3   ♡ A Q 10 9 6 5   ◇ 8 2   ♣ 6

Partner might have a fair hand with a spade suit and game might be missed. A hand with four spades is seldom suitable for the weak two-bid. Exchange the spade and club holdings and this hand would fit the weak two-bid standard.

VULNERABILITY AND MATCH-POINT CONSIDERATIONS

Like any preëmptive bid, the weak two-bid anticipates a possible double, so a weak two-bid is usually stronger when the bidder is vulnerable than when he is not vulnerable, but there are some respects in which the considerations applying to a weak two-bid are exactly the opposite of those applying to a three- or four-bid.

For example, a three-spade bid is far more likely to be doubled for penalties than a three-diamond bid, so a vulnerable player will bid three diamonds on a weaker hand than he requires for a three-spade bid.

But a weak two-bid may be made in spades with a hand that would be passed if the suit were diamonds. On the following hand two spades might be bid, first hand, not vulnerable, against vulnerable or nonvulnerable opponents:

♠ Q 10 9 8 6 3   ♡ 8 6   ◇ 7   ♣ K 10 9 8

Change the suits, leaving the cards the same:

♠ 8 6   ♡ 7   ◇ Q 10 9 8 6 3   ♣ K 10 9 8

On this hand it is hardly worth while to bid two diamonds. The opponents are less likely to be shut out, so there is the same risk with less to gain; if partner should have great strength it will avail much less, because five diamonds will be so much harder to make than four spades would be on the preceding hand; and if partner wishes to sacrifice against a major-suit game he must go one trick higher than would be necessary on the spade hand.

The weak two-diamond bid, for these reasons, is seldom heard in rubber bridge. In duplicate games with match-point scoring it is used more often when not vulnerable against vulnerable opponents, but largely because it avoids one danger of a psychic one-diamond bid: Partner is immediately warned of weakness and will not be likely to overbid on a very strong hand.

The weak two-heart bid should be slightly stronger than the weak two-spade bid, because it has less shut-out effect but undertakes the same risk.

Generally it is best to adhere to the classic requirements, a good six-card suit with a trick and a half (7 to 9 high-card points) in the hand.

RESPONDING TO THE WEAK TWO-BID

There are two possible objectives in responding to a weak two-bid: one is defensive, the other offensive. As suggested earlier the partner of the weak two-bidder may increase the level of the preëmpt by making a simple raise. He may also raise to game, either as a preëmpt or with the expectation that game will be made. The ambiguous character of the game raise makes it doubly difficult for the opponents to know when to enter the auction, since the responder could raise a weak two-heart bid to game with either of these hands:

1.	♠ 7		2.	♠ A K 7
	♡ K 8 7 5			♡ J 8 7 5
	◇ 9 6 2			◇ K Q 6
	♣ K 8 6 4 2			♣ K Q 4

When the responder has an in-between hand and either does not know whether to bid a game or does not know which game to bid, he can make a forcing bid to request more information from the opener. A new suit bid is generally considered natural and forcing, although a growing number of players treat it as non-forcing.

The bid of two no-trump is conventional and forcing. It asks opener to bid a new suit if he has better than a minimum weak

two-bid, to rebid his suit if he has a minimum, or to rebid three
no-trump if his suit is solid (e.g., A-K-Q-10-3-2).

THE OGUST TWO NO-TRUMP CONVENTION

In practice, contrary to the classical requirements, there is considerable variation both in the high-card content of weak two-
bids and in the location of the high-card strength. To cope with
the wide range of hands that the weak two-bidder may hold,
Harold Ogust developed a convention to codify the opener's
answers to his partner's two no-trump inquiry.

For example, when opener bids two hearts responder may have
a rather ordinary hand such as

♠ A K 7 3   ♡ 8 7 5   ◇ A 6   ♣ Q J 8 2

There are many correct weak two-bids opposite which responder's
hand will produce game. Using the Ogust convention, following
a two no-trump response the opener has four bids available to
announce whether his suit is "good" or "bad," and whether his
hand is minimum or maximum.

Opener rebids three clubs to show a bad hand with a bad suit,
a hand such as

♠ 8 4   ♡ Q J 10 4 3 2   ◇ K 4   ♣ 7 3 2

A three-diamond rebid * shows a good hand with a bad suit,
for example,

♠ 8 4   ♡ Q J 9 4 3 2   ◇ K 4   ♣ A 7 3

A three-heart rebid * shows a bad hand with a good suit, for
example,

♠ 8 4   ♡ A K J 4 3 2   ◇ 5 4   ♣ 9 5 3

(If opener's heart suit were solid, of course, he would rebid three
no-trump.)

---

* Some partnerships reverse the meanings of the three-diamond and
three-heart responses.

A three-spade rebid shows a good hand with a good suit, such as

♠ 8 4   ♡ A K 10 4 3 2   ◊ 5 4   ♣ K 10 7

With the information provided by the Ogust rebids the responder should be able to make a reasonably intelligent decision whether or not to bid a game, and if so, where.

5

THE TWO-CLUB FORCING BID

Use of the weak two-bid virtually demands that an opening bid of two clubs be a very strong, usually a game-forcing, bid; but the popularity of the two-club bid is not exclusive to those who use weak two-bids. Many of the world's most successful players combine the forcing two-club bid with strong two-bids in the other suits.

The two-club convention is this: An opening bid of two clubs is forcing to game (with one occasional exception that will be noted later). The two-club bid does not necessarily show a club suit. The bidder may even be void in clubs. It does show an unusually strong hand, especially in aces and kings.

The partner of the two-club bidder must make an artificial response of two diamonds if he wishes to deny strength. If he bids another suit, or bids two no-trump, he shows some strength of his own and the rest of the bidding is likely to be pointed toward a slam.

The history of the two-club convention is obscure. It was originated in the early days of contract bridge, around 1930, probably by David Burnstine, then a member of the Four Horsemen and later of the Four Aces. Milton Work, the senior prophet of the predecessor game of auction bridge, espoused the bid, but temporarily it lost favor as Ely Culbertson and his forcing two-bid (in every suit) became ascendant.

The advantages claimed for the two-club bid are twofold. First, it often saves a round of bidding, especially when the bidder's principal strength is in spades or hearts and not in the minor suits. Second, it frees the bids of two spades, two hearts, and two diamonds for other uses.

The most popular use of these other two-bids today is in the weak two-bid, a mild shut-out bid, described in the preceding section.

But Mr. Burnstine's original two-club bid was combined with other two-bids (spades, hearts, diamonds) that were strong but not game-forcing.

By this interpretation a strong but nonforcing two-spade bid might be made on

♠ A K Q 10 6 5   ♡ 9 5   ◇ A Q 10   ♣ K 5

This hand might make game opposite any hand that has a small amount of spade support or high cards insufficient for a response to a one-bid, for example:

♠ J 8 2   ♡ 10 8 7 3   ◇ 5 4   ♣ Q 9 6 2

On these combined hands game might be made by a winning finesse or a favorable lead, and such games should be bid.

With no support in trumps or outside high cards the responder may pass the strong but nonforcing two-bid or may drop it short of game.

The advantage of the strong, nonforcing two-bid is largely negative. It permits one-bids to be made on weaker hands and it permits the one-bidder's partner to pass more readily without fear of missing game, since the range of the one-bid is more limited.

A variation of these methods—with the strong two-bid forcing for one round but not forcing to game—is part of the Acol system used by many of the leading British players.

The disadvantage of the forcing two-club bid is a practical one: the average player hates artificial bids. If he bids clubs he wants to have clubs, not spades or hearts or diamonds. However, this consideration does not bother the expert.

HOW THE TWO-CLUB BID WORKS

Requirements for the two-club bid can hardly be expressed in points, or at least not in high-card points. A hand that qualifies for the forcing two-bid (page 50) is a proper hand for a two-club bid, but an advantage claimed for the two-club bid is that some hands that do not qualify as forcing two-bids are safe two-club bids.

The typical two-club hand will include:

Usually, second-round control or better in every suit; never weaker than a singleton or Q-x in any suit.

One long, solid suit, or two strong five-card or longer suits, or at least 21 points in aces and kings.

Any of the following hands would be a two-club bid for the majority of the experts who use that bid (but it should be noted that today's experts do not demand nearly so much as previous generations of experts):

1.	♠ A 6	2.	♠ A Q J 8 5	3.	♠ A K 6 4 3
	♡ K J 4		♡ A K Q 10 4		♡ 6
	◇ A 3		◇ A 8		◇ A K 5
	♣ A K Q J 7 5		♣ 7		♣ A K 8 7

The partner of the two-club bidder must respond two diamonds unless he has, in high cards, at least an ace and a king; or K-Q and king; or three kings; or at least a five-card suit headed by A-J or K-Q with a queen outside.

Opening bid and first response out of the way, both partners bid normally. The opener's first rebid shows his real suit. Traditionally any rebid in a suit by opener, such as

SOUTH	NORTH
2 ♣	2 ◇
2 ♠	

indicates that opener has a good enough hand to make game all by himself, and North is required to bid again and keep the bidding open until game is reached. The responder, if he started with two diamonds, shows his real suit; or support for the opener's suit, if he can; or greater weakness by bidding no-trump.

According to more modern practice, the two-club opening ceases to be forcing if the opener merely rebids the same suit:

SOUTH	NORTH
2 ♣	2 ◇
2 ♠	2 N.T.
3 ♠	

This practice increases the number of hands that can be opened with two clubs to include some that are similar to the intermediate hands discussed on page 52.

LATER BIDS BY RESPONDER

There is no doubt that these restrictions often serve to clarify the meanings of rebids. For example, a hand bid to a slam in a New York tournament:

NORTH
♠ 5
♡ K J 10 8 7 6 3
◇ 8 4 3
♣ 9 6

WEST
♠ 3
♡ 9 2
◇ J 10 7 2
♣ A Q 10 5 4 2

EAST
♠ J 9 7 6 2
♡ 4
◇ K 9 5
♣ K J 7 3

SOUTH
♠ A K Q 10 8 4
♡ A Q 5
◇ A Q 6
♣ 8

Both sides were vulnerable. The bidding:

SOUTH	WEST	NORTH	EAST
2 ♣	Pass	2 ◇	Pass
2 ♠	Pass	4 ♡	Pass
6 ♡	Pass	Pass	Pass

There could be no question of a grand slam; since North had responded two diamonds in the first place, he could not hold both the ace of clubs and the king of hearts.

But since North had jumped his bid on the second round, he

had to have a very strong heart suit and that ought to produce a slam, which South accordingly bid.

The contract was a lay down, despite the bad spade break. East opened a low club, and after taking his ace West shifted to a trump. North had only to trump his losing club in dummy and discard his diamonds on the high spades, after drawing trumps.

A diamond opening by East would have made greater demands on North's skill, but a good declarer should have made his contract with no greater difficulty.

Of course, the first-round diamond finesse could not be taken by anyone who does not peek. If the finesse lost, a club would defeat the contract. So the diamond ace would be put up.

The spade ace would be cashed next, for a 6-0 break in a suit is sufficiently unlikely to be disregarded in nearly all cases. The spade ace would win and a low spade would be led from dummy, with North prepared to trump with the heart ten if West followed; but West would have to discard or trump, so North could safely trump with any heart sure to win.

A heart lead to dummy's queen, a ruff of the spade eight in North's hand, and another heart lead to dummy would establish the ten of spades and also draw trumps. Two diamonds would go off on the K-Q of spades and one club on the ten of spades and North would surrender a club trick, taking the rest and making his contract. The 2-1 break of the East-West hearts made establishment of the spade ten unnecessary, since North could ruff his second club in dummy, but this line of play might have been needed if hearts had broken 3-0.

TWO CLUBS AS A TWO NO-TRUMP BID

The two-club forcing bid in its most popular application is not necessarily forcing to game. It may be made either on a typical two no-trump hand or on a game-going powerhouse, and no one but the opener knows which it is until the opener rebids. Sometimes not then.

SOUTH	WEST	NORTH	EAST
2 ♣	Pass	2 ◇	Pass
2 N.T.			

South holds just what a traditional two no-trump opening used to show—about 23 or 24 high-card points. Responder is not forced to bid over two no-trump, but he should bid again if he has as much as a couple of queens, or a queen and a jack.

The great value of using the two-club/two no-trump bid to show a hand of 23 to 24 points is that a two no-trump opening can be made on a slightly weaker hand, about 21 to 22 points. This permits opener's hand to be described with greater precision, which is more and more desirable as the bidding approaches the game level.

A positive response by North creates a game-forcing situation, even if South's rebid is two no-trump:

South	West	North	East
2 ♣	Pass	2 ♡	Pass
2 N.T.			

North must bid again and both North and South must continue bidding until game is reached. The trick and a half or more shown by North's two-heart response must produce a play for game, even if South had the minimum for his two-club bid.

6

NEGATIVE AND RESPONSIVE DOUBLES

IN THE summer of 1957 Alvin Roth took a plane to Europe to play a set game (rubber bridge, at high stakes) with Tobias Stone against an Italian pair. While on the plane it occurred to Mr. Roth that it would be more valuable to double an opponent's overcall for takeout than for penalties. When Mr. Roth landed he told Mr. Stone about his idea and they immediately adopted it. Both give it much of the credit for the fact that they won the match by a big margin.

DEFINITION AND REQUIREMENTS

The Roth-Stone negative double—originally (and still, in Europe) called "sputnik" after the Russian satellite launched at about the same time—is an immediate double of an opponent's overcall in a bidding situation such as the following:

SOUTH	WEST	NORTH	EAST
1 ♣	1 ♠	Double	

or

SOUTH	WEST	NORTH	EAST
1 ♠	2 ♣	Double	

According to bidding rules that were universally unchallenged from 1930 or before until 1957, North's double in either case must be for penalties and South is expected to pass. Roth and Stone construe North's double as a takeout double, over which South is expected to bid again. Furthermore their interpretation of the negative double goes all the way up to the four-level. If West's overcall had been three diamonds, or even four spades, North's double would still have been for a takeout. However, many partnerships agree on lower levels, e.g., "negative through three diamonds."

174

Unlike other takeout doubles, the negative double does not discourage a penalty pass. In fact, the negative double invites a penalty pass if the moderate strength it shows seems insufficient for a game but the opposing contract can probably be defeated. The negative double is not made on very strong hands. By doubling West's overcall, North in the foregoing bidding sequences showed that he had some strength but not enough to make a free bid in a suit or no-trump.

The Roth-Stone requirements for the negative double are 7 to 10 high-card points including 1 or 2 quick tricks. The double that was effectively made in the following deal was typical.

NORTH
♠ K 10 9 8
♡ 6 4 2
◊ Q J
♣ K J 9 8

WEST
♠ 6 4
♡ A K Q 10 9 8 5
◊ 7 5
♣ 3 2

EAST
♠ Q J 5 3 2
♡ J 7
◊ 6 4 3 2
♣ 6 5

SOUTH
♠ A 7
♡ 3
◊ A K 10 9 8
♣ A Q 10 7 4

This deal occurred in a tournament and Tobias Stone, North, was paired with his wife, Janice Stone, South. The bidding, with South dealer and North-South vulnerable, was:

SOUTH	WEST	NORTH	EAST
1 ◊	3 ♡	Double	Pass
6 ♣	Pass	Pass	Pass

Other pairs were prevented from bidding their slam by West's preëmptive overcall, over which North would have had no good bid if a double would have been construed as a penalty double. (In some cases West bid four hearts instead of three, but using negative doubles North still could have doubled and the double would have been even more likely to result in a slam contract.) With 10 points in high cards, North had exactly what South could expect; and since South knew that these high cards were chiefly in suits other than hearts, they were almost sure to be useful. The contract was a laydown, South having twelve tricks after West took the first heart trick.

ARGUMENTS PRO AND CON

Originally the argument in favor of the negative double went like this: Bridge players no longer make weak overcalls, so the penalty double of a simple overcall has become a wasted bid. It may as well be applied to a useful purpose.

To this original argument the rebuttal is: Yes, but if you remove the only possible deterrent to weak overcalls—the hairtrigger penalty double—your opponents will again go wild with overcalls as they did, years ago, before the mass of bridge players learned that it can be profitable to double low bids.

And finally, the counterrebuttal is: The negative double does not materially lessen the possibility of penalizing the opponents if they make weak overcalls. The responder could not double an overcall without strength in the opposing suit. The opening bidder is mathematically about as likely as the responder to hold strength in the opposing suit, and if he does have this strength he can pass the negative double for penalties. There is even an advantage in a case like this:

SOUTH	WEST	NORTH	EAST
1 ♡	2 ◊	Double	Pass

If North's double were known to be for penalties, and East knew it, East's pass would take on a special meaning. It would mean that he could stand the double, or at least that he had no obvious rescue suit. But when North's double is for a takeout,

East has no reason to rescue because South will probably bid. If South nevertheless passes for penalties, West cannot tell how willing East may be to play at a two-diamond contract.

The penalty pass of the double was effective in the following deal, played by Messrs. Roth and Stone.

NORTH
♠ 7
♡ K J 10 2
◇ A K J 6 5
♣ K 4 3

WEST
♠ Q J 9 2
♡ 8 6
◇ 10 9 3
♣ Q 8 7 2

EAST
♠ 8 6
♡ A Q 9 4 3
◇ Q 7 2
♣ A 6 5

SOUTH
♠ A K 10 5 4 3
♡ 7 5
◇ 8 4
♣ J 10 9

North dealt. East-West were vulnerable. This deal was played in that first game in which the negative double was tested. Mr. Stone was North and Mr. Roth South, and the bidding was:

NORTH	EAST	SOUTH	WEST
1 ◇	1 ♡	Double	Pass
Pass	Pass		

South was strong enough to bid one spade, but he preferred to double so as to show that his hand was not very strong. He planned to bid spades later. However, North's heart strength was so great that he foresaw greater profits in passing for penalties and he was right. North-South won three diamond tricks, three heart tricks, and two tricks in each of the other suits, and East was down 1,100 points. The only possible North-South game was three no-trump played by North. It probably would not have been made against the best defense, and even if made it would have been worth less than 500 points.

TREATMENT OF LENGTH IN OPPONENT'S SUIT

The responder cannot use the negative double when he has a natural penalty double of the suit in which the opponent over-calls. If the bidding goes:

SOUTH	WEST	NORTH	EAST
1 ♡	2 ◇		

North must pass the following hand, on which in other systems he would make a penalty double:

♠ K 10 3   ♡ 5 4   ◇ K 10 8 7   ♣ K 6 4 2

North hopes his partner can reopen with a takeout double:

SOUTH	WEST	NORTH	EAST
1 ♡	2 ◇	Pass	Pass
Double	Pass		

South's double is for a takeout, of course, but North will pass it for penalties.

This appears to answer the final aspect of the charge that the negative double lets the opponents overcall too freely. In fact, however, it does not quite answer it.

South's takeout double indicates that his opening bid was some-what better than a minimum. The double is stronger than, for example, a two-heart rebid.

In this sequence:

SOUTH	WEST	NORTH	EAST
1 ♠	2 ♣	Pass	Pass
Double			

the double is stronger than a rebid of two spades, two hearts, or two diamonds would be.

In the Roth-Stone bidding system opening bids are strong and the opening bidder is very likely to be able to reopen with a double. In systems that stress light opening bids, the use of the negative double will unquestionably cost some opportunities for lucrative penalty doubles, and if the negative double is grafted onto such systems some resourceful opponents may be able to get into the bidding with overcalls more often than they do now.

THE RESPONSIVE DOUBLE

The responsive double is a double in response to partner's take-out double, when partner has doubled the opening bid and the opener's partner has raised:

SOUTH	WEST	NORTH	EAST
1 ♠	Double	2 ♠	Double

East's double is not for penalties. It shows general support for the three suits other than spades. East is not strong in high cards; as with the negative double, he will usually have 7 to 10 points in high cards, usually not so many as 10. A sample hand cited by Roth and Stone for East's double is

♠ x   ♡ Q x x x   ◇ K x x x   ♣ Q x x x

As stated earlier (page 107), a cue-bid is widely used to carry this message, but in this bidding the cue-bid would have to be three spades, which drives East-West pretty high, and if North's raise had been a jump to three (or even four) spades a cue-bid would have been out of the question while the responsive double would be just as effective as it is at the two-level.

This use of the responsive double deserves its newly acquired popularity. Seldom will one wish to double such a raise for penalties.

RESPONSIVE DOUBLE OVER PARTNER'S OVERCALL

The responsive double can also be used when partner has over-called and the opening bid has been raised, as in this bidding:

SOUTH	WEST	NORTH	EAST
1 ◇	2 ♣	2 ◇	Double

Some but not all of those who use the responsive double treat East's double as responsive and not as a penalty double. This is logical, for there can seldom be an opportunity to make a profitable penalty double of a low contract when one opponent has bid a suit and the other has raised it.

The Roth-Stone description of East's double is: "[East] requests [West] not to rebid his own suit unless it is self-sufficient. He may bid any three-card suit with assurance of support." The example they give for East's hand is:

♠ K 10 9 x x   ♡ K J 10 x x   ◇ x x   ♣ x

It must appear, then, that this is one responsive double that should not be passed for penalties; but then, West would have passed one diamond instead of overcalling if he had held great length in diamonds. This problem will seldom arise when an opposing suit has been bid and raised.

For many years the future of this type of responsive double as a regular bidding tool was doubtful. Nevertheless it has remained a part of the game and can be expected to increase the number of its adherents among at least a minority of the players, and most of those the best players.

7

THE FORCING ONE
NO-TRUMP RESPONSE

In a few systems, and among a few other players who do not fully accept those systems, a response of one no-trump to partner's opening major-suit bid is forcing for one round.

This method is treated here among the bidding conventions, rather than among the standard practices described in Part I of this book, because the few systems that use the forcing no-trump response are not the most widely played systems: Roth-Stone, Kaplan-Sheinwold, Stayman, perhaps two or three others, all involving a taboo against opening, four-card major suits.

Like so many other bidding developments of this bridge generation, the forcing no-trump response is a Roth-Stone innovation. It is probably the most brilliant idea bridge has seen since the days of the pioneers, back in the 1920s and early 1930s. Its praiseworthiness is all the greater because when it was introduced it seemed like heresy to all experts and probably it still does to most experts.

The forcing no-trump response occurs in the following situation:

South	West	North	East
1 ♡ *or*	Pass	1 N.T.	Pass
1 ♠			

Now South must bid again.

Theoretically, this is unsound. In pure bridge theory every no-trump bid (unless used artificially, like the Blackwood convention) is a limited bid and passes control to the partner. A bid that is forcing *ipso facto* retains control.

But in practice the forcing one no-trump response to a major works perfectly and furthermore it has succeeded in resolving a dilemma that for many years had seemed insoluble.

The dilemma arose principally with such hands as this:

♠ 6　♡ 10 4　◊ A 9 8 6 3 2　♣ J 7 5 2

Partner opens with one spade, the next hand passes. Under the bidding systems that have been used for more than thirty years *and are still being used by 95 percent of all bridge players,* any action taken on this hand is likely to be wrong. A pass might leave the partnership to play a spade contract when a diamond contract would be much better; and a pass might even cost a game, if partner has a very strong or unbalanced hand that fits diamonds. A one no-trump response gives the desirable message of weakness, but with a minimum partner may pass one no-trump, which is the last place at which the responder wishes to play the hand. A two-diamond response is conventionally forcing and promises more strength than this hand has, so the partnership is almost sure to get too high.

The desideratum is to get to two diamonds, and stop there if partner is not very strong, without restricting partner's license to go on if his hand warrants going on.

In the early years of contract bridge a two-diamond response would not have been defined as forcing; but the opening bidder always bid again anyway, because so often two diamonds would have been bid on a much stronger hand. Authorities defined a standard situation called the sign-off:

SOUTH	WEST	NORTH	EAST
1 ♠	Pass	2 ◊	Pass
2 N.T.	Pass	3 ◊	Pass

By this three-diamond rebid North showed weakness and asked South to pass. Sometimes South dutifully passed but three diamonds went down one when two diamonds could have been made if there had been any way to stop there. More often South could not be talked out of his strong hand, persisted to three no-trump or some other impossible bid, and went down several—unless North wearily bid four diamonds to go down two, doubled this time.

This problem, at least, has been solved by making the one no-

trump response forcing. The hand that has just been under discussion occurred as the South hand in the following deal.

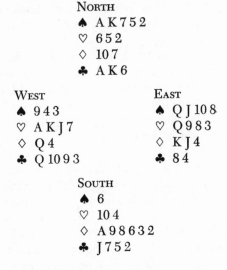

NORTH
♠ A K 7 5 2
♡ 6 5 2
◇ 10 7
♣ A K 6

WEST
♠ 9 4 3
♡ A K J 7
◇ Q 4
♣ Q 10 9 3

EAST
♠ Q J 10 8
♡ Q 9 8 3
◇ K J 4
♣ 8 4

SOUTH
♠ 6
♡ 10 4
◇ A 9 8 6 3 2
♣ J 7 5 2

North dealt. Neither side was vulnerable. The bidding was:

NORTH	EAST	SOUTH	WEST
1 ♠	Pass	1 N.T.	Pass
2 ♣	Pass	2 ◇	Pass
Pass	Pass		

North had to bid over South's no-trump response. North's two-
club rebid was of a kind often used by those who have adopted
the forcing no-trump response. It is a convenient way to show the
location of the opening hand's outside strength, and it permits the
responder to rebid at a low level—in this case, the lowest level
because North's outside strength was in clubs and South's suit
was diamonds. But it does not guarantee a biddable suit.

The two-club rebid was not forcing and South could have
passed it, with his four-card club support. No great damage
would have been done if South had passed, for North would
probably have wangled out eight tricks at clubs. But two diamonds, which South decided to bid, proved to be better.

There was no question about North's passing two diamonds. South had shown weakness with his no-trump response and now he could neither pass two clubs nor support spades by going back to two spades. Obviously he wished to play diamonds.

West started with the king and ace of hearts and led a third round, which South trumped.

South's technique was good. He wished to establish a long spade, so he led his singleton spade to dummy and trumped a low spade in his hand before surrendering the lead. If South had started leading trumps too early, a club lead by East would have driven out one of the club entries South would need later to reach an established spade in dummy.

After trumping the spade, South led a low diamond. Just in case one opponent had K-Q-J-x in diamonds, he played to keep a trump in dummy to control another heart lead and also to keep the diamond ace in his hand to control the trump suit.

West put up the diamond queen and led the nine of spades, and South played low in dummy and trumped in his hand. Then South cashed the diamond ace and led a club to dummy. One of South's clubs went off on the spade king and another on the spade seven, which East trumped high. South had a trump and the club ace in dummy for the last two tricks and made three. He would have made his contract, two diamonds, even against a bad trump break.

The forcing one no-trump response is not used over an opening minor-suit bid, because it is not necessary. A one-over-one response can be made on a weaker hand and will keep the bidding lower.

North was not required to pass two diamonds. With a very strong hand, and especially with some high diamond, North could have tried once more. For example, with K-x in diamonds North would have raised to three diamonds. Then South could have gone on with a much better diamond suit, such as A-Q-x-x-x-x.

It should not be inferred that the forcing one no-trump response is perfect. Some hands appear, especially misfits, that are bound to get too high and this device is powerless to prevent it. But seldom do weak hands get more than one trick higher than necessary when the forcing one no-trump response is used.

8

TRANSFER BIDS

TRANSFER BIDS have been perhaps the most controversial of the
new bidding conventions in contract bridge.

The purpose of a transfer bid is to transfer the contract—that is,
the right to be declarer—from one partner to the other. For example, South opens with one no-trump and North holds such a hand
as this:

♠ 76   ♡ Q 10 8 7 6 2   ◇ 8 4 3   ♣ K 8

It is almost sure that the North-South hands will play best with
hearts trumps, but since South has a strong hand in high cards,
and North a weak one, it will be better if South is declarer so that
the opening lead will be made to his strong hand and so that the
exact nature of his high cards will be concealed. The North-South
object, therefore, is to reach a heart contract with South as declarer, and the transfer bids are a device to achieve this end.

A transfer bid is a response in the suit next-lower in rank than
one's real suit. On the hand shown above, for example, the real
suit is hearts, therefore the holder of the hand would bid diamonds. This would force the no-trump bidder to bid the next-
higher suit, hearts, and become declarer at that suit.

The invention of transfer bids is generally credited to Davd
Carter, a Missouri man, but they became popular chiefly in the
Southwest and often they are called the Texas convention. In
Europe the convention is called simply "Texas." Some of the
transfer bids, especially those made at the two-level, are also
called Jacoby transfers because Oswald Jacoby has been their
principal proponent.

In their simplest form transfer bids are made only at the four-
level. If South opens one no-trump and North responds four diamonds, South must bid four hearts; if North responds four hearts,
South must bid four spades.

For a four-heart response North may have a hand such as this:

♠ K J 9 7 6 5 2   ♡ 8   ◇ Q 6 4   ♣ 8 3

Opposite a hand strong enough for an opening no-trump bid, the hand shown will almost surely produce a game but will not produce a slam. The combined hands may play one trick better if the strong no-trump hand is declarer.

But the heart hand shown earlier:

♠ 76   ♡ Q 10 8 7 6 2   ◊ 8 4 3   ♣ K 8

is not quite strong enough to insist on game if the no-trump hand is a minimum and lacks a fit with hearts. The Jacoby transfer bids were designed for such hands.

THE JACOBY TRANSFER BIDS

Jacoby's extension of this principle makes it apply to the two-level:

If over one no-trump the responder bids two diamonds, the no-trump bidder must bid two hearts; two hearts, two spades; two spades, the no-trump bidder shows whichever minor suit he prefers. The response of two clubs is reserved for the Stayman convention, described earlier in this book.

Responses of three in a suit—three diamonds, hearts, or spades —are normal forcing bids.

Responses of four in a suit are again transfer bids, except four clubs, which is the Gerber convention.

Use of transfers at both the two- and the four-level gives the partnership a great deal of flexibility in describing hands with slam interest, without slam interest, two-suited hands, and relatively balanced hands. For example, game-going hands can be expressed as those without slam interest by making the transfer at the four-level, or as hands with slam interest by making the transfer at the two-level and then raising to four. Thus

SOUTH	NORTH
1 N.T.	2 ◊
2 ♡	4 ♡

shows a much better responding hand than

SOUTH	NORTH
1 N.T.	4 ◊

After a two-level transfer, if the opener's partner "raises" his real (or "anchor") suit it is a simple game invitation in the suit. If he rebids two no-trump he shows 5-3-3-2 shape and gives opener the option of playing a game or a part-score, in either the anchor suit or no-trump. Responder might hold a hand such as

♠ K 5   ♡ K Q 10 7 3   ◇ 7 4 2   ♣ 9 8 6

A new-suit rebid after a transfer bid would be natural and forcing, and allows game to be reached in the anchor suit, in the new suit or in no-trump. For example,

SOUTH	NORTH
1 N.T.	2 ◇
2 ♡	3 ◇

Responder might have

♠ 6 4   ♡ K Q 10 7 3   ◇ A 7 4 2   ♣ Q 6

EXAMPLE OF THE JACOBY TRANSFER BID

The Jacoby transfer bids led to a very pretty result in the deal that included a hand shown earlier. The deal was:

NORTH
♠ 7 6
♡ Q 10 8 7 6 2
◇ 8 4 3
♣ K 8

WEST
♠ A 10 4
♡ A 9
◇ K 9 6 2
♣ J 7 4 2

EAST
♠ Q J 9 5 3
♡ 5 4 3
◇ 10 5
♣ Q 9 6

SOUTH
♠ K 8 2
♡ K J
◇ A Q J 7
♣ A 10 5 3

South dealt. East-West were vulnerable. Mr. Jacoby held the North hand, and his partner, South, was his son, James Jacoby, who followed in his father's footsteps by winning several national championships while still in his twenties, and has twice been a world champion. The bidding was:

SOUTH	WEST	NORTH	EAST
1 N.T.	Pass	2 ◊	Pass
2 ♡	Pass	3 ♡	Pass
4 ♡	Pass	Pass	Pass

The two-diamond bid was the transfer bid; the two-heart bid was the forced response. The three-heart rebid by North was a simple invitation to South to go on if he had a good fit for hearts or a relatively strong no-trump hand.

Jim Jacoby had an exceptionally strong no-trump hand; he had 18 high-card points, and the best players today seldom bid no-trump with more than 17 points. Therefore his acceptance of the game invitation was automatic.

West played safe by opening the ace of hearts and continuing with the nine. Any other lead from his hand seemed dangerous, and although as it happened he could have opened diamonds or clubs with impunity, a spade lead would have wrecked the defenders' chances from the start.

South, who had unblocked by throwing his king of hearts on the first trick, won the second trick with dummy's queen of hearts and drew the last outstanding trump with dummy's ten, on which he discarded a spade, as did West. Then South took the king and ace of clubs and trumped a club in dummy, on the bare chance that both the queen and jack would fall. They did not, and South tried a diamond finesse, leading low from dummy and playing the queen. West could not dare refuse this trick, so he won with his king and got out of the lead with the jack of clubs, which dummy trumped.

Dummy now had one trump left, and South led it and discarded his remaining low spade. West could not part with a diamond, for that would establish South's low diamond; so West blanked his ace of spades. South led the eight of diamonds from dummy, won with the ace and threw West in by leading the king of spades. West had to lead from the 9-6 of diamonds into South's J-7, and South made his game contract.

THE CONTROVERSIAL ASPECTS

The American Contract Bridge League, after somewhat reluctantly sanctioning transfer bids at the four level ("Texas"), for years barred the Jacoby transfer bids. Their principal reason was that such bids are too confusing to opponents unaccustomed to them.

But transfer bids at any level, including the four-bids that are permitted, seem to confuse even the players who use them. In the heat of play, it is hard to remember that a perfectly normal-sounding bid does not mean what it says.

John Crawford and Tobias Stone, playing for the United States in an international match, lost a game because Mr. Crawford forgot and bid four in his real suit, hearts, instead of bidding four diamonds. Terence Reese and Boris Schapiro, of Britain, so often forgot the Texas convention that eventually they agreed that the forgetful partner would pay the other one pound. Money regularly changed hands.

Such cases have caused some expert pairs to abandon transfer bids, while casual players shy away completely—as they do from most artificialities.

But transfer bids are nevertheless gaining in popularity among tournament players, who have grafted the usual crop of extensions and modifications on them.

9

THE UNUSUAL NO-TRUMP

THE UNUSUAL no-trump originated in the Roth-Stone system about 1950. The convention created no stir then, probably because it had no catchy name. It received the catchy name when it was adopted into the Kaplan-Sheinwold system about 1954.

In its simplest form, the unusual no-trump is as follows:

If a player bids two or three (or, exceptionally, four) no-trump when he cannot have a hand strong enough to play such a contract, he shows a hand with great length in both of the minor suits, diamonds and clubs. Usually he will have at least five cards in each minor suit.

The no-trump bidder's partner must then bid his "best" (longer) minor suit, even if he has only two or three cards in it.

The unusual no-trump is forcing. It cannot be passed.

In the first book on the Roth-Stone system, published in 1952, this convention was described casually and without title, via the following bidding sequence:

SOUTH	WEST	NORTH	EAST
Pass	Pass	1 ♠	Pass
1 N.T.	Pass	2 ♠	Pass
Pass	2 N.T.	Pass	

What should East do now? East's hand is powerful, in view of his previous passes:

♠ x x x   ♡ A J 10 x x   ◇ Q 9   ♣ K 10 x

If West had a genuine two no-trump bid, East would have more than the values required to bid game at no-trump or hearts. But West cannot have a genuine two no-trump bid because he passed originally and there is no such thing as a hand that can make two no-trump yet is too weak for an opening bid. Therefore West is asking to be taken out of his no-trump contract.

Opposite a normal takeout bid, such as a double, East would unhesitatingly bid his very good heart suit. In this case he must not. This is the respect in which the unusual no-trump ceases to be a logical bidding message and becomes a convention, or arbitrary message. Being an "unusual," or nongenuine, no-trump overcall, West's bid of two no-trump demands a minor-suit response; and Mr. Roth's official answer to the question was, "Three clubs. No choice. Partner is requesting a minor suit."

West's hand, to justify his bid of two no-trump, would be expected to be the following or its equivalent:

♠ x x   ♡ x   ◇ K J 10 x x   ♣ A Q x x x

Such a hand would be minimal, and acceptable only when not vulnerable, except in match-point duplicate bridge where an opposing part-score must be contested even at some risk. If the opponents have not already passed the hand out at a low contract, the unusual no-trump bidder should be stronger—perhaps with a 6-5 two-suiter such as

♠ x   ♡ x   ◇ K Q 10 x x x   ♣ A J 9 8 x

CALLING FOR UNBID SUITS

From its original use to show a two-suiter in the minor suits, the unusual no-trump has developed in many partnerships as a convention to show a two-suiter in the two unbid suits, when the opponents have shown strength and have bid only two suits. An example is the following deal.

NORTH
♠ A 10 8 4 3
♡ J 10 9
◇ K 6 3
♣ J 6

WEST
♠ 5
♡ Q 8 6 4 3 2
◇ 9
♣ K 10 7 4 3

EAST
♠ J 9 6
♡ K 7
◇ 10 8 5 2
♣ A Q 9 2

SOUTH
♠ K Q 7 2
♡ A 5
◇ A Q J 7 4
♣ 8 5

South dealt. North-South were vulnerable. The bidding was:

SOUTH	WEST	NORTH	EAST
1 ◇	Pass	1 ♠	Pass
3 ♠	3 N.T.	4 ♠	5 ♣
Pass	Pass	Double	Pass
Pass	Pass		

West's unusual no-trump bid—three no-trump—was used to show a two-suiter in the two suits North-South had not bid. Since East had quite a good hand, the result was excellent for East-West. They lost only one spade, one heart, and one diamond trick and were down one, 100 points as they were not vulnerable. At this small cost they prevented a vulnerable game their opponents could have made, worth 650.

The North-South bidding is not exempt from criticism. South's pass of five clubs, which would be meaningless in the average game, carried a distinct message in the expert circles in which it was made. It was a forcing pass, meaning that South could stand a five-spade contract if North could bid it. Probably North should have bid five spades, but East or West could have bid six clubs, going down two tricks or 300 points and still saving 350 points.

A most extreme use of the unusual no-trump occurred in the following deal.

```
                    NORTH
                    ♠ K
                    ♡ K 6
                    ◊ A 9 8 5 4 3
                    ♣ 10 8 7 4

      WEST                         EAST
      ♠ Q 8 5                      ♠ 10 9 7 6 3 2
      ♡ 10 8 4 3                   ♡ Q J 9 7 5 2
      ◊ Q J 6                      ◊ 10
      ♣ 9 6 2                      ♣ ———

                    SOUTH
                    ♠ A J 4
                    ♡ A
                    ◊ K 7 2
                    ♣ A K Q J 5 3
```

South dealt. North-South were vulnerable. The bidding reached the significant point as follows:

SOUTH	WEST	NORTH	EAST
2 ♣	Pass	2 ◊	Pass
3 ♣	Pass	4 ♣	Pass
4 N.T.	Pass	5 ◊	Pass
5 N.T.	Pass	6 ♡	6 N.T.

The opening two-club bid was not the artificial forcing bid used by many experts but was the natural strength-showing bid used by the majority of players, showing a genuine club suit and a probable game-going hand. The two-diamond response by North was a positive response, showing strength; North's "bust response" would have been two no-trump. The bids of four and five no-trump were Blackwood bids, and when North had shown one ace and two kings facing an opening two-bid East could tell that South was fairly sure to bid a grand slam.

It is almost axiomatic in bridge that there is no such thing as a bad sacrifice by a nonvulnerable player against a vulnerable grand slam that his opponents can make. The vulnerable grand slam is worth at least 2,140 points, and against such a score a nonvulnerable pair can bid seven and go down eleven tricks and still show a profit. The only reason there are not more sacrifices against grand-slam bids is that hope springs eternal and there is always a chance that the grand slam may be beaten.

South did bid seven clubs, and West, reading East's bid of six no-trump as the "unusual no-trump," calling for a response in one of the unbid suits, bid seven hearts and played the hand there, doubled, going down five, or 900 points.

North and South could have made seven clubs easily. They could have made seven no-trump by a squeeze but it is mathematically unsound to bid grand slams that depend on successful squeezes or finesses.

THE UNUSUAL NO-TRUMP AS A CONVENTION

The unusual no-trump described (sans name) by Roth and Stone in 1952 was interpreted by logic. Now the takeout message is assigned to it arbitrarily, so that many and perhaps most of the experts bid as follows:

SOUTH	WEST	NORTH	EAST
1 ♠	2 N.T.		

West's two no-trump is the unusual no-trump. It shows that West has a two-suiter in the minor suits and is willing to go as high as three in the one that best fits East's hand.

The argument used to justify this interpretation is that West could double first, to show strength, and later bid no-trump if he had a genuine two no-trump hand.

The advantage of the bid is that West avoids being shut out of the bidding. If West passed on the first round, North might bid two or three spades and South might bid four and West could not safely come in. If West overcalled with two diamonds on the first round and the bidding reached four spades by the time it came around to him again, it might not be safe for him to bid *five* clubs. So East, who might have a fine fit for clubs, could never learn about the two-suited nature of West's hand.

With the unusual no-trump used as an immediate jump overcall, West can show the nature and approximate strength of his hand with a single bid and without being forced too high.

The strength required varies according to vulnerability, as is the case with all overcalls. The hand shown earlier in this section—

♠ 74   ♡ 6   ♢ K J 10 7 3   ♣ A Q 9 5 2

—would be good enough only if not vulnerable or if reopening the bidding against opponents who have already stopped at a low contract and cannot have great strength. A vulnerable player should usually have a 6-5 hand or a very strong 5-5:

♠ 6   ♡ 5   ♢ K Q 10 8 7 5   ♣ A J 10 7 3

or

♠ 6   ♡ 9 4   ♢ A Q 10 7 6   ♣ A K J 5 2

The bid is somewhat safer if the opponents' suit has been raised, for then partner is unlikely to have length in that suit and is more likely to fit one of the minors. In the following situation:

SOUTH	WEST	NORTH	EAST
1 ♠	Pass	2 ♠	2 N.T.

East does not need quite so much as West needed for his immediate jump to two no-trump in the preceding bidding diagram. The fact that West has passed is not a consideration. In overcalling one does not rely on finding more in the hand of a partner who has not yet been heard from than in the hand of a partner who has passed.

Not everyone has adopted the jump two no-trump as part of the unusual no-trump convention. Many of the older players like two no-trump to be a genuine bid in such a case, made perhaps on a hand like this:

♠ Q 63   ♡ A Q   ◇ A K Q 8 6 2   ♣ Q 5

This would be an immediate jump overcall of two no-trump over one heart. It could be very slightly stronger—say, a king instead of one of the queens. At any rate it invites a very light raise to game.

Over a weak two-bid, an overcall of two no-trump is always genuine; over a strong two-bid it is always unusual.

SOUTH	WEST	NORTH	EAST
2 ♡	2 N.T.		

If North-South use weak two-bids, West should have such a hand as the one shown just above. If North-South use strong two-bids, West's two no-trump is the unusual no-trump, preparing for a sacrifice against a game or slam contract.

PROS AND CONS OF THE UNUSUAL NO-TRUMP

The major advantage of the unusual no-trump is that in one bid it gives one's partner a choice of suits to support, before the opponents, who have the higher-ranking suit(s) have a chance to raise the level of the bidding so high that both suits cannot be shown.

However, this one bid that gives partner such precise information also alerts the opponents. Therefore, if the side that called on the unusual no-trump does not buy the contract, the bid has become a liability rather than an asset.

In each of the examples given earlier, the unusual no-trump bidder had either a good playing hand or a hand so extreme in distribution that a profitable sacrifice was likely if partner fit either of his suits. However, consider what is likely to happen if the no-trump bidder has a poor hand and the opponents buy the contract:

NORTH
♠ A J 7 2
♡ A K
◇ A 10 7 5 4
♣ 8 5

WEST
♠ Q 9 6
♡ J 10 7
◇ Q J 8
♣ Q 10 9 2

EAST
♠ 5
♡ Q 8 6 4 3
◇ 9 2
♣ K J 7 4 3

SOUTH
♠ K 10 8 4 3
♡ 9 5 2
◇ K 6 3
♣ A 6

North dealt. North-South were vulnerable. The bidding:

NORTH	EAST	SOUTH	WEST
1 ◇	Pass	1 ♠	Pass
3 ♠	3 N.T.	4 ♣	Pass
4 ◇	Pass	4 ♠	Pass
5 ♡	Pass	6 ♠	Pass
Pass	Pass		

West leads the jack of hearts. In the absence of any adverse bidding, declarer's normal play would be to cash the ace and king of trumps rather than to take a finesse. On this deal, however, declarer was forewarned that East had at most three cards in the spade and diamond suits, since his unusual no-trump bid announced at least ten cards in the other suits.

Declarer therefore cashed the king of spades, and when both opponents followed low, he took the precaution of leading a diamond to the ace and a low diamond back, to get as complete a count as possible of East's hand. When East followed to both diamonds, the spade finesse through West was clearly marked. If East had ruffed the second diamond no harm would have been done since declarer must lose a diamond anyway; if East had discarded on the second diamond, declarer would have been back to guessing whether to finesse or to play for the queen of spades to drop.

This was a case in which the unusual no-trump side did not buy the contract, and its use may have cost them 1,530 points because it gave the declarer a clear indication of how to play the hand, whereas without adverse bidding he might easily have gone wrong.

RESPONDING TO THE UNUSUAL NO-TRUMP

Strict discipline is required in responding. The longer minor suit must be bid, even on a hand like this:

♠ K 10 8 6 2   ♡ A J 5 3   ◇ 7 5 4   ♣ 3

The response must be three diamonds, not three of either major and not pass.

While the unusual no-trump seldom shows a real powerhouse, it is after all a hand capable of undertaking a three-level contract. If the responder has a good minor-suit fit and a smattering of high-card strength, he must make a jump response:

♠ A 5 4   ♡ 9 7 5 2   ◇ 8   ♣ A 9 7 5 2

This hand calls for a jump to five clubs over an unusual no-trump. With the king instead of the ace in clubs, five would still be the bid unless the unusual no-trump were a "balancing" bid (to reopen the bidding).

One cannot count points in responding to the unusual no-trump. Only an ace is a dependable trick in a major suit. A king may be worthless, because partner may have a singleton; a queen almost surely *is* worthless; and even K-Q may be worth no more than two small cards. But any strength in either minor is worth a great deal and the queen of the other minor is almost as good as an ace.

EXTENSIONS OF THE UNUSUAL NO-TRUMP

A few experts still limit the unusual no-trump to the minor suits; the majority apply it also to the unbid suits; and a few use it for almost any two-suiter, following these rules:

1] If the opponents have bid two suits, it shows the other two.

2] If the opponents have bid only hearts, it shows the two minors.

3] If the opponents have bid only one suit but that suit is spades, diamonds, or clubs, it shows *any two* of the other three suits. Partner responds in his best *minor*. A suit rebid by the no-trump bidder now shows that the two-suiter was composed of hearts and the other minor.

This device is intended to cover cases in which a five-card heart suit is too weak to bid over a difficult contract such as two spades, but the second suit makes it likely that there will be some safe spot.

SOUTH	WEST	NORTH	EAST
1 ♠	Pass	2 ♠	2 N.T.

East holds

♠ 5   ♡ K 10 8 5 2   ◇ A K Q 8 6   ♣ Q 2

East will pass a minimum response of three diamonds, will bid three diamonds over three clubs, and will bid four hearts over a jump response of four diamonds.

Most players think this is carrying a good thing too far, but they feel the same way about most of the elaborate conventions now being used.

10

FISHBEIN CONVENTION AND
OPTIONAL DOUBLES

THERE IS hardly a greater problem in contract bridge than that of the fairly strong hand against which an opponent makes an opening preëmptive bid, such as three spades or four hearts.

To some extent the problem is insoluble, because the high opening bid has preëmpted the bidding rounds in which partners usually exchange information. Nevertheless there have been numerous attempts to overcome the difficulty with artificial bids over the opponent's preëmptive bid.

One of these is called the Fishbein convention, having been suggested by Harry J. Fishbein of New York. The Fishbein convention, which is now seldom used and has been abandoned even by Mr. Fishbein, is used only against preëmptive three-bids and minor-suit four-bids and only by the player immediately after the preëmptive bidder. It works like this:

If your right-hand opponent opens with a three- or four-bid, and you want your partner to show his best suit, you overcall with the next-higher suit-bid. Over three diamonds you would bid three hearts; over three spades, four clubs.

If you double, it is for penalty.

If you bid no-trump, you want to play the hand there and your partner may pass.

In this situation West's overcall is a Fishbein convention bid:

SOUTH	WEST	NORTH	EAST
3 ♡	3 ♠		

In this situation East's overcall is not:

SOUTH	WEST	NORTH	EAST
3 ♡	Pass	Pass	3 ♠

East has made a natural overcall, showing a spade suit and inviting West to raise to game if he can but permitting him to pass.

The three-spade overcall by West in the former situation may not be passed. If North passes, East must respond as he would to a double, showing his best suit. Of course, West is expected to have strength in spades, as in the other unbid suits, but if East's best suit is spades he does not simply pass because West has promised spade support. He is supposed to bid four spades.

Among tournament players the opening three-bid is often very weak; the suit is broken and the rest of the hand is next to hopeless. Mr. Fishbein in his book on the Fishbein convention, cited the following hand on which forty-seven out of fifty-two players in a national tournament opened the bidding with three spades:

♠ K J 9 7 6 4 2   ♡ 5   ◊ J 5 3 2   ♣ 8

Fishbein wanted to be able to double that hand for penalties if he sat over it, so he devised his convention. He did not apply the convention to the player who is *under* the three-bidder (as in the second bidding situation shown on page 200), because trump strength under the bidder is worth less and opportunities for penalty doubles are accordingly fewer.

A typical Fishbein (penalty) double of a three-spade bid is:

♠ A J 8 7 2   ♡ 3   ◊ A K J 4   ♣ K Q 10

The doubling hands speak for themselves. They are good hands with trump length and strength. Using the Fishbein convention, one will rarely be in doubt as to when he should double.

The strength required for the takeout overcall, such as three hearts over the opponent's three diamonds, varies with vulnerability. Among the keenest players it varies also according to the bidding habits of their opponents, but vulnerability is the essential consideration when playing in good company.

The very weak three-bid is made only when not vulnerable and usually only when playing against vulnerable opponents. When a good player bids three and is vulnerable, he expects to win at least seven tricks and his hand will not be the dangerous one cited from the national tournament but rather something like this:

♠ K Q 10 9 8 7 6 ♡ 5 ◇ Q J 10 9 ♣ 8

Little profit can be expected from a penalty double of such a bid, and indeed even nonvulnerable good players generally exercise greater care if they are likely to be doubled for penalties. Thus the opportunities for the immediate penalty double have become less frequent and the Fishbein convention has lost currency.

Nevertheless, the best opportunity for the Fishbein convention arose in a National tournament in 1970 when Marty Cohn, known among tournament players for a certain imaginativeness in his bidding, opened with a three-heart preëmpt on a suit of three hearts headed by the jack. He caught Peter Leventritt, his left-hand opponent, with seven hearts to the ace, king, and queen, and with no conceivable bid, because Mr. Leventritt and his partner Howard Schenken were playing takeout doubles; Mr. Schenken could hardly be expected to pass such a double. It must surely be right to play Fishbein over Marty Cohn.

THE OPTIONAL DOUBLE

The majority of the experts do not use the Fishbein convention or any other convention (including the once prevalent custom of bidding three no-trump over a three-bid as a takeout double) in defending against a preëmptive bid. They double.

The expert relies on a double, plus partner's "feel" of the situation, plus the intuition of both partners, to land them in the proper spot. Such confidence is not always justified in the event, but the fact remains: It is the experts' approach.

The full details of the experts' usual method is something you will never read about in any book, including this one, because nearly everything depends on each partner's appraisal of the situation as of the time he takes action—or declines to take action.

THE INDEFINABLE DOUBLE DEFINED

Briefly, the experts play any double of an opening three- or four-bid as a takeout double. Partner is asked to bid, even on a very weak hand. But partner need not bid if he does not want to.

The experts' philosophy of defense against preëmptive bids is something like this:

1] Profits are meager when you double the preëmptive bid of a good player, and the risk is great. Therefore, one does not double solely for the purpose of increasing the value of the penalties but to enlist partner's collaboration in finding the best contract.

2] A double of a preëmptive bid merely expresses the opinion that the doubler's side, and not the opponents', holds the superior cards.

3] This being the case, the doubler's partner should take the double out unless he has a good reason to leave it in.

For example, South deals and bids four hearts; West doubles; North passes. East, the doubler's partner, is expected to bid four spades on a hand like this:

♠ 9 x x x x   ♡ x x   ◊ J x x x   ♣ x x

(And there is no particular reason why the nine of spades should have been specified in the example hand. Any five small spades would do.)

The double is passed when the doubler's partner has his principal length in the opponents' suit, or when he has either a weak or a fair hand with no suit to bid.

If a rule must be made, it is this: The doubler's partner takes out the double into any five-card suit that he can bid without increasing the contract. He would bid four spades over a doubled four hearts with any five spades; but he would pass with a five-card diamond suit in a weak hand, because he would have to bid five to show it. He would bid a four-card suit if his hand were stronger; for example, over four hearts doubled he would bid four spades on this:

♠ J x x x   ♡ x x   ◊ K x x x   ♣ Q x x

The justification of this method is that the expert either is, or considers himself to be, intuitive. The method is theoretically unsound, because of cases like the following:

NORTH
♠ A 9 3 2
♡ A 4
◊ J 6
♣ Q 10 9 6 3

WEST
♠ K 10 8
♡ 7
◊ A Q 7 5 4
♣ A 7 5 2

EAST
♠ Q J 7 6 4
♡ 8 2
◊ K 10 8 3
♣ J 4

SOUTH
♠ 5
♡ K Q J 10 9 6 5 3
◊ 9 2
♣ K 8

South, vulnerable or not, deals and bids four hearts. East-West are vulnerable. West must pass; he is not strong enough to double when the double would invite a response on a weak hand. North passes; he is satisfied with the contract. What is East to do?

The expert will assure you that East bids if he should, and passes if a bid would be wrong; somehow or other, he knows what to do. The expert will further assure you that he does not get into trouble on these hands.

It is true that players have been known to reopen the bidding on the East hand, and trouble seldom results. Nevertheless the expert's argument is unconvincing. Whether or not he has the intuition to select the best course, a run-of-the-mill player has not. He needs a better method.

On this particular deal, it is profitable for East to bid. If left alone, South will make four hearts. If East bids four spades, he will make it or South must bid five hearts and go down.

Therefore the recommended system is either one of the artificial ones, mentioned above, or the "optional double," in which the doubler has about 3½ tricks—enough to make it probable that the contract will be beaten if the double is passed—and his partner must have a trick or so, and a five-card suit, if he wishes

to bid; a hand like East's in the deal shown above. But the purpose here is to report what is being played, and not to teach
what ought to be played, and the fact is that in expert games a
double of a preëmptive bid is primarily a takeout double.

THE FOUR NO-TRUMP OVERCALL

Traditionally a four no-trump overcall of an opponent's opening four-bid (whether made by the next bidder or by fourth hand
after two passes) has served as a gigantic takeout double. The
same definition has been given to a five no-trump overcall of a
preëmptive five-bid. But seldom does a player have a hand so
strong that he can force a response at the five-level from a partner who may have a totally worthless hand; and considering that
an opening five-bid in itself is rare, occasions to use a five no-
trump overcall are in effect nonexistent.

When the four no-trump overcall is used in its book meaning
to show a powerhouse, almost always it is made over a four-spade
bid—over which it is, after all, the cheapest bid that can be made
—and it is based on a hand with a long diamond or club suit plus
strong support in hearts if partner has a five- or six-card heart
suit.

The following hand would be an ideal four no-trump over an
opponent's four spades.

♠ 3   ♡ A K J 5   ◇ A K 10 4   ♣ A Q J 7

Even this hand will hardly be secure for eleven tricks if partner
must respond in a weak four-card suit, and an unusual degree of
security is needed when one not only risks going down at his own
contract but relinquishes a sure penalty score against the opponents. Many experts would merely double four spades.

Therefore the four no-trump overcall, under the influence of
the popular "unusual no-trump," has become a bid to show a
two-suiter. It usually shows eleven cards in two suits. It may not
be passed, as a three no-trump bid may be, even if partner has a
stopper in the opponent's suit.

Over four hearts, four no-trump can be assumed to show both

minors; over four spades, it should have hearts plus one minor. It
may be a genuine two-suiter:

♠ 5   ♡ A Q J 6 3   ◊ A Q J 10 7 5   ♣ 3

or it may contain a long minor suit that would warrant an overcall at the five-level plus strong support for the other major if
partner has a five- or six-card suit, as in the following deal.

NORTH
♠ 8 6 2
♡ J 8 7 5 3 2
◊ 6
♣ A J 3

WEST
♠ 9 4 3
♡ K 9
◊ K
♣ Q 10 8 7 6 4 2

EAST
♠ A K Q J 10 7 5
♡ 4
◊ 10 9 4 2
♣ 9

SOUTH
♠ ———
♡ A Q 10 6
◊ A Q J 8 7 5 3
♣ K 5

East dealt. North-South were vulnerable. The bidding:

EAST	SOUTH	WEST	NORTH
4 ♠	4 N.T.	5 ♠	6 ♡
6 ♠	Pass	Pass	Double
Pass	Pass	Pass	

Both sides did well on this one. The fact that North found his
hand good enough for a six-heart bid shows how much he re-
spected the four no-trump overcall. North-South would have
made six hearts, of course. East-West took a smaller loss at six
spades, and only the best defense put it down 700 points.

South opened the ace of diamonds and continued with the
queen, despite dummy's void. Dummy's three of spades was

overtrumped by North, who returned the two of spades. East won and led a heart.

South put up the ace of hearts and led his low club, and North was in with the ace to lead another trump, so East could not trump a diamond with the high spade in dummy. East did discard a diamond on the king of hearts, but he still had one diamond to lose.

11

LANDY AND OTHER COUNTERS
TO ONE NO-TRUMP

It is always dangerous to overcall one no-trump, because the no-trump bidder's partner can double so easily. He knows his partner has at least two cards in the overcaller's suit, because opening no-trump bids are not made on unbalanced distribution. He knows the odds heavily favor his partner's having an honor in the overcaller's suit.

If South opens with one no-trump and West overcalls with two diamonds, North can and should double with a hand like this:

♠ A 8 ♡ K 7 4 3 ♢ 10 7 6 2 ♣ J 7 6

Assuming that South has a standard no-trump hand of some 16 points, the combined North-South hands have 24 points in high cards and six or more diamonds and it is unlikely that West will win eight tricks.

West knows all this, of course, and probably he has a hand on which he cannot be badly hurt, but it is the readiness of North to double that requires him to have such a hand. If North stopped doubling freely, West could overcall more freely.

There are many cases in which West would be unable to overcall because he has no trump suit strong enough, and would be unable to double because a double of one no-trump is primarily a penalty double, but still East-West could compete profitably against the no-trump bid if they could *safely* find their best-fitting suit.

This is an old problem against all bids of one no-trump, whether they are strong or weak, and whether they are opening bids, responses, or rebids. The problem was intensified when the weak one no-trump opening of 12 to 14 points came into common use in the 1950s, for there are necessarily more hands with which one might compete against a weak no-trump than a strong one.

Lessening the requirements for a double of one no-trump does not solve the problem. A double of one no-trump should remain a penalty double. But a takeout double is needed too.

The simplest of the substitutes for the takeout double is the Landy convention, named for Alvin Landy, who from 1951 until his death in 1967 was executive secretary of the American Contract Bridge League, and had been for many years a high-ranking American tournament player.

Mr. Landy devised his convention originally as a defense against the weak no-trump, bid on a hand such as this:

♠ K Q x x   ♡ 10 x x x   ◇ A Q x   ♣ J x

The Landy convention is this: A two-club overcall of an opponent's opening one no-trump bid does not show a club suit but asks partner to bid his best suit. (If his suit is clubs, he may pass; but he should prefer a major.)

The two-club overcall has been widely adopted and has been generally extended for use against the strong opening no-trump bid of 15 or more points, as in the following deal:

NORTH
♠ 8 5 4 2
♡ K
◇ 9 5 4
♣ K 9 8 3 2

WEST
♠ K J 9 6 3
♡ Q J 9 4
◇ 8
♣ Q J 5

EAST
♠ 10
♡ 10 8 7 5 3
◇ A K J 10 6 3
♣ 7

SOUTH
♠ A Q 7
♡ A 6 2
◇ Q 7 2
♣ A 10 6 4

South dealt, both sides were vulnerable, and the bidding was:

SOUTH		NORTH	EAST
SOUTH	Pass	NORTH	EAST
1 N.T.	WEST	Pass	2 ♣
Pass	2 ♠	Pass	3 ◇
Pass	3 ♡	Pass	Pass
Pass			

Some play that the Landy convention applies only to a two-club bid by the next opponent (in this case, West). Most players, like East-West in this deal, use it also as a reopening bid.

West had the right kind of hand for a Landy two-club bid, but not enough high-card points. About 13 points are needed, except with a two-suiter such as East's.

East could not double, for he had no reason to believe he could defeat a no-trump contract; and he did not wish simply to bid two diamonds, since hearts would be a better trump if West happened to have biddable strength in hearts. The conventional two-club bid solved his problem.

East's premises were correct. South could easily have made one no-trump and might have made two. Two diamonds would not have been the best East-West contract and a two-diamond contract might even have gone down, if the defense were perceptive enough. West did make the response most unwelcome to East when he bid two spades, but East had diamonds as an escape suit, and West, knowing that the two-club bid probably showed a two-suited hand, found the best contract by bidding his secondary heart suit.

At three hearts West had to lose only the two high trumps and the two black singletons, and the score for three hearts was top on the board.

The Landy two-club takeout bid over one no-trump has become conventionalized to the extent shown in the deal above. The two-club bid denies sufficient strength (16 or more points) to double one no-trump for penalties. When the two-club bidder rescues his partner's takeout suit he shows a two-suiter that includes an escape suit strong enough to bid independently.

Often the decision between a double of one no-trump and a two-club overcall for a takeout is a close one. The following deal occurred when North-South were using weak no-trump bids, rather than the strong no-trump used by North-South in the preceding deal.

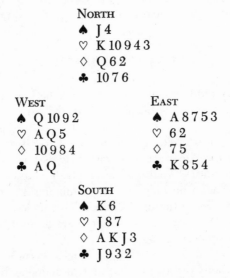

NORTH
♠ J 4
♡ K 10 9 4 3
◇ Q 6 2
♣ 10 7 6

WEST
♠ Q 10 9 2
♡ A Q 5
◇ 10 9 8 4
♣ A Q

EAST
♠ A 8 7 5 3
♡ 6 2
◇ 7 5
♣ K 8 5 4

SOUTH
♠ K 6
♡ J 8 7
◇ A K J 3
♣ J 9 3 2

South dealt. Neither side was vulnerable. The bidding:

SOUTH	WEST	NORTH	EAST
1 N.T.	2 ♣	2 ♡	2 ♠
Pass	Pass	Pass	

West might have been more inclined to double a strong no-trump bid for penalties than to double the weak no-trump bid by South. Against a strong no-trump West could expect both the A-Q combinations to be almost as good as ace-kings. Against a weak no-trump he could expect North to hold at least one of the kings in those suits and perhaps both.

East-West reached their best contract. They made three spades easily. With the opposing hearts placed so advantageously for him, North could not have gone down more than one trick at three hearts and would have made the two-heart contract.

If West had doubled one no-trump, East might have passed and the result would have been a poor one for East-West unless

West chose a spade lead; or East might have jumped to three spades, because the double shows more strength than the two-club overcall, and West might have raised to four spades, and at four spades East-West would have gone down. However, four spades would not be a bad contract at rubber bridge.

LANDY MODIFICATIONS

As with every bidding convention that has had much circulation, the Landy principle has been modified and extended in various ways.

Ripstra is an extension developed by J. G. Ripstra, a former president of the American Contract Bridge League. The over-caller still promises length in both major suits, but with the Ripstra convention he bids his longer minor suit, and in theory suggests shortness in the unbid minor. This undoubtedly is more enlightening but it does remove one more natural bid, two dia-monds, from a player's repertory.

Astro, named after Paul Allinger, Roger Stern, and Lawrence Rosler, uses both the two-club and two-diamond overcalls, the former showing hearts and a minor suit, the latter spades and one of the other three suits. It works well, and as with many of the conventions described in this part of the book it poses only the problem of how far one wishes to go in the use of special conventions.

Brozel is a never convention devised by Bernard Zeller in which each two-level overcall shows a two-suited hand:

> 2 ♣ shows hearts and clubs
> 2 ◇ shows hearts and diamonds
> 2 ♡ shows hearts and spades
> 2 ♠ shows spades and a minor
> 2 N.T. shows clubs and diamonds

A double is penalty-oriented and shows a one-suited hand. If the partner of the doubler does not want to defend he bids two clubs and passes the doubler's rebid.

12

SHORT-SUIT TRIES FOR
GAMES AND SLAMS

FOR MORE than fifty years, the primary purpose of opening bids and responses has been to show long suits. A player's first bid is expected to be in his longest suit. This is logical; such a suit can become an acceptable trump suit. But it is surprising how many hands there are in which it is almost (not quite) as important to exchange information on short suits. That mystical quality of bridge hands called a "fit," with which few bidding systems deal adequately, depends principally on whether and where each partner has a singleton.

The Culbertson asking bids of 1936, which still deserve admiration though they were a bit too involved to win widespread acceptance, were an effort to locate singletons for slam-bidding purposes.

More recently there has been some experimentation with bids to show singletons below the game level, to help decide whether to bid game or stop short. Adoption of such methods is doubtful, not only because artificialities are unpopular but because the value of the methods themselves is doubtful. The information may not help the bidding side as much in the bidding as it helps their opponents in the defense.

BIDDING FOR GAME

Singleton showing designed for game rather than slam bidding has been used in the Kaplan-Sheinwold system.

In standard practice, a player's second bid shows his secondary strength—a suit that is not quite as long or strong as the suit he bid first, but still a good suit. For example:

♠ A Q 9 7 4   ♡ Q 7 5   ♢ A Q 6 3   ♣ 5

213

On this hand a player will open with one spade and if his partner raises him to two spades he will make a tentative try for
game by bidding three diamonds. His partner is expected to return to three spades if he had a weak raise and to jump to four
spades if he had a strong raise.

Messrs. Kaplan and Sheinwold reversed the time-honored principle by making the opener's second bid show his weakness. On
the hand above, the rebid would be three clubs. The responder
should now bid game if he has several losers in clubs but should
sign off if he has high cards in clubs and weakness elsewhere.

The following deal carries the principle one step further.

NORTH
♠ 10 9 7 4 2
♡ 4
♢ Q 7 3
♣ 8 7 5 2

WEST
♠ 8
♡ K 10 7 6
♢ A 8 6 5 2
♣ K 10 4

EAST
♠ A 3
♡ Q 9 8 2
♢ 9 4
♣ A Q J 9 3

SOUTH
♠ K Q J 6 5
♡ A J 5 3
♢ K J 10
♣ 6

South dealt. Both sides were vulnerable. The bidding:

SOUTH	WEST	NORTH	EAST
1 ♠	Pass	2 ♠	Pass
3 ♣	Pass	3 ♡	Pass
4 ♠	Pass	Pass	Pass

The essential bid here was South's rebid of three clubs. It
showed that South had a singleton club and a desire to reach
game if the North-South hands fitted. Those who are interested in

using the proposed convention in its simplest form may adopt it only up to this point, since the great majority of hands will require no more information.

But in this case, North's three-heart bid gave additional information. It meant that North had raised originally on so weak a hand that he still could not risk a game contract, even though his weak clubs fitted well with South's singleton; but that he had a singleton heart, and if this fact made the fit even better, South should bid the game.

The singleton heart did fit with South's hand and South did bid game. If North's singleton had been in diamonds, South would have signed off at three spades. At four spades, South had to lose only a club, a diamond, and the ace of trumps.

Or was that all? If West opened a low diamond, East could get a diamond ruff to defeat the contract. The North-South bidding was sufficiently revealing to suggest this defense.

ITALIAN SINGLETON-SHOWING BIDS

In the Roman Club system used by some members of Italy's formidable "Blue Team," opening two-bids are used to show the distribution of the bidder's hand.

The strong two-bid, as used by the majority of players, will not often occur once a session. The weak two-bid, used by some players in reaction to this fact, is usually a bit too low to be effective as a shut-out bid. The Romans use all two-bids to show distribution.

Opening bids of two hearts, two spades and two no-trump are used to show biddable club suits plus one outside suit. (An opening one-club bid cannot be made in the Roman system on a standard hand, because one club is their artificial forcing bid.) So two hearts shows clubs and hearts, two no-trump shows clubs and diamonds. These bids do not actually show singletons, but when a hand is long in two suits it is short in the other two.

Especially interesting are their two-club and two-diamond bids, which show hands distributed 4-4-4-1 or 5-4-4-0. Two clubs shows a biddable hand up to 16 points in high-card strength; two diamonds shows a stronger biddable hand, with 17 or more high-card points.

The idea of using opening bids to show hand patterns was undoubtedly original with Harold W. Bissell of New York in his book published by Columbia University Press in 1936, but nearly twenty years elapsed before the idea was adopted by a team strong enough to exploit it.

In the 1959 world championship matches the distributional two-bid helped the Italians in the following deal:

NORTH
♠ A J 10 8
♡ K 8 7 6 2
◊ A K Q 5
♣ ———

WEST
♠ K Q 7
♡ A 10 9 4
◊ 9 4 2
♣ 10 7 3

EAST
♠ 6 3
♡ Q J 5 3
◊ J 10 6
♣ A K 9 4

SOUTH
♠ 9 5 4 2
♡ ———
◊ 8 7 3
♣ Q J 8 6 5 2

East dealt. Neither side was vulnerable. The Italian bidding:

EAST	SOUTH	WEST	NORTH
Pass	Pass	Pass	2 ◊
Pass	2 ♠	Pass	4 ♠
Pass	Pass	Pass	

North's two-diamond bid showed a strong hand with three suits of at least four cards each. North's singleton or void might have been in spades, but South tried his four-card spade suit first; if North had rebid in another suit or in no-trump, South could then have bid clubs with assurance that there would be a good play for five clubs, since North would have to have at least four of them. Since the spade response happened to fit North's hand, North bid game at once.

West opened the two of diamonds. Dummy won and South started a cross-ruff, trumping four hearts in his hand and three clubs in dummy. Then South cashed dummy's two other high diamonds and finally made the ace of trumps for his eleventh trick.

When the American players held the North-South cards, North opened with one heart and South passed. Neither can be criticized by the terms of the bidding methods Americans use, but the fact remains that one heart went down a trick while the Italians were making game on the same cards, and the Italians gained 500 points.

BIDDING FOR SLAM

In recent years several conventions have been devised to show singletons in an effort to reach slam. The most used of these conventions are discussed in section 15 of this part.

13

THE GRAND SLAM FORCE

THE FRENCH bridge newspaper *Le Bridgeur*, like nearly all other bridge periodicals, conducts regular bidding competitions.

In presenting one set of bidding problems *Le Bridgeur* (in 1962) stated that there are only two conventions it assumes everyone uses: the takeout double and the grand slam force.

Le Bridgeur made no mistake, so far as its enlightened readers are concerned. Everyone does use the takeout double. Every expert does use the grand slam force.

This makes the grand slam force the Cinderella among bidding conventions.

When the grand slam force was introduced in 1936 it was greeted with disdain by nearly all experts and it encountered almost universal nonacceptance among the bridge-playing masses. Now the vast majority of American experts use it and apparently the same is true on the Continent.

Ely Culbertson introduced the grand slam force in the first edition of his *Gold Book*, published in 1936, now out of print.

The grand slam force is a free bid of five no-trump after a trump suit has been agreed upon by the partnership. The five no-trump bid requires partner to bid seven if he has two of the three top honors in the agreed trump suit—A-K, A-Q, or K-Q. Having none of these trump combinations he must bid six.

The implied accolade given to the grand slam force by *Le Bridgeur* in 1962 was balanced by an error made by that same publication in 1961.

Then (in 1961) the grand slam force was referred to in *Le Bridgeur* as *"le coup Joséphine."* This name attributed invention to Josephine Culbertson (Mrs. Ely Culbertson). I would and should be the last person to deny Mrs. Culbertson any credit due her, since she and I were bridge partners, business partners, and close friends for many years, but this is not one of the credits due her.

In preparing his *Gold Book,* Ely Culbertson was assisted by an impressive staff of experts that included (among others) Richard L. Frey, A. Moyse, Jr., Theodore Lightner, Sam Fry, Charles Vogelhofer, A. Mitchell Barnes, Josephine Culbertson herself, and incidentally Albert Morehead.

Every one of these without exception strongly opposed Mr. Culbertson's grand slam force, for which he was solely and obstinately responsible. Mrs. Culbertson not only was among the opponents, she had the unique advantage of being able to voice her opposition in bed.

But Mr. Culbertson, who was the boss, had seen this deal come up recently (as of then):

NORTH
♠ A K 9 5 3
♡ 8 7 3
◇ 1 0 9 8 7 2
♣ ———

WEST
♠ J 10 8
♡ A Q 6 5 2
◇ 3
♣ 10 7 6 2

EAST
♠ ———
♡ K J 10 9 4
◇ Q 5 4
♣ J 9 8 4 3

SOUTH
♠ Q 7 6 4 2
♡ ———
◇ A K J 6
♣ A K Q 5

South dealt. East-West were vulnerable. The bidding was:

SOUTH	WEST	NORTH	EAST
1 ♠	Pass	4 ♠	Pass
6 ♠	Pass	Pass	Pass

North-South had a laydown for a grand slam but South, on the information he had, gambled slightly when he bid a small slam.

With Mr. Culbertson's proposed grand slam force the bidding would be:

SOUTH	WEST	NORTH	EAST
1 ♠	Pass	4 ♠	Pass
5 N.T.	Pass	7 ♠	Pass
Pass	Pass		

And, of course, if North had lacked the ace or king of spades he would have signed off at six spades, which South in the absence of information had in effect bid anyway.

To make seven spades, after West opens the heart ace, requires only care, but a careless player might go down by trying to trump three hearts in his hand.

The sure winning play is to trump the heart, draw three rounds of trump, and then cash the diamond ace. If both opponents follow, three of dummy's diamonds are discarded on the high clubs and the ruff of one of South's diamonds in dummy must establish the other for South's thirteenth trick. If either opponent shows out on the diamond ace, the other opponent's queen can be trapped by a straight finesse or a trump finesse.

Soon afterward there was a deal in which a player's suit was A-J-5-4-3-2 and the player knew his partner had only two-card support; but he used the five no-trump bid, found that his partner had K-Q doubleton, and so reached a grand slam.

Impressed by these examples, Mr. Culbertson put the grand slam force into his book—as an "optional" convention—in defiance of the advice of all his advisers.

But the grand slam force seemed to be a failure, as mentioned above, and in Mr. Culbertson's private marked copy of the 1941 edition of the *Gold Book,* opposite the space allotted to this convention, is his handwritten note: "condense? or omit?"

The resurgence of the grand slam force undoubtedly began in 1941 when Lee Hazen and Richard L. Frey formed a new partnership and had a remarkable series of successes in major tournaments. One of the bidding tools they used was the grand slam force, Mr. Frey apparently having withdrawn his earlier objections to it.

Attention of the world's experts was drawn to the bid by a few dramatic cases in which Frey-Hazen reached grand slams that their opponents missed. Adoption of the bid was gradual, but by the time Ely Culbertson died in 1955 there was no doubt that the grand slam force was one of his greatest successes.

EXTENSIONS OF THE GRAND SLAM FORCE

Many extensions of the grand slam force have been proposed and others are still being proposed. Probably none improves materially on Mr. Culbertson's own recommendation, published in the 1945 edition of the *Gold Book:*

"[In response to five no-trump:]

"If the agreed suit is spades, bid six hearts to show five spades headed by ace or king; six diamonds to show four spades headed by ace or king; six clubs to show any five spades.

"If the agreed suit is hearts, bid six diamonds to show ♡ A x x x x or ♡ K x x x x; six clubs to show ♡ A x x x or ♡ K x x x.

"If the agreed suit is diamonds, bid six clubs to show ◊ A x x x x or ◊ K x x x x."

This takes care of cases in which the player who bids five no-trump needs only to know that the combined hands have at least ten trumps, including the ace and king, in which case the odds are almost 4 to 1 that no trump trick need be lost.

Such a response was used in the following deal.

```
                    NORTH
                    ♠ A J 6 5 4
                    ♡ 6 2
                    ◊ ────
                    ♣ A K Q 8 6 5

   WEST                         EAST
   ♠ Q 10                       ♠ 9
   ♡ Q 9 7 4                    ♡ J 10 8 5
   ◊ Q 6 4 2                    ◊ A J 10 9 8 5 3
   ♣ J 9 4                      ♣ 3

                    SOUTH
                    ♠ K 8 7 3 2
                    ♡ A K 3
                    ◊ K 7
                    ♣ 10 7 2
```

South dealt. East-West were vulnerable. The bidding was:

SOUTH	WEST	NORTH	EAST
1 ♠	Pass	3 ♣	3 ◊
Pass	Pass	3 ♠	Pass
4 ♡	Pass	5 N.T.	Pass
6 ♡	Pass	7 ♠	Pass
Pass	Pass		

South's six-heart bid told North he could expect five or more spades to the king in South's hand, and since South's earlier cue-bid in hearts had shown the heart ace, the grand slam in spades was almost sure. As it turned out, North-South had thirteen top tricks.

GRAND SLAM FORCE AFTER BLACKWOOD

Sometimes the solidity of the trump suit is not the partnership's only concern. For instance, when one player's hand is not strong enough to cause him to cue-bid his aces, his partner may need to use Blackwood. Now, after the ace-showing response to Black-wood, five no-trump is no longer the grand slam force but is an inquiry for kings.

A solution adopted by many experts is for the Blackwood bidder to bid six clubs over the ace-showing response as the grand slam force (unless, of course, the agreed-upon trump suit is clubs).

Such an agreement would take care of the following hands:

WEST	EAST
♠ A Q 9 6 3	♠ K J 8 2
♡ Q J 3 2	♡ A 8
◇ 7 4	◇ A K Q J 4 3
♣ A 5	♣ 6

The bidding would go:

WEST	EAST
1 ♠	3 ◇
3 ♡	3 ♠
4 ♠	4 N.T.
5 ♡	6 ♣
7 ♠	

14

SLAM DOUBLE CONVENTIONS

THE LIGHTNER slam double convention is more a principle than a convention. Anyone could have and should have thought of it. However, Theodore Lightner did think of it first, and despite its logical basis, he had to argue its merits for two or three years before it was generally adopted by other experts. Since there are no possible arguments against it, he was bound to be successful eventually; and for the last forty years the slam double convention had been accepted without question by all expert players.

The principle, briefly stated, is this: When competent opponents bid a slam voluntarily (that is, not as a sacrifice) they are pretty sure to be within a trick or two of making it. It cannot often pay to double them for the sole purpose of increasing the score for undertrick penalties. Therefore the double can best be used to guide partner's opening lead.

Consequently, when a defender who is not on lead doubles a slam contract his purpose is to call the leader's attention to the proper opening lead. He would not have to call the leader's attention to a normal opening lead, so a double of a slam contract asks for some unusual opening lead.

There should be no set rules as to what should be led when a slam contract is doubled. The winning lead is not necessarily the declarer's second suit or dummy's first suit. The defender who has the lead is expected to look at his hand, decide what he would have opened normally, and then open something else.

Mr. Lightner figured this out in 1928 or 1929, when contract bridge was in its infancy. He tried to sell the idea to his bridge partner, Ely Culbertson, who was then codifying the bidding system that became the basis of expert bidding. Unfortunately, Mr. Lightner's first demonstration was far from successful. The opponents bid a slam and he doubled, because an unusual opening lead from Mr. Culbertson was the best hope of defeating the

contract. Mr. Lightner forgot that it was not his partner's lead,
but his own. With the lead in his own hand, there was no hope of
defeating the contract. The opponents redoubled and scored
several hundred extra points. Mr. Culbertson became so preju-
diced against the convention that it was four years before he
would listen to Mr. Lightner's arguments again. However, by
1933 Mr. Culbertson succumbed and adopted the Lightner slam
double convention, and since then there has not been a dissenting
vote.

An illustration of the working of the convention might be found
in this bidding:

SOUTH	WEST	NORTH	EAST
1 ♠	Pass	2 ♣	2 ♡
3 ♣	Pass	4 ♠	Pass
4 N.T.	Pass	5 ♡	Pass
6 ♠	Pass	Pass	Double
Pass	Pass	Pass	

West has the lead, holding the following hand:

♠ 6 3   ♡ 3   ◊ J 10 7 6 5 2   ♣ 10 7 6 3

West's "normal" lead would be his singleton heart, since his
partner bid the suit. However, his partner's double tells him not
to make this lead. Casting about for another lead, he will think
first of his long diamond suit, in which East may be void. But can
North-South have seven diamonds between them, and East be
void? Unlikely. Then he remembers that North has bid clubs and
South has raised them freely. West has four of them; East may be
void. West opens a club and, sure enough, East is void and
trumps. East proves also to have the ace of diamonds, which
defeats the contract. The normal heart lead would have failed
because East did not have the ace of hearts. The diamond lead
would have failed because then East would never have had the
chance to ruff a club. Only an opening club lead could have
earned the setting trick.

Some effort has been made to conventionalize the slam double
even further and make it call for a lead in the first suit bid by
dummy. In the previous example it would have worked. But

many cases indicate that this may be carrying matters too far. Almost always the opening leader, if warned that he must make an unusual lead, can figure out what kind of hand his partner has and what suit should be opened. West did so in this deal, which occurred in a pair tournament:

<pre>
                       NORTH
                       ♠ K Q J
                       ♡ 7
                       ◇ Q J 7 5
                       ♣ A K Q 5 2

    WEST   EAST
    ♠ 6 4   ♠ 8 3 2
    ♡ K Q 8 4 2   ♡ J 9 6 5 3
    ◇ K 8 6 3   ◇ ──────
    ♣ 8 3   ♣ J 10 9 7 6

                       SOUTH
                       ♠ A 10 9 7 5
                       ♡ A 10
                       ◇ A 10 9 4 2
                       ♣ 4
</pre>

South dealt. Neither side was vulnerable. The bidding:

SOUTH	WEST	NORTH	EAST
1 ♠	Pass	3 ♣	Pass
3 ◇	Pass	3 ♠	Pass
4 ◇	Pass	4 N.T.	Pass
5 ♠	Pass	5 N.T.	Pass
6 ♣	Pass	6 ♠	Double
Pass	Pass	Pass	

When East doubled the slam, West could immediately rule out a heart lead. Hearts, the only unbid suit, would be his natural opening. The slam double never calls for a trump lead; so West's choice was narrowed to diamonds and clubs.

In the bidding, South's five-spade response to the Blackwood bid of four no-trump showed that South had started with three aces. By responding six clubs to five no-trump, South showed that he did not have a king, but still South was marked with at least 12 points in high cards.

East could not have A-Q in dummy's club suit—which might be one reason for doubling—because then North could not have been strong enough to make a forcing jump response at his first turn and push on to a slam later.

Nor could East be void of clubs when West had only two.

West therefore decided that East must be void in diamonds and wanted a diamond opening. North had cleverly tried to forestall such a conclusion by concealing his good support for his partner's rebid diamond suit, but the message got through despite his effort.

When West opened the three of diamonds, East trumped it and that gave the defenders one trick.

East led back the jack of clubs and dummy was in. Since South had three low diamonds in his hand and could not discard more than two of them on dummy's clubs, the contract had to go down one.

South tried. After winning the club jack with dummy's queen, he trumped a low club with the spade nine and drew two rounds of trumps with the spade jack and queen in dummy. This exhausted the East-West trumps. Two diamonds were discarded on the ace and king of clubs, and if the East-West clubs had been divided 4-3 instead of 5-2, the last diamond would have gone off, too. Since the clubs did not break evenly, South had to give West the setting trick with the diamond king.

Without East's double, West would never have opened a diamond from his king into a rebid suit. He would have led the heart king.

South could have made six diamonds, but in tournament play the higher-scoring major-suit contract is preferred.

THE LIGHTNER DOUBLE APPLIED
TO LOWER CONTRACTS

The slam-double principle has come to be applied to lower contracts. A double of three no-trump, for example, when neither defender has bid, shows strength in dummy's suit and suggests, even if it does not demand, a lead in that suit.

In every case, an unexpected double tells the doubler's partner not to make what could be expected to be his normal lead.

In the next deal the double by East carried that message at a game contract in a major suit.

NORTH
♠ 10 8 4
♡ K J 9
◇ A Q 6 3
♣ K 8 4

WEST
♠ J 3
♡ 7
◇ J 9 8 7 4 2
♣ Q 6 5 2

EAST
♠ A Q 9 7 5 2
♡ A 6 5 2
◇ ———
♣ 9 7 3

SOUTH
♠ K 6
♡ Q 10 8 4 3
◇ K 10 3
♣ A J 10

North dealt. Both sides were vulnerable. The bidding was:

NORTH	EAST	SOUTH	WEST
1 ◇	1 ♠	2 ♡	Pass
3 ♡	Pass	4 ♡	Pass
Pass	Double	Pass	Pass
Pass			

Without East's double, West would have opened the jack of spades, the suit East had bid. South would have had no difficulty in making four, probably five, against this opening lead.

On the spade opening East would take his ace and lead back a spade, hoping West had a singleton. South would win his spade king on the second lead and lead trumps until East took his ace.

After taking the ace of hearts East would continue spades and South would trump.

South would lead his remaining trumps and West would be squeezed. To hold four diamonds, West would have to reduce his hand to two clubs. South would then cash three top diamonds and the ace and king of clubs, West's queen of clubs would fall, and the defenders would never get another trick.

But when East doubled the four-heart contract, West inferred some defensive feature of East's hand not shown by the moderate overcall of one spade. He opened a low diamond and East trumped.

Now East's problem was to get West back into the lead so that he could trump another diamond. To effect this, East led a low spade.

South put up the king of spades and won the trick, knowing from East's overcall where the ace of spades probably was. But when South started the trump suit East got the first trick with the heart ace and led another low spade.

This spade lead put West in with the jack and West led another diamond, which East trumped for the setting trick.

The double of four hearts on East's hand must be treated as a gamble that will sometimes go wrong, giving declarer's side a bigger score for making a doubled or redoubled contract plus even a bonus for an overtrick. East had no assurance that the contract could be defeated or even that the double would guide West to a diamond opening. But the reward when the double succeeds is the saving of game and rubber, a total gain of 820 or more points, and that justifies taking some chances.

THE "UNDOUBLE" SLAM DOUBLE

While there is no doubt that all expert players use the Lightner double in most slam situations, within the past decade a few have given a different meaning to doubles of slams reached after competitive auctions in which their side may want to sacrifice. For example (North-South are vulnerable):

NORTH	EAST	SOUTH	WEST
1 ♣	2 ♠	4 ♣	4 ♠
	(*weak*)		
4 N.T.	Pass	5 ◊	Pass
6 ♣			

If six clubs can be made, East and West undoubtedly can profit by sacrificing. But if East and West have two defensive tricks they do not want to sacrifice.

In these situations, where the partnership has bid and supported a suit and the hand "belongs" to the other side, some players use the double of a slam not to suggest a lead, but to exchange information on the number of defensive tricks held.

The most logical way to play these cooperative slam doubles is for the partner having the first call (here, East) to double the slam if he has two defensive tricks; with one or no tricks he should wait to see what his partner has to say. The partner in the pass-out seat (West) passes, of course, if his partner has shown two tricks.

However, if his partner has shown one or no tricks by passing, the pass-out partner will: (1) pass if he has two defensive tricks (ending the auction with the opponents in an unmakable slam); (2) sacrifice if he has no defensive tricks; (3) double if he has one defensive trick. This last bid gives the ball back to the immediate-seat partner, who will pass if he has one defensive trick, and "undouble" (i.e., sacrifice) if he has no defensive tricks.

15

MORE INFORMATIVE TRUMP RAISES

UNTIL ABOUT fifteen years ago Standard bidders had almost no way of making an immediate forcing raise of partner's opening bid of one in a suit except by bidding three of the suit. This standard response revealed that responder's hand was worth about 13 to 15 points, but did little to clarify his distribution or the texture of his trump holding.

Similarly, when many experts adopted limit jump raises as part of their methods, some substituted three no-trump as their forcing raise of opener's suit, which gave no better description of the responding hand than did standard methods. Other experts who adopted limit raises elected not to have any immediate forcing trump raise but to handle such hands by indirect bidding.

After the Italian Blue Team started winning one world championship after another and enjoying superior results on their slam decisions, American bridge writers began to take a closer and more critical look at the slam bidding of the American experts. One of the principal places needing improvement was trump raises.

To facilitate good slam bidding a partnership needs: (1) to be able to fix the trump suit in a way which both forces game and suggests slam interest; (2) to determine whether or not the trump suit is reasonably solid; (3) a way to ferret out slams that depend more on "fit" than on raw power—and, conversely, a way to discover when too much of the partnership's power is wasted.

With these goals in mind, a variety of conventions have been developed which at once establish the trump suit and either give or solicit additional specific information. Among these, the most widely used are the Swiss convention, the Jacoby two no-trump response to an opening bid of one of a major, and Splinter bids.

THE SWISS CONVENTION

The Swiss convention is used primarily by partnerships using limit jump raises. It consists of a response of four clubs or four diamonds to an opening bid of one heart or one spade, to show a hand which is committed to playing in game at opener's suit and is willing to consider slam. Its high-card strength is usually in the 13-to-15-point area, and its pattern is usually balanced, since responder would tend to bid a long side suit if he had one, in order to help his partner assess the value of his high cards.

There are a number of ways to play the Swiss convention, and the distinction between what a four-club bid shows and what a four-diamond bid shows is a matter of partnership agreement. Some players feel it is most important to distinguish between a strong raise made on key controls and one made on other values. Control Swiss uses one four-of-a-minor bid to show either three aces or two aces and the trump king; a bid of four of the other minor shows any other strong raise. (Any partnership electing to use this convention should be careful to settle which minor shows which hand!)

Since there are other ways to determine below the slam-level what or how many aces the partnership has, probably a more valuable way to use the Swiss convention is to establish the solidity of the trump suit. Trump Swiss uses one four-of-a-minor bid to show either four trumps headed by at least two of the top three honors, or five trumps headed by at least the ace or the king. Four of the other minor suit is bid to show any other strong raise.

In a recent tournament South opened the following hand with one heart, and would have had a difficult rebidding problem if he had not been using the Trump Swiss convention:

♠ 8   ♡ J 8 7 4 3   ◇ A Q 8 5   ♣ A K 6

A standard forcing raise of three hearts would leave South wondering whether or not to try for slam: six could be virtually laydown if responder held

♠ A 5 3   ♡ K Q 6 5   ◇ K J 9 3   ♣ 8 3

But five could be in jeopardy if responder held instead

♠ K Q 5   ♡ K 10 6 5   ◊ K J 9 3   ♣ Q 8

On the actual deal, North jumped to four clubs, which the partnership had agreed promised either four trumps headed by at least two of the top three honors, or five trumps headed by at least the ace or the king. With this assurance about the trump suit, South started a cue-bidding sequence that led to slam. Here was the complete deal:

NORTH
♠ A 5
♡ A 10 9 5 2
◊ K 3 2
♣ J 8 3

WEST
♠ K Q 7 4 2
♡ Q 6
◊ 9 6
♣ 10 5 4 2

EAST
♠ J 10 9 6 3
♡ K
◊ J 10 7 4
♣ Q 9 7

SOUTH
♠ 8
♡ J 8 7 4 3
◊ A Q 8 5
♣ A K 6

East dealt. Neither side was vulnerable. The bidding:

EAST	SOUTH	WEST	NORTH
Pass	1 ♡	Pass	4 ♣
Pass	4 ◊	Pass	4 ♠
Pass	5 ♣	Pass	5 ◊
Pass	6 ♡	Pass	Pass
Pass			

South won the opening spade lead and ruffed a spade so that he could lead a low heart toward the dummy, inserting the nine when West played low—a safety play if West held all three out-

standing hearts. South won East's diamond return and pulled the
last trump. Now he would make his slam if diamonds broke 3-3,
or if the queen of clubs was singleton or doubleton or lay in the
hand that was long in diamonds.

South began running trumps, reaching this position:

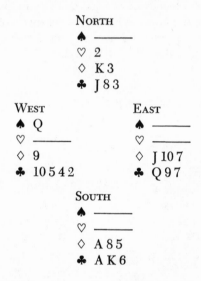

NORTH
♠ ———
♡ 2
◇ K 3
♣ J 8 3

WEST
♠ Q
♡ ———
◇ 9
♣ 10 5 4 2

EAST
♠ ———
♡ ———
◇ J 10 7
♣ Q 9 7

SOUTH
♠ ———
♡ ———
◇ A 8 5
♣ A K 6

On the lead of dummy's last heart (with South discarding a club)
East was squeezed. Whether he threw a club or a diamond, declarer had the rest of the tricks.

A third variety of the Swiss convention attempts to combine
key features of the first two versions, by using a four-club bid to
show good controls and a four-diamond bid to show good trumps.
This method is sometimes difficult to apply since some hands
qualify for both a four-club and a four-diamond response, and
some hands qualify for neither.

THE JACOBY TWO NO-TRUMP RESPONSE

This convention was devised by Oswald Jacoby for use in con-
junction with limit raises, and is designed to create a game-forcing
situation while requiring the opening bidder to clarify his distribution and/or his strength.

After an opening bid of one of a major suit, a response of two no-trump is a forcing raise, unlimited in strength. Opener shows his distribution as follows: with a singleton, opener bids three of his singleton suit; with a void, opener bids four of his void suit. If he has no singleton or void, opener shows the strength of his hand by bidding four of his suit with a minimum hand and no slam interest, or by bidding three of his suit with strong slam interest (at least a king better than a minimum opening bid), or by bidding three no-trump with a sound opening bid (14 to 15 points).

Here is one of the hands cited by James Jacoby as an example of the effectiveness of this convention:

WEST	EAST
♠ A	♠ 8 4 2
♡ A 6 4 3 2	♡ K Q 10 8 5
◇ K 7 5 2	◇ A Q 6
♣ K 5 4	♣ A 6

WEST	EAST
1 ♡	2 N.T.
3 ♠	4 N.T.
5 ♡	5 N.T.
6 ♡	7 ♡

West opens the bidding with one heart and East bids two no-trump asking about opener's distribution and strength. Opener's three-spade bid shows a singleton spade. Now it is safe for East to use Blackwood since he knows the partnership does not have two quick spade losers. West's response to four no-trump is five hearts, revealing that his singleton spade is the ace, and this makes it obvious that the two kings shown by the six-heart response to five no-trump are the two minor-suit kings. East can count thirteen tricks, and so bids a 99 percent sure grand slam on a hand with which many pairs would not reach even six.

SPLINTER BIDS

As with the Jacoby two no-trump response, Splinter bids recognize that one of the keys to good slam bidding is the ability to check for wasted strength. Splinter bids provide somewhat greater flexibility than the Jacoby two no-trump response because, while the Jacoby bid unearths opener's singletons or voids, opener learns nothing about responder's distribution. Splinter bids allow responder to show his side singleton or void, either immediately or on a subsequent round of the bidding, and allow the opener to show support for the responder's suit while indicating opener's singleton or void.

A Splinter bid is an *unusual* jump,° usually a double jump, into a singleton or void suit. It guarantees a good fit for partner's suit and strength equivalent to that of the standard forcing raise. For example, if opener bids one spade responder would jump to four clubs with

♠ K Q 8 5   ♡ Q 7 4 3   ◇ A J 6 2   ♣ 5

Players who do not use the Swiss convention find it advantageous to use the Splinter bid, not only because it gives meaning to an otherwise virtually unused bid but also because it differentiates a distributional forcing raise from a balanced forcing raise.

A Splinter bid was used on the following hand:

NORTH
♠ A K 9 7 3
♡ K 8 5
◇ 10
♣ K 7 5 2

WEST
♠ 10 8
♡ J 9 7 6 3
◇ Q 7 2
♣ Q 10 4

EAST
♠ J
♡ Q 10 4 2
◇ 9 5 4 3
♣ A 9 8 6

SOUTH
♠ Q 6 5 4 2
♡ A
◇ A K J 8 6
♣ J 3

° Whether the auctions one heart/three spades and one spade/four hearts are Splinter bids or preëmpts is a matter which should be discussed and agreed upon.

South dealt. North-South were vulnerable. The bidding:

SOUTH	WEST	NORTH	EAST
1 ♠	Pass	4 ♦	Pass
4 ♡	Pass	5 ♣	Pass
6 ♠	Pass	Pass	Pass

South knew from North's four-diamond Splinter bid that the partnership had some duplication of values; however, South's distribution was good enough to warrant a slam try despite the duplication. When North answered South's four-heart cue-bid by cue-bidding five clubs, which could have shown the club ace, South simply bid the slam.

Six spades would have been much safer if played from the North position, but there was no way this could be arranged. As it was, if West led a club, South would have to guess whether West was leading from the ace or from the queen in order to make his contract. With any other lead South could discard a club from his hand on dummy's king of hearts. If trumps broke 2-1 he could simply cross-ruff for twelve tricks. If trumps broke 3-0 the contract would be made if diamonds broke 4-3, or if the queen fell singleton or doubleton, or if the club ace were in the West hand.

Until clarified, the unusual jump shows a singleton. But if on the next round the Splinter bidder rebids the suit in which he has jumped he promises a void. For example:

WEST	EAST
1 ♠	4 ♣
4 ♡	5 ♣

East's five-club bid shows a void:

♠ K Q x x x   ♡ Q x x x   ♦ A J x x   ♣ ———

Splinter bids can be used by both the opener and the responder at a later round of the bidding. Again, the Splinter is an *unusual* jump; it guarantees a fit for partner's last-bid suit and shows a singleton or void in the suit in which the jump is made. For example,

SOUTH   NORTH
1 ♠   2 ◇
4 ♣

A three-club rebid by opener would normally show better than a minimum opening and would practically commit the partnership to game. Therefore, opener's four-club bid is an unusual jump, showing support for diamonds and a singleton or void in clubs, perhaps a hand such as

♠ A J x x x   ♡ A K x   ◇ K Q x x   ♣ x

In the following auction responder's jump shows strong support for hearts rather than for opener's first suit:

SOUTH   NORTH
1 ♠   2 ◇
2 ♡   4 ♣

Responder might have this hand:

♠ K x   ♡ K J x x   ◇ A J x x x x   ♣ x

FRAGMENT BIDS

Splinter bids are also sometimes called Antifragment bids, because when the concept of using an unusual jump to show distribution was first introduced by Monroe Ingberman, he proposed to jump in a real, although not biddable, suit rather than the short suit, and he called this jump a Fragment bid. Typically the Fragment bidder would have a suit of his own, good support for his partner's suit, and at most three cards in the suit in which he made his unusual jump.

Using Fragment bids, the opener would bid the hand

♠ A J x x x   ♡ A K x   ◇ K Q x x   ♣ x

(discussed above) as follows:

SOUTH	NORTH
1 ♠	2 ♦
4 ♡	

If opener cue-bid clubs on the next round he promises a club void.

16

THE FLANNERY TWO-DIAMOND
CONVENTION

ONE TYPE of hand bridge players have found difficult to bid over the years is a hand of average opening strength containing four spades and five hearts. For example, South holds:

♠ A Q 10 6   ♡ K Q 8 5 3   ◊ K 7   ♣ 9 7

South cannot open the bidding with one heart and rebid two spades over North's response, because that would be a reverse and South's hand is not strong enough to warrant forcing North to take a choice at the three-level.

If North-South are playing four-card majors, of course, South could make the "prepared" opening of one spade and rebid hearts. But if he does this, North will take a preference to spades with equal length in spades and hearts, because he will not know whether South has the hand shown above, or

♠ A Q 10 6 3   ♡ K Q 8 5   ◊ K 7   ♣ 9 7

Most players* think the lesser evil is to open one heart and rebid hearts, taking the risk of "losing" the spade suit on a hand such as

SOUTH	NORTH
♠ A Q 10 6	♠ K 4 2
♡ K Q 8 5 3	♡ 6 2
◊ K 7	◊ A Q J 6 3 2
♣ 9 7	♣ 8 4

* Among experts this majority is bolstered by five-card majorities and others who expect the responder to show any four-card spade suit, sometimes in preference to a longer minor.

240

On this hand the only makable game for North-South is likely to be four spades. Yet many pairs would fail to reach four spades after the auction starts

South	North
1 ♡	2 ◊
2 ♡	

One solution to this problem is the Flannery two-diamond convention, devised by William Flannery of McKees Rocks, Pennsylvania: An opening bid of two diamonds shows a hand of 11 to 15 points with four spades and five hearts.

The responder knows the exact distribution of opener's major suits and can place the final contract by bidding two or four of either major; can invite game by bidding three of either major; or can ask for additional information about opener's distribution and strength by bidding two no-trump.

Over responder's two no-trump (forcing), opener shows his distribution. If he has a three-card minor suit he bids it at the three-level; if he has a four-card minor he bids it at the four-level. If opener is 4-5-2-2, he rebids three hearts with a minimum hand (11 to 13), and bids either three spades or three no-trump with a maximum (14 to 15). Opener's choice between rebidding three spades and three no-trump depends on the location of his high-card strength. With a concentration of strength in his short suits he would bid three no-trump.

The Flannery device was almost too good a convention on the following hand:

West	East
♠ A963	♠ K87542
♡ A10853	♡ K6
◊ 4	◊ A95
♣ A74	♣ KQ

This hand was dealt in the Spingold Teams at the 1971 Summer Nationals in Chicago. At one table, the defending Spingold champions of 1970, a team of young New York experts, used the

Flannery convention, which seemed ideally suited for this hand, to reach the fine contract of seven spades. Their auction was:

WEST	EAST
2 ◇	2 N.T. (*asking clarification*)
3 ♣ (*4-5-1-3 shape*)	4 N.T. (*Blackwood*)
5 ♠	7 ♠

This contract depended only on a 2-1 trump break, assuming no side suit could be ruffed on opening lead—a better than 77 percent grand slam. Unfortunately for the defending champions, however, the spades broke 3-0 and the slam failed.

At the other table their opponents were not using Flannery and had little chance to reach the grand slam; in fact, they bid conservatively to only four spades, reaching an inferior contract but gaining 11 IMPs (international match points). Had they bid the virtually guaranteed small slam they would have gained 14 IMPs.

In spite of their loss on this deal, the defending Spingold champions, playing the Precision club, won this match by 1 IMP, and went on to win the Spingold again.

17

STRONG CLUB SYSTEMS

THE PAST decade has seen a growing number of tournament players turn to strong artificial club systems—a fundamental change from the past. While there was an artificial club system in the early 1930s—the Vanderbilt club, invented by the originator of contract bridge, Harold Vanderbilt—the strong forcing club had fallen into disuse in this country for about thirty years.

Interest in forcing club systems was revived in the early 1960s by the winning streak of Italian teams, using the Neapolitan and Roman club systems, and by the publication of Howard Schenken's "Big Club" system.

More recently the spark of interest has been fanned to fever heat by the development of the Blue Team club and the success of the Precision club system. Blue Team club is based on the old Neapolitan club system as gradually revised by Benito Garozzo, a member of the world championship Italian teams in 1961 to 1969 and 1972. The Precision system, devised principally by C. C. Wei, gained international prominence in 1969 when the Chinese team using it was runner-up in the world championship—the highest finish ever by a non-European, non-North American team.

Each of these club systems uses devices to enable the partnership to conduct precise investigation after a one-club opening. But a major advantage over traditional methods accrues when the bidding is opened with one diamond, one heart, or one spade; failure to open with one club has limited the opening hand, which leads to greater accuracy.

The major drawback of the club systems is their use of a substantial number of artificialities, putting a great deal of strain on each partner to remember what each bid is supposed to mean. Needless to say, the best system in the world loses effectiveness if one partner's memory fails under pressure.

BLUE TEAM

The principal features of the Blue Team club system are control-showing responses to a one-club opening, a tendency to canapé—that is, to bid short suits before long suits—when the bidding is opened with one diamond, one heart, or one spade, and a special two-diamond opening to show a three-suiter with 17 or more points.

A one-club opening normally shows 17 or more high-card points. Responses show controls by steps, counting each king as 1 control and each ace as 2, as follows:

1 ◇	0–2 controls, less than 6 points
1 ♡	0–2 controls, 6 or more points
1 ♠	3 controls
1 N.T.	4 controls
2 ♣	5 controls
2 ◇	6 controls
2 N.T.	7 controls

The responses of two hearts and two spades over one club are reserved to show a weak hand with a six-card suit.

ORANGE AND BLACK

When the Dallas Aces won the world championship for the United States in 1970 one of the three pairs used a variation of Blue Team club. By 1971 two pairs of the Aces were using Blue Team variations, one called the Black club and the other called the Orange club.

The following Orange club hand contributed to the Aces' victory over France in the finals of the 1971 world championship.

NORTH
- ♠ A J 10 4 2
- ♡ 7
- ◇ J 9 4 3
- ♣ K J 2

WEST
- ♠ K 8 7 3
- ♡ 10 6 2
- ◇ K 6 5
- ♣ 9 6 3

EAST
- ♠ Q 9 5
- ♡ Q J 5 4 3
- ◇ 10 8 2
- ♣ 8 7

SOUTH
- ♠ 6
- ♡ A K 9 8
- ◇ A Q 7
- ♣ A Q 10 5 4

North dealt. North-South were vulnerable. The bidding:

NORTH	EAST	SOUTH	WEST
Pass	Pass	1 ♣	Pass
1 ♠	Pass	2 ♣	Pass
2 ♠	Pass	3 ♡	Pass
4 ♣	Pass	4 ◇	Pass
4 ♡	Pass	4 N.T.	Pass
6 ♣	Pass	Pass	Pass

South's one-club opening showed 17 or more points, and North's response showed 3 controls. The next four bids were natural, and after North supported clubs, South began cue-bidding. North cooperated by cue-bidding four hearts. South's four no-trump bid was not Blackwood but a general slam invitation, which North accepted because he had good trumps.

South won the opening trump lead in the dummy, led a heart to the ace, and ruffed a heart. He then led a diamond to the ace and ruffed his remaining low heart. He cashed the ace of spades and ruffed a spade to get back to his hand, pulled trumps, and conceded a diamond to make six.

When the hand was replayed, the French pair sitting North-South stopped at three no-trump, and the Aces gained 12 IMPs.

SCHENKEN (BIG CLUB)

As with the Blue, Black, and Orange clubs, the Schenken one-club opening shows 17 or more points. Schenken responses show points rather than controls. The one-diamond response is negative and shows 0 to 6 points; a two-club response is semipositive, showing 7 to 8 points. Any other response is positive and natural, showing 9 or more points and committing the partnership to game.

In order to locate specific high cards, the Schenken system uses a special two-diamond opening. Responses at the two-level show one specific ace. If the responder has two aces he must jump in the higher-ranking suit if his aces are in touching suits, jump to four clubs if he has the black aces, and jump to three no-trump if he has nontouching aces.

Schenken retains such traditional treatments as four-card major-suit openings and strong one no-trump openings.

PRECISION

The forcing club system most rapidly gaining in popularity is the Precision system. The chief reasons for its popularity are its basic naturalness and the greater frequency of occurrence of the one-club opening.

Precision rejects control-showing responses in favor of showing real suits. Unlike Schenken and the other club systems, the minimum for a Precision one-club opening is 16 points, and since 16-point hands occur about twice as frequently as 17-point hands, Precision allows one club to be opened much more often.

In response to a one-club opening a one-diamond bid is negative, less than 8 points, and bids of one heart, one spade, two clubs, and two diamonds are forcing to game, showing 8 or more points and at least a five-card suit. A one no-trump response shows 8 to 10 points with even distribution.

With a hand worth a positive response but having 4-4-4-1 distribution, a convention called the "impossible negative" is used: responder bids one diamond over one club, and then over opener's rebid responder jumps in the suit of his singleton. If his single-ton is in opener's suit, responder shows it by jumping in no-trump.

An alternate method for showing a hand of 4-4-4-1 distribution, introduced in Simplified Precision and widely adopted, is for responder to make an immediate jump in his singleton suit—the unusual positive. All in one bid, this tells the one-club opener that responder holds 8 or more points in a hand the distribution of which is also precisely defined.

In compensation for giving up control-showing responses, Precision uses a system of asking bids which can begin at a relatively low level. After a positive response of one of a major or two of a minor, a simple raise by opener is an asking bid requesting responder to reveal how long his suit is and how many high honors he has in it. Subsequently, bids of new suits by opener are also asking bids, inquiring whether responder has first-, second-, or third-round control of the new suit.

Precision adapts some of the fundamentals of the Kaplan-Sheinwold system. It uses intermediate no-trump openings of 13 to 15 points, five-card major-suit openings to which a one no-trump response is forcing (see page 181), and inverted minor-suit raises (see page 250).

The following deal is an example of the Precision system in action.

NORTH
♠ 4 2
♡ A K 5 3 2
◊ 7 6 3
♣ A 8 4

WEST
♠ 9 7 6
♡ 4
◊ K 10 8 4
♣ Q J 10 5 2

EAST
♠ 10 5
♡ J 10 9 8
◊ Q J 9 5
♣ 9 6 3

SOUTH
♠ A K Q J 8 3
♡ Q 7 6
◊ A 2
♣ K 7

South dealt. Both sides were vulnerable. The bidding:

SOUTH	WEST	NORTH	EAST
1 ♣	Pass	1 ♡	Pass
2 ♡	Pass	3 ♡	Pass
3 ♠	Pass	4 ♣	Pass
5 ♣	Pass	5 N.T.	Pass
7 ♠	Pass	Pass	Pass

After North's positive response of one heart, showing 9 or more points and five or more hearts, South could envision a grand slam if North held the top heart honors and the ace of clubs. He therefore embarked on a series of asking bids designed to find out about these honors, and on the way, to find out whether North also had spade support.

South's two-heart bid theoretically confirmed the heart suit as trumps and asked North to clarify his heart holding. North's three-heart response showed a five-card suit headed by two of the top three honors. Three spades by South was an asking bid in spades, and North's four-club response showed third-round control—here obviously a doubleton since South had the queen.

Finally, South made an asking bid in clubs and North's five no-trump response showed at least three clubs headed by either the ace or the king. South could now count thirteen tricks provided neither defender was void in hearts or spades. He therefore jumped to the grand slam in spades, the partnership's best suit.

18

OTHER BIDDING CONVENTIONS

OPTIONAL RESPONSES TO ONE-BIDS

Limited jump raise in majors

A raise of an opening one heart to three hearts, or of one spade to three spades, shows four-card trump support and 10 to 12 high-card points, but is not forcing.

South opens one spade, North responds three spades. North holds:

♠ Q 10 6 3   ♡ A 7   ◇ K Q 8 6   ♣ 8 5 4

South may pass a minimum.

Two no-trump as a limit raise

Players using the limited jump raise in a major, customarily use two no-trump as a limit raise after an opponent has made a takeout double. The requirements are the same as for a jump raise without competition.

South opens one spade and West doubles. North would bid two no-trump with

♠ Q 10 6 3   ♡ A 7   ◇ K Q 8 6   ♣ 8 5 4

This allows North to jump directly to three spades over the double with a more preëmptive hand which is weaker in high-card strength, such as

♠ Q 10 6 3   ♡ 7   ◇ K 9 8 6 3   ♣ 8 5 4

Three no-trump forcing response

Players using the limited jump raise in a major often use three no-trump as a game-forcing response showing strong, four-card or longer trump support and 13 to 15 high-card points.

South opens one spade, North responds three no-trump. North holds:

♠ K J 5 4 2   ♡ 6   ◊ A K 7 3   ♣ Q 6 3

South must rebid and may bid four spades on any biddable suit.

Inverted minor raises

In this popular method, a jump raise of one club to three clubs or one diamond to three diamonds is preëmptive, showing length in trumps but a weak hand in high cards (usually 8 points or less in high cards); a single raise, from one club to two clubs or from one diamond to two diamonds, shows 10 points or more and perhaps only strong three-card trump support.

1.	SOUTH	WEST	NORTH	EAST
	1 ◊	Pass	3 ◊	

2.	SOUTH	WEST	NORTH	EAST
	1 ◊	Pass	2 ◊	

NORTH HOLDS:

1.		2.	
♠	8	♠	Q 6
♡	Q 8 4	♡	A 10 8
◊	K J 8 6 2	◊	K 9 4 3
♣	J 7 5 4	♣	K 8 6 2

Preëmptive raise in competition

This convention makes any single raise over an opponent's overcall weak (8 points or less in high cards) but adequate trump support is required.

SOUTH	WEST	NORTH	EAST
1 ♡	2 ◇	2 ♡	

NORTH HOLDS: ♠ 6 3 2
                 ♡ J 8 5 3
                 ◇ 6
                 ♣ Q J 7 5 2

Drury convention

This is a bidding device introduced by Douglas Drury for use over partner's third- or fourth-hand opening bid, to determine the soundness of the bid. A two-club response to the opening bid asks the opener to clarify his hand. If opener has made a substandard bid he rebids two diamonds; any other rebid verifies a sound opening. The two-club response is artificial (not promising club strength) and is forcing.

SOUTH	WEST	NORTH	EAST
Pass	Pass	1 ♠	Pass
2 ♣	Pass	2 ◇	

NORTH HOLDS: ♠ Q J 10 8 2
                 ♡ A J 3
                 ◇ 9 5
                 ♣ K 9 4

OPTIONAL RESPONSES TO ONE NO-TRUMP

Modified or extended Stayman

The many variations of the Stayman convention (page 151) have two main branches: (1) two diamonds, as well as two clubs, as a forcing response to one no-trump; (2) special meanings given to certain rebids. Some of the principal variations are:

Weak and strong responses. Either two clubs or two diamonds asks for a major-suit response, but two clubs shows 9 points or less and is non-forcing; two diamonds shows 10 points or more and is forcing to game.

Asking for better major. A two-club response requires opener to rebid in a four-card major; a two-diamond response shows at least one five-card major in the responding hand, probably two five-card majors, and requires opener to bid his longer or better major, even if it is only a three-card holding.

Murray convention. (Eric Murray of Toronto.) A two-diamond response requires opener to show his best major, as in the preceding paragraph. Responder's rebid at the three-level is invitational but not forcing. If responder's rebid is two no-trump, opener must show his four-card suit(s), beginning with the lowest.

Rebid to show both majors. By opener: Over the Stayman response, a rebid of three clubs by opener shows that he has two four-major majors. *By responder:* After the Stayman response and opener's two-diamond rebid, a certain rebid by responder (three clubs, three diamonds, or two no-trump, depending on the system being used) requires opener to show now his longer or better major.

Opener's rebid to define his hand. Over the two-club response, opener (lacking a four-card major) rebids two diamonds with a minimum no-trump and two no-trump with a maximum. This was part of the original Stayman convention. It has been abandoned by most experts but still is widely used.

Preëmptive responses. Any jump to three of a suit over partner's opening one no-trump bid is weak and demands that opener pass.

Flint convention. (Jeremy Flint of England.) Over an opening two no-trump, a three-diamond response requires opener to bid three hearts. The three-diamond response is designed for weak hands, such as

♠ 87   ♡ 1085432   ◇ J73   ♣ 102

Responder will pass three hearts. If his suit were spades, he will bid three spades and opener must pass. If he has a strong hand, or a diamond suit, he can continue bidding to game or beyond.

TWO-BID CONVENTIONS

Two-club and two-diamond convention

In several variations of the two-club forcing bid (page 168), two diamonds also is a forcing bid.

Two Clubs—forcing for one round. Negative response is two diamonds. (Any positive response is forcing to game.) If over two diamonds opener's rebid is two no-trump, he shows a 22-to-24-point no-trump hand; if his rebid is a suit he shows a strong suit or two-suiter. Neither bid is forcing.

EXAMPLES:

♠ A Q 6   ♡ K 10 4   ◇ A K Q 7   ♣ K J 3   *Two-clubs*
♠ K Q J 10 8 4   ♡ 6 3   ◇ A K 5   ♣ A 3   *Two clubs*
♠ ——   ♡ K Q J 10 6 3   ◇ A K Q 10 5   ♣ 4 3   *Two clubs*

Two Diamonds—forcing to game. Negative response is two hearts but ace-showing responses are used by most players. Usually at least 23 points in high cards and no less than second-round control in any suit.

EXAMPLES:

♠ A K Q 3   ♡ K Q 10 9   ◇ A K 5 4   ♣ A   *Two diamonds*
♠ A K J 5   ♡ A   ◇ 6   ♣ A K Q 8 7 5 3   *Two diamonds*

Two-club and two-diamond conventions are used with either the weak or the intermediate two-bid.

Intermediate two-bids

In some systems in which the artificial forcing two-club bid is used, an opening bid of two spades, hearts, or diamonds shows a strong but not game-forcing hand. It is used on two types of hand:
    (a) Playing strength that warrants game, but not enough in high cards for a two-club bid.

♠ 6   ♡ KQJ873   ◊ AKQ65   ♣ 4   *Two hearts*
♠ A   ♡ 63   ◊ AKQ97652   ♣ Q3   *Two diamonds*

(b) Enough in high cards for a two-club bid, but too little in playing strength to force to game.

♠ AQ763   ♡ AK542   ◊ AQ   ♣ 6   *Two spades*
♠ AK62   ♡ 6   ◊ AK54   ♣ AK63   *Two diamonds*

Responses. Responder may pass a hopeless hand. A response of two no-trump shows a weak hand but gives the opener a chance to bid a second suit, which responder may be able to raise but may pass. *Any other response is forcing to game.*
Partner opens two hearts (intermediate two-bid).

♠ K632   ♡ 74   ◊ 862   ♣ 8763   *Pass*
♠ 10753   ♡ 8   ◊ K852   ♣ Q763   *Two no-trump*
♠ 854   ♡ J76   ◊ A8753   ♣ 87   *Three-hearts*
♠ KQ10864   ♡ 63   ◊ 75   ♣ K76   *Two spades*

OPTIONAL RESPONSES TO DOUBLES

The following are special responses to takeout doubles, used by many players.

Cue-bid response to takeout double

In response to partner's takeout double, a bid in the doubled suit is itself a takeout bid, asking the doubler to bid his best suit. This response is in general use.

The doubler's partner should have at most two cards in the doubled suit, at least one four-card major suit, and 8 or more high-card points.

SOUTH	WEST	NORTH	EAST
1 ◊	Double	Pass	2 ◊

EAST MAY HOLD: ♠ J732
♡ 10964
◊ 63
♣ AK5

Herbert convention

This convention, introduced by Walter Herbert, uses the next-higher suit as a negative response to any forcing bid. In the U.S. the convention is chiefly popular in responding to a forcing two-bid.

SOUTH	WEST	NORTH	EAST
2 ◇	Pass	2 ♡	

The two-heart response is used instead of two no-trump to show a weak hand. North does not promise length or strength in hearts.

A two no-trump response may be used to show a genuine suit in the next-higher suit.

Partner makes a forcing two-diamond bid. Respond:

♠ 8 6 4 3   ♡ 6 2   ◇ 7 5 3   ♣ 10 8 6 2   *Two hearts*
♠ 8 6   ♡ A Q 8 7 5   ◇ 7 5 3   ♣ Q 7 2   *Two no-trump*

The Herbert convention is also used in responding to a takeout double. The lowest possible suit response shows a very weak hand with no preference among the unbid suits and asks the doubler to bid the suit he prefers (or to pass, if he wishes).

SOUTH	WEST	NORTH	EAST
Pass	1 ♡	Double	Pass
1 ♠			

South need not have spades. He shows weakness and invites North to choose the suit.

OTHER BIDDING CONVENTIONS

Asking cue-bids

These bids are played chiefly on the U.S. Pacific Coast.

A low-level cue-bid (in the opponents' suit, or in a suit in which the bidder cannot have genuine biddable strength) does not show

control of that suit but invites partner to bid three no-trump if he
has at least a partial stopper.

	SOUTH	WEST	NORTH	EAST
1.	1 ◇	Pass	1 N.T.	Pass
	2 ♣	Pass	2 ♠	Pass

	SOUTH	WEST	NORTH	EAST
2.	1 ◇	1 ♠	2 ◇	Pass
	2 ♡	Pass	2 ♠	Pass

In each case South is asked to bid no-trump if he has any
strength in spades. In the first example, North cannot have a
spade suit or he would have responded one spade; in the second,
North cannot be strong in spades or he would have bid no-trump;
in either case, North cannot have a very strong hand or he would
not have made, as his first response, a bid that could be passed.

Psychic controls

Most players use psychic bids infrequently, if ever. Those who
do use psychic bids may use one of various devices to identify
the psychic when the partner of the psychic bidder has a big
hand. There are three conventions in use for this purpose, to be
used over partner's jump in a new suit.

1] A rebid in no-trump at the lowest level. Any other bid shows
a sound opening.

2] A rebid of the original suit or no-trump, whichever is the
cheaper.

3] The cheapest rebid possible.

SOUTH	WEST	NORTH	EAST
1 ♡	Pass	3 ♣	

Having opened a psychic heart bid, South would:

1. Rebid 3 N.T.   2. Rebid 3 ♡   3. Rebid 3 ◇

Bar bids

According to this convention a rebid in the same suit, after a
single raise by partner, is preëmptive and requires partner to pass.

SOUTH	WEST	NORTH	EAST
1 ♥	Pass	2 ♥	Pass
3 ♥	Pass	*Must pass*	

SOUTH	WEST	NORTH	EAST
1 ♥	Pass	1 ♠	Pass
2 ♠	Pass	3 ♠	Pass
Must pass			

Four clubs and four diamonds as strong major-suit preëmpts

A number of experts use a convention to distinguish weak four-level major-suit preëmpts (on which opener will need plenty of help to make even four) from strong preëmpts which have slam possibilities. Most players who use this convention open a natural four hearts or four spades to show a weak preëmpt, such as

♠ K Q J 7 5 4 2   ♥ 6   ◇ K 9 4   ♣ 3 2

They open with an artificial four-club bid to show a strong preëmpt in hearts and a four-diamond bid to show a strong preëmpt in spades. For example, South would open four diamonds with

♠ A K J 9 5 4 3 2   ♥ 8   ◇ A 6   ♣ 9 4

PART III

THE PROCESS OF CARD VALUATION

1

APPROACH TO HIGH-CARD VALUATION

I⟶ is trite but true that hand valuation is "mental play." To estimate the trick-winning value of his hand, the player must foresee
the conditions that will obtain when the cards are actually played.
The better the player, the more accurate his valuation; for he can
foresee only those plays which he can actually execute.

The expert recognizes two kinds of trick-winning strength:
high-card and distributional. Basically the plays that establish
distributional trick-winners are more complex than the plays that
establish high-card trick-winners. Any beginner can lead out an
ace; far greater proficiency is required to establish a deuce as the
thirteenth card of its suit and then win a trick with it. So it is in
hand valuation. The average player readily grasps the fact that
an ace will win a trick; he cannot so readily grasp the fact that a
hand distributed 5-4-3-1 is more promising than a hand distributed 5-3-3-2 because the four-card suit in the former distribution
may yield a trick-winner.

In their valiant efforts to educate the average bridge player by
substituting rule for reason, bridge writers have made many
efforts to formulate hand valuation. Some have sought a mathematical or "point-count" basis; others have tried to translate the
experts' "mental processes" into tables of quick tricks or honor
tricks.

In a point-count formula, each high card from the ace down-
ward to the jack or ten is given a rating in points. The original
schedule of this sort rated the ace as 7, the king 5, the queen 3,
the jack 2, and the ten 1.* In other counts the assigned values are
6,4,3,2,1; 4,3,2,1 . . . ; 3,2,1,½ . . . ; etc. Since none of these schedules is entirely accurate and any will yield a rough approximation
of relative values, it matters little which is used. The popularity of

---

* See also page 22.

a point-count formula seems to depend on ease of counting and perhaps on other, psychological factors; the 4,3,2,1 count has become standard (and is used in this book wherever "points" are mentioned) although it probably is not quite so accurate as the 6,4,3,2,1 and 3,2,1,½ formulas.

Except in making an opening bid, the player can get little competent guidance from a quick-trick table. This is not only because the high-card counts fail to reflect distributional values, which have a decisive influence on bidding; but even more because the high cards themselves do not have constant values. Their values depend upon the contract, the holdings of all four players at the table, and the line of play that must consequently be adopted— and these conditions vary from deal to deal.

Thus it can seldom suffice to say, "Such-and-such a bid requires four honor tricks." The question would arise, "What kind of honor tricks?"

FIRST PRINCIPLE OF VALUATION

The value of a high card in any one suit depends on the number and nature of the high cards held in the other suits. In different circumstances a queen may be equivalent to an ace; an ace may be worth more or less than a K-Q. Two aces in a given hand may be inadequate; two K-Q's may be inadequate; and yet the combination of *one* ace and *one* K-Q may be ideal.

Beyond all such considerations are the cases—and they play a major role in expert competition—in which no formula can even approximate the trick-winning power of a hand. This is the "mental play" referred to before.

NORTH
- ♠ Q 10 2
- ♡ 10 8
- ◇ A Q J 6
- ♣ Q 10 8 2

WEST
- ♠ A
- ♡ A 6 5 3
- ◇ 9 7 5 3 2
- ♣ K J 6

EAST
- ♠ 8 7 5 3
- ♡ Q J 9 7 2
- ◇ ———
- ♣ 9 5 4 3

SOUTH
- ♠ K J 9 6 4
- ♡ K 4
- ◇ K 10 8 4
- ♣ A 7

South dealt, both sides were vulnerable, and the bidding went:

SOUTH	WEST	NORTH	EAST
1 ♠	Pass	2 ◇	Pass
3 ◇	Pass	3 ♠	Pass
4 ♠	Double	Pass	Pass
Pass			

South went for 1,100, and what valuation system could rate West's hand highly enough to predict even a one-trick defeat of the contract?

But because of North's diamond bid and South's diamond raise, West expected his partner to have at most a singleton in diamonds. West could therefore open a diamond; regain the lead on the first round of trumps; lead a second diamond for his partner to trump; and get in once again with the ace of hearts to give his partner a second ruff.

West's double was based upon mental play of a most elaborate sort, tantamount to a play-by-play forecast. But such a forecast is largely an unconscious and automatic one, for West did not repeat the series of plays to himself. He knew that a trump stopper and a quick entry outside, combined with a singleton in his partner's hand, add up to four tricks, and four tricks are enough to warrant doubling.

West opened the nine of diamonds, a suit-preference signal indicating that he preferred a heart to a club return. His hopes were more than realized when East was able to trump on the first round, not the second.

East read the suit-preference signal and led back the queen of hearts. South played low; there was not the remotest chance that East had the heart ace, and South did not wish to create two heart entries for West in case West had A-J. So the queen of hearts won the trick.

East continued with the heart jack and West took his ace, then led the deuce of diamonds for East to trump.

The next lead by East was a club, and South had a problem because he could not see his opponents' hands and could not know that his play would make no difference. If East had started with only three spades, and if West had the club king (as indicated by his leading the ◇ 2, another suit-preference signal), South could save a trick by putting up his club ace and leading trumps. If East had the club king, South might save two tricks by playing his low club.

South decided to play his club ace and lead a spade. West took his spade ace, gave East a third diamond ruff, and won his king of clubs for the defenders' seventh trick.

The process of valuation by "mental play" permitted not only the diamond lead that gave the defenders a four-trick set but also West's double, which gained at least 700 points for the defenders.

2

TIMING VALUE OF HIGH CARDS

ANY HIGH card may have a dual function: as a trick-winner and as a stopper. Usually it performs both of these functions. Occasionally its sole value will be as one or the other.

When a high card serves primarily as a stopper, its value is solely one of timing. Depending upon the contract, it may be required to win a trick on the first round, or on the second round, or on a later round, *or not at all.* A card may serve its purpose by preventing the opponents from making a damaging lead. It would win a trick if they made that lead; therefore they do not make that lead; therefore the card never wins a trick. But it may have been worth more than an ace.

Any bridge player understands the essential nature of timed stoppers at slam contracts:

WEST	EAST
♠ A K Q 8 5 4	♠ J 9 6 3 2
♡ 7 3	♡ A K Q J 8 5
◇ K 4 3	◇ 8
♣ K 7	♣ 2

The East-West cards will readily produce twelve or more tricks, but cannot make a slam because the opponents have two aces. Here it would be ridiculous to insist that two kings are worth 6 points and an ace only 4 points. One more ace in West's hand, instead of the kings of diamonds and clubs, would permit the slam to be made but the hand's count would be 2 points less.

The average player recognizes the timing function of high cards in slams; the expert extends the same recognition to lower contracts.

WEST	EAST
♠ A 8	♠ 10 9 4 3
♡ A 6	♡ J 10 5 2
◇ A K Q J 6 5 2	◇ 8 7
♣ Q 5	♣ J 4 3

To West, playing at a three no-trump contract, ♣ Q 5 is worth virtually as much as the club ace would be. West needs no additional trick-winners to make his contract; he has nine tricks in spades, hearts, and diamonds. All he needs is to stop the club suit, and the queen when combined with the guarded jack in dummy is sufficient to that task.

Yet it must be noted that the nature of West's entire hand determines the value of that queen. If West did not have nine tricks in the other suits, the queen would not assume so exaggerated an importance.

By the 4, 3, 2, 1 count, the club queen counts 2 points in West's hand, the spade or heart king would count 3 points; but the club queen limits the opponents to two club tricks and probably is worth three tricks in all while the spade or heart king might be worthless if North-South could start off by running five club tricks against a no-trump contract.

Translating the value of the club queen into total points, at the no-trump game contract it is probably worth 500 + 30 points (value of the game plus 30 points for a no-trump trick)—but only because West can win nine tricks in the outside suits. If West lacked the ace of spades or hearts, the club queen would be worth at most 30 points. If diamonds were trumps, the club queen would be worth *nothing;* West's holding of ♣ Q 5 would be worth no more than a holding of ♣ 6 5, for the opponents would win exactly two club tricks in either case.

In nearly every valuation method including the 4, 3, 2, 1. K-Q is rated higher than an ace—5 points against 4 points—because K-Q may win two tricks, while an ace can win only one. But there are many cases in which the holder does not need to win two tricks. All he wants is one trick—but he wants to win that trick fast.

DUMMY
♠ 6 3
♡ J 10 6 5
◇ 9 6 5
♣ J 10 4 3

DECLARER'S HAND
No. 1
♠ A K
♡ K Q 4
◇ K Q J 10 4 3
♣ A 5

DECLARER'S HAND
No. 2
♠ A K
♡ A 8 4
◇ K Q J 10 4 3
♣ A 5

With hand No. 1, declarer cannot make three no-trump. The opponents will open spades; continue spades when they get in with the diamond ace; and defeat the contract when they get in with the heart ace. With hand No. 2, declarer can make three no-trump, for he will win the opening spade lead, establish his diamonds, and run out his nine tricks when he wins the second spade lead. Here the ace is worth at least one trick, and perhaps 530 points, more than the K-Q-x.

In actual bidding, this distinction should be recognized and utilized by the expert. For example:

EAST	SOUTH	WEST	NORTH
1 ♠	Double	2 ♠	Pass
Pass	?		

Now South, holding hand No. 1, should not bid three no-trump; for, knowing from North's pass that North can hardly have an ace, South foresees the dissipation of his two spade stoppers before he can establish and win nine tricks. He doubles again or bids diamonds. But if he holds hand No. 2 South should jump to three no-trump, knowing that against the anticipated spade opening he can take in nine tricks before his opponents can defeat him.

The expert is not so painstaking as to forecast a play-by-play result for each deal. He has learned, however, that *every contract requires a certain balance of trick-winning cards and timing cards.*

DUMMY
♠ 6 3 2
♡ J 6 2
◇ 9 6 5
♣ J 10 4 3

DECLARER'S HAND No. 1	DECLARER'S HAND No. 2
♠ A K 8	♠ A K 8
♡ K Q 4	♡ A 8 4
◇ K Q J 10 4	◇ K Q J 10 4
♣ A 5	♣ A 5

Now the ♡ K Q 4 appears far more valuable than the ace. With hand No. 1, declarer will probably make a game at no-trump, since he can establish two heart tricks, four diamonds, two spades, and one club, nine tricks in all. With hand No. 2, declarer will probably go down at three no-trump, for he can establish no heart trick in addition to his ace, and can consequently muster only eight tricks.

NUMBER OF STOPPERS NEEDED—THE "WEAK SUIT"

For the successful fulfillment of any contract, declarer's side needs a certain number of stoppers in the suit or suits the defenders choose to lead. The exact number of stoppers depends in any given instance upon how many tricks declarer needs, and how many times he must lose the lead in establishing them.

The defenders have the opening lead and usually can get the lead two or three times again (at game contracts, once or twice again) while declarer is establishing his tricks. Therefore:

At trump contracts, declarer must usually be prepared to draw the opposing trumps and have two extra trumps to act as stoppers-at-large. Against normal distributions this requirement is met by a combined trump length of eight or more cards. Hence bidding is designed to discover at least an eight-card trump suit.

At no-trump contracts declarer's side must usually have at least two stoppers in the shortest combined suit. No-trump bidding can seldom be so arranged as to reveal the exact location of miscellaneous high cards in short, and therefore unbiddable, suits. Experience proves, however, that it is unsafe to initiate a game-going no-trump contract with more than one "weak" suit.

A weak suit may be defined as a short suit containing no more than one possible stopper. The holding A-10-x, K-J-x, or better *may* become two stoppers; but A-6-2 or K-6-2 will not, and these are therefore weak suits.

One weak suit is acceptable; partner is likely to provide a second stopper in it. Two weak suits are dangerous; partner is unlikely to have protection in both, unless, of course, he has already promised such protection by his bids.

We may now return to the valuation and consequent bidding of the hands previously shown:

1.	♠ A K 8	2.	♠ A K 8
	♡ K Q 4		♡ A 8 4
	◊ K Q J 10 4		◊ K Q J 10 4
	♣ A 5		♣ A 5

A player may choose, with hand No. 1, to make an opening bid of two no-trump. He has only one "weak suit"—clubs. With No. 2 he would prefer an opening bid of one diamond. He has two weak suits and will postpone suggesting a no-trump game unless his partner has indicated ability to stop at least one of them.

Thus in some cases K-10-9 or Q-J-x-x may appear more valuable, and may better justify a bid, than an ace, though both of the former combinations rank below the ace in all formulas.

SOUTH	WEST	NORTH	EAST
1 ♠	Pass	2 ◊	Pass
2 ♡	Pass	2 N.T.	Pass
3 ◊	Pass		

North should not bid three no-trump with this hand:

♠ 96   ♡ A 7   ◇ K J 10 6 5   ♣ A 8 3 2

South's bidding has shown strength in the other three suits, and consequently weakness—probably a small singleton—in clubs. North has only one club stopper and cannot reasonably expect to run nine tricks before letting his opponents get the lead. If North is loath to give up hope of game, he must bid four clubs or four diamonds. But suppose North has this:

♠ 96   ♡ A 7   ◇ K J 10 6 5   ♣ K J 8 2

Now North's best bid, and best hope of game, is three no-trump. North would as readily bid three no-trump with ♣ Q J 10 2 or even ♣ Q J 7 2. The club suit promises to produce two stoppers, giving North time to establish his diamond suit and, with the tricks he expects in South's heart and spade suits, to amass nine tricks before the opponents get in again to run clubs.

UNIQUE VALUE OF THE ACE

Nevertheless the value of the ace is unique, because no other card fully satisfies the requirement of time and delivers a sure trick as well.

Among all the high-card holdings, only aces are essential to game contracts. While it is far from impossible, rarely can a game be made when the opponents hold a majority of the aces. Consider this hand:

♠ A K Q J 10   ♡ 6   ◇ K Q   ♣ K Q J 10 5

This hand failed to make a four-spade contract, though the dummy held three spades and the opposing spades were divided 3-2. The opponents had three aces; and with the opening lead and with each of the aces they led hearts, forcing declarer to trump. Eventually he ran out of trumps, before he had established a trick with his ◇ K Q. If he had held ◇ A 2 instead, he would have made his contract. The full deal was:

NORTH
♠ 9 6 3
♡ 10 7 4 2
◇ 10 5 4
♣ 8 4 3

WEST   EAST
♠ 8 2   ♠ 7 5 4
♡ A K 8 3   ♡ Q J 9 5
◇ J 9 7 6   ◇ A 8 3 2
♣ A 7 2   ♣ 9 6

SOUTH
♠ A K Q J 10
♡ 6
◇ K Q
♣ K Q J 10 5

South dealt. Neither side was vulnerable. The bidding:

SOUTH	WEST	NORTH	EAST
2 ♠	Pass	2 N.T.	Pass
3 ♣	Pass	3 ♠	Pass
4 ♠	Pass	Pass	Pass

West opened the heart king and East played the queen, asking
for a low heart lead next, so West led the heart three. Dummy
played low and South trumped East's nine with the ten of spades.
   South drew trumps in three rounds, but this left him with only
one trump. When South next led the king of clubs, West took the
ace and led the ace of hearts. South won this with his last trump.
   Now South ran his four good clubs, leaving only the ◇ K Q in
his hand. East discarded down to ◇ A and ♡ Q. South's final
lead of the ◇ Q gave East the last two tricks.
   South could have played much more cleverly, although in this
case it would not have helped him to do so. After trumping the
second round of hearts and leading only two rounds of spades,
South should have shifted to the king of clubs, which would have
lost to the ace. After trumping a third round of hearts, South

should have continued to lead clubs, leaving one opposing trump outstanding.

If West had held not only three clubs but also three trumps, this would have made the contract. On the fourth club lead, South could overtrump in dummy if West trumped or discard dummy's last heart if West did not trump; either way, South could no longer be forced to trump a fourth heart lead and would have time to establish the one diamond trick he needed.

But West did not have the three-card trump holding. East had it, so even if South had perceived and pursued this plan it would not have worked. East would have trumped the third round of clubs and cashed the ace of diamonds for the setting trick.

THE TWO-ACE REQUIREMENT

Declarer's side need not have a majority of the aces, but it should have at least two of them in the combined hands before undertaking a game contract on the "book" requirement of 26 points.

That is why experts hesitate to make opening bids on strong hands that lack aces, and hesitate to pass relatively weak hands containing two or more aces.

1. ♠ A Q 6 4 2   2. ♠ K Q 10 9 5
    ♡ A 6 5   ♡ K J 7
    ◇ 9 7 4 3   ◇ Q J 9 7
    ♣ 7   ♣ 6

Many experts who will bid on No. 1 will pass on No. 2. Yet No. 2 counts 2 points more and in trick-winning power is at least one trick better, probably two or more tricks better.

A CLASSIC FREAK . . .

There was a classic hand in which a player held 150 aces but could not defeat an opposing three no-trump contract:

NORTH
♠ K 10 2
♡ Q J 9 5
◇ K J 10 6
♣ K 8

WEST
♠ A 6
♡ A 8 7 4 2
◇ A 8 3
♣ A 5 4

EAST
♠ 9 7 4 3
♡ 10 3
◇ 7 5 2
♣ 9 7 6 2

SOUTH
♠ Q J 8 5
♡ K 6
◇ Q 9 4
♣ Q J 10 3

North dealt. The bidding was:

NORTH	EAST	SOUTH	WEST
1 ◇	Pass	2 N.T.	Pass
3 N.T.	Pass	Pass	Double
Pass	Pass	Pass	

West led the four of hearts and South took East's ten with his king and led spades until West took his ace on the second round.

Then West cashed the ace of hearts and led another heart, which dummy won, South discarding a diamond.

South led clubs until West took his ace, and at this point South had nine tricks with three spades, three clubs, and three hearts. West could take his ace of diamonds now or later. The four aces were the only tricks he could get.

. . . AND ITS PRACTICAL COUNTERPART

The deal just shown was a freak, but occasionally players can recognize and exploit a similar pattern:

NORTH
♠ Q 9 6 4
♡ A 7
♢ Q J 10 2
♣ K Q J

WEST
♠ A J 10
♡ 10 8 6 3 2
♢ A 5 3
♣ 8 6

EAST
♠ 8 5
♡ Q 5 4
♢ 9 8 6 4
♣ A 5 4 2

SOUTH
♠ K 7 3 2
♡ K J 9
♢ K 7
♣ 10 9 7 3

With neither side vulnerable, the bidding went:

NORTH	EAST	SOUTH	WEST
1 ♢	Pass	1 ♠	Pass
2 ♠	Pass	2 N.T.	Pass
3 N.T.	Pass	Pass	Pass

Rarely would an expert pair relinquish an opportunity to play in a major suit divided 4-4 (of which more later), but North could recognize this as a case in which South's spades were weak and the other suits were solid. North was right, because at four spades South would have had to lose two trump tricks and two aces and could not have made game. South made three no-trump, though it was not without its pitfalls.

West opened the three of hearts and South won East's queen with his king. South led the king of diamonds, which held, and another diamond, taken by West's ace. A second heart lead took out dummy's ace.

After cashing two more diamonds and discarding two spades, South led a spade to his king. West's ace won and now West had no quick entry to his hearts so he continued with the spade jack. This was won by the queen in dummy.

The king of clubs lost to East's ace, and dummy was thrown back in with a club. A spade lead from dummy gave the defenders their fourth and last trick, for South still had the high heart.

Solid as the North-South hands were, the power of the three aces was so great that if South had slipped even slightly he would have failed to make game. For example, if South had led a club instead of a spade from dummy after cashing his diamonds, he would have gone down. East would have taken his ace of clubs, a heart lead would have knocked out South's last stopper, and West would have had two good hearts and the ace of spades for three more tricks.

In no-trump bidding it is well to be sure that the combined hands have at least two aces and to look for another spot if they have not.

3

VALUATION OF HIGH-CARD COMBINATIONS

THE TRICK-WINNING power of a high-card combination is measured by four different standards:

Trick-winning potential;
Ease of establishment;
Combining quality;
Security.

The *potential* of a high-card combination is the maximum number of tricks it may produce. It is in trick-winning potential that K-Q-x is superior to A-x-x. Opposite partner's strong one no-trump bid, hand No. 1 below is a sound raise, hand No. 2 is a quick pass, though each counts 8 points:

	1.		2.	
	♠	A 6 3	♠	A 6 3
	♡	Q 8 5 4	♡	8 5 4 2
	◇	J 9 5	◇	9 5 3
	♣	J 4 2	♣	A 4 2

Hand No. 2 can produce only two tricks; hand No. 1 may produce three or four tricks.

Trick-winning potential also makes honors in combination more valuable than scattered honors. For example,

♠ K x x   ♡ J x x

will produce one trick 50 percent of the time, with no legitimate chance for two tricks. Yet

♠ K J x   ♡ x x x

will produce one trick 75 percent of the time and two tricks 25 percent of the time.

It is *ease of establishment* to which the expert refers when he speaks of his ability to "handle" a combination of cards. Though it would appear that K-Q-x is as good as K-Q-J if the ace is known to be at the holder's right, K-Q-J is patently superior. To establish K-Q-J as two tricks, the holder need only lead them out. To establish K-Q-x he must lead toward them twice; if entries are lacking, K-Q-x cannot be "handled" for two tricks.

The expert gauges the trick-winning power of any combination by his knowledge of suit-establishment technique. Unless he can "handle" the suit, he assigns little value to it. A poll of experts once revealed that the majority favored opening on hand No. 1 below; a pass on No. 2.

	1.	♠ A J 5	2.	♠ A J 5
		♡ K Q 8 4		♡ K Q 8 4
		◊ Q 10 4 3		◊ Q 8 4 3
		♣ 8 7		♣ 8 7

Obviously the distinction must be explained by the presence of the ◊ 10 in hand No. 1, since all the other cards are identical. But the expert is not thinking of the individual cards. He is thinking of how he will play the combination if he becomes declarer.

FIGURE 1	FIGURE 2
5 2	5 2
N	N
W E	W E
S	S
Q 8 4 3	Q 10 4 3

There is no standard suit-establishment play by which South can hope to develop a trick-winner in Figure 1. The hope that East will hold both the ace and king is too remote to be leaned upon. (The odds are 3 to 1 against it.)

In Figure 2 South can finesse through East for the jack, with an eventual trick in sight if East holds K-J or A-J in the suit. Because he can foresee a way of playing the suit, South considers it valuable.

The *combining quality* of high cards is measured by the chance that they may be improved by unbid and unbiddable cards in partner's hand. Here is found another point in favor of Q-10-4-3 over Q-8-4-3. If partner should hold the jack of the suit, the Q-8 combination gains little in value, while the Q-10 combination becomes a sure trick.

Similarly, A-10-2 is considered by the expert to be worth, in trick-winning value, almost twice as much as A-3-2; for the former will produce an extra stopper opposite Q-x, J-x, or 9-x-x-x, while the latter will gain nothing in value if partner holds the jack or nine and will gain but a dubious possibility of an extra trick if partner holds the queen.

The suit K-Q-x-x is doubly superior to the suit A-x-x-x, first in trick-winning potential, as has been shown, and also in combining quality; for A-x-x-x does not gain in value if partner holds J-x, while opposite K-Q-x-x the J-x may be worth a trick.

The *security* value of a high card is found in the degree of the probability that it will win a trick. As an assurance of one trick, Q-J-10 is better than K-J-x though it counts one point less; Q-J-x, never rated higher than K-x-x, is superior to it as a stopper and is on occasion so acknowledged in expert bidding—or should be.

NORTH
- ♠ Q 8 5
- ♡ 8
- ◊ A 4
- ♣ A K J 10 7 5 3

WEST
- ♠ K 7 2
- ♡ A Q J 9 7 2
- ◊ Q 7 3
- ♣ 8

EAST
- ♠ A 10 9
- ♡ 10 6 5
- ◊ J 10 9 5
- ♣ 9 6 4

SOUTH
- ♠ J 6 4 3
- ♡ K 4 3
- ◊ K 8 6 2
- ♣ Q 2

North dealt. Both sides were vulnerable. The bidding:

NORTH	EAST	SOUTH	WEST
1 ♣	Pass	1 ◇	1 ♡
3 ♣	Pass	3 N.T.	Pass
Pass	Pass		

From the bidding, West could read the nature of the North-South hands; North must have a very long, strong club suit, and South must have the king of hearts, without which he could not have bid no-trump after West's heart overcall. West wished to put his partner in the lead for a heart return through South's king. Diamonds seemed like a poor lead in view of South's earlier diamond bid, so West opened the deuce of spades.

East took his spade ace and led the ten of hearts, and it made no difference whether South covered. West ran six heart tricks, then cashed the spade king, and South was down 400 points.

In this case, Q-J-x would have been a much safer heart stopper for South than the king. Unless West had A-K-10 in hearts and East could get the lead twice to lead through South, the Q-J-x would be a stopper. East needed both ace and king of spades to hurt ♡ Q J x—an unlikely chance. East needed only one entry to destroy the value of the heart king.

South did not need a heart trick. He had nine tricks—seven clubs and two diamonds—as soon as he got the lead, and he had only to prevent his opponents from running five tricks before he could get in. With Q-J-x as his heart holding, South would have made his game, for the defenders could have taken only two spade and two heart tricks.

Also, Q-J-x is superior to a king in combining quality, since the presence of the ten in partner's hand will make the assurance complete.

4

EFFECT OF THE RANK OF LOW CARDS

EVERY CARD has, theoretically, a greater value than any lower-ranking card. A position can be arranged in which a three is of greater value than a deuce:

NORTH
♡ 8 7 6

WEST   EAST
♡ 5 4   ♡ J 10 9 2

SOUTH
♡ A K Q 3

West opens the ♡ 5, East must cover dummy's card and South wins. Upon North's gaining the lead twice more, the process is repeated until South holds and leads the ♡ 3, which wins the trick from East's ♡ 2.

Usually any distinction in value between two low cards is owing to the vagaries of distribution and cannot be foreseen:

NORTH
♠ Q 4 3
♡ 10 8 7

WEST   EAST
♠ 7 2   ♠ J 10 9
♡ 9 5   ♡ A K Q J 4 3

SOUTH
♠ A K 8 6 5
♡ 6 2

Spades are trumps. West opens hearts and East plays three rounds. On the third round South can win the trick by ruffing with the ♠ 8. He could not have done so had he held, instead, ♠ A K 7 6 5.

Rarely can such fine shadings in the relative values of spot cards control a choice between bidding and passing. There are, nevertheless, many cases in which the superior timing value of an eight or nine over a lower card may be recognized in the bidding. The holding A-Q-9 is frequently one full trick better than the holding A-Q-8. The former may permit a double finesse if partner has 10-3-2. A throw-in play may be possible with A-Q-9 that would not be possible with A-Q-8 or lower. Here is another case:

NORTH
♠ 6 3 2

WEST   EAST
♠ K 7 5   ♠ J 10 8 4

SOUTH
♠ A Q 9

The ♠ 2 is led from the North hand. If East plays low, South may finesse the nine, forcing out West's king and giving South two tricks in the suit. If West puts up the ten or jack, South covers with the queen. West can win with the king, but now South has a tenace over East and will get two tricks in the suit.

Obviously, if South had only A-Q-8 in the suit, he could win only one trick, his ace. His queen would be killed by the king in any event, and East would still have the suit stopped.

In that case the nine is demonstrably superior to the eight. Similarly, having an eight, instead of a lower card, is not without its value in many cases.

NORTH
♣ 7

WEST   EAST
♣ Q 9 8 6 2   ♣ A 10 4

SOUTH
♣ K J 5 3

At no-trump, West opens the ♣ 6. East wins with the ace and returns the ten. If South covers with the jack, West can force out his only club stopper immediately. If South puts up the king, and East has one entry, West's entire club suit will be realized.

Consider the difference if South held the ♣ 8:

NORTH
♣ 7

WEST   EAST
♣ Q 9 6 5 2   ♣ A 10 4

SOUTH
♣ K J 8 3

West opens the ♣ 5; East wins with the ace and returns the ten. *South covers with the jack.* Now West cannot lead the suit again because it would give South an extra club trick. East may have an entry, but he must use it to get the lead again, and now when he leads the ♣ 4 South still has the suit stopped by putting up his king.

This is the exact principle which, at times, makes the famous Bath coup such an effective timing play.

NORTH
♠ 8
♡ 7 4 2
◇ Q 10 7 5 3
♣ K 9 5 2

WEST   EAST
♠ K 10 7 5 2   ♠ Q J 9 4 3
♡ K Q 10 9   ♡ 8 6 5
◇ 9 4   ◇ A 6 2
♣ 10 3   ♣ 8 7

SOUTH
♠ A 6
♡ A J 3
◇ K J 8
♣ A Q J 6 4

South dealt, with neither side vulnerable. The bidding:

South	West	North	East
1 ♣	1 ♠	2 ♣	2 ♠
3 ♠	Pass	4 ♣	Pass
5 ♣	Pass	Pass	Pass

THE BATH COUP

The Bath coup was originally used to trick the opponent into leading into a tenace, but it has its straightforward uses too, as this example shows.

West opens the king of hearts. If South wins it, he will go down; because when East gets in with the diamond ace he can lead a heart to give West two tricks in the suit. If South ducks the first heart, he cannot be defeated. West cannot continue the suit, and when East gets in for the first and last time it will be too late, for the second heart trick will not be established for the defenders.

It is no doubt possible to compute the relative values of all cards—Dr. Emanuel Lasker attempted it and perhaps succeeded —but the respective values so established are useless in hand valuation. They are too indefinite, for they are subject to some degree of modification on every hand. Authorities seldom attempt to rate the ten and lower cards, having to fall back on "body" to describe the relative advantage of holding nines, eights, sevens, and sixes instead of an equal number of deuces, threes, fours, and fives.

A single ten or lower card in the hand seldom controls a player's bid. The presence in his hand of several such cards may be decisive. Suppose South bids one heart and West one spade. North will usually pass No. 1, below, and will usually bid one no-trump (or, against vulnerable opponents, double) with No. 2.

	1.		2.	
	♠	K 6 4 3	♠	K 9 8 4
	♡	5 3	♡	10 7
	◊	A 10 6	◊	A 10 6
	♣	Q 7 6 2	♣	Q 9 7 2

Hand No. 2 is stronger by one ten, two nines, and an eight. North may expect at least one of these four cards to win a trick or to furnish an extra stopper or to facilitate the handling of an establishable suit. *The hand that has "body" is therefore the hand in which high spot cards are the rule rather than the exception.* Such a hand may often be rated about 3 points higher than its high-card point count.

Jacks and lower cards are third- and fourth-round stoppers and are useful only when such stoppers are needed. With surplus trumps to act as stoppers-at-large in all side suits, a player does not need "fillers."

♠ A K Q J 8 4 3   ♡ J 10   ◇ J 10   ♣ J 10

With spades trumps, the J-10's are hardly worth more than 3-2's would be. But this is not so unless the trump suit is very strong.

NORTH
♠ 10 8 4
♡ K 6
◇ A 10 8 3
♣ Q J 7 3

WEST
♠ 6
♡ A 8 7 3
◇ 9 7 5 2
♣ 9 8 6 2

EAST
♠ J 9 7 2
♡ 10 9 5
◇ K Q 6 4
♣ A 5

SOUTH
♠ A K Q 5 3
♡ Q J 4 2
◇ J
♣ K 10 4

South plays four spades, and West opens the ◇ 2, which dummy's ace wins. If North's diamonds were any weaker—if even they were A-10-7-3—South could not make his contract. With two aces and a trump trick, the defenders could force South to trump two diamonds, after which he would have insufficient trumps to prevent a final diamond trick from being cashed. With

North's diamonds as strong as they are, the defenders cannot lead them three times without establishing dummy's ten, whereupon their setting trick is gone.

In actual play the $\diamond$ 10 will never win a trick and the importance of the $\diamond$ 8 will be a potential one only, for the defenders will shift suits rather than establish the $\diamond$ 10. This need not blind the bidder to the true value of such cards.

5

LONG-SUIT TRICKS

DISTRIBUTIONAL VALUES are, in the expert mind, no different from high-card values. Both are means of winning tricks and of stopping the opponents from winning tricks. In trick-winning power South's cards in the following examples are of identical value:

1.
	NORTH	
	♠ 4 3 2	
WEST		EAST
♠ J 10 9 8		♠ 7 6 5
	SOUTH	
	♠ A K Q	

2.
	NORTH	
	♠ 9 8	
WEST		EAST
♠ A K Q		♠ J 10
	SOUTH	
	♠ 7 6 5 4 3 2	

Either combination will produce three tricks for South. No. 1, however, will produce three tricks without establishment; No. 2 requires for establishment three losing leads, and these must be compensated by three stoppers in other suits. Distributional values must therefore be appraised in accordance with the number of stoppers in other suits. These stoppers may be high cards; they may equally well be trumps, which are equivalent, in timing value, to aces. In No. 2 above, South has three sure tricks if spades are trumps, for then the suit supplies its own stoppers. Again:

1.		2.		3.	
♠	A K Q J 10	♠	A K Q J 10	♠	A K Q J 10 2
♡	6	♡	6	♡	6
◇	K Q	◇	A 2	◇	K Q
♣	K Q J 10 5	♣	K Q J 10 5	♣	K Q J 10

Hand No. 1 was previously shown as having failed to make four spades. It was noted that if declarer had held hand No. 2 he could have made four spades. The same is true of No. 3. The potential winners in the three hands are precisely the same, but either the ace in No. 2 or the extra spade in No. 3 gives declarer trump control, which with No. 1 he lacks. Here the extra trump is exactly equivalent to an ace.

TRUMP CONTROL

The value of any long side suit at a typical trump contract depends upon the holder's *trump control.*

A side has trump control when it can continue to ruff an opposing strong suit until its own side-suit strength has been established and all possible tricks won. Trump control usually consists of nine trumps in the combined hands and is deemed to be absolute when the combined hands have ten trumps. Experience has demonstrated that with these trump holdings a partnership can establish the maximum value of its side suits without running out of trumps. A combined holding of eight cards, though it is the standard minimum for a satisfactory trump suit, cannot be relied upon for establishment of a long, weak side suit in which two or more tricks must be lost.

A long suit of freakish length in one hand may supply trump control all by itself:

1.	♠ A K Q 8 7 5 3	2.	♠ A K Q 8 7
	♡ 9		♡ 9 8 2
	◇ 8 6 4 3		◇ 8 6 4 3
	♣ 2		♣ 2

With hand No. 1, the player counts his diamond length as one full trick because he has trump control. He will bid on the absolute assumption that his hand will win eight tricks. With No. 2 he counts the diamond suit as being of little value because he will have used up all his trumps before he can establish and win a trick with the fourth diamond. But at any time that partner raises spades, the diamond suit in No. 2 assumes the same one-trick rating that it has in No. 1.

Thus, to the expert, distributional values are sometimes equivalent to high-card values, sometimes worth less, sometimes worth more, depending upon how many stoppers—whether furnished by aces or by trump control—he has.

1.	♠ A K Q 6 5	2.	♠ A K Q 6 5
	♡ A 8 4		♡ A 8 4
	◇ 9 6 5 3		◇ 9 6 5
	♣ 7		♣ K 7

Suppose either of the above hands to be South's in the following bidding sequence, with East-West vulnerable:

SOUTH	WEST	NORTH	EAST
1 ♠	Pass	Pass	Double
Pass	2 ♡	2 ♠	3 ♡
Pass	4 ♡	Pass	Pass

North should now consider a four-spade sacrifice bid on No. 1; he should pass on No. 2. He does not expect to defeat the contract with either hand, for North's first pass has warned him of a total absence of defensive assistance. He does fear, with No. 2, that he will lose seven tricks and go down 700 points; the club king may not win a trick. He has no such fear on No. 1, for with a four-card spade holding in North's hand he has trump control and can confidently expect to win a low-card trick in diamonds, either by establishing his last diamond or by ruffing it in dummy after the opponents' trumps are drawn.

The "losing-trick count" so often praised by expert players— F. Dudley Courtenay, founder of the "Official system" of the early '30s, has been the principal apostle—assumes no more than three losing tricks in any suit. No other valuation system so closely conforms to expert practice when there is trump control, or is farther off the mark when there is not.

EFFECT OF ENTRIES ON LONG-SUIT VALUATION

At no-trump contracts both stoppers and entries affect distributional values. A long suit is more valuable if it contains its own entry.

FIGURE 1

NORTH
◇ 10 8 6 4 2

WEST   EAST
◇ K J 3   ◇ Q 9

SOUTH
◇ A 7 5

FIGURE 2

NORTH
◇ A 8 6 4 2

WEST   EAST
◇ K J 3   ◇ Q 9

SOUTH
◇ 10 7 5

The combined North-South holdings in the two figures are apparently identical, but the diamond suit in Figure 2 is far more valuable at no-trump. In either case, the suit may be established after losing two rounds and winning one (with the ace). In Figure 1, after this process, North must have a side entry or the two remaining cards cannot be cashed. If North has no side entry, or if he has an entry that the opponents can knock out before the diamond suit is established, the suit is worthless. In Figure 2, by ducking the first two leads and winning the third with the ace it is possible to provide entry to the established cards regardless of the defense.

Of the following hands, No. 1 was shown as a proper pass of a strong one no-trump bid. No. 2 would be a proper raise; No. 3 would be a doubtful raise.

1. ♠ A 6 3   2. ♠ A 6 3   3. ♠ A 6 3
    ♡ 8 5 4 2   ♡ 9 5 3   ♡ 9 5 3
    ◇ 9 5 3   ◇ A 8 5 4 2   ◇ 8 5 4 3 2
    ♣ A 4 2   ♣ 4 2   ♣ A 4

No. 2 contains, besides the two aces, two possible distributional tricks—the long cards in diamonds—and in a suit that provides its own entry. No. 3 has the same two possible distributional tricks and most players would raise on it but they should recognize the danger that both aces may be gone before the long diamonds can be made good.

Except in freak cases, distributional strength cannot exist in one hand alone, but is made up of a combination of the two partnership hands.

1.   ♠ A K 4 3   2.   ♠ A K 4 3 2
     ♡ A Q 7 5   ♡ A Q 7 5 4
     ◇ A 6 3   ◇ A 6
     ♣ 4 2   ♣ 4

To the expert, No. 1 is a dangerous hand, despite its high-card strength; No. 2 is a powerful hand. The reason is that No. 2 will probably produce four or five distributional tricks in addition to its high cards, while No. 1 is unlikely to produce more than one. But this original appraisal is based upon the mathematical likelihood that partner will have at least three cards in either spades or hearts. If the bidding proves this assumption to be false, and if partner reveals that he has a two-suited hand composed of diamonds and clubs, then No. 1, which will support partner's suits better, becomes by far the superior of the two hands.

HOW SCORING AFFECTS LONG-SUIT VALUATION

In deciding how many tricks a long suit will win, the expert visualizes the various possible distributions of the other players' hands and the suit-establishment methods he may employ. The spade suit A-Q-x-x-x, as trumps, may win four tricks (if partner holds three spades and a finesse for the king wins); it may win three tricks (if in the same circumstances the finesse loses); it may win only two tricks (if partner is short in spades and an opponent holds ♠ K J 10 x). It is not true, however, that the expert values such suits "optimistically" if he is not vulnerable and "pessimistically" if he is vulnerable. He notes all contingencies at all times. His bids do depend, of course, on how great and how likely his possible loss is, and on how much he stands to gain by risking such a loss.

Let us say South holds:

♠ 7   ♡ A K J 8 6 4   ◇ Q J 7 3   ♣ A 3

South may win six tricks in hearts; he may win only four. He may win two tricks, or one trick, or no trick in diamonds (depending on whether or not his partner holds a diamond honor, on finding entries to his partner's hand, and on how long his trump control will last if he must repeatedly ruff spade leads). South's trick-winning power, then, may vary from five to nine tricks. He gambles on winning the maximum if he stands to profit greatly; he refuses to gamble if he stands to gain little. Suppose the bidding to be, with neither side vulnerable:

SOUTH	WEST	NORTH	EAST
1 ♡	Pass	Pass	Double
Redouble	1 ♠	Pass	2 ♠
Pass !			

If South bids three hearts he may make it, but he may as easily go down 500 points. He will not risk 500 points to make a part-score or to prevent his opponents' making a part-score. But suppose other bidding:

SOUTH	WEST	NORTH	EAST
1 ♡	Pass	1 N.T.	3 ♠
4 ♡ !			

Since North's one no-trump response did not necessarily promise more than one trick, South's four-heart bid risks almost as much as a three-heart bid would have risked in the previous bidding situation. But, while South's risk is still at least 500 points, his possible profit is now a game worth about 500 points.

The expert does not—or at least should not—risk when there is little or nothing to gain. In the following deal there was a "field-

er's choice" situation, in the experts' vernacular. But somehow
the casual player finds a suit such as South's irresistible.

NORTH
♠ J 10 9 2
♡ 5 3
◇ 6 4 3
♣ Q 10 9 2

WEST
♠ K 8 5 4
♡ K 9 8 2
◇ K 5
♣ 7 6 4

EAST
♠ A Q 6 3
♡ 7
◇ A 9 8 2
♣ K J 8 5

SOUTH
♠ 7
♡ A Q J 10 6 4
◇ Q J 10 7
♣ A 3

South dealt, both sides were vulnerable, and the bidding was:

SOUTH	WEST	NORTH	EAST
1 ♡	Pass	Pass	Double
Pass	1 ♠	Pass	2 ♠
3 ♡	Double	Pass	Pass
Pass			

West led the spade four and East took the ace. Since West's
spade bid marked him with four and South with a singleton, East
shifted to the two of diamonds. South played the ten, West the
king. A diamond return to the ace and a continuation gave West
a diamond ruff.

West led the club seven, the ten and jack went on, and South
won. Next came the ace and queen of hearts, West taking the
latter.

A club lead put East in again and West ruffed the last diamond.
South was down three, 800 minus his honors, 700 net—and East-
West could not make a game.

South's three-heart bid gave his opponents a fielder's choice. If they wished to go on to three or more spades, South's bid could not stop them. If they found it more profitable to double, they could double—as they did.

If South felt a compulsion to rebid his hand, he might far better have bid two hearts over the takeout double. West might have been too weak to make a free bid (he wasn't—he would have bid two spades anyway—but he might have been) and if so the two-heart bid might have prevented East-West from finding their spade fit. And if South was doomed to be doubled, at least it would have been one level lower and would have saved him (and poor North) 300 points. But the important thing is that the two-heart bid might have accomplished something. The three-heart bid could not.

6

CONSIDERATIONS IN SELECTING
A TRUMP SUIT

IT IS almost axiomatic that a partnership should have numerical superiority in any trump suit it selects, and whenever possible this should be clear-cut superiority. A combined holding of seven cards is considered hardly adequate. Eight cards are generally accepted as the minimum for a satisfactory trump suit.

A combined holding of fewer than eight cards may nevertheless be playable, *depending upon the manner in which the trump cards are divided between the partnership hands.* Consider the six trump cards A, K, Q, J, 6, 2. If the division is A-K-Q in one hand, J-6-2 in the other, it is no trump suit at all. If the division is A-K-Q-J in one hand, 6-2 in the other, the suit will prove satisfactory only in freak cases, of which the following is the only representative type:

WEST	EAST
♠ A K Q J	♠ 6 2
♡ 6 3	♡ 8 5
◇ Q 8 5 4	◇ K 7 6 3
♣ K J 6	♣ A Q 10 7 2

With normal breaks in all suits, these hands will produce game at spades and at no other contract. But such contracts can be made so rarely that bidding methods are not designed to reach them. The holding A-K-Q-J is at best sufficient to draw the opponents' trumps, and leaves nothing over to stop their strong suit. If the combined hands happen to have high-card stoppers in all the

294

other suits, a no-trump contract may be played with equal profit and greater safety. In fact, the spade contract in the above example is always dangerous, for a 5-2 division of the opposing trumps will slaughter it.

Highly expert players can sometimes recognize an opportunity to play with six combined trumps divided 4-2. The following deal, played by William Root (South) and Harold Harkavy (North) in a game in Florida, produced one of those rare cases.

NORTH
♠ A Q
♡ Q 8 4
◇ 7 5 3
♣ A Q J 9 6

WEST
♠ 8 7 5
♡ K 3 2
◇ A K Q 10 8 4
♣ 7

EAST
♠ 6 4 3 2
♡ J 10 9 6
◇ J
♣ 10 8 5 3

SOUTH
♠ K J 10 9
♡ A 7 5
◇ 9 6 2
♣ K 4 2

North dealt. Neither side was vulnerable. The bidding:

NORTH	EAST	SOUTH	WEST
1 ♣	Pass	1 ♠	2 ◇
Pass	Pass	3 ♣	Pass
3 ♠	Pass	4 ♠	Pass
Pass	Pass		

North bid three spades on a two-card trump holding because his two trumps were both high cards and because he had not raised to two spades over two diamonds; therefore South could not expect to find a great deal of trump support in North's hand.

South bid four spades, gambling on finding no more than four trumps in either opponent's hand. The odds are about 2 to 1 against an opponent's having five trumps when there are six or seven trumps outstanding.

The contract was made with ease. West won the first three tricks by cashing his high diamonds, but then West could not lead another diamond because dummy could trump it while South discarded. So West led his seven of clubs.

This club lead was won by dummy's jack. Dummy's ace of spades was cashed, then the spade queen was overtaken by South's king and South continued with his jack and ten of spades, drawing the last of East's trumps. Four more clubs and the ace of hearts made ten tricks.

The essential requirements when one wishes to play for a game with only six trumps, divided four and two, are: First, if either partner can be forced to trump, it must be the dummy, with the two-card trump holding; and, second, the six-card combined holding must include at least the ace, king, and queen of trumps.

In such cases, a major-suit game with a six-card combined trump holding is often the only game contract that can be made. In this case North-South could not have made three no-trump because West could have run six diamond tricks, and they could not have made five clubs with three quick diamond tricks to lose.

5-1 AND 6-0 DIVISIONS

Divide the given six trumps A-K-Q-J-6 in one hand, deuce in the other, and the trump position is somewhat better, but not much. There will be only one extra trump for use as a stopper, and this is seldom sufficient. On part-score hands, such a suit may be the best available; and on very strong hands—when the side suits are solid or are quickly establishable—it may be preferable to a no-trump contract. It must be noted, however, that declarer must not lose the lead more than once in establishing his tricks:

WEST	EAST
♠ A K Q J 6	♠ 2
♡ 8	♡ A 5 3
◊ K 10 9 5	◊ J 8 7 2
♣ 9 8 4	♣ A K 10 5 2

With a 4-3 spade break and a 3-2 club break, West can make four spades; his one extra trump is sufficient to establish his ten tricks, for he need lose the lead only once. A no-trump game would hardly be possible with the single heart stopper. But here again the spade contract, while it is the best hope of game, will be costly if the trumps break badly.

When the six trumps A-K-Q-J-6-2 are all in one hand, it is usually a satisfactory trump suit. The top cards will draw the opposing trumps and leave declarer two additional trumps to act as stoppers-at-large, and in most cases two stoppers are enough. Nevertheless, a six-card length opposite a void can be depended upon only when the suit is very strong in high cards—almost never weaker than A-K-Q-x-x-x or K-Q-J-10-x-x.

What has been said of a six-card combined holding may almost be said of a seven-card combined holding, so far as bidding purposes are concerned. Seven trumps in almost any division *may* be adequate, but they cannot be depended upon. Unless the partners together have all the top cards, or one partner has a strong six-card suit, search should be made in the bidding for a longer trump suit.

In fact, if safety were the only consideration, the longest combined holding would always be most desirable, for there is then less to fear from a bad break. But conditions do not always make caution profitable.

SUPERIORITY OF THE EVENLY DIVIDED TRUMP SUIT

Often, and at some risk, a major suit may be selected in preference to a minor, a seven- or eight-card combined length in preference to a nine- or ten-card. The longest available trump suit is not necessarily the most favorable.

NORTH
* ♠ J 7 4 3
* ♡ K J 6 5
* ◇ 9 5 3
* ♣ Q 7

WEST
* ♠ 10 9 5
* ♡ 9 2
* ◇ J 10 6 2
* ♣ K 10 6 5

EAST
* ♠ 8 2
* ♡ 3
* ◇ A Q 8 7 4
* ♣ J 9 8 4 2

SOUTH
* ♠ A K Q 6
* ♡ A Q 10 8 7 4
* ◇ K
* ♣ A 3

With the ten-card heart suit as trumps, the North-South hands produce only eleven tricks. With the eight-card spade suit as trumps, they produce twelve tricks and make a small slam; for three rounds of spades draw trumps, after which the heart suit provides a discard for North's losing club and permits dummy to ruff a club that would otherwise be lost.

This fact was not recognized in the bidding, which was (with South dealer and both sides vulnerable):

SOUTH	WEST	NORTH	EAST
2 ♡	Pass	3 ♡	Pass
4 N.T.	Pass	5 ♣	Pass
6 ♡	Pass	Pass	Pass

Having received assurance of heart support, as well as a positive response to his two-bid, South was so well satisfied with his trump suit that he saw no reason to look for another. He made a mistake.

It would not have cost South anything to bid three spades before bidding four no-trump, nor North anything to raise the spades to four, confirming four-card support for that suit too. South could then have made his Blackwood bid, intending to bid seven hearts if North showed an ace and six otherwise—but six spades, not hearts.

In such a case, and in nearly all cases in which one cannot count thirteen top tricks, it is not the number of trumps but the division of trumps that determines the choice of suits. Of alternative trump suits, when one suit is evenly divided between the partnership hands and the other is unevenly divided, *the evenly divided suit is usually more productive of tricks.*

Thus, the preceding example did not illustrate the advantage of an eight-card suit over a ten-card suit; it illustrated the advantage of an even division of trumps over an uneven division. As between an eight-card length divided 4-4 and a ten-card length divided 5-5, the ten-card length is invariably superior.* But as between a 6-4 or 5-4 or 5-3 trump suit and a 4-4 trump suit, the 4-4 suit will often produce at least one extra trick.

CASES IN WHICH A 4-4 TRUMP SUIT IS BEST

There are various hand types on which the superiority of the 4-4 trump suit may be recognized in the bidding.

First type of hand on which the 4-4 trump suit is superior: Any hand that requires one or more ruffing tricks to fulfill its contract.

A suit divided 4-4 can win no more than four tricks if it is not trump. If trump, it can win those same four tricks in one hand and add one or more tricks by ruffing in the other hand.

Of course, a 5-3 trump division can produce more than five tricks *if ruffs may be taken with the three-card holding.* This, however, is possible less than half the time. When both a 5-3 and a 4-4 trump suit are available, one partner must *ipso facto* hold 5-4 in those two suits. This is the partner who will be short in the other two suits, and who must most often ruff. If his five-card suit is made trumps, he gains nothing by ruffing unless he can ruff *three times,* which is unusual. He can win a maximum of five trump tricks in the 5-3 suit and four tricks in the 4-4 suit. If his 4-4 suit is made trumps, he can still get five tricks from his 5-3

---

* Barring freak cases, seldom detectable during the bidding, in which an opponent can ruff the 4-4 suit and not the 5-5 suit. But the danger of a ruff in the side suit is almost six times as great when the 4-4 suit is trump.

side suit and he will usually get five or more tricks from his 4-4 trump suit.

Against a 5-3 trump suit, the defenders can often lead trumps until the shorter hand has no more, and thereby destroy ruffing power. Against a 4-4 trump suit they cannot do so; there is no "shorter" hand:

NORTH
♠ Q 8 7
♡ K 7 5 4
♢ 10 9 4 2
♣ 10 8

WEST
♠ 5 3
♡ 10 8 2
♢ K J 6 3
♣ A Q 9 2

EAST
♠ J 10 2
♡ J 9
♢ A Q 7 5
♣ K J 6 5

SOUTH
♠ A K 9 6 4
♡ A Q 6 3
♢ 8
♣ 7 4 3

Given a 3-2 break in both hearts and spades, the North-South hands cannot make four spades if West opens a trump and if the defenders continue to lead trumps at every opportunity. The declarer (South, undoubtedly) can win five spade tricks and four heart tricks for a total of nine; but he cannot get a tenth trick by ruffing a club in dummy, for by the time he has rid dummy of clubs dummy's trumps also will be gone.

No lead and no defense can beat four hearts. After South has drawn trumps in three rounds and has run five spades, South's remaining heart will trump a diamond and North's remaining heart will trump a club.

Second type of hand on which the 4-4 trump suit is superior: Any hand that has ample trick-winning power but a possible shortage of controls. This is sometimes the case at game contracts; it is so often the case at slam contracts that the evenly divided suit should almost always be preferred.

WEST	EAST
♠ K Q J 6	♠ 5
♡ A 8	♡ K Q J 7 3 2
◇ K Q 6 3	◇ A 9 5 4
♣ 8 5 2	♣ A 7

Against any opening but a club, six hearts would be easy; but assuming a club opening, the only possible slam is at six diamonds, which can be made if the diamonds break 3-2. Declarer can win the club opening, draw trumps in three rounds, and discard West's two clubs on the long hearts. East-West do not need an extra trick; they have a superfluity of tricks. But East-West do need *time*, and this time is supplied by the unevenly divided side suit, which furnishes discards and restores control to declarer's side.

East, having heard a diamond bid plus some indication of heart support from West, should bid the slam in diamonds, not in hearts.

Such obvious examples as the foregoing have not failed to make their impression on expert players. Most experts, however, have construed the examples to indicate a specific advantage for the 4-4 suit. This is false, of course. Whatever is said of the 4-4 suit applies with even greater force to the 5-5 trump suit as against any less evenly divided suit:

WEST	EAST
♠ ———	♠ 4 3
♡ 6 3	♡ A 7
◇ A K Q 5 4	◇ J 8 6 3 2
♣ A 10 8 7 5 3	♣ K Q 9 4

WEST	NORTH	EAST	SOUTH
1 ♣	1 ♠	2 ♣	2 ♠
3 ◇	Pass	4 ◇	Pass
4 ♠	Pass	5 ♡	Pass
?			

As between bidding seven clubs and bidding seven diamonds, West should choose the diamonds. Even if East proves to have the same number of supporting cards in clubs and diamonds, the diamond suit will be the more evenly divided and should make the superior trump suit.

The evenly divided diamond suit produces a grand slam, whereas the unevenly divided club suit would not. After drawing trumps, West can discard dummy's low heart on the fifth round of clubs. If East had only four diamonds, and three hearts, the diamond suit would still make the grand slam, for both of East's small hearts could be discarded. The 5-4 trump suit would still be superior to the less evenly divided 6-4 trump suit.

Third type of hand on which the 4-4 trump suit is superior: Any hand on which declarer and dummy each has a weak suit that can be stopped only by ruffing.

WEST	EAST
♠ A Q J 6 3	♠ 9 7 2
♡ A 10 7 4	♡ K 6 5 3
◇ 9 5 2	◇ 10
♣ 8	♣ 9 7 6 5 3

The East-West hands were played, in a duplicate game, in spades at some tables, in hearts at others. A spade contract developed only eight tricks; a heart contract nine tricks. The opponents had a choice of suits with which to force declarer. At spades, they properly forced the long trump hand. West was able to establish a third trick in hearts, but he did not have enough trumps, after ruffing repeated club leads, to draw the opponents' trumps and cash his last heart. At hearts, West was able to establish his spades, take two rounds of trumps, and then run the spades.

The point here is: With the 4-4 trump suit it does not matter to declarer which hand the opponents choose to force. With the 5-3 trump suit it does matter.

The expert players of Boston were incredulous when the following deal occurred in a tournament there some forty years ago.

NORTH
♠ K 10 3
♡ 9 8 4 2
◇ 10
♣ A J 10 8 2

WEST
♠ J 4
♡ A K J
◇ J 6 5 4 3 2
♣ 7 4

EAST
♠ Q 7 2
♡ Q 5
◇ K Q 8 7
♣ 9 6 5 3

SOUTH
♠ A 9 8 6 5
♡ 10 7 6 3
◇ A 9
♣ K Q

South dealt. Both sides were vulnerable .The bidding:

SOUTH	WEST	NORTH	EAST
1 ♠	Pass	2 ♣	Pass
2 ♡	Pass	3 ♡	Pass
3 N.T.	Pass	4 ♡	Pass
Pass	Pass		

No one in conservative Boston had ever heard of bidding as weak a suit as South's hearts, and if a Bostonian had even thought of such a bid he would have expected some God of Bridge to emanate in a flare of lightning and strike him dead.

It was even worse when the Bostonians learned that the crass New Yorker who bid the hearts had made his four-heart game.

They could not believe their ears when they heard that everyone who had tried for four spades or three no-trump had gone down.

And they were downright indignant when they laid out the four hands and discovered the four hearts could not be beaten and that it was the only game that could be made. At spades, South had to lose three hearts and a trump trick. At no-trump, with a diamond opening, North-South could take only eight tricks; then East-West would get in and take the rest with diamonds and hearts.

Against four hearts West opened the four of diamonds. South took his ace and led a trump. The best available lead for the defense was another diamond. Dummy trumped and led another heart.

West could take both his remaining trumps and then lead a third round of diamonds to force out South's last trump, but then South would have the rest with five good clubs and two top spades.

From this and other sensational examples, extremists in all countries soon developed the Cult of the Four-Card Major, and they began to bid four-card spade and heart suits regardless of their weakness. Many of them still do. The answers to a questionnaire recently (1961) circulated among bridge experts internationally revealed that many experts will respond or rebid in any four-card major, however weak. Some will open the bidding in such a suit.

Alas, both the doctrine and the ritual of the 4-4 Major Cult went a bit too far.

WHEN A 5-3 TRUMP SUIT SHOULD BE PREFERRED

The frequent and obvious superiority of the 4-4 trump suit has become too well known. Into the expert dogma has crept the tenet that the 4-4 suit should *always* be preferred. The use of the word "always" is just as dangerous in this case as it is elsewhere in bridge analysis. The cases in which a 5-3 or 6-2 suit is superior may not occur very often, but when they do occur they can usually be recognized during the bidding.

The 5-3 trump suit is usually superior to the 4-4 trump suit when the combined hands have an abundance of winners in the other two suits.

Cases that fit this description are rare. For one thing, both of the available trump suits must be majors; as between a major and a minor, the major will usually be preferred whether it is 5-3 or

4-4. Also, the presence of superfluous stoppers can seldom be recognized except when one partner has made a strong no-trump bid. But there are times when the bidders may realize that the 4-4 suit can hardly be superior, while the 5-3 suit *may* be.

NORTH
♠ A J 4 3
♡ A J 6
♢ Q J 10
♣ K J 5

WEST
♠ 10 7
♡ K 8 4
♢ K 8 4
♣ 9 8 7 3 2

EAST
♠ Q 8 2
♡ 9 5
♢ A 9 7 5 3
♣ A 10 6

SOUTH
♠ K 9 6 5
♡ Q 10 7 3 2
♢ 6 2
♣ Q 4

North deals and bids one no-trump; South responds two clubs (Stayman) and North rebids two spades. South should now bid three hearts, and if North raises to four hearts (showing three-card support) South should pass.

By one line of bidding or another, most expert pairs will reach and play four spades on the North-South cards. Yet a four-spade contract requires successful finesses in both spades and hearts (and, as the cards lie, would undoubtedly go down). A four-heart contract requires the success only of the heart finesse, since two of South's low spades can be discarded on North's third diamond and third club. Three no-trump cannot be made because East will open diamonds and eventually win four diamonds and the club ace. The only game is in hearts, the 5-3 suit, not in spades, the 4-4 suit, *and South should expect this and bid for it.*

The point is that here it is unnecessary either to ruff or to discard the two side suits, and it is in facilitating additional ruffs and discards that a 4-4 division of trumps is principally valuable.

The 5-3 trump suit should be preferred when it is very strong, the 4-4 suit is or may be weak, and the combined hands contain so many high cards in all suits that trump losers are the greatest danger.

In the following deal, played in a tournament in England, both members of the bidding side might have applied this principle but neither did.

NORTH
♠ K 8 5 2
♡ K Q J 7
◇ A 5
♣ J 10 7

WEST
♠ Q 10 9 4
♡ 10 6 5 2
◇ J 8 6
♣ 8 3

EAST
♠ J
♡ A 9 4 3
◇ Q 9 7 4 2
♣ 6 4 2

SOUTH
♠ A 7 6 3
♡ 8
◇ K 10 3
♣ A K Q 9 5

South dealt. Neither side was vulnerable. Seven expert pairs bid the North-South hands. One bid them like this:

SOUTH	WEST	NORTH	EAST
1 ♣	Pass	1 ♡	Pass
1 ♠	Pass	4 ♠	Pass
4 N.T.	Pass	5 ◇	Pass
5 ♠	Pass	Pass	Pass

Since South must lose two spade tricks and the ace of hearts, he cannot make five spades. No possible bidding result is better calculated to give a bridge player nightmares than to bid five in a major suit and go down one. Yet three of the expert pairs bid, and failed to make, five spades; three others bid six spades and were down two.

And all the time the North-South hands were a laydown for six clubs.

South wins the first trick unless West opens hearts, in which case South wins the second trick. The jack of clubs is taken, then the ace and king of diamonds cashed and a diamond ruffed with the club ten. The seven of clubs is led. South draws the East-West trumps, and two spades from South's hand will go off on two hearts in dummy. The heart ace is the defenders' only possible trick.

The pairs that bid the North-South cards to five spades in the bidding shown above went back over their bids and found every one of them defensible. If called upon to bid the same hands again, they might reach the same contract.

It is probable that most good American pairs would play the North-South hands in some spade contract, because of the general predilection for major suits and also because "it is well known" that a 4-4 trump suit is better than a 5-3 trump suit.

Given the first three rounds of bidding shown above, South had no reason to fear bidding a slam, with one ace located in North's hand. South had second-round control in the fourth suit, whichever suit it might be. But South did have reason to fear the spade suit because his spades were so weak. Therefore South should have bid six clubs (instead of five spades), showing that his clubs had the tops though his spades did not.

And North, who also had reason to fear the spade suit but who had support for a strong club suit, should have passed for that very reason.

Not even the best breaks would have permitted a slam in the 4-4 spade suit. The slam could have been made in clubs even against a 5-0 trump break if the dangerous opponent's hand had comprised five clubs, three hearts, three diamonds, and two spades —the most likely division of cards, in the circumstances.

The 5-3 trump suit may be superior for a game contract, because it is safer, when the 4-4 suit would have to be selected for a slam contract because it is the only chance.

NORTH
OPENING HAND
♠ A K 6 5
♡ A 6
◇ K Q J 5
♣ A J 9

SOUTH
RESPONDING HAND
No. 1
♠ 10 7 4 3
♡ K Q J 10 2
◇ 6
♣ 8 7 4

SOUTH
RESPONDING HAND
No. 2
♠ Q 7 4 3
♡ K Q J 10 2
◇ 6
♣ 8 7 4

The opening bid is two no-trump. The responder, with hand No. 1, should not try for a slam. Expecting three hearts in the opening hand, and superfluous stoppers in the other suits (because of the two no-trump bid) the responder should prefer to play the hand at four hearts:

NORTH	EAST	SOUTH	WEST
2 N.T.	Pass	3 ♡ *	Pass
3 ♠	Pass	4 ♡ !	Pass
Pass	Pass		

It may be observed that a club opening and a 4-1 spade break (a 32 percent chance) will probably defeat four spades; nothing is likely to defeat four hearts.

With responding hand No. 2 the situation is different. Now the spade suit seems solid and a slam seems possible. So, over North's three-spade bid, South raises to five spades. If North can bid again, a slam will probably be made; but it can be made only in the 4-4 suit. After a club opening, North will need to draw trumps and discard his losing clubs before conceding a diamond trick.

* No doubt most experts would make a Stayman three-club response, which might do no damage but can hardly help since South can make his decision before North rebids.

Controls are vital in slam bidding and it can rarely pay to surrender the chance of discarding on the unevenly divided long suit.

Regardless of the nature of the hand, a 4-4 trump suit must be regarded with suspicion if its high-card strength is concentrated in one hand. If the hand with the high trumps must stand repeated forces, a trick may be surrendered. *When such a situation can be foreseen, the 5-3 suit should be preferred.*

NORTH
♠ A 8 2
♡ 10 7 4 3
◇ Q 10 6 4
♣ 10 3

WEST
♠ J 6
♡ J 9 5
◇ K 8 7 5
♣ A 7 6 5

EAST
♠ Q 7 4
♡ 8 2
◇ A J 9 2
♣ J 9 4 2

SOUTH
♠ K 10 9 5 3
♡ A K Q 6
◇ 3
♣ K Q 8

When this hand was played, South bid one spade and North raised to two spades; South bid three hearts and North raised to four hearts, where the hand was played. West opened the diamond five. East won dummy's ten with the jack and led back his low diamond, which South had to ruff. Now South had to give up a trick in either spades or clubs, whereupon a diamond continuation would force out one of his high trumps and establish West's heart jack as the setting trick.

Four spades would have been easy, of course, because South could stand two forces, or even three, without sacrificing a high trump. And accurate trump valuation would have placed South in four spades. It was obvious from this hand that if anyone would have to trump diamonds, he would; and he could not afford to use his high hearts for that purpose.

It is only when *essential* high trumps must be wasted in ruffing that the 4-4 suit should be avoided. If one partner holds A-K-Q-x and the other holds J-10-9-x, it does not matter which partner must ruff—the other partner can supply equivalent top strength. Also, when there will be no apparent need to ruff with the high trumps it would be pointless to avoid the suit on the grounds that it is "too strong."

	WEST	EAST
♠	A K Q 6	8 7 4 3
♡	J 8 7 5 3	A 9 4
◇	Q J 4	K 6
♣	2	K Q J 5

East bids one club, West one heart; East raises to two hearts, and West bids two spades. East raises to three spades. West should bid four spades. He will hardly be forced to ruff clubs, the suit East has bid. There is a better play in spades, as there usually is in the 4-4 suit; for one of East's hearts may be discarded on the third round of diamonds.

WHEN 6-2 IS SUPERIOR TO 5-3 OR 4-4

There is finally the choice between alternative eight-card trump holdings of which one is divided 4-4 or 5-3 and the other 6-2.

On two-suited hands that require all or most of the winning tricks to come from the two long suits, *the trump suit that is more unevenly divided should be selected.* That is, 6-2 is better than 5-3 and 5-3 is better than 4-4.

When the combined hands are strong—game-going—the two prospective trump suits may play equally well and the object is not to select the better trump suit so much as to select the higher-scoring trump suit. A 5-3 major suit would take preference over a

6-2 minor suit, and a 4-4 major suit over a 5-3 minor suit. When the hands are very strong—slam-going—a 4-4 suit may produce more tricks even than a 6-2 suit, as has been shown.

But this assumes good suit breaks, or so many high-card controls that good suit breaks are not needed. Few of the 4-4 trump suits shown in previous examples would have played better than the alternative 5-3, 5-4, or 6-2 suits if the opposing trumps had not been divided evenly (3-2) and against bad trump breaks the 4-4 suits could have been hurt much worse. When breaks are bad or the opponents have the preponderance of the high-card strength, the longer suit in a two-suited hand may or may not produce more tricks but *it is always safer.*

A two-suited hand in which the long suits are 5-4 or 6-5 must be short in one or both of the other two suits. When the opponents are strong in these other suits they will lead them, and declarer's only stoppers will be his trumps. The greater length he has in trumps, the more stoppers he will have; that is, his trumps will last longer. One extra stopper may make a difference of several tricks in the play of the hand.

This fact has a profound influence on sacrifice bidding.

NORTH
♠ A 6 2
♡ 8 6 4 3
♢ 10 6
♣ J 10 7 2

WEST
♠ 10 5
♡ Q J 10 7 2
♢ A Q 4
♣ A 6 4

EAST
♠ 9 7 3
♡ A K 5
♢ 8 2
♣ K Q 9 3 2

SOUTH
♠ K Q J 8 4
♡ 9
♢ K J 9 7 5 3
♣ 8

In this deal East-West were vulnerable, North-South were not. North-South chose to sacrifice rather than permit East-West to play and make four hearts. In both spades and diamonds North-South held eight cards, and a four-spade sacrifice was one trick lower than a five-diamond sacrifice. Nevertheless, diamonds were the only safe choice.

The fact is well demonstrated in this deal in which both spades and diamonds "broke"—were 3-2 in the opponents' hands.

At four spades North-South would probably win only five tricks, going down five—a most unprofitable sacrifice. With a heart opening and continuation South would have to ruff; after going over to the spade ace and losing a finesse for the diamond queen he would have to ruff again; after giving up his second losing diamond he would have to ruff a third time. Now he could not draw trumps. By other play South might get six tricks, but the loss of 700 points would still be unprofitable.

There is also the matter of entries to be considered. Assuming that the long side suit can be established, it cannot be run unless there is entry to it. With a two-suited hand, declarer's cards in his side suit or suits are usually gone immediately, and his only means of reëntry is often a trump. If his trumps have all been dissipated by repeated ruffing, he cannot gain entry to his side suit after he establishes it. In this deal, even if dummy had held ♠ A 10 6 and South could have drawn trumps, he could not then have gained reëntry to the four established diamonds.

At five diamonds North-South would probably win nine tricks, going down only two at a contract one trick higher, and effecting a very profitable sacrifice. South would ruff the second heart lead and give up a trump trick; ruff the third heart lead and give up another trump trick; and still have enough trumps to ruff again, draw the last opposing trump, and run his spades without contest. A spade opening and continuation by West, the only defense that would cost South an extra trick, would be difficult in actual play, and against that defense South would be down only three, a profitable sacrifice of 500 points.

The decision is easy for the player who holds the 6-5 two-suiter (South, in the foregoing deal) if he knows his partner to have at least two diamonds and probably not more than three spades; and sometimes the bidding does reveal such information. In such a case the six-card suit is the automatic choice. But usually the decision rests on the bidder's partner, in this case North.

A good North will recognize the situation and will place the contract in diamonds, going one trick higher in a suit in which he has conspicuously weaker support. The bidding might be, with West dealer:

WEST	NORTH	EAST	SOUTH
1 ♡	Pass	2 ♣	2 ♢
Pass	Pass	2 ♡	2 ♠
4 ♡	Pass	Pass	4 ♠
Double	5 ♢ !	Double	Pass
Pass	Pass		

From South's rebid of his second suit at the four-level, North may assume South's 6-5 distribution. Though longer in spades, North must take the contract to five diamonds.

North should not do this on a strong hand. On weak hands, a desire for safety compels selection of the 6-2 suit.

Readers should not too hastily condemn East-West for failure to bid five hearts and score the vulnerable game they could make. Neither East nor West could be confident of making five hearts. Both knew they could beat four spades or five diamonds, even if they did not know by how much. My observation convinces me that the biggest winners, in both rubber and tournament bridge, take the sure plus score.

COMPARISON OF 5-4 AND 4-4

The case for the 5-4 suit, as against the 4-4 suit, is the same as the case for the 5-3 suit but just a little bit better. The extra trump in the 5-4 suit provides better control and reduces the danger of a bad break.

If declarer will need one discard (it is the most he can get) for control or trick-winning, he must willy-nilly play in the 4-4 suit. If he has ample controls and tricks in the side suits, the 4-4 suit cannot be superior and may be inferior, as it would have been in the following deal.

NORTH
♠ K 8 6 3
♡ A K Q 6
◇ K Q J 2
♣ 8

WEST
♠ Q J 2
♡ 7
◇ 10 7 5 4
♣ Q J 10 4 3

EAST
♠ 9
♡ J 10 4 2
◇ 9 6 3
♣ K 7 6 5 2

SOUTH
♠ A 10 7 5 4
♡ 9 8 5 3
◇ A 8
♣ A 9

South dealt. Both sides were vulnerable and North-South had 80 on the score. The bidding:

SOUTH	WEST	NORTH	EAST
1 ♠	Pass	3 ♡	Pass
4 ♡	Pass	5 ♠	Pass
6 ♠	Pass	Pass	Pass

Since both members of the North-South pair knew the facts about trump suits, North made his slam invitation in spades and South accepted it in spades.

The play at six spades was easy enough. West led the club queen. South won the first trick with his ace, led a low spade to dummy's king, and led a spade back. A spade trick then had to be given up to West's queen but that was all. One of South's low hearts went off on one of dummy's high diamonds, South's losing club was ruffed in dummy, and South had the rest.

Six hearts would have been a losing contract for North-South, because of the coincidence of a 3-1 spade break and a 4-1 heart break. There were not enough high diamonds in the North hand to provide discards for all three of South's losing spades, so eventually North-South would have had to lose a spade trick in addition to the inescapable trump trick. Result, down one for a loss of 100 points instead of a vulnerable slam bid and made for a profit of 1,430 points.

In this case:

WEST	EAST
♠ A Q 8 6 4	♠ K 10 7 2
♡ K Q J 6	♡ 10 9 5 4
◇ ———	◇ 8 5 3
♣ A 10 7 5	♣ 6 2

The 5-4 spade suit is superior because West has three diamonds to trump and the four-card suit may not stretch far enough. *A player should not willingly play with a four-card trump holding if he has a void suit.* His partner should keep this principle in mind when showing preference.

WHEN A 4-3 TRUMP SUIT IS PREFERRED

Even the best players, bound to the dogma that a sound trump suit must have a combined length of at least eight cards, overlook many cases in which a combined seven-card holding divided 4-3 would be their best trump suit and provide their best contract.

The 4-3 trump suit is usually selected only when it is a major, when no-trump is out of the question because some suit is unstopped, and when there seems little chance of getting eleven tricks in a longer combined minor suit. In other words, it is a less dangerous version of the situation shown on page 294.

In the case most often neglected, the 4-3 trump suit is superior because one or two ruffs with the short (three-card) trump holding add essentially to declarer's trick-taking power.

The 4-3 spade suit was correctly selected in the following deal, and while there were collateral reasons for preferring it, the suit would in any event have been the best choice.

NORTH
♠ K 6 5
♡ J 6 5 4
◇ A K 7 5 4
♣ 3

WEST	EAST
♠ 10 9	♠ 8 7 4 2
♡ A Q 8	♡ 10 9 7 3
◇ J 9 8 2	◇ 10
♣ J 9 6 4	♣ 10 8 7 2

SOUTH
♠ A Q J 3
♡ K 2
◇ Q 6 3
♣ A K Q 5

East dealt. East-West were vulnerable. The bidding:

EAST	SOUTH	WEST	NORTH
Pass	2 N.T.	Pass	3 ♣
Pass	3 ♠	Pass	4 ◇
Pass	4 ♠	Pass	5 ♠
Pass	6 ♠	Pass	Pass
Pass			

North wisely preferred to have South the declarer, but if this had been his only reason he could have made six no-trump the contract. The principal thought in North's mind was that his low spades might add one or two tricks by ruffing clubs. North did not know South's club suit was so strong, but the one club ruff that North did get proved decisive. No such advantage could attach to the diamond suit, for any ruffs would have to be made with the long diamonds and add no tricks to the total.

The result proved North right in every respect. Six no-trump could not be made because there simply were not twelve tricks. Six diamonds would have been beaten speedily by a heart opening, but even if the heart ace had been in East's hand, a six-diamond contract would have been doomed by the 4-1 break. The heart ace plus a trump trick would have had to be lost.

The six-spade contract weathered both storms.

West opened the spade ten and dummy's king was put up. South took his club ace and trumped his club five, then led dummy's last spade and drew trumps. West discarded a heart and club, dummy two hearts.

South cashed his last two clubs. West could follow to the first, while a diamond was thrown from dummy. (South did not know diamonds would not break, but by relinquishing his chance for an overtrick he maintained his best play for the contract.) On the last club West had to part with the heart queen to keep his diamond stopper.

Now the contract was safe. The heart six was discarded from dummy and South led his low heart, dropping West's ace and making his remaining cards good.

The squeeze helped, but at worst South would have had a play to find the ace of hearts onside.

A 5-1 spade break would have defeated the contract, but it must be remembered that the odds are 5 to 1 against anything worse than a 4-2 break when you have seven trumps. The odds are only 2 to 1 against a bad break when you have eight trumps.

THE CONSPIRACY AGAINST MINOR SUITS

The scoring laws of contract bridge arbitrarily make diamonds and clubs the "minor" suits, in which eleven tricks are needed for game.

There being no rational reason why one suit should count more than another, countless reformers have proposed equalizing the count of the four suits.

Yet the scoring differential between major and minor suits, illogical though it may seem, is one of the primary reasons why contract bridge became and has remained the most popular card game. To equalize the suits would be, practically, to legislate the no-trump game contract out of the game. Nearly always a partnership has a good fit in one of the four suits, but when the fit is in a minor suit the tendency is to play at three no-trump rather than play at five of the best minor.

The reformers have a sound argument, nevertheless, when they say that bidding systems so emphasize the major suits and no-trump that good players seldom know how to reach a game-going bid of five in a minor suit when that is the best contract.

In the following deal several good North-South pairs actually bid to four spades, stopped there, and went down two tricks. It never occurred to them to play at five of a minor.

NORTH
♠ 10 7 6 2
♡ K 3 2
♢ 7 4 3
♣ A K 5

WEST
♠ 8 4
♡ A Q 10 9 4
♢ A 6
♣ 10 8 7 3

EAST
♠ J 9 5 3
♡ J 8 6 5
♢ Q 9 2
♣ 9 2

SOUTH
♠ A K Q
♡ 7
♢ K J 10 8 5
♣ Q J 6 4

South dealt. North-South were vulnerable. The bidding was:

SOUTH	WEST	NORTH	EAST
1 ♢	1 ♡	1 N.T.	2 ♡
3 ♣	Pass	3 ♢	Pass
4 ♢	Pass	5 ♣	Pass
5 ♢	Pass	Pass	Pass

Few players bid so aggressively as did North and South with only a minor suit to land in, while customarily experts bid their cards in this way when their suit is spades or hearts. But South's contract was a good gambling one, requiring only a successful finesse for fulfillment.

The finesse worked but better defense would have put South to a guess and he might have guessed wrong.

The ace of hearts was opened and won the first trick. West then led the club three and dummy's king won.

South led a diamond from dummy, finessing the jack.

If West had not won this trick with the ace of diamonds, he might have beaten the contract.

When West took his diamond ace, South had no problem. He won a club continuation, finessed again through East's queen of diamonds, and had the required cards to draw trumps and claim the remainder with high spades and clubs.

Suppose West had played low on the first diamond trick. Now South would have known only where the queen of diamonds was. He would not have known which opponent held two diamonds nor which opponent had the diamond ace.

South could have overcome this defense only by a perfect guess, whereby he would have led a low diamond after winning with his ten, dropping West's ace. But probably South would have led his other low club to dummy's ace, to take another diamond finesse. This time West would have had to take his ace— but this time West could lead a third round of clubs, which East would ruff for the setting trick.

7

VALUATION BASED ON
PARTNER'S HAND

In appraising any card, or his hand as a whole, the expert leans heavily upon the hand he expects his partner to hold. His picture of partner's hand may come from the bidding, or lack of bidding, or the natural expectation that partner will hold one-third of whatever high-card strength is held by the other three players.

When partner is known to be weak, the trick-taking power of most high-card combinations drops sharply.

West	North	East	South
2 N.T.	Pass	Pass	

East's pass, in this situation, is made only on a worthless hand, and West may find his own hand two tricks weaker than he thought it was.

West	East
♠ A K J 6	♠ 8 2
♡ K Q 10	♡ 8 7 5 4
◇ Q 10 6 5	◇ 9 8 4
♣ A K	♣ J 8 4 3

West may quite reasonably have hoped to win three spade tricks, two heart tricks, two club tricks, and one diamond. This appraisal was, however, based upon two expectations.

The primary expectation in valuation is that declarer can gain entry to his partner's hand, to finesse if he so chooses. An entry-less dummy may reduce the power of such a tenace as A-Q-10 from two or three tricks to one trick. In the case of the example above, lack of an entry prevents West's finessing for the spade queen or for the diamond jack, or leading up to his ♡ K Q 10.

The second expectation in valuation, and often the far more important one, is that declarer and dummy will have at least one suit they can lead without unnecessarily establishing tricks for their opponents. Suppose in this case East held ◊ J 4 3 2. By leading diamonds West could throw his opponents into the lead and they would probably then lead one of the other suits. Except in unusual cases he would gain a trick by their leads.

Forced to lead from his own hand, West may find his trick-taking power reduced from the original eight-trick estimate to an ultimate five or six tricks.

Such a bidding situation often opens to a defender (South in the bidding sequence above) an opportunity for a lucrative double. South, knowing that West would probably have bid more than two no-trump if he had held eight *sure* tricks, may double on the assumption that West held no more than eight *probable* tricks, some of which by reason of East's pass have become improbable. With a smattering of strength, as in the following hand, it may pay South to double:

♠ 10 9 3   ♡ J 7 4   ◊ A J 7   ♣ Q 10 9 2

Every now and then the double will give North-South an un-earned game, but far more often it will pick up an extra 200 or 300 points.

When partner is known to be strong, there is automatic appreciation of values in the appraisal both of high cards and of long suits.

1.	♠ K 6 3	2.	♠ 8
	♡ Q 8 5 2		♡ 10 8 7 6 3 2
	◊ K 7		◊ 9 7 5 4 3
	♣ 9 6 5 3		♣ 10

No. 1 is worth a trick if partner passes; it is worth at least three tricks if partner opens with a two no-trump bid; it justifies a slam try if partner opens with a game-forcing bid or a three no-trump bid. When the opponents are known to have their share of the high cards, kings and queens lose part of their combining value, since partner may have nothing with which they can combine; they lose part of their trick-winning power, since they may be captured by opponents' higher honors. When the opponents are known to be weak and partner to be strong, these circumstances are reversed.

No. 2 is worthless and dangerous if partner passes, and should not be bid; it is promising and should be bid at least twice if partner makes a moderately strong bid such as a takeout double; it warrants insistence on a game contract if partner makes a very strong bid such as two no-trump. In the latter case, when partner is known to be strong and to have some strength in hearts, trump control should be expected, permitting the diamond suit to be established. If partner happens not to have the tops in diamonds then he will be able to stop the spade and club suits, so that the trump control will not be weakened by repeatedly having to ruff the opponents' strong suits.

REAPPRAISAL OF HIGH CARDS

Partner's distribution has an effect on the valuation of high-card holdings both defensively and offensively.

A player should not double his opponent's contract in the expectation of winning two tricks with ♡ A K 6 4 2 if his partner has raised hearts; partner probably has heart length and one opponent probably has a singleton.

If partner makes an opening bid of four hearts, ♠ Q J 10 x x x is virtually worthless, and might almost as well be ♠ 7 6 5 4 3 2; for partner probably has no more than a doubleton spade and would lose two tricks in either case. But ♠ K x x x x x has some value, for if partner has a doubleton spade and the ace is onside he may save a trick.

When a player has shown that his strength is in one very long suit (as by a preëmptive bid) or that he has a two-suiter, the timing function of high cards in side suits becomes paramount. If one partner opens or overcalls and then bids up to three spades, singlehanded, the other partner should raise with two aces but not with two K-Q holdings. The bidder will probably have a singleton in at least one of the K-Q suits. In this case a K-Q will be of no value, since partner would lose one trick, and no more than one trick, in the suit anyway.

There is little value to ◇ J 6 if partner bids spades and hearts, but a great deal of value to it if partner bids clubs and the opponents bid spades and hearts, for then partner probably has side strength in diamonds and the jack has combining power.

Before partner is heard from, Q-J-10-x-x-x is a far better suit than K-x-x-x-x-x, for it can be "handled." The former suit sometimes justifies a bid when the latter would be passed.

	1.		2.	
♠	6		♠	6
♡	Q J 10 8 7 5		♡	K 8 7 5 3 2
◇	A 7		◇	A 7
♣	J 10 7 3		♣	J 10 7 3

Over an opponent's one-spade bid, No. 1 warrants a vulnerable two-heart overcall; No. 2 suggests a pass. The apparent superiority of Q-J-10-x-x-x may end, however, when partner's distribution and high-card holding become known.

If partner raises hearts, the suit headed by the king becomes superior. Suppose partner holds four small hearts; then Q-J-10-x-x-x will still lose two tricks, but K-x-x-x-x-x may lose only one.

If partner gives a double raise in hearts, the superiority of K-x-x-x-x-x may be reckoned a full trick. Suppose partner holds A-x-x-x; then a finesse will be required to clear the Q-J-10-x-x-x suit without loss, but no finesse will be needed with K-x-x-x-x-x.

DUPLICATION OF VALUES

Duplication of values can destroy the effect of any system of valuation.

Values are said to be duplicated when one partner has high-card control in a suit in which the other partner has distributional control, or when the two partners have distributional values in the same suit.

A bidding system should be designed to reveal duplication of values quickly, whenever it is possible to do so.

The following is a case of high-card duplication:

WEST	EAST
♠ A K Q	♠ ——————
♡ 9 3	♡ J 6
◇ Q J 4 3	◇ A K 10 9 6
♣ Q 10 4 2	♣ A K J 9 6 5

If East-West play at a club or diamond contract, West might as well have ♠ 4 3 2 as ♠ A K Q, assuming that the opponents will open hearts and win the first two tricks. If West had ♡ A instead of ♠ A K Q (5 points less) or if East had ♠ J 6 and a void in hearts, the East-West hands would produce a grand slam. With the spade duplication they cannot produce even a small slam.

When these hands were bid, the East-West pair found it possible to detect the duplication and avoid the losing slam. Their bidding was:

WEST	NORTH	EAST	SOUTH
1 ♣	Pass	2 ◇	2 ♠
Pass	Pass	3 ♠	Pass
3 N.T.	Pass	4 ♣	Pass
4 ◇	Pass	5 ♣	Pass
Pass	Pass		

West's bid of three no-trump was a warning of duplication. Later West should and would have bid four hearts instead of four diamonds if he had held the heart ace, and four no-trump (which in this situation should not be Blackwood) if he had held the heart king. West's failure to make either of these bids constituted sufficient warning to East that there might be two heart tricks to lose, so East proceeded cautiously with his five-club bid and West confirmed his fears by letting it rest there.

Obviously West's A-K-Q in spades were not worthless. If he had actually held 4-3-2 instead of A-K-Q, North-South would have had ten solid spades plus nine solid hearts and could have made five-odd in one of the majors (or defeated a sacrifice six-club contract).

Note also that the ten-card club suit was a better trump suit than the nine-card diamond suit. With diamonds trumps there would have been a greatly increased chance that North-South defensively could win two hearts plus a club ruff, preventing East-West from making even a game.

Duplication of distribution is far more insidious than high-card-plus-distribution duplication. It is not so easy to detect, except when clues are provided by the opponents' bids, but it can be similarly damaging.

For such a case as the following no one has proposed a remedy.

West	East
♠ A Q 10 6 3	♠ K J 7 5 4
♡ K J	♡ A 8
◇ A 6 3	◇ J 7 5
♣ 7 4 3	♣ A 10 6

West opened one spade, East raised to three spades, and West bid four—routine bidding.

There was virtually no play for the contract. West had to lose two diamond tricks and two club tricks.

If either partner had held his doubleton in any suit but hearts, the game would have been a laydown.

Three no-trump is a laydown and is the safest game contract, but no bidding system provides for a no-trump game with a 5-5 major-suit fit.

Experts perforce treat such cases as unlucky breaks, shrug their shoulders, bear the loss, and go on to the next deal. A system designed to detect such cases of duplication would be self-defeating. It would consume bids that can be put to better purposes.

But warnings from the opponents' bidding are not overlooked.

South	West	North	East
1 ♡	1 ♠	2 ♡	4 ♠

South holds:

♠ 9   ♡ K Q J 10 6 3   ◇ A Q 4   ♣ 9 7 3

The singleton spade is far more dangerous in South's hand than three small spades would be. North probably has a singleton or at most a doubleton in spades. If East-West have winning cards in clubs or diamonds they will get them; if North has a long minor suit South may be powerless to prevent a ruff.

In the following deal the bidding revealed high-card duplication of an unusual kind: two many tricks in a suit in which they were not needed.

NORTH
♠ A Q 6
♡ 8 7 5 4
♢ 5 3
♣ K 10 8 3

WEST
♠ 10 9 8 5 4 2
♡ Q
♢ A K Q 6 2
♣ 9

EAST
♠ 3
♡ 10 6 3 2
♢ 10 9 4
♣ Q 7 6 4 2

SOUTH
♠ K J 7
♡ A K J 9
♢ J 8 7
♣ A J 5

South dealt, with both sides vulnerable. The bidding began:

SOUTH	WEST	NORTH	EAST
1 ♡	1 ♠	2 ♡	Pass
2 N.T.	Pass	3 ♣	

When South could bid two no-trump after West's spade over-call, North (who was Richard Frey) feared that his side had too much strength in spades and might be unprotected in one of the other suits. Therefore North tested the situation by showing his club stopper and South got the message and bid four hearts.

At no-trump, a contract North might ordinarily have welcomed with his balanced hand, West would have run off the first five tricks in diamonds. The four-heart contract was unbeatable, but good defense did force South to locate the club queen.

West took the first trick with the diamond king and shifted to the spade ten. West too had heard the bidding. South had shown spade strength and might have all four missing spades. If so, East could ruff the spade, put West back in with a diamond, and get another spade ruff for the setting trick.

East could not ruff the first spade trick but the lead was nevertheless West's best by far. South won with the spade jack but now he could not lead diamonds to set up a ruffing position for his third diamond without giving the trick back via a spade ruff by East.

However, when South cashed the heart ace and saw West's queen fall, he decided to trade tricks with East after all. If he drew all of East's trumps, as he easily could, he would himself be out of trumps and could not afford to lose the club finesse and have the rest of the diamond suit run against him.

So South cashed the heart king and led the diamond jack. West won and gave East his spade ruff. East led back his last heart and the contract depended on South's finessing clubs the right way.

South might easily have gone wrong. West had overcalled when vulnerable and was marked with several high cards. West had shown six spades and a diamond suit, but West had held a singleton heart and his diamonds might have been only four long. In that case West would have held two clubs and East four clubs, and while mathematics would make the odds 2 to 1 that East had the club queen, the bidding would make it likely that West had Q-x in clubs.

The five of clubs was led to dummy's king. South's decision was not affected by West's play of the nine. West would have had to play the nine from Q-9 but he would have played the nine anyway from 9-x. South finally decided to go along with mathematics. He finessed through East for the club queen, making the contract. South's play was correct, because it exploited the additional possibility that West had started with five diamonds and one club, as he had.

Some players would have bid one no-trump originally with South's hand, but the majority of experts have decided that an 18-point hand is too strong. They bid one no-trump on 15 to 17 points or only on 16 or 17 points.

8

RECONCILIATION OF OFFENSIVE
AND DEFENSIVE VALUES

THE EXPERT first sees his hand as an offensive weapon and unconsciously labels it "strong hand" or "weak hand."

In this first appraisal a strong hand is one with which the holder
can do some bidding and expect, or hope, to secure the contract
and make it.

There is no strong hand that does not have some high-card
strength but there are hands that have much in high cards and
still are "weak."

	1. STRONG HAND	2. WEAK HAND
♠	A 9 7 6 4 2	A 9 7 6 4
♡	A 10 6 5 3	A 6 2
◇	8	A 8 5
♣	6	6 2

Hand No. 1 will probably win eight or nine tricks in whichever
of its long suits partner can better support, even if partner has
no high-card strength. This hand, given a trump fit, has both
timing value (aces and trumps to stop the opponents' suits) and
trick-winning value (long cards that can be established). Unless
partner has shown a misfit, as by bidding the minor suits, hand
No. 1 should be bid up to the three-level.

Hand No. 2 is a doubtful bid at anything above the one-level
and a dangerous hand even there. In high cards it is at least 50
percent better than No. 1, but what does it matter that there is
ample time to develop its trick-winners? There are almost no
trick-winners to develop.

Valuation systems rely upon the expectation that a 16-to-18-
point hand (or a 4 to 4½ quick-trick hand) will be strong. Usually
this expectation will be justified, but not always.

In the previous examples, the superior distribution of hand No. 1 made it a strong hand, but distribution need not be the determining factor. In the following examples, one 15-point hand is strong and another 15-point hand of the same distribution is weak.

	3. STRONG HAND	4. WEAK HAND
♠	K Q 9 8	A K 5 3
♡	A 10 9 6	A K 7 2
◇	K J 3	7 6 5
♣	Q 8	J 4

Hand No. 3 is superior because of the presence of intermediates; because it has no hopelessly weak suits; because its offensive prospects do not depend on finding a good fit with any specific suit or suits in partner's hand. The holder of hand No. 3 knows that an opponent cannot confidently bid five on a hand like this:

♠ 6   ♡ 5   ◇ A K Q J 4   ♣ A K Q 9 7 2

—and make it, redoubled. Against hand No. 4 an opponent might do just that.

Nor can hand No. 4, any more than the previous hand No. 2, safely enter the auction against opponents' bidding at any level higher than a one-bid or a double of a one-bid. Hand No. 3 can, if need be, but it is unlikely that against hand No. 3 the opponents will do much bidding.

Yet point-count valuation would rate hands 3 and 4 the same and quick-trick valuation would make No. 4 one full trick stronger.

THE MEASURE OF A STRONG HAND

Such anomalies in the popular valuation methods can be avoided if the player always applies dual valuation to his hand, offensive and defensive.

By such dual valuation hand No. 1 is not a strong hand, despite the expert's desire to consider it so.

The decisive measure of a strong hand is this: *It must be able to penalize the opponents if they outbid it.*

The following declarer's hands are close to being equivalent only offensively (and No. 2 is superior offensively because it is less often subject to a bad trump break).

DUMMY
♠ 8 6 4 3
♡ A 4
◊ J 10 7 5 4
♣ 7 6

DECLARER'S HAND No. 1	DECLARER'S HAND No. 2
♠ A K 10 5	♠ K Q 9 7 5 2
♡ K Q 6	♡ 6
◊ A 2	◊ A 2
♣ A 8 5 4	♣ A 8 5 4

Either No. 1 or No. 2 appears likely, opposite the dummy shown, to produce a game at spades. No. 1 has nevertheless a vast margin of superiority, for it promises six or more defensive tricks, as compared with two or at most three such tricks for No. 2. Against No. 2 the opponents can often find a profitable sacrifice bid; against No. 1 they cannot. The holder of No. 1 will probably score 450 to 600 points, the holder of No. 2 may score only 100 or 200 points.

The formulas prescribe dependence on quick tricks—that is, on high-card strength alone—for defensive purposes. It is true that at the start of the auction a player has no basis for assigning defensive value to anything but a high card. But as the bidding reveals the hand types that have been dealt, defensive valuation becomes a process no different from offensive valuation. The value of any card is exactly the same to one side as to the other. The card declarer most needs to make his contract, the defenders most need to defeat it.

South	West	North	East
1 ◇	Pass	1 ♠	Pass
2 ♣	Pass	3 ♣	Pass
5 ♣	Pass	Pass	Pass

East holds:

♠ K Q 6 2   ♡ A K 6 4   ◇ 9 7 5   ♣ 7 4

He cannot double despite his three "quick" tricks, for South, having displayed length in two suits, must be short in at least one of the other suits. East may get no spade trick; he may get one heart trick.

In another case, despite absence of high cards, a player may judge his hand to be defensively powerful:

South	West	North	East
1 ◇	1 ♡	2 ♣	Pass
2 ◇	Pass	2 N.T.	Pass
3 N.T.	Pass	Pass	Double

East holds:

♠ J 6   ♡ J 9 5   ◇ Q J 10 8   ♣ K 10 9 4

He has, by any count, no more than 1½ "quick" tricks. But North has contracted to win nine tricks, and where are these tricks coming from? Not from spades; neither North nor South was strong enough in spades to bid the suit. Not from hearts; West bid them. Not from diamonds or clubs, since North cannot establish either suit without giving East two tricks in it.

Because it is so clearly understood that no hand can be described unqualifiedly as strong unless it satisfies both offensive and defensive requirements, players hesitate to make bids that are conventionally strength-showing unless they have considerable defensive strength. In consequence, experts have come to depend upon their partners' strength-showing bids to guarantee defensive strength, and lean heavily upon this inferred guarantee in future doubling and slam bidding. Two famous players reached a losing slam through the bidding of the following hand:

♠ A Q 10 9 7 5 3   ♡ K Q 6 4   ◇ 3   ♣ 8

The holder of the hand opened with one spade; his partner responded two diamonds and he jumped to three spades. No lesser bid would properly have portrayed the offensive power of his hand, yet his limited defensive power should have warned against the bid. His partner expected about four tricks in top cards and went to six no-trump, which was down four. If the opponents had been bidding and had reached five clubs his partner might have doubled them with equally poor results.

THE RANK OF THE SUITS AS A FACTOR IN BIDDING

There is still another standard for defensive valuation: the rank of the suits. The profit potential of any hand is largely dependent upon the rank of its longest suit.

If one's long suit is spades, the defensive strength can be reckoned one trick higher than if one's long suit is diamonds or clubs. In some cases the superiority of the spade suit can be stated in an exact number of points. The following deal is an example:

NORTH
♠ 8 6 4 3
♡ A 4
◇ J 10 7 5 4
♣ 10 7

WEST
♠ J 10
♡ K J 9 7 3
◇ K 8 6 3
♣ K 6

EAST
♠ A
♡ Q 10 8 5 2
◇ Q 9
♣ Q J 8 5 4

SOUTH
♠ K Q 9 7 5 2
♡ 6
◇ A 2
♣ A 9 3 2

South was the dealer and both sides were vulnerable. The bidding was:

SOUTH	WEST	NORTH	EAST
1 ♠	Pass	2 ♠	Pass
4 ♠	Pass	Pass	Pass

West chose to open the seven of hearts, but it made no difference what he led. South could easily make four spades, losing to the ace of trumps, plus a diamond trick and one club trick. After trumps were drawn, there were two trumps left in dummy to take care of South's other two clubs.

Probably East-West should not have let themselves be shut out of the bidding. It would be dangerous for West to make an overcall at the two level, but many players would enter the bidding over two spades with the East hand. Some might choose to double, some might bid two no-trump—the "unusual no-trump," which is used to show a two-suiter and ask partner to bid.

In this case East was afraid South might bid four spades and West might bid five diamonds, a suit East could not support. As the cards lay, this might readily have happened, because the unusual no-trump usually shows minor-suit strength. West would expect East to hold length in diamonds rather than length in hearts. On this reasoning, a takeout double by East would be better.

Users of the light takeout double would get into the bidding on this hand—West could double, planning to bid hearts if his partner responded in clubs—but the light double has been largely superseded by the Michaels cue-bid, for which West's hand is not strong enough.

The fact remains that East-West had a game in hearts—at four hearts they could have lost only three tricks, to the three North-South aces—and they never got into the bidding.

Even if East-West had entered the bidding they would have had to lose, because they could not outbid South's spades. By making four spades, South scored 620 points, but at best East-West would have had to sacrifice at five hearts, go down one trick doubled, and lose 200.

EFFECT OF A SHIFT OF SUITS

The following layout of the cards is exactly the same as the deal shown before except that this time East-West have the spades and North-South have the hearts.

NORTH
♠ A 4
♡ 8 6 4 3
◇ J 10 7 5 4
♣ 10 7

WEST
♠ K J 9 7 3
♡ J 10
◇ K 8 6 3
♣ K 6

EAST
♠ Q 10 8 5 2
♡ A
◇ Q 9
♣ Q J 8 5 4

SOUTH
♠ 6
♡ K Q 9 7 5 2
◇ A 2
♣ A 9 3 2

Again both sides are vulnerable. This time the bidding must be different. South opens with one heart. West, who was not strong enough to bid two hearts over one spade, is strong enough to bid one spade over one heart. Once West enters the bidding, East will carry him to four spades. Even if West did not overcall with one spade, East with his spade strength would consider it safe to double when North raised to two hearts.

The bidding would probably be like this:

SOUTH	WEST	NORTH	EAST
1 ♡	1 ♠	2 ♡	4 ♠
5 ♡	Double	Pass	Pass
Pass			

South would make the same ten tricks as before, but this time he would be down one, doubled and vulnerable, and would lose 200 points.

The value of the spade suit in such a case is therefore at least 400 points, for the side that has the spades will be plus 200 points instead of minus 200 points. The value can go still higher, for in the first deal South was permitted to play at four spades and score 620, and in the second deal East-West might possibly be permitted to play at four spades and score 620. North might consider his hand too weak to give a free raise in hearts, and in that case South probably would not risk a sacrifice five-heart bid; but today there are few players who would not raise freely on the North hand.

The value of the higher-ranking suits is a practical consideration in many bids. One example is when a player decides whether or not to open the bidding fourth-hand on a borderline hand. With such a hand as this, it is customary to pass:

♠ 7 3　♡ 6 4　◇ A Q 8 3　♣ A J 9 6 2

The remaining high cards can be assumed to be more or less evenly divided among the other three hands. The opponents probably have a satisfactory spade or heart suit and can outbid the diamond and club suits, making it more likely that they will make a part score. If fourth hand had his strength in the majors instead of the minors, he would open the bidding. If one of his suits were spades, he would bid, as in this hand:

♠ A Q 8 3　♡ 7 3　◇ 6 4　♣ A J 9 6 2

Here the spade suit will probably outbid the opponents if the strength is evenly divided; the hand with the spades is worth one more trick defensively than the hand without spades.

EFFECT OF THE RANK OF THE SUITS AT LOWER LEVELS

Not only in competitive bidding does the rank of the suits exert its influence. At every stage the thinking player must consider the likelihood that his opponents can enter the bidding cheaply, or outbid him in a contested auction, with a higher-ranking suit. Pervading his thoughts at all times must be the question "Who has the spades?"

As one example only: Bridge books uniformly tell what is required to give a single raise when partner makes an opening suitbid.

It is as absurd to generalize on single raises as it is to say there are five vowels in the English language. Just as the vowel A differs in *father, cat, ball,* the expert's single raise varies according to the suit his partner has bid and what he has in other suits.

A raise of one spade to two spades has a powerful preëmptive effect. The opponents must go to three to overcall. Among all the single raises, this one may show the least trump support. Experts have been known to bid it on hands like this:

♠ Q3   ♡ 1086   ◇ 9763   ♣ Q852

or

♠ 10865   ♡ 7   ◇ 83   ♣ Q97653

The essential requirement is that the responder be able to pass the opener's new-suit rebid with relative safety, even if the suit is short or weak, or to go safely back to the first suit.

A raise of one heart to two hearts may have a similar preemptive effect, but only if the responder has the spade suit protected. On the following hand, which ideally meets the book requirements for a single raise in hearts, an expert did not raise partner's one heart to two:

♠ 6   ♡ J854   ◇ K76   ♣ Q8643

He bid four hearts. Two hearts might not have shut out the opponents' spade suit. But he would have bid two hearts on the following hand.

♠ QJ3   ♡ J854   ◇ Q8643   ♣ 6

This time the opponents probably would have no spade suit.

A raise of one diamond to two diamonds can have only one of three purposes: (1) to show distributional trump support in case five diamonds is the only game; (2) to prepare for a sacrifice; (3) to promise solidity for a long suit in partner's hand in case partner may wish to run a string of diamonds at no-trump. Here again the advisability of the bid depends on how much one must fear the opponents' major suits. With

♠ 10 7 6 3   ♡ Q 8 5 2   ◊ Q 10 8 6   ♣ 5

one would respond one heart (or, as some play it, one spade) and never two diamonds. With

♠ 5   ♡ Q 8 5 2   ◊ Q 10 8 6   ♣ 10 7 6 3

many experts would bid one heart because they are bound to systems in which failure to bid a four-card major denies having one, but two diamonds is a better bid.

A raise of one club to two should never be as weak as a single raise in spades may be, because there is little preëmptive value. Nor can the trump length be less than four cards when one raises a club bid, because despite all disclaimers in bridge books (including this one) one is permitted to remember that his partner may have opened on a short club suit. The raise to two clubs does have some preëmptive value and any other response should be preferred only when there remains some hope of finding a major-suit fit. With

♠ 7 2   ♡ 8 6 3   ◊ A 10 8 4   ♣ J 10 8 3

a raise of partner's club bid to two clubs is better than a one-diamond response, which can lead nowhere if not to two clubs (response one diamond, rebid one spade, responder's rebid two clubs). But with

♠ 8 6 5 3   ♡ 7   ◊ A 10 8 4   ♣ J 10 8 3

the response is one diamond, because it is better to hope for a spade rebid by partner than to rely on a two-club bid to shut out an opposing heart suit.

TWO MAJORS AND TWO SIGNALS

The rank of the suits, plus two basic card-playing conventions, affected the results of this deal:

NORTH
♠ A 8 3
♡ 7 5
◇ K 10 9 8
♣ J 10 4 2

WEST
♠ 6 5 4
♡ A J 10 9 4 2
◇ 2
♣ 8 7 5

EAST
♠ 7 2
♡ 8 6 3
◇ A J 6 4
♣ A K Q 3

SOUTH
♠ K Q J 10 9
♡ K Q
◇ Q 7 5 3
♣ 9 6

North dealt. East-West were vulnerable. The bidding was:

NORTH	EAST	SOUTH	WEST
Pass	1 ◇	1 ♠	3 ♡
3 ♠	4 ♡	4 ♠	Double
Pass	Pass	Pass	

In the system played by East-West, the three-heart bid was "weak," showing just about the kind of hand West had. This is logical, since a two-heart bid would be not only forcing but on the strong side for a two-over-one, as explained on page 00. But in standard American bidding the three-heart bid is still defined as a powerhouse, game-forcing bid.

West could have made four hearts, losing two spades and one heart, so South did not miscalculate greatly when he decided to sacrifice at four spades. But West was on top of the situation when he doubled despite his paucity of high cards. By doubling he warned East not to bid five hearts, which could not be made; and the singleton diamond promised several tricks because on the bidding East was due to have the diamond ace.

The deuce of diamonds was duly opened and East won and returned the four of diamonds for West to trump.

The four of diamonds was the suit-preference signal, invented by Hy Lavinthal in 1934, which has influenced the card-playing habits of expert bridge players throughout the world more than any other development in this century. By leading his lowest diamond, East instructed his partner to return the lower of the two available suits other than trumps—in this case, clubs rather than hearts.

West trumped with the spade five, starting a trump echo. The trump echo, a high-low play with two small trumps, informs partner that one has an additional trump and wishes to ruff with it.

Obedient to East's suit-preference lead, West led the club eight. East took the trick with his queen and led the diamond six. West trumped with the spade four, completing the trump echo.

Another club lead and East was in again, with the club king. The trump echo having told East that West had another spade, East led his fourth diamond and West got a third diamond ruff, then cashed the heart ace to put South down four. The net score of 600 (700 less 100 honors) gave East-West a good profit, and at duplicate bridge the score of 700 would have been better than making four hearts—and probably a top.

Without the trump echo by West, East might not have led that fourth diamond. On the bidding South could easily have had a six-card spade suit. If West could not trump another diamond, it would be important for East to lead a heart and get the heart ace while there was still time. Otherwise South could establish the club jack in dummy and discard a heart on it.

PART IV

THE THEORY AND
STRATEGY OF BIDDING

1

THE OBJECT OF BIDDING

EVERY DEAL of the cards provides some final contract that is theoretically ideal for each side, and some final contract that is theoretically ideal for both sides.

Assume a deal in which North-South can make four spades, and East-West can make four hearts. Both sides are vulnerable.

At four hearts, East-West can score 620 points. This is their ideal contract. At four spades, North-South can score 620 points. This is their ideal contract. But at four spades East-West would *lose* 620 points. Therefore, if North-South bid four spades, the best East-West can do is bid five hearts, be doubled, and go down one, losing only 200 points; and if East-West do bid five hearts, the best North-South can do is double, scoring 200 points.

Five hearts doubled, then, is the theoretically ideal contract, the product of the best efforts of both sides.

The bidding science is complex because every bid should have a dual objective. There is equal advantage in exploiting one's own cards and in frustrating one's opponents.

Imagine a series of two deals, of which the first will produce a game for North-South, the second a game for East-West. If the East-West bidding prevents North-South's reaching game on the first deal, the East-West profit is about 500 points. If the East-West bidding arrives at the game on the second deal, the East-West profit is again about 500 points. Assuming that the luck of the deal evens up in the long run, obstructive tactics on inferior cards will yield as great a profit as precise bidding of superior cards.

Bidding, then, is a code conceived to enlighten the partner while mystifying the opponents. Its conversations deal in nuance and indirection. The bids that comprise its vocabulary may not be defined, only interpreted.

If a bidding system is properly constructed, its bids will tell partner only what he needs to know and will withhold all information of any value from the opponents.

NORTH
♠ Q 6 5 2
♡ A 9
♢ A K 10 8 3
♣ 10 2

WEST
♠ 10 8 4
♡ Q 8 6 4
♢ Q 9 6
♣ K 6 5

EAST
♠ J 9 3
♡ 10 7 3 2
♢ J
♣ A Q 9 8 3

SOUTH
♠ A K 7
♡ K J 5
♢ 7 5 4 2
♣ J 7 4

North deals and bids one diamond. South responds two clubs. It is his proper systemic bid.

The response of two clubs should denote a desire, or at least a willingness, to play a club contract; but in the early rounds bids do not have denotations, only connotations. The two-club response connotes a desire to have North rebid. What prompts that desire North does not know and need not know.

Any other response selected by South would send a false message. A response of two no-trump would require a game and promise a stronger hand than South has, especially in clubs. A raise to two diamonds would show a weaker hand than South has, and a raise to three diamonds would show greater concentration of strength in the diamond suit. A response of one spade or one heart would suggest the possibility of a major-suit game contract if North has fair support (perhaps Q-x-x) for the major suit. North would not raise a minor suit to game without much better support than that.

The two-club response serves every purpose. It gives the impression of general strength, which South has. It requires a rebid from North, which is desirable because South can see strong hope for game opposite an opening bid. It leaves the opponents in the dark. They will hesitate to lead clubs, because South may have (and usually will have) a genuine club suit, and without a club lead North-South may make a game that would otherwise be impossible.

After the two-club response North rebids two diamonds, South bids two no-trump, and North raises to three no-trump. A club opening would give the defenders five tricks and defeat the contract, but West has no reason to lead clubs and selects the four of hearts. This lead gives South three heart tricks, and after trying the ace and king of diamonds and finding that the suit does not break, South tries the ace, king, and queen of spades and finds that that suit does break, so the spade six is his ninth trcik.

The two-club response was not designed as a deceptive bid to inhibit a club lead, because at that juncture South did not know a club lead would be damaging. South merely selected a bid that gave as much information as he considered necessary to his partner, and no more. Such advantage as accrued from misleading his opponents was a by-product.

FRUSTRATION OF THE SYSTEM MAKERS

The record of any championship bridge match turns out to be a record of experts' errors. Games are bid that cannot be made, games that could be made are not bid, slams go down because they are placed in the wrong hand or wrong suit, and the catalog could be extended indefinitely.

The errors, conspicuous and widely published, constitute an irresistible challenge to conscientious souls who thereupon besit themselves at their card tables to chart the new and perfect bidding system.

Invariably the system makers try to make their systems so informative that each player may reveal his exact holding to his partner, thus to reach eventually the ideal double-dummy contract for the partnership. Variously, the system makers have devised bids to locate the aces, kings, and queens, and the distribution of the four suits in the partnership hands. If such information might be exchanged, they have believed, contract bridge bidding could become a perfect thing.

Yet widespread though this belief is, the reasoning behind it is utterly fallacious.

If two partners are to reveal to each other their exact holdings, then by the properties of the game they must make the same revelation to their opponents. The information would usually be of greater value to the opponets than to the partners themselves.

Suppose the East-West partners could show each other the following:

WEST	EAST
♠ K Q 8 7 4	♠ A J 6 3
♡ A 6	♡ K 4
◊ Q 10 8 2	◊ J 9 7 3
♣ A 9	♣ 8 7 5

Playing at double-dummy, East-West should not score a game at spades more than one time in ten. The other nine times, North-South will be able to win two diamond tricks and get a diamond ruff immediately, after which West still has a club trick to lose. If the East-West hands are not exposed, however, East-West will make four spades more than half the time, for the opening leader will not be in a position to lead a diamond against them. If any other suit is opened, West will obtain the lead and draw trumps, whereupon the diamond danger is removed.

The factor most often overlooked by the system-makers is that the bidding side—that is, the side with the superior cards—almost never needs precise information.

A bid is a bet, and a bet is a good bet if it stands to take 51 percent or more of the purse. Perhaps it is comforting to know that the chance of victory is 60 percent or 85 percent or 100 percent, but the practical advantage is nil because with 51 percent one should make the bet anyway.

As soon as a bidding side discovers that it has about an even chance to make game, it should bid game. If it appears that game should not be bid the partnership should stop at the lowest safe part-score. As soon as it discovers that it has a 51 percent chance to make a small slam, it should bid the slam. As soon as it discovers that it has a 70 percent chance to make a grand slam, it should bid the grand slam. Any further exchange of information can help only the opponents.

Artificial bidding devices such as the Blackwood convention are frequently needed to determine the advisability of bidding a slam, but only to the extent to which they reveal a positive expectancy of success.

2

MATHEMATICS AND BRIDGE

THE SCIENCE of contract bridge may have a root in mathematics, but if so the root is a slender one at best. Both in bidding and in play, the only mathematics required to justify correct technique is simple arithmetic.

The bridge expert does proceed on certain assumptions that have a mathematical basis. He knows that the odds favor certain contingencies and oppose others. He knows that winning the first game of a rubber has a total value of approximately 450 points, but only 100 or 120 of these points (the trick score) are immediately set down on the score sheet. His knowledge of the odds and of the existence of unscored values must have come from mathematical calculations.

It is yet an error to suppose, as many do, that the bridge expert must be an accomplished mathematician. Not five in one hundred are deserving of this designation, and that any bridge expert knows mathematics is purely coincidental. Every expert leans far more heavily upon experience and observation than upon any probabilities he may know or assume. Whatever mathematical information applies to bridge science must be constantly modified by other knowledge: The relative degrees of skill of the players, the bids and plays they make, and the way they make them.

Since bridge mathematics is so crude in form and so rough a guide, the term itself becomes misleading when applied to bridge, and it is better to use a term from the vernacular: *figuring*. Any pertinent figuring in bridge may be done on the spur of the moment and in the head of one trained to think in bridge terms.

All the figures that govern bidding science arise from the contract bridge scoring table. Every bid puts at stake a certain number of points, in accordance with the existing schedule. The declarer's possible gain is determined by the values established for tricks and the bonuses awarded for winning the rubber or making a slam. The declarer's possible loss is stated in the table of under-trick penalties.

VALUES OF GAMES, SLAMS, AND PART-SCORES

Suppose North-South win the first game in a rubber.

As few as 100 points (the necessary trick points) may be scored, but North-South have simultaneously won an unscored equity in the rubber bonus. The rubber bonus eventually may be either 500 or 700 points.

Two more completed games may be required to finish the rubber, so the North-South equity is calculated on all the ways in which two games can be won.

	RUBBER BONUS SCORED BY	
	NORTH-SOUTH	EAST-WEST
North-South wins next, loses last *	700	
North-South wins both	700	
North-South loses next, wins last	500	
North-South loses both		500
	1900	500

Since the side that wins the first game of a rubber will win the rubber in three of the four cases, the odds in favor of its winning the rubber are 3 to 1.

Since in each group of four cases following the first game the side that won the first game will score 1,900 points in bonuses and lose back 500 points, the net value of the first game is 1,400 divided by 4, or 350 points.

The strictly mathematical 350-point value must, however, be modified by the fact that the side that wins the first game becomes vulnerable and is exposed to greater undertrick penalties. The disadvantage is not fully balanced by the fact that a vulnerable side can earn larger bonuses for slams and overtricks at doubled and redoubled contracts, for these occur far less often.

---

* In practice, of course, if North-South win the next game the last game will not be played. However, both of the 2nd-3rd game possibilities begin-ning with a North-South win are shown above since the likelihood that North-South will win that next game is twice as great as the likelihood of either 2nd-3rd game combination following a North-South loss.

Calculating along these lines, the bridge lawmakers of the pioneer days established 300 points as the equity value of the first game. It is an arbitrary figure, but it is probably as good as any. It has persisted in tournament scoring as the bonus for a nonvulnerable game and in rubber bridge scoring as the bonus for having the only game in an unfinished rubber.

Whatever the value assigned to the first game, the equity value of the second straight game must be the difference between the first-game value already won and the 700-point rubber bonus that will be scored when the second game is won.

If mathematically it is worth 350 to win the first game, then it is worth only 350 to win the second game and score the 700-point bonus. Given a choice between making four spades and scoring 120 plus a 700 rubber, or defeating the opponents by 500 points, a side would profit slightly by taking the penalty, for the game would have a true value of only 120 + 350 or 470 net. But if the first game was worth only 300, then the second straight game is worth 400 and the game is worth more than the penalty by 520 to 500.

No one figures quite so closely, nor should. The personal factor is always more important: With a superior partner one takes the penalty and prolongs the rubber; with an inferior partner one takes the game, ends the rubber, and gets a cut for a new partner.

When both sides are vulnerable, the game is worth exactly 500 points, for now the mathematical aspect is *a posteriori*. What went before has been wiped off the board.

Similarly the value of a slam is the precise amount of the slam bonus. A superstitious player may consider that his loss has been the greater if he bids a slam, goes down, and later loses a rubber he could have won by stopping short of the slam; but mathematically his losing slam try has cost him only his game, not the rubber.

The value of a part-score is indeterminable. In the laws it is set at 50 points. Good rubber bridge players agree in setting it higher than that but they cannot agree on how much higher. John Crawford has estimated the value of a part-score at 200 points against players who will compete rather than let the game go cheaply; he expects to make that much extra profit by doubling and penalizing their overbids. But while the opinion of such a player must be treated with respect, it must be noted that 200 points is the value to Mr. Crawford. The part-score does not necessarily have so great a value to a player less able to exploit it.*

THE PERSONAL FACTOR

The personal factor modifies to a large extent anything that may be written on contract bridge bidding. True, there is what may be called an expert "system" of bidding, and in this system each bid has its own distinct meaning. The ultimate meaning, however, can be assigned to any bid only when it is made by a certain player against certain opponents in a certain situation. Posing a problem of bidding to ten different experts, one may expect and receive some uniformity of reply. If an identical problem were presented to the same ten players, but each time in conditions of actual play, three, four, or five different decisions might result.

To a certain extent the strategy of the bridge player must resemble that of the poker player, who seeks to lure his opponents into error. The term *poker bridge*, however, is applied only to the use of stratagems other than legal bids and plays; to bluffing, making misleading remarks, feigning discomfiture or confidence, and other histrionics. Ethically the bridge player may build up a good hand only by means of misleading bids and passes.

The expert bridge player may eschew the normally correct bid when he feels that his partner may misunderstand it or that his opponents may learn too much from his making it. In these cases he violates the written system but he is in actuality true to the system, though only to the unwritten part of it.

---

* Mr. Crawford's appraisal nevertheless has strong support. According to Alan Truscott, the British international player, "A part-score when both sides are vulnerable is certainly worth much more than in other situations. [Jean] Besse [Swiss champion] calculated it at 220 after investigating a large number of rubbers, and *it cannot be less than 150.*" The statement in italics is Mr. Truscott's opinion. My estimate is 100 to 110 points, based on the only fully recorded series of 300 rubbers that I know about, the 150 rubbers of the Culbertson-Lenz match and the 150 rubbers of the Culbertson-Sims match. Granted that all the players in these matches were expert and conservative, and also that there is less emotional incentive to save a rubber when it is known to be only one rubber in a long series, the fact remains that I found relatively few cases in which the part-score affected the winning of the rubber or induced the opponents to sacrifice by more than one trick.

Intuition, or perhaps inspiration, is always sufficient to dislodge a bid that is mathematically sound in favor of one that has no mathematical justification. There is no way to criticize the intuitive bid except by its result:

♠ J 10 8 4   ♡ A K J 8 5 2   ◇ A Q 6   ♣ ———

An expert held this hand, when his opponents were vulnerable and he was not. He occupied the West position in the following bidding sequence:

South	West	North	East
1 ♠	Pass	2 ♣	Pass
2 ♠	3 ♡	3 ♠	Pass
4 ♠	5 ♡		

Almost undoubtedly West could not make the five-heart contract, and could defeat the four-spade contract. The five-heart bid, then, could have been based only upon a conviction that North or South would proceed to five spades. What prompted this conviction? Perhaps a knowledge of the opposing players, perhaps their demeanor when they made their previous bids; it does not matter. South did go to five spades, was doubled, and was down 800 points.

A bold bid, which mathematically is a poor risk, may be good tactics against timid opponents who will not double. A bid or pass may often be mathematically unsound but tactically excellent. For example:

South	West	North	East
1 ◇	1 ♠	2 ♡	2 ♠
3 ♡	Pass		

If North holds this hand, he may be quite sure that he can make a four-heart contract:

♠ 6 3   ♡ A Q 10 9 7 4   ◇ J 8 4 3   ♣ 8

Yet North, in defiance of mathematics, may choose to pass. If he bids four hearts, his opponents are fairly sure to bid four spades, a contract North-South may be unable to defeat; while North cannot feel confident of making five hearts if he should later have to bid it. If North passes at three hearts, his opponents will probably let him play it, rather than risk having a game made against them. If North passes three hearts and makes an apparently unwilling bid of four hearts over three spades, his opponents may pass or double. It becomes tactically sound for North to pass and take a sure plus score.

NORTH
♠ 9 7 4 3
♡ A 6 5
♢ 6 5
♣ K J 9 5

WEST
♠ A Q 10 5 2
♡ 8
♢ 10 7 4 2
♣ 8 6 3

EAST
♠ K J 6
♡ J 10 4
♢ K 3
♣ A Q 10 7 2

SOUTH
♠ 8
♡ K Q 9 7 3 2
♢ A Q J 9 8
♣ 4

East dealt. North-South were vulnerable. The bidding was:

EAST	SOUTH	WEST	NORTH
1 ♣	1 ♡	1 ♠	2 ♡
2 ♠	3 ♡	Pass	Pass
Pass			

West opened the eight of clubs.

The par score on this hand would be for East-West to play four spades doubled and go down one. In this case South beat par by an unusual bid. Although he was almost sure he could make four hearts, he bid only three hearts because he knew East-West would sacrifice at four spades if forced to that level.

To South's opponents it appeared that South's hand was doubtful, so they let him play three hearts. It was an excellent score. With proper defense, South could make exactly four hearts and West could make exactly three spades.

3

THE PRINCIPLE OF GAIN VS. RISK

KNOWING THE number of points he is putting at stake, the expert selects his bid (or play) by balancing possible gain against estimated risk. Every bid (and every play) should be a good bet.

For a good bet, *the ratio of possible gain to possible loss must be greater than the ratio of the expectancy of loss to the expectancy of gain.*

Suppose a player can gain 500 by doubling if his double succeeds but will lose 300 if his double fails. His ratio of possible gain to possible loss is 5 to 3. And suppose he calculates that in seven deals his double will succeed three times and fail four times. The ratio there is 4 to 3. The ratio of possible gain to possible loss is greater, therefore the double is a good bet. In seven instances the player will gain 500 points three times, for a profit of 1,500, and will lose 300 points four times, for a loss of 1,200. Over the course of the seven occasions he will be 300 points better off by doubling than by not doubling.

It is psychologically difficult for most players to endure the losses, even if intellectually they know their profits are greater; and it is seldom practical for a player to figure so closely that he knows precisely where his advantage lies. Nevertheless there are situations easily recognizable and frequently occurring in which the expectancies can be exactly ascertained.

SOUTH	WEST	NORTH	EAST
1 ♠	Pass	2 ♡	Pass
3 ♡	Pass		

Let us suppose that North, whose turn it is to bid, knows that he can make the contract of three hearts. If he can win a certain finesse he will make four hearts. There is exactly as much chance that the finesse will win as that it will lose. Should North bid four hearts, or should he pass?

The calculation is easiest at team-of-four play with total-point scoring, because the value of a part-score is fixed by law at 50 points, but the same principle applies to rubber bridge.

Both sides are vulnerable, so by making four hearts North can score 500 rubber-bonus points plus 120 trick-score points; if he bids four hearts and goes down one he will lose 100 penalty points; if he passes he will surely score 90 trick-score points plus 50 points reckoned as the value of making a part score. North now figures gain vs. loss:

By bidding four hearts North stands to *gain* 480 points (the difference between 620 he may score and 140 he could have scored anyway). He stands to *lose* (by risking his sure part-score) 240 points (the penalty of 100 plus the 140 he could have scored at three hearts).

In effect, then, North is offered 480 to 240, or 2 to 1, on an even-money or 1-to-1 bet. The superiority of bidding the game is in the ratio of 2 to 1, and the expert player invariably bids the game. To translate into points the advantage of the game-bidder over the player who stops short of game, one may examine a series of two hands:

If game is always bid:

First attempt (finesse wins)	Second attempt (finesse loses)	Net result
+ 620	− 100	+ 520

If game is never bid:

First attempt (finesse wins)	Second attempt (finesse loses)	Net result
+ 170	+ 140	+ 310

Over the series of two hands, the aggressive player scores 520 points, or an average of 260 points per hand. The conservative player scores 310 points, or an average of 155 points per hand.

Yet the statement or belief that "all experts are aggressive" is only conditionally true. Consider the same bidding situation, in which North has a choice between bidding four hearts and stopping at three hearts; and suppose that the game depends upon winning both of two finesses. The ratio of gain to loss remains the same, 480 to 240; but the expectancy of success is entirely different. The odds against winning two consecutive finesses are 3 to 1, so this time the bidder is offered only 2 to 1 on a 1-to-3 chance. The superiority of *not* bidding the game is as 3 to 2, and the "aggressive" player, over a series of four hands, could score a net of only 220 points as against his "conservative" fellow's 320. Aggressiveness, then, can be a bridge virtue or a bridge vice, depending upon the mathematics.

These examples, however, are oversimplified. Bidding is not so accurate that a player can often know his contract will depend solely upon winning a finesse. Even if, at double-dummy, the finesse would be the only possibility, the opponents' hands may be such that they cannot find their best line of defense, and the contract will succeed though the finesse may fail. Most experts realize that mathematically a nonvulnerable game should not be bid in reliance upon finding a 3-3 suit break, but seldom does the expert particularly care. He knows how often he can overcome a less favorable break, and he bids the game anyway.

Somewhat more dependence is placed upon mathematical considerations in deciding whether or not to bid a slam, it being assumed that game could surely be made. The mathematical advisability of the bid may vary with conditions of vulnerability and with the denomination—minor suit, major suit, or no-trump—to be played; but the variance is insignificant. The expert has learned that he needs anything better than a 50-50 chance to bid a small slam.

An example in which neither side is vulnerable may serve as well as any other to illustrate the procedure.

North-South can make five clubs, not vulnerable. They will make six clubs if a finesse succeeds. The finesse, of course, has a 50 percent probability of success. Should six clubs be bid?

North-South stand to *gain* 500 points, the slam bonus, by bidding six clubs—if the finesse wins.

North-South stand to *lose* 350 points (game value) plus 100 (trick-score) plus 50 points (penalty) by bidding six clubs—if the finesse loses. The total is 500.

It is therefore immaterial whether North-South bid six clubs or stop at five. They are offered a 50-50 bet on a 50-50 chance; if they do bid six clubs they might as well be matching coins or cutting cards on a sheer gamble.

It would be the same if North-South needed to win two finesses out of three, another 50-50 chance.

In a major suit or at no-trump, the risk is slightly greater than the possible gain—550 as against 500—and theoretically North-South should not bid the slam if it depends wholly upon winning a finesse. But there is always the possibility of the opponents' making a poor opening lead, or slipping in some other respect.

Nevertheless it is not the expert's practice to bid any slam whose success depends on a finesse. Psychologically a losing slam may have a bad effect on partner. He may take wild chances to make good the loss.

Here as elsewhere, the human element must be considered. An expert will bid a close slam if he knows his opponents to be poor players who may drop a trick in their defense. He will bid a doubtful slam if he has a good partner against weaker opponents, for if the slam fails he will still have the good partner.

THE QUESTION OF THE GRAND SLAM

A grand slam try is mathematically a good bet if the odds are somewhat better than 2 to 1 in favor of making it, but psychologically it is the worst risk of all and few experts will undertake much less than a sure-thing grand slam except when playing with an equally expert partner.

Not vulnerable, if you can make a small slam in a major suit you will score 500 slam bonus, 180 trick score; 300 value of game, total about 1,000 points. Bidding and making a grand slam will add only 500 points, the difference between the 500-point small slam bonus and the 1,000-point grand slam bonus, the other scores remaining the same. Bid the grand slam and go down one and you lose nearly 1,100 points—the 1,000 points you could have scored plus the undertrick penalty. The ratio of risk to gain is 1,100 to 500, or 2+ to 1, and you need a 2+ to 1 chance of making. Add in the psychological considerations and you need at least 3 to 1. A grand slam bid should never be made dependent on winning a finesse, or even on getting a 3-2 break in an eight-card combined trump suit (odds 68 to 32, or slightly better than 2 to 1).

Vulnerable, the score for a small slam is at best 750 + 500 +

180 or 190, total 1,430; the gain by bidding a grand slam is 750 (difference between 750 and 1,500 bonus), and the risk is the value of the small slam plus 100 or more points in undertrick penalties, total 1,500+ points. Again the mathematical ratio is 2 to 1, and an expert wants at least a 3 to 1 chance before he bids the grand slam. The psychological hazard is even greater because partner will see himself losing the rubber, not merely a game and small slam.

THE FIVE-OR-SEVEN HAND

The mathematical basis of slam bidding changes entirely on a type of hand, frequently encountered, called the five-or-seven hand.

NORTH
♠ K J 6 3
♡ 5
◇ A Q J 10 6 5
♣ 7 2

WEST
♠ 5
♡ Q 10 8 3
◇ K 8 2
♣ K Q J 8 3

EAST
♠ 9 8
♡ K J 9 7 6 2
◇ 9 4
♣ 10 9 4

SOUTH
♠ A Q 10 7 4 2
♡ A 4
◇ 7 3
♣ A 6 5

South plays a spade contract. West opens the king of clubs. If the diamond finesse wins, South can make seven spades. If the diamond finesse loses, South cannot make six spades. Obviously North-South should stop at four or bid seven, but any intermediate bid is unintelligent because it accepts the maximal risk in exchange for less than the maximal gain.

INFLUENCE OF THE SCORING LAWS

The influence of the scoring table on bidding tactics is profound and decisive, for the scoring table determines the objectives of contract bridge bidding. These are:

1] *Safety*—for the undertaking of any bid entails a risk of under-trick penalties if the contract is not made.

2] *Game*—for only by bidding a game can the partnership profit in addition to the trick score.

3] *Slam*—for a successful slam contract again adds bonus points to the trick points.

Of these objectives, the game is of first and paramount importance. It is a positive goal, whereas safety is a negative goal; that is, when a player tries for game he is trying to win points, whereas when he seeks safety he is trying only to avoid losing points. Also, game is the first goal in sequence. As between two part-score contracts that can be made, it matters little which is finally settled on; but a player must reach a game before he can bid a slam. Finally, the game is the goal most frequently attainable. More than 50 percent of all deals will result, if properly bid and played, in a game for one side or the other, whereas fewer than 5 percent will yield a slam. The expert's first thought in bidding is, "Can I make a game?" and his first and automatic analysis of any deal is, "There is a game in it" or "There is not a game in it."

There is constant conflict between the goal of game and the goal of safety. However powerful an incentive game may be, penalties are almost an equally powerful threat. Suppose the bidding to be:

SOUTH	WEST	NORTH	EAST
1 ♣	Pass	1 ◇	Pass

and South holds:

♠ Q J 5   ♡ A 3   ◇ J 2   ♣ A K Q 6 4 3

What shall be South's rebid? South has a reasonable hope of winning eight tricks in his hand, and if his partner can supply one trick—not too ambitious an expectation—a game may be made at no-trump. On the basis of this hope South wishes to make a strong rebid. But all these expected tricks are contingent upon North's holding certain cards. In the fear that North may not hold these cards, South hesitates to commit himself to a game contract. Consider that North may hold either of the following hands:

	1.		2.	
	♠ K 6 3		♠ 8 7 6 3	
	♡ Q J 7		♡ Q 6 5	
	◇ Q 7 6 4 3		◇ K Q 6 4 3	
	♣ 9 2		♣ 2	

If South chooses the goal of safety and contents himself with a rebid of two clubs, and if North holds hand No. 1, North will pass and a game will be lost, whereas North would have raised a two no-trump rebid. But if South, choosing the goal of game, does bid two no-trump, and if North holds hand No. 2, North will raise to three no-trump and a three- or four-trick penalty may result, whereas a two-club contract could have been made.

Fear is another vicious influence on the bidder. Suppose South opens with one spade, West overcalls with two hearts, North doubles and East holds:

♠ 7 5 3   ♡ ———   ◇ Q J 9 8 6 4   ♣ 8 7 5 2

East, fearing the penalty at two hearts, often seeks to rescue with a three-diamond bid—a bid he would never make except for the double, yet which is rendered all the more dangerous when, by doubling, North has shown his partner that he has some dependable trick-taking power.

The costliest mistakes in expert bidding come of an unwillingness to pass, whether it is greed, fear or system that fathers the impulse to bid. A bid impelled by greed may trade a profit for a loss, while a bid impelled by fear may turn out to be a move from the frying-pan to the fire.

SACRIFICE BIDDING

For many years no one but the experts understood the principle of sacrifice bidding. The average player—like the wholly untutored player even today—considered it mildly disgraceful to bid any contract and fail to make it.

The spread of duplicate bridge enlightened the bridge masses, and now nearly all players (at least, all players capable of reading this book) understand the paradox by which one can lose points and still show a profit.

Briefly, the justification of the sacrifice principle is this:

Every contract fulfilled has a certain point value to the successful bidders. It is always worth while to submit to a penalty rather than let a contract be made by the opponents, provided the point value of the penalty does not exceed the point value of the opponents' contract.

Suppose a case in duplicate bridge in which North-South, vulnerable, bid four spades and can make it. East-West are not vulnerable and can win eight tricks with diamonds as trumps. If East-West bid five diamonds they will be doubled and will go down three.

If East-West pass they will lose 120 points trick score plus 500 points game bonus, a total of 620. If East-West bid five diamonds they will be set 500 points, an actual gain of 120.

This comparison is simply made at duplicate, when the full value of every contract is immediately scored. It is not so obvious at rubber bridge, where the actual value of many contracts is greater than the number of points immediately scored.

If North-South can make two spades, for a trick score of 60 points, it might appear in rubber bridge that East-West would lose by bidding three diamonds and going down 100 points. Actually East-West would show a profit because a part-score has an additional value at least sufficient to make the two-spade contract worth—as it is in duplicate—somewhat more than 100 points. Good rubber bridge players willingly go down 200 points to prevent their opponents' getting a part-score.

The exact hidden value of a part-score is indeterminable. A part score does not substantially increase the prospect of scoring a game—statistics on about 2,000 deals indicated that only one in seven part-scores results in a game that would not have been made anyway—but if properly exploited it may often force the opponents into unsound contracts. The unscored value of making a game is easier to calculate. (See the discussion of these values on page 349.)

Considering any single hand, it cannot pay to go down more than 500 points to prevent an opposing game. This does not mean, however, that it cannot pay to risk more than 500 points, even when the opponents are by no means sure to make a game. The following hand is an excellent opening bid of four diamonds, even when vulnerable:

♠ 8   ♡ 62   ♢ KQJ97543   ♣ 96

The hand may win only seven tricks, and go down 800 points— in freak cases it may go down 1,100 or even 1,400—but such a contingency depends upon finding partner with a worthless hand, the diamonds bunched behind the declarer, and the opponents in a doubling mood. The expert observes that he gains from the bid more often than he loses, and he makes the bid no matter what the analysts may tell him.

It is not necessarily important that a bid gains on nine hands out of ten, or that it loses on nine hands out of ten. The question is, how much does it gain (or lose) on the nine? how much does it lose (or gain) on the tenth? A bid that gains 50 points per hand on nine hands and loses back 500 on the tenth is a losing bid.

Not mathematics but experience must determine the soundness of such bidding. Unconsciously, the expert retains the impression of what has happened over a series of ten, twenty, or fifty hands on which a given bidding technique was used; and of whether he has shown a net gain or a net loss from its use. In his unconscious computation the expert must observe not only what happens when he uses the bid in question, but also what would have happened had he not used it. It is by this unconscious recollection of past events that the expert usually determines the advisability of his sacrifice bids and of obstructive bids that may be the more effective when they are mathematically unsound.

Simplicity and convenience are considerations that modify the dictates of mathematics in bidding. It is proper to take greater chances in game-bidding when both sides are vulnerable than in any other vulnerability conditions, but no such distinction is made in expert bidding. Not even the most experienced partnership could conveniently adjust itself to so constantly changing a set of standards.

There is a psychological barrier to the use of many bids that are, in practice, profitable. It is a barrier that always deters the average player and is not without its effect upon the expert. A bid that would pay well in the long run but occasionally results in an 1,100-point loss will usually be dropped from use. Even the expert is too impressed by the one tragic failure to remember a slow accumulation of smaller profits.

INSURANCE

Valuation methods are not often so accurate that a player can know exactly how many tricks the respective sides can win at a given contract. A good player often essays a bid that will surely lose points in preference to a pass that may gain points, because of a disproportion in quantities.

Suppose the opponents bid a vulnerable slam worth 1,430. You believe you can defeat the slam, earning a plus score of 100; but if you are wrong you will lose the 1,430. If you make a sacrifice bid of six or seven you will surely go down 100 or 200 points, but that is all you can lose.

A pass is in effect a bet of 5 to 1 or as much as 7 to 1 that you will beat the slam. If you think the opponents might make their slam one time in six or seven tries you are better off to sacrifice and limit your loss.

This is called "taking out insurance." You pay a premium of 100 or 200 points to guard against the larger loss.

South's bid in the following deal was an insurance bid. In this case it paid.

NORTH
♠ 8 5 3
♡ 8 5 4
◇ J 8 5
♣ K 6 4 2

WEST
♠ A Q 7 6 4 2
♡ A Q 10 9 6 2
◇ ———
♣ 7

EAST
♠ K J 10 9
♡ J 2
◇ Q 10 7 6 2
♣ 9 3

SOUTH
♠ ———
♡ K 7
◇ A K 9 4 3
♣ A Q J 10 8 5

West dealt. East-West were vulnerable. The bidding was:

WEST	NORTH	EAST	SOUTH
1 ♠	Pass	2 ♠	2 N.T.
6 ♠	Pass	Pass	7 ♣
Double	Pass	Pass	Pass

South trusted to the assumption, usually dependable, that West would not have bid six spades if he had not expected to make it, for West might have bought the contract at a lower and surer level.

If West could make six spades, South would lose about 1,400 points (in rubber bridge depending on whether West had honors, in duplicate bridge exactly 1,430 points). South accepted a probable loss of 100 to 700 points less 100 honors to avoid this risk.

West might have achieved the maximum of two tricks down, 300 points, if he had made a different opening lead; but West made his safest lead, the heart ace, which won the first trick and defeated the contract immediately. Then West led the spade ace.

South trumped with the club eight, saving the five in case he needed an extra entry to dummy. The club queen was cashed and the club ten led to dummy's king.

On the lead of the diamond five from dummy, East played the deuce. South followed through on his previous assumption that West could make six spades, and since West had revealed one club loser, West had to be void in diamonds. So South played low, the diamond five won the trick, and the remaining tricks were safely South's, with two trumps left in dummy to take care of South's two other small diamonds.

Putting up the diamond ten on dummy's lead of the five would not have gained a trick for East. Having saved the five of clubs, South could get back to dummy to lead the jack and catch East's queen.

The net score was zero—down 100 offset by 100 honors. It was cheap insurance.

How about West's refusal to take out insurance, when he doubled seven clubs instead of bidding seven spades (or letting East do it)?

West risked a loss of more than 1,500 points if South's distribution were 7-6-0-0—an unlikely contingency but one that has been known to occur. West surrendered a chance to score more than 2,200 points, for if North opened any suit but clubs West could have made seven spades.

The insurance premium, if West had bid seven spades, would have been only 100 or 200 points, the amount he would have lost by going down one.

In the long run West would profit by bidding seven spades.

4

A PRACTICAL VIEW OF
BIDDING THEORY

ALL BRIDGE experts, however many thousands they number, grasp the theory underlying the play of the cards. Only a few hundred are thoroughly versed in the theory of bidding.

The latter are often at a loss to understand how they can ever have difficulty in defeating provincial opponents who violate bidding theory with almost every breath. In this feeling the top-notchers seriously overestimate the practical importance of bidding theory.

An understanding of bidding theory is not always essential to good bidding. It is essential to "perfect" bidding, but perfection in bidding, like perfection in any human undertaking, is itself something that exists only in theory. From a practical standpoint, bids that are theoretically unsound are frequently as effective as bids that are theoretically unexceptionable. For example:

♠ A Q 8 5 2   ♡ A J 8   ◇ 10 8   ♣ K Q 6

Assume that North holds this hand, and hears South, his partner, make an opening bid of one spade. Any player who is capable of accurate hand valuation—as all experts are—can see that a slam is quite probable. How the player goes about trying for the slam is seldom important. Among experts whose grasp of theory is scant, the bidding may be:

SOUTH	WEST	NORTH	EAST
1 ♠	Pass	3 ♠	Pass
4 ♠	Pass	5 ♠	

From the standpoint of theory, North's raise to three spades is incorrect, even though the double raise is treated as a game-

366

forcing bid. A double raise is a limited bid, showing a maximum of 16 points in combined high-card and distributional values. North has 16 points in high cards alone and should fake a response of three clubs to show that his strength is not limited.

From the standpoint of theory, North's five-spade bid is impossible; it is highly inconsistent; it is "trap bidding."

From the practical standpoint it is unlikely that the bid will do any damage. Occasionally South will go on to six spades and make it, occasionally South will pass and will make the five-spade contract. No better result than these could be achieved by the more refined methods of those experts who understand the theory behind their bids.

Nevertheless knowledge of bidding theory has its value. There will be some cases, few but important, when the South player in the above example will pass five spades and go down one. He would have made a game if theoretically sound bidding had stopped him at a four-spade contract. Other factors being equal, occasional dividends of this sort over a series of many hands are sufficient to give 99½ percent of the big championships to ½ of 1 percent of the expert players.

The following is comedy bidding, but in its hyperbole it serves to emphasize the consequences of bids made in ignorance or in disregard of theory.

South	North
1 ♠	1 N.T.
2 ♠	2 N.T.
3 N.T.	4 N.T.
5 N.T.	6 N.T.

The humorous aspect of this bidding is in its cadence when one reads it aloud. The significance of the bidding is in its flouting of theory. South's two-spade bid should have shown a fairly weak hand; North's one no-trump bid should have shown a fairly weak hand. How could a player with a weak hand make a slam try? How could the combination of two weak hands produce twelve tricks at no-trump? The contract was doubled and down five.

In an expert game in which one of the four players is stronger on bidding theory than the others, the superior player will frequently make profitable doubles when his hand seems by no means to warrant doubling. His explanation will be, "I didn't like the bidding." This remark may be paraphrased to read, *I have detected a contradiction, a basic inconsistency, in my opponents' bids.* A good player might reasonably have doubled six no-trump, in the preceding example, on no other justification than the apparent aimlessness of the bidding. In the following example such a double paid 500 points.

South	West	North	East
1 ♡	Pass	1 ♠	Pass
1 N.T.	Pass	2 ◇	Pass
2 ♡	Pass	2 ♠	Pass
2 N.T.	Pass	3 ◇	Pass
3 N.T.	Double		

West doubled on

♠ 6 3   ♡ K J 7 4   ◇ J 10 9 3   ♣ K Q 6

West had 10 points and his partner had not bid. No bridge book could dare advise a double on 10 points (or 2 honor-tricks).

But though the strength of West's hand suggested no double, the bidding did. South's bidding was originally weak; North's bidding throughout disclosed unwillingness to raise no-trump. If South realized the implications of North's bids, and was nevertheless strong enough to bid three no-trump, he must have underbid his hand to begin with.

This is a case in which a little learning is most dangerous, for West would probably not have doubled ignorant opponents on identical bidding. The inexpert player, who is not always capable of proper hand valuation, often underbids a hand that has game possibilities. The expert almost never does.

So, confronted by inconsistent bidding that proves his opponents were either underbidding originally or overbidding ultimately, the acute expert may assume that good opponents have done the latter but that weak opponents may have done either.

5

BASIS OF PARTNERSHIP BIDDING

OF ALL factors that influence bidding theory, the partnership factor is least appreciated, though it should be the most easily understood. It is the partnership factor that produces this basic tenet of bidding theory: *Each partner can speak for himself; therefore each partner must be permitted to speak for himself.* There must be no attempt to usurp each partner's prerogative of bidding his own cards.

Any bid entails some risk. To compensate for this risk, the bidder must have some strength. The least extent of his strength is determined by logic but is so well established that it has become conventional. Every bid—except certain responses to forcing bids—guarantees some conventional "minimum." *Each player is supposed to bid only on the values in his own hand plus the minimum he may assume—on the basis of previous bids—in his partner's hand.*

If the partner has more than the minimum previously guaranteed, it is assumed he will bid again. This principle may be evoked in the bidding of the following hand:

$$\spadesuit \text{ A Q 4} \quad \heartsuit \text{ K 6} \quad \diamondsuit \text{ K Q 6} \quad \clubsuit \text{ A J 7 5 3}$$

On this hand the expert of any class bids one club. Suppose his partner responds one diamond.

The expert who is weak on bidding theory is accustomed next to jump to three no-trump. His partner need have only A-x-x-x-x in diamonds and a queen or perhaps even a J-10 outside to produce an acceptable play for the game. It is reasonable to assume this much strength in the partner's hand, and the game will usually be made.

Nevertheless the theoretically correct rebid is two no-trump. If the partner does hold $\diamondsuit$ A x x x x and an outside queen or J-10, he will raise to three no-trump. If his holding is any less, the three no-trump contract probably cannot be made.

On this reasoning the rebid of three no-trump is indefensible. It stands to accomplish nothing the two no-trump rebid would not equally well have accomplished. It stands to lose in those cases in which it results in a penalty that would not have been suffered at two no-trump.

Suppose the foregoing hand to occur when the cards have been dealt as follows:

WEST	EAST
♠ A Q 4	♠ K 7 6 2
♡ K 6	♡ Q 8
◇ K Q 6	◇ A 8 7 4 2
♣ A J 7 5 3	♣ Q 4

West having bid one club and East one diamond, if West's rebid is three no-trump, East should bid a slam. By a three no-trump rebid West would, in effect, say, "I expect a good chance for game even if you have the minimum on which you could have made the one-diamond response."

If West had such a hand—with his club suit headed by A-K, perhaps—the slam should be made with ease. When West does not have such a hand, East's slam bid will be beaten and a game will be lost.

Such bids as a jump to three no-trump on West's hand, which would be the attempt of one player to bid his partner's cards as well as his own, lead to most partnership misunderstandings in expert games. At the root of these particular misunderstandings is a more general one, a fallacious belief that an expert should visualize his partner's hand and bid on the strength of it.

The premise is correct, the conclusion wrong. The expert should seek to visualize his partner's hand, and should then make his bidding sympathetic to his partner's problems, but he must not bid on his partner's cards. His partner, working from knowledge and not conjecture, is better able to do that for himself.

This does not necessarily mean that a player should never bid on the hope of finding unrevealed values in his partner's hand.

Sometimes a keen realization of probabilities will dictate a sheer gamble on finding partner with specific strength that his previous bidding has by no means revealed. For example:

♠ K Q J 8 6 5 3   ♡ Q 3   ◇ A K 5 3   ♣ ———

The holder of this hand bids one spade; this is overcalled with two clubs, his partner passes, and his right-hand opponent raises to three clubs. The hand shown justifies a rebid of four spades, vulnerable or not.

For the four-spade contract some assistance is required, and it is true that no assistance is ever guaranteed by a partner who does nothing but pass. But the required assistance may consist in many forms that are not biddable by partner—the queen of diamonds; or a doubleton diamond and 10-x in spades; or the J-10 of diamonds and the king of hearts; or miscellaneous cards that happen to "fit." Holding such cards would not have warranted a bid over the two-club overcall, wherefore there is still a chance that partner may hold them. Surely half the time partner will have something to assist the four-spade contract, and this expectancy justifies a try for game.

South's decision was made in this deal:

NORTH
♠ 10 9
♡ 10 8 7 5 2
◇ Q 8
♣ Q 10 7 6

WEST
♠ A 4
♡ K 6
◇ J 10 6 2
♣ A K J 8 2

EAST
♠ 7 2
♡ A J 9 4
◇ 9 7 4
♣ 9 5 4 3

SOUTH
♠ K Q J 8 6 5 3
♡ Q 3
◇ A K 5 3
♣ ———

South dealt, neither side was vulnerable, and the bidding went:

SOUTH	WEST	NORTH	EAST
1 ♠	2 ♣	Pass	3 ♣
4 ♠	Double	Pass	Pass

West opened the king of clubs.

South ruffed the first club and played the queen of diamonds and then cashed the ace of diamonds. Now he ruffed his small diamond. When next he played spades, West won and gave his partner a diamond ruff, defeating the contract.

After ruffing his small diamond in dummy, South should have returned to his hand via a club ruff and ruffed his diamond king with the spade ten. Then he could have lost only two hearts and the ace of trumps.

There was a chance to make this contract even if West opened the ace and another spade. South should win in dummy and lead a low heart. If the defenders do not switch to diamonds soon enough—for example if East takes his heart ace and leads a club —a squeeze develops on West. South runs all his spades and West must throw a diamond to save his club or club and heart stoppers.

RESTRICTIONS ON BIDS

The guiding principle in partnership bidding should then be expressed as follows: A player must not make a bid in dependence upon cards his partner may hold, *if his partner, holding those cards, could reasonably be expected to make the bid for himself.*

In the case of high cards and measurable distributional strength, partner can recognize and bid his own values. There should be no gambling on finding aces and kings, or trump length, in partner's hand. A gambling bid is justified only when it seeks to find distinctly unbiddable values in partner's hand.

The partnership factor exerts much restraint on bidding. Each bid must be made in full awareness of the message it will carry to the partner, and in full preparation for any action partner may take on the strength of that message.

The fact that some contract is superior may not be sufficient excuse for bidding it. Holding the following hand, when his partner makes an opening bid of one spade, a player may feel fairly sure that two diamonds would be a better contract than one spade:

♠ ——— ♡ 7 5 3 ◇ 10 9 7 6 4 3 2 ♣ 8 7 5

Nevertheless he must pass. He cannot bid two diamonds, for his partner would have no way of knowing that the two-diamond bid is designed only to provide a safer contract. The consequence of the two-diamond bid might be a final contract of two or three spades, or of four diamonds, which would be far more dangerous than one spade. In these circumstances, the best contract, two diamonds, is unattainable. If the opponents so will, the hand must be played at an inferior one-spade contract. If this be a weakness in expert bidding methods, at least it is a proper subordination to the more important partnership factor; and experience in play has not shown the passing of such hands to be ultimately costly.

6

OBSTRUCTIVE BIDDING

THE MAJOR object in the building of any bidding system is to permit valuable information to be supplied to the bidder's partner and at the same time withheld from his opponents. Fortunately for the system maker, the achievement of this apparent paradox is not overwhelmingly difficult.

Undeniably an exchange of information between partners is necessary. There are few cases in which one partner alone can decide the best final contract.

1. ♠ A K 10 9   2. ♠ K Q J 10 9 8 7
   ♡ A K 8 4   ♡ 8 3
   ◇ A Q J 10   ◇ 7 5
   ♣ 6   ♣ 5 3

The player who holds hand No. 1 is willing to insist on reaching a game, but he must know his partner's distribution before he can decide the suit at which the contract is to be played.

The player who holds hand No. 2 is willing to insist on spades as the trump suit, but he must know his partner's high-card strength before he can decide how high to go.

For these choices precise information is not necessary. The partners need not waste time seeking absolute assurance that they can make game. A game should be bid when there is but a fair (50% ±) chance that it will be made. If it appears that game should not be bid, it is desirable to stop at the lowest safe contract, and the two partners need not know whether they will win seven, eight, or nine tricks. As between two or more prospective trump suits, it is enough merely to know which is best, and there need be no effort to determine the exact length and strength of each.

The information exchanged between partners sometimes is purposely kept vague. This does not prevent their reaching the most desirable contract, and it permits them to devote a part of their bidding energy to the thwarting of their opponents.

The essential requirement of every bid in contract bridge is that it be obstructive. When a partnership has the superior cards, it may choose its bids so as to mislead, or at least so as not to assist, the opponents' defense. When a partnership's cards are inferior to, or no better than, their opponents' cards, they must so bid as to discourage or hamper their opponents' bidding.

DEFINITION OF OBSTRUCTIVE BIDS

An opening bid or response is satisfactorily obstructive when it is dangerous to overcall it.

Overcalling is dangerous in direct proportion to the danger of being doubled; hardly ever is an appreciable loss suffered from playing an undoubled contract. The degree of danger of being doubled depends, in most cases, upon the number of tricks bid for. It would appear that it is no greater overbid to bid for seven tricks (one-odd) when able to win only five than to bid for ten tricks (four-odd) when able to win only eight. In either case, the result will be a two-trick penalty. In practice, however, the former is no overbid because it will not be doubled; the latter is an overbid because it will be doubled.

Assume that a player, in overcalling, undertakes a contract he cannot make. He will be doubled almost invariably if his overcall is a four-bid; usually, if it is a three-bid; frequently, if it is a two-bid; and almost never if it is a one-bid.

An opening bid or response of two or more odd tricks is inherently obstructive. Often it does not leave the opponents time enough to discover their best trump suit and the extent of their combined strength. Thus they are doubly handicapped: To overcall is dangerous and must be balanced by a chance to find a profitable contract they can make; therefore to overcall is futile even when there is a contract they can make, if they are unable to reach that contract. Faced with such a doubtful choice, they frequently decide not to bid. Consider again these hands (from page 88):

WEST	EAST
♠ A 9 7 4 2	♠ 10 8 6 3
♡ A K 10 8 6	♡ 7 5
◇ K 6	◇ A Q 4 2
♣ 9	♣ 8 6 5

Suppose South, not vulnerable, makes an opening bid of four clubs. West may suspect that his side can make four-odd in whichever major suit East can better support. For West to show both his suits, however, would require two bids. This would necessitate a contract of five-odd, which might go down. For West to attempt, by guessing, to select the best suit would be equally dangerous. Finally, there is the danger that East can support neither suit, and that North can double and severely penalize any overcall. West may find in these circumstances that it is safer merely to double South's four-club bid. If East passes, East-West will probably collect a penalty of 300 points, perhaps less 100 honors —poor pay for the spade game they could have reached and made if South had passed.

To the two-, three-, four-, and higher bids that stand as inherently obstructive must be added the bid of one no-trump. For one thing, a two-bid is required to overcall it; but even more important is the manner in which it increases the danger of being doubled.

NORTH
♠ 8 4
♡ 8 5 4 2
◇ K 9 4 2
♣ Q 7 4

WEST	EAST
♠ Q 9 7 2	♠ A 10
♡ J 10 3	♡ K Q 6
◇ J 6 5	◇ Q 10 8 7
♣ K 10 9	♣ A J 5 3

SOUTH
♠ K J 6 5 3
♡ A 9 7
◇ A 3
♣ 8 6 2

If East should make an opening bid of one club or one diamond, South may overcall with a bid of one spade, and West will hardly double. For all West knows, East may have a worthless singleton in spades, and North-South will have enough spade strength to make the contract with ease.

If East should make an opening bid of one no-trump, South cannot overcall it with a bid of two spades; for not only would the contract be one trick higher, but West's double would become automatic. West would know, from the no-trump bid, that East holds some spade strength. A two-spade overcall would be doubled and would go down three tricks, 500 or 800 points.

For this reason South dare not overcall a no-trump bid; yet consider the possible consequences to South of his failure to overcall. If the West and North hands were exchanged, East-West could make one no-trump while North-South could make two spades. By his failure to overcall South would lose 40 points plus the value of the part-score, instead of scoring 60 points plus the value of the part-score—an ultimate difference of perhaps 300 points. Such is the value, in this case, of the obstructive function of East's opening bid.

WHY ONE-BIDS ARE GIVEN A WIDE RANGE

The inherently obstructive bids are only occasionally available. In most hands that are strong enough to bid, the trump suit is too uncertain or the hand is too weak to bid more than the allowed minimum. This means a one-bid in a suit; and the one-bid is not high enough to be inherently obstructive. It does not sufficiently discourage an overcall; it does not rob the opponents of the bidding rounds they need to find their best trump suit. Yet the one-bid, to meet the test of a proper systemic bid, must in some way be made obstructive.

What cannot be done by force can often be done by indirection. In the case of the opening one-bid, the purpose is accomplished by creating uncertainty in the opponents' minds. When the opponent must guess, he may guess wrong; and often, rather than risk the consequences of incorrect action, he will take no action at all. To create this uncertainty, to necessitate this guess, the opening one-bid is given as wide a range as possible.

In general expert practice, either of the following hands would be opened with a bid of one heart:

1.	♠ 6	2.	♠ A 3
	♡ A K 8 6 5 3		♡ A Q J 7 2
	◊ Q J 5		◊ A K 8 3
	♣ 8 4 2		♣ Q 7

Suppose South has made an opening bid of one heart; West, his opponent, must consider whether or not to overcall.

If South holds hand No. 1, West can probably overcall without serious risk of having to play his contract doubled. If South holds hand No. 2, an overcall by West may result in a double and a disastrous penalty.

This uncertainty alone is a serious deterrent upon West, but far more important to West is this: Without knowing the nature of the opening hand, he cannot gauge the extent of his possible gain. If hand No. 1 prompted South's bid, it is quite possible that East-West can reach and make a game, and this possibility justifies some risk. If hand No. 2 prompted South's bid, game is entirely out of the question for East-West, and if West overcalls he will be in the position of having risked without hope of gain. The expert's psychological make-up being what it is, the unwarranted risk would be seriously detrimental to his self-respect if not to his bridge score.

This psychological factor should not be underestimated. The expert abhors a guess. It may be that he would gain in the long run by overcalling even when the overcall entails some risk—though in the early days of contract bridge weak overcalls were so consistently punished that they were soon abandoned—but the occasional large loss is always more impressive than a series of smaller gains. Thus, while the obstructive function of the one-bid is largely illusory, it is nonetheless effective.

The wide range given to opening one-bids is a matter of necessity as well as of strategy. A single bid cannot completely inform the partner—it can tell of high-card strength or of distribution, but not of both. Therefore the introductory bids are purposely kept vague, since they can be nothing else to partner and should be, ideally, nothing else to the opponents.

THE CODE BIDS

The "mathematical" systems disregard this tenet of theory and so lose much of their effectiveness. Consider the following bidding according to one of the systems in which the preliminary bids precisely define the hands on which they are made.

South	West	North	East
1 ♣	Pass	1 ♠	

Now, according to the "code bids" followed in such systems, South is known to have two aces and a king, or the equivalent; at most, three aces. North has an ace and a queen or the equivalent. East can read with entire confidence his partner's high-card holding, and may frequntly decide to enter the bidding in the secure knowledge that he cannot be caught and punished.

Consider the same bidding when one-bids in suits are given a wide instead of a narrow range. South and North have both bid, yet East knows almost nothing of their holdings. Either or both may be strong; either or both may be weak. If both are weak, they may be headed for a contract above their trick-taking potential, and for East to bid would rescue them; if both are strong, for East to bid would be dangerous. If their hands are but of average strength, for East to pass may cost his side a part-score, especially if East has some such borderline holding as

♠ 6   ♡ A Q 8 6 2   ◇ K 10 4 3   ♣ J 8 2

The bidding proceeds and still little light is thrown on the North-South holdings until it is too late:

South	West	North	East
1 ♣	Pass	1 ♠	Pass
2 ♠			

Now South has limited his hand to a certain extent, but there is still no information on North's hand; and West, though he knows South has no powerful holdings, cannot dare bid for fear

North's first bid has concealed a high-card holding of several tricks. Finally the uncertainty ends, but still not to the entire satisfaction of East:

South	West	North	East
1 ♣	Pass	1 ♠	Pass
2 ♠	Pass	Pass	

East now realizes that neither North nor South has a very strong hand; but by this time East is discouraged from overcalling simply because the auction has reached so high a level. Granted North-South are not very strong, does that necessarily mean East-West can win nine or more tricks?

Thus the unlimited one-bids are designed as a stopgap to confuse the opponents until, on the second round of bidding, those bids which are inherently obstructive come into use.

It may be argued that the "code bids" of the Italian and similar systems could be made similarly obfuscating if the code were frequently violated; that is, if a player with a strong holding occasionally made a bid purporting to show a weak hand. This argument is unexceptionable, but it is the same as the discredited argument for psychic bids, which have been generally abandoned: If bids were so used the partner would be equally deceived. The cost of the deception would be to hinder the bidding partners' efforts to reach their own best contract. The psychic bid plays a small part in any system but is singularly destructive in the code or artificial systems.

No code system ever succeeded against good opposition until the Italians, with a combination of good players, strict discipline, and floundering opposition, won a series of world championships. No one else has matched their successes and it appears wiser to rely on methods that are theoretically sound than on devices that have been effective only when employed by certain players.

THE REPLY TO THE WIDE RANGE OF ONE-BIDS

The obstructive value of the nearly unlimited low bid has proved to be so great that the expert's only defense is a reply in kind. The passes of the defending side are given almost as wide a range as the bids of the opening side. For example, South makes an opening bid of one diamond; West with the following hand is strong enough to overcall with relative safety, but he does not overcall, he passes.

♠ A K Q   ♡ 87   ◇ J 9 8 4   ♠ A K 4 2

The effect of the pass, from the direct standpoint, is this: North-South may, because of West's silence, overbid weak holdings and be doubled. If West entered the bidding immediately, then North-South could refrain from further bidding and could never be doubled.

The indirect value of the pass is this: The opening side is discouraged from too aggressive bidding, for fear its opponents may be lying in ambush. Thus the following holdings may fail to reach a game:

WEST	EAST
♠ 6 3	♠ A J 10 7
♡ A K Q 9 4 3	♡ 10 2
◇ K 10 3	◇ J 8 7
♣ K 5	♣ Q 6 4 3

West bids one heart, East one spade, West two hearts. East passes; what else can he do? Yet any expert, looking at the East-West hands and and knowing that it is profitable to be at game if there is almost a 50 percent chance to make it, would elect to play at three no-trump or four hearts rather than stop at a part-score.

If the passes of North and South were more a guarantee of weakness than in practice they are, East-West might reach their game. West could make a stronger rebid; two no-trump, for example, or three hearts. Or East could bid two no-trump over the two-heart rebid. It is the fear of finding partner expectedly weak, and an opponent expectedly strong, that discourages such aggressive bids.

Unhappy examples such as this one do not convert many experts to the code-bid systems but they have won many adherents to the systems (such as Acol in England, and the Vanderbilt and

Schenken systems) that place a low limit on the strength that can be shown by a one-bid. If West's opening one-heart bid had limited his hand to 15 points, as it would in some systems, West could have jumped to three hearts for his rebid without misrepresenting his hand.

The theory of deceptive-obstructive bidding is not repudiated by the code systems but it is not carried quite so far.

7

LIMITED AND UNLIMITED BIDS

LIMITED AND unlimited are relative terms in bridge. No two hands are exactly alike. Furthermore, the same hand may vary in strength between one bidding situation and another. A limited bid, then, does have some range; an unlimited bid does have certain limits. For purposes of definition, a bid is limited when the weakest hand on which it may be made, and the strongest hand on which it may be made, are no more than one trick apart; a bid is unlimited when its weakest and strongest examples may be more than one trick apart.

Thus: South opens the bidding with one heart. North, his partner, can hardly "limit" South's strength. South may have from a four- to an eight-card heart suit; he may have only two quick tricks but he may have five; he may have only 12 or 13 points but he may have 20 points; he may be unable to make his seven-trick contract without considerable assistance, but he may have enough playing strength to guarantee a ten-trick game without support. Actually there is a bottom limit to South's strength, and a top limit; but they are so far apart that practically the bid is unlimited, for it tells too little to give North any notion of the best final contract.

Ideally, any low bid should be unlimited and any high bid should be limited. The limited bid is always desirable, for it better informs the partner, and the information it gives should be forgone only for purposes of obstruction. The low bid cannot be made obstructive unless it is unlimited, but the high bid can.

Any high opening bid (three or more) is strictly limited. It may be a weak bid, like a shut-out four-spade bid; it may be a powerful bid, like a slam-try five-spade bid; it is still a limited bid. It must be noted that a limited bid is not necessarily weak, nor an unlimited bid necessarily strong.

A low bid should be unlimited because many holdings require

383

two or more bids before the partnership can proceed intelligently to a proper contract. The following example was previously cited (page 376):

♠ A 9 7 4 2
♡ A K 10 8 6
◇ K 6
♣ 9

It was found impossible to bid this hand adequately over an opening four-club bid. The hand suggests a series of two bids, one in spades, one in hearts, so that partner may choose between the suits. The first bid should be made at a low level, leaving room to make the second bid without risking a penalty.

It follows that any low bid carries the implication that the hand may have undisclosed strength, and that the bidding is purposely being kept low so that additional information may be given later.

This principle applies, however, only to a low bid in a suit that has not previously been bid. When a player reverts to a suit that has previously been bid, he clearly implies that he has found an acceptable trump suit and that further distributional information is unnecessary. In this circumstance, why not show the full strength of the hand?

1.	SOUTH	WEST	NORTH	EAST
	1 ♡	Pass	1 ♠	Pass
	2 ♡			
	(or 2 ♠)			

2.	SOUTH	WEST	NORTH	EAST
	1 ♡	Pass	1 ♠	Pass
	2 ◇			

In No. 1, South limits his hand far more strictly than he does in No. 2. If South in No. 1 were extremely strong, why should he not bid three or four hearts? or three or four spades? South can be interested in no other suit, for if he were he could have bid that suit. But South in No. 2 may have left much about his hand unspoken. He may have a club suit that he has not yet had time to show; he may be waiting to learn whether or not North can support hearts or diamonds, or rebid spades. It is not a certainty that

South in No. 2 has a strong hand, any more than it is ever a certainty that an opening bidder has a strong hand; but it is a possibility. South in No. 1 cannot have a very strong hand; he has made
a limited bid. Consequently North will make every effort to rebid
in No. 2 but will not fear to pass in No. 1.

Therefore any bid in a suit previously bid (by either partner)
is a limited bid; any bid in a new suit (not previously bid) is an
unlimited bid, as these terms were defined earlier in this section.
This means, it must be remembered, only that an unlimited bid
has a range of more than one trick.

FORCING AND NONFORCING DOUBLE RAISES

Theoretically no natural bid that limits the strength of a hand
should be forcing. If the bidder's partner knows what to expect,
he should be able and entitled to make his own decision.

A player limits his hand to some extent whenever he fails to
make the strongest bid he might make in the circumstances.

SOUTH	WEST	NORTH	EAST
1 ♡	Double	1 ♠	Pass

North's hand is limited by the fact that he did not redouble.
However strong North's later bids may sound, South must keep
this fact in mind. South may pass the one-spade bid, "one-over-
one" though it may seem, because North has limited his hand.
North cannot have more than 9 or 10 points (he probably has less)
and South may know that this is too little for game.

The Acol and other systems that use a nonforcing double raise
are sounder in theory than the Standard American system that
makes a double raise forcing to game. Being a bid in a suit previously bid, the double raise is limited; and being limited, it
should not be forcing.

American experts do use the double raise as forcing, but they
mean by this that it is forcing within limits. Its forcing effect is
based on the assumption that the opening bid was of conventional
strength. On rare occasions when the opening bid was a psychic,
the double raise can be passed, forcing or not. A jump in a new

suit, which is by definition unlimited, cannot be passed even if the opener did not have a genuine bid.

This distinction is kept in mind by the opener, even when he has a genuine bid (as he usually has) and the responder must not disappoint him.

	SOUTH	WEST	NORTH	EAST
1.	1 ♠	Pass	3 ♠	

	SOUTH	WEST	NORTH	EAST
2.	1 ♠	Pass	3 ◇	

Conventionally, North's two responses would appear to carry identical meanings. Both show strong hands; both are "forcing to game." But the former, the raise in the same suit, is a limited bid; the latter an unlimited bid. The expert does not make the double raise on a hand that is more than one trick (or 2 or 3 points) stronger than the possible minimum. True to the theory, he keeps the raise as a limited bid and uses the jump takeout when he needs an unlimited bid:

1.	2.
♠ K 8 7 5 2	♠ K Q 7 5 2
♡ A Q 6	♡ A K 6
◇ 8 4	◇ 8 4
♣ K 6 5	♣ A 6 5

Hand No. 1 would justify a double raise of partner's one-spade bid; therefore hand No. 2 would not. There is too great a range between the two hands for both to satisfy the requirements of a limited bid. Since no conventionally sound response is available on hand No. 2, the expert would respond with a jump to three clubs, conforming to theory and making an unlimited bid even at the expense of misinforming his partner as to his club holding.

NO-TRUMP BIDS AS LIMITED BIDS

Any bid in no-trump, whether an opening bid of one or more no-trump, a raise in no-trump, or a rebid or response in no-trump, is invariably a limited bid.

There is a basic theoretical justification for this. The only reason some bids must be unlimited is that it is impossible to show strength and distribution with the same bid. The no-trump bid describes its distribution and implies that it has no further distributional information to give. Therefore the quantity of the no-trump bid can and should show the full strength of the bidder's hand.

There is a further practical reason why any no-trump bid must be limited. No-trump is the easiest denomination for the opponents to double, which makes it too dangerous a bid to keep vague.

1.	SOUTH	NORTH		2.	SOUTH	NORTH
	1 ♠	2 ♠			1 N.T.	2 N.T.

In No. 1, North may gamble a bit to raise the opening spade bid. If South has a very strong hand, the raise may keep the bidding open to game; if South has a very weak hand he may pass *and the opponents probably cannot double.* Even if they have great power in aces and kings, the opponents must fear that North-South have enough trump length and distributional power to win eight tricks.

In No. 2, North cannot so gamble. If the raise proves to be unwise speculation on the strength of South's hand, North-South will be at the mercy of their opponents; for either of the opponents can safely double a no-trump contract with strength in any suit or suits.

Suppose South makes an opening bid of one no-trump; and suppose South's hand might be either of the following, or anything in between:

1.		2.	
♠	A Q 6	♠	A Q 6
♡	A 7 2	♡	A J 7
◊	J 8 5 3	◊	K 10 9 2
♣	K 5 4	♣	K Q 5

North, after the one no-trump bid, would have no notion what to do with the following hand:

♠ K 7 3   ♡ 10 3   ◊ Q 7 6 4   ♣ A 7 6 2

If North raises to two no-trump and South has hand No. 1, the opponents may double and collect a two- or three-trick penalty; but if in view of this danger North passes and South happens to have hand No. 2, the pass will surrender a sure game. This dilemma is precluded by so limiting the one no-trump bid that its strongest and weakest examples are never more than 2 points or ½ trick apart, wherefore the partner always knows whether or not he can profitably raise.

8

FORCED AND FREE BIDS

EVERY BID supposedly implies some minimum trick-winning strength. The implication of strength exists, however, only when the bid is made willingly and not perforce. Obviously a player needs no strength to bid when he is forced to bid. It takes no expert to detect the difference between the two following situations:

1. SOUTH	NORTH	2. SOUTH	NORTH
1 ♡	2 ♠	1 ♡	1 N.T.
2 N.T.		2 N.T.	

In No. 1 South had to bid, so he need have no more for his two no-trump bid than he had for his one-heart bid. In No. 2 South might have passed one no-trump, so his voluntary increase in the contract promises extra strength.

The amount of strength implied by any bid depends upon whether the bid is *forced* or *free*.

A *forcing* bid is a conventional command to partner. The adjectival form *forced*, however, applies not only to bids made in response to a command but also to bids made because partner has urged them or because it would be unsafe or unprofitable to pass. While only one of the three following situations is forcing, in each of them the last bid is a forced bid:

1. SOUTH	WEST	NORTH	EAST
1 ♠	Pass	3 ◇	Pass
3 ♠			

2. SOUTH	WEST	NORTH	EAST
1 ♠	Pass	1 N.T.	Pass
2 ♡	Pass	2 ♠	

3. SOUTH	WEST	NORTH	EAST
1 ♡	Pass	1 ♠	

In No. 1 South rebids in obedience to his partner's forcing bid. In No. 2 North may be rebidding only because, being offered a choice, he considers a spade contract safer than a heart contract. In No. 3 North may be responding only because he does not know how strong South's hand is and does not want to lose a chance for game in case South is exceptionally strong.

The distinction between a forced bid and a free bid is this: *A forced bid is made in dependence upon partner's hand. A free bid is based upon strength that the bidder has in his own hand and has not previously shown.*

In No. 1, South's bid of three spades did not mean that South's hand justified a nine-trick contract. North had already established the level of the contract. In No. 2, South had committed his side to an eight-trick contract in any event, and North's return to two spades was made in dependence upon South's previous commitment. In No. 3, North bid only after South had already expressed willingness to play for seven tricks.

The fact that a bid is made in a forcing situation does not necessarily make it a "forced bid." It is a forced bid only if it undertakes no risk that has not already been undertaken by partner. If it does accept additional risk, by unnecessarily increasing the contract or by undertaking an unnecessarily dangerous contract, it is a free bid, regardless of the situation in which it is made.

SOUTH	WEST	NORTH	EAST
1 ◇	Pass	2 ♣	Pass
2 ♠			
(free bid)			

South's rebid of two spades shows greater strength than South needed for his one-diamond bid. South was forced to make some rebid, it is true; but he was not forced to make a strength-showing rebid, nor one that would be dangerous if made on a weak hand. Therefore his two-spade rebid is a free bid.

A forced bid may be made even when holding additional strength.

SOUTH	WEST	NORTH	EAST
1 ♠	Pass	3 ♡	Pass
3 ♠			

South's rebid is forced, and he may have no more than a minimum opening bid. Yet he may have a powerful hand, and take this opportunity to show that his spades are strong enough to rebid. South's hand may be either of the following, or anything in between:

1. ♠ A Q 10 6 5   2. ♠ A K Q 8 6 4
    ♡ 9   ♡ J 3
    ◇ K Q 7 2   ◇ Q J 7
    ♣ 7 3 2   ♣ A 4

The distinction of the forced bid, however, is this: While North is aware that South may have hand No. 2, North must not depend upon finding anything better than hand No. 1. In fact, if South is a player who makes psychic bids, North must consider the possibility that the one-spade bid was a psychic. A forced bid may conceal values not previously shown, but it never guarantees them. *Every forced bid is a possible minimum.*

Consider the following bidding:

SOUTH	WEST	NORTH	EAST
1 ♠	Pass	2 ♣	Pass
2 ♠	Pass	3 ♡	Pass
4 ♡	Pass	5 ◇	Pass
5 ♡	Pass	6 ♡	Pass
Pass	Pass		

Discussing the bridge hand that was bid in this way, one expert may ask another, "What was the bidding on that hand?" and the other will reply, "One spade—six hearts." Many bids intervened between one spade and six hearts, but the experts understand each other perfectly. North might almost as well have bid the small slam directly over the opening one-spade bid. All of South's subsequent bids were forced bids and gave no greater impression of strength than had the one-spade bid. North's bids may have been correct, but if so he should have held something at least this strong:

♠ 6 3   ♡ A K Q 3   ◇ A   ♣ K Q 10 5 4 2

South's bidding did give some extra information: It showed that he could support a four-card heart suit. A forced bid always tells something about the bidder's distribution and the location of such strength as he has.

1.	SOUTH	WEST	NORTH	EAST
	1 ♡	Pass	1 ♠	Pass
	1 N.T.			

2.	SOUTH	WEST	NORTH	EAST
	1 ♡	Pass	2 ♣	Pass
	2 ♢			

In No. 1, South does not show additional strength by his no-trump rebid, but does imply that he has no-trump (balanced) distribution. In No. 2, South does not show additional strength but does say that part of the strength he has already shown is in diamonds.

While a forced bid never affirms additional values, it may deny them. Any forced bid that is not itself forcing denies the ability to make a stronger bid.

SOUTH	WEST	NORTH	EAST
1 ♠	Pass	3 ♡	Pass
3 ♠			

In this case, previously shown, while South's rebid does not affirm additional strength, neither does it deny it. North is sure to bid again, and South may be withholding information until a later turn. But in this case:

SOUTH	WEST	NORTH	EAST
1 ♠	Pass	1 N.T.	Pass
2 ♡	Pass	2 ♠	

South need not bid again, therefore North denies ability to make a free bid, such as a raise to three spades or three hearts, or a bid of two no-trump.

THE THEORY OF THE POSSIBLE MINIMUM

Properly defined, a forced bid is one that is made in compliance with partner's demand or request *and* that declines to guarantee values not previously shown. There are two situations in which a forced bid may be made.

1. *A forced bid may be made when partner has either demanded or urged that the bidding be kept open.*

Any bid that is conventionally forcing demands that the bidding be kept open. Unless, in keeping the bidding open, the partner goes out of his way to show additional values, his bid must be deemed a forced bid.

SOUTH	WEST	NORTH	EAST
1 ♠	Pass	3 ♠	Pass
4 ♠			

(forced bid)
or 3 N.T.
(forced bid)
but 4 ◇
(free bid)

North's forcing raise demands a game, and when South merely bids game he makes a forced bid. When South makes a bid that is unnecessary to the reaching of the game, and that gives information that can be of value only in reaching a slam, he makes a free bid and shows additional values.

Any bid so highly unlimited that it may conceal a game-going hand urges that the bidding be kept open. Therefore a response to such a bid is a forced bid.

In the Standard American System, with the one-over-one and two-over-one responses treated as forcing, the only such bid is the opening suit-bid of one. When one spade (or any other one-bid in a suit) is bid, the partner knows it may be weak but that it may likewise be very strong, either in high cards or in distribution; anything up to and including the following hands.

1. ♠ A K 6 3   2. ♠ K Q J 8 6 5
    ♡ A Q 10 2   ♡ A K Q 6 4
    ◊ J 3   ◊ 8 3
    ♣ A J 6   ♣ ————

If the one-spade bid was made on hand No. 1, game at no-trump or in a suit could be made with scanty support; if the one-spade bid was made on hand No. 2, game would require only three-card support in one of the major suits. Therefore the partner's obligation to keep the bidding open, while not absolute, is very strong. Any response that does no more than keep the bidding open is a forced bid.

SOUTH	WEST	NORTH	EAST
1 ♡	Pass	1 ♠	
		or 1 N.T.	
		or 2 ♡	

Any of North's responses may have been made solely through reluctance to pass; made, that is, because South's bid urged a response. Therefore any one of North's responses is a forced bid *and a possible minimum.*

The several responses are not identical in meaning. The spade response is unlimited, the heart raise and the no-trump response limited; the *usual* strength shown by the two-heart raise is greater than the *usual* strength shown by the no-trump response, in that the raise does at least promise a fit; but the three responses have in common the fact that they *may* be equally weak.

When there is no necessity to keep the bidding open any response is a free bid:

SOUTH	WEST	NORTH	EAST
1 ◊	1 ♡	1 ♠	
		or 2 ◊	
		or 1 N.T.	

West's overcall having already "kept the bidding open" (assured South a chance to rebid), North's bid in any case implies that *North* accepts the risk involved in the contract he names. In other words, that North makes a free bid.

There is no such thing as a forced bid over an opponent's intervening bid.

SOUTH	WEST	NORTH	EAST
1 ♠	Pass	3 ♣	3 ♦

Any bid South makes now is a free bid.

To deny additional strength when there has been an intervening bid, one need only pass.* A double, however, does not rank as a bid; it may be a sign of weakness:

SOUTH	WEST	NORTH	EAST
1 ♠	Pass	2 N.T.	3 ♦
Double			

South may be doubling because he fears for the success of any contract North may undertake, and wishes to forestall North's rebid. But the double does not deny additional strength in South's hand, for South may have a powerful hand on which he selects a double of three diamonds as the most lucrative contract.

PREFERENCE BIDS

2. *A forced bid may be made whenever partner has offered a choice between two or more contracts, of which one may be safer than the others.*

Any time a player bids two different suits he requests his partner to *show preference.* If his partner does no more than show which bid he prefers, he makes a forced bid.

SOUTH	WEST	NORTH	EAST
1 ♠	Pass	1 N.T.	Pass
2 ♥	Pass		

* The amount of "additional strength" shown, however, depends on partnership understanding. Increasingly players give free raises merely to confirm a fit in partner's suit and promising no high-card strength—a device suggested by the frequent necessity for sacrifice bids in duplicate bridge.

If North can better support one of South's suits than the other, he must not willingly permit South to play the inferior suit. North may pass if he prefers hearts, but must return to two spades if he prefers spades. A bid of two spades by North would therefore be a forced bid. To make a free bid North must raise; and while a bid of three hearts is a free bid, a jump to three spades is necessary to make an equivalent free bid and at the same time show preference for spades. If a choice of suits is given by means of a forcing bid—

South	West	North	East
1 ♠	Pass	1 N.T.	Pass
3 ♡	Pass		

—since North may not pass, he makes a forced bid whether he bids three spades or raises to four hearts. A jump to four spades, or a bid in diamonds or clubs to give information unnecessary to a game contract, would constitute a free bid.

AVOIDING AN UNSAFE CONTRACT

A choice between a suit and a no-trump contract is offered whenever a suit has previously been bid and raised, and a no-trump contract is then offered by one partner or the other.

1.	South	North	2.	South	North
	1 ♠	2 ♠		1 ♠	3 ♠
	2 N.T.	3 ♠		3 N.T.	4 ♠

In either case North may have to return to spades for no other reason than that he cannot safely pass the no-trump contract; therefore in either case North's last bid is forced and shows no values not already guaranteed.

Since a no-trump contract is inherently unsafe if played without support, a player may be "forced" to change a doubtful no-trump contract to a safer suit contract, even when no suit has been raised.

SOUTH	WEST	NORTH	EAST
1 ♠	Pass	1 N.T.	Pass
2 ♣ *or*			
2 ♠			

Though North's one no-trump response was neither forcing nor highly unlimited, South may have to return to a suit contract because his hand cannot support a no-trump contract.

Either of the two following hands would justify a suit rebid by South.

1.	♠ A Q 10 8 6 2	2.	♠ A 10 6 5 2
	♡ K J 6		♡ A 7 3
	◇ 9		◇ 5
	♣ Q 4 3		♣ K Q 4 3

Either the two-spade rebid, which would be made with hand No. 1, or the two-club rebid, which would be made with hand No. 2, is a forced bid and a possible minimum, though either may conceal some additional strength.

A double may evoke a forced bid, either because the double urges a bid or because it makes a pass dangerous:

1.	SOUTH	WEST	NORTH	EAST
	1 ◇	Double	Pass	1 ♠

2.	SOUTH	WEST	NORTH	EAST
	1 ♠	4 ◇	4 ♠	5 ◇
	Pass	Pass	Double	Pass
	5 ♡			

In No. 1 West's double conventionally expresses preparation to have East bid a weak hand, and East's one-spade bid guarantees nothing. In No. 2, South's bid of five hearts may have been made only to escape the danger of the opponents' makng five diamonds, and cannot be taken as a sign of additional strength.

THE FORCING PASS

Either a bid or a double may be a forced bid, and a possible minimum, when partner has made a forcing pass.

The forcing pass is made by a player who has shown such great strength that his side can surely make game or penalize the opponents.

SOUTH	WEST	NORTH	EAST
2 ◇	2 ♠	Pass	3 ♠
(forcing)			
Pass	Pass		

North must either bid or double, in this instance because South's two-diamond bid was forcing to game and game has not been reached. If North bids three no-trump, four diamonds, four hearts, on four clubs, he indicates his distribution but promises nothing in high cards.

North may hold:

1.	♠ K6	♡ 7532	◇ 7	♣ 1086532	*Three no-trump*
2.	♠ 8	♡ QJ9763	◇ 54	♣ J943	*Four hearts*
3.	♠ 87	♡ 10843	◇ 1063	♣ J754	*Four diamonds*
4.	♠ 8	♡ Q843	◇ 1076	♣ J7543	*Four diamonds*
5.	♠ 975	♡ 8643	◇ 6	♣ J7543	*Double*

Suppose the bidding continues:

SOUTH	WEST	NORTH	EAST
2 ◇	2 ♠	Pass	3 ♠
(forcing)			
Pass	Pass	4 ◇	4 ♠
		(forced)	
Pass	Pass		

Again North is forced to bid or double, because South showed so much strength by his opening bid that he must be able to beat

four spades—if he cannot make five diamonds. South's pass merely
states that he wishes North to make the decision. North may hold:

1.	♠ 8 7	2.	♠ 8	3.	♠ 8
	♡ 10 8 4 3		♡ Q 8 4 3		♡ 8 6 4 3
	◊ 10 6 3		◊ 10 7 6		◊ 8 5 4 2
	♣ J 7 5 4		♣ J 7 5 4 3		♣ 9 6 4 3

With No. 1, North doubles. He has too little to relish undertaking a five-diamond contract and he expects South to win at
least four tricks in top cards. With No. 2 or No. 3, North bids
five diamonds. He has enough support to expect the contract to
be made and it should be more profitable than defeating four
spades. The important thing is that South may not pass.

The forcing pass may result from strong bidding by the combined hands.

SOUTH	WEST	NORTH	EAST
1 ♣	2 ♡	3 ♡	Double
	(weak)		
3 ♠	Pass	4 ♠	5 ♡
Pass	Pass		

North must bid or double. South has not abandoned the contract. He has merely asked North to make the decision.

In either bidding situation North's bid (or double) is a forced
bid, promising no more than North could be expected to have in
the light of his previous bids or passes.

FREE BIDS AS SLAM TRIES

Any bid except a forced bid shows additional strength; therefore
a bid that is not forced may be read as a slam try when it is
above game.

SOUTH	WEST	NORTH	EAST
1 ♡	4 ◊	4 ♡	5 ◊
5 ♡	Pass		

West's four-diamond bid was a weak bid, and so might have been East's raise to five diamonds, especially if East-West were not vulnerable. But North's four-heart bid was a strong bid, for North would have no need to sacrifice in view of South's opening bid, which presumably showed enough defensive strength to defeat a high opposing contract.

Therefore a pass by South would have been forcing, requiring North to bid or double.

When South bid five hearts it was a free bid, promising extra values. South might have held:

♠ K 10   ♡ A Q 10 6 3   ◊ 5 4   ♣ A Q 6 3

A bid by a player who could have made a forcing pass is a strength-showing bid, and at the game level or higher it is a slam try.

North could bid six hearts on this hand:

♠ A 8 7 3   ♡ K J 9 7   ◊ K 3   ♣ K J 5

Like most five-bids made as slam tries, South's bid invited North to bid six only if North had at least second-round control of the opponents' suit, in this case diamonds.

The foregoing situation must not be confused with this one:

SOUTH	WEST	NORTH	EAST
1 ♠	4 ◊	4 ♡	5 ◊
Pass	Pass	5 ♡	Pass

Now South may not bid six hearts, whatever his hand. His forcing pass asked North to make the decision, North made it, and South must abide by it.

Any bid by South over five hearts would be an example of "trap bidding." North would be the trapped player. Consider North's problem *before* he bid five hearts. North might know he could make five hearts; but if North bid it he would lose because South might carry him to six, down one—and if North failed to bid it he would lose because he would miss the game he could make. North would be trapped—bound to lose whatever he did. To preclude such a contretemps, North must be accorded the assurance that South will pass.

9

THEORY OF THE STEP SYSTEM

IN 1934 A BRITISH bridge writer published a book on a bidding method that he called the "step system." * Each partner showed the strength of his hand by the number of bidding "steps" by which he increased his contract. Thus a one-heart response to a one-club bid would show a stronger hand than a one-diamond response, because the former increases the bidding level by two steps, the latter by only one.

The experts scoffed. They said, any suit-bid at a given level is the same as any other suit-bid at the same level. But they were guilty of a half-truth; and in the years that followed they learned to adopt a style of bidding that itself embraces a step system.

Every bidding level is subdivided into five steps. The one-odd level consists of one club, one diamond, one heart, one spade, and one no-trump; every other level is similarly subdivided. Bidding should be so designed as to conserve these steps. In his interpretation of another player's bid, one must consider whether it is conservative or profligate of steps.

In the early stages of the bidding, a waste of steps can prevent a partnership's finding a safe trump suit at the lowest possible level. In the upper bidding levels, a waste of steps diminishes the information that may be exchanged before the contract is finally decided.

Suppose North deals and bids one club, holding:

* Arthur Carson-Roberts: satirically, as the *reductio ad absurdum* of the then current passion for overrefined bidding conventions. Since Carson-Roberts was an ingenious analyst, his satire, like Swinburne's parodies, had much "method in't."

♠ 8 3
♡ A K 8 6
◇ J 5
♣ A 10 8 5 2

SOUTH MAY HOLD: *or* SOUTH MAY HOLD:

1.   ♠ A J 6 4   2.   ♠ A J 6 4
      ♡ 5 3   ♡ 10 7 5 3
      ◇ Q 6 4 3   ◇ Q 6 4 3
      ♣ Q 7 4   ♣ 6

In each case South has a stronger spade than diamond suit, yet for South to bid one spade might be costly. North cannot dare bid two hearts over one spade, for fear South has hand No. 1, whereupon the very lowest contract at which the partnership can stop would be three clubs, and three clubs may go down. Yet if North accordingly rebids one no-trump, South will pass with hand No. 2, and the pass will be costly because a two-heart contract would be far better than a one no-trump contract.

A one-diamond response on either South hand eliminates these dangers. North may now bid one heart safely, whereupon South may bid one spade with hand No. 1, or raise to two hearts with hand No. 2. Whichever hand South holds, the partnership will easily stop at two-odd in its best combined trump suit, and make the contract. The one-diamond response saves two *steps* over the one-spade response, and the availability of those two extra steps for further bidding may often be worth 200 points or more.

THE "SHORT CLUB" AND OTHER UNBIDDABLE SUITS

Conservation of steps often dictates the bidding of "unbiddable" suits. With the following hand, the best response to a one-club bid is one diamond:

♠ A 8 6 3   ♡ 10 9 4 2   ◇ K 4 3   ♣ 6 3

A one-heart response could mislead partner as to the strength of the heart suit; a one-spade response could shut out a heart con-

tract as in the previous example. The one-diamond response relinquishes no bidding opportunity, because it wastes no steps.

The "half-truth" previously referred to is this: The possible
maximum shown by any unlimited bid at a given level is always
the same, no matter how many steps are consumed in making the
bid. A one-diamond response to a one-club may be just as strong
as a one-spade response. An opening one-club bid may be just as
strong as an opening one-spade bid, and may on occasion be
stronger. *But the possible minimum shown by any bid varies with
the number of steps it consumes.*

	1.		2.	
♠	A K 6 5		♠	9 8 2
♡	A 7		♡	A 7
◇	7 6 4 3		◇	7 6 4 3
♣	9 8 2		♣	A K 6 5

Many an expert will pass originally on No. 1, but will bid one
club on No. 2. A one-spade bid consumes so many steps that
future bidding may get too high for safety; a one-club bid leaves
plenty of room for safe bidding at a low level.

Therefore an opening one-club bid may be made on a weaker
hand than an opening one-spade bid; its *possible minimum* is
lower.

But the possible maximum of the one-club bid is higher, because of the step system. An expert might consider the following
hand unsuitable for a forcing two-bid or a two no-trump bid,
because of the weakness in hearts:

♠ A K Q J   ♡ 7 4 2   ◇ A Q   ♣ A K 7 5

But he would fear to bid one spade, which his partner would
pass on a hand like this:

♠ 6 4 3   ♡ 8 3   ◇ K J 7 5 4 2   ♣ 6 2

Therefore he bids one club, the easiest bid for his partner to respond to. This is the step system at work. The frequent use of a
"short" (fewer than four cards) club suit is also attributable to the
step system:

1.　♠ A K Q J　　2.　♠ 10 9 6 3
　　♡ 7 4 2　　　　　♡ A 8 5 4
　　◊ A K Q　　　　　◊ A K
　　♣ K 8 3　　　　　♣ Q 6 3

An expert might open one club on No. 1 because it is so strong and on No. 2 because it is so weak.

The propriety of keeping the bidding open is frequently determined by the step system. Suppose the opening bid of one club.

1.　♠ Q J 6 4 3　　2.　♠ 8 6 3
　　♡ 9 7 4 3　　　　♡ 9 7 4 3
　　◊ 8 6 3　　　　　◊ Q J 6 4 3
　　♣ 2　　　　　　　♣ 2

Hand No. 1 should be passed; the only possible response is one spade, which is an unmitigated gamble on finding partner with spade support. Hand No. 2 warrants a response of one diamond, for then a spade or heart rebid may be passed more safely than could the one-club bid. A one no-trump rebid by the opener will show balanced distribution and if it is doubled it can be rescued with a two-diamond bid, for the opener will have at least two-card support.

While any forced bid is a "possible minimum" and suggests that the partner be cautious, a bid that is not only forced but also frugal of steps suggests especial caution.

1.　♠ A K 6 3 2　　2.　♠ 10 6
　　♡ A 8 5　　　　　♡ K J 4
　　◊ K J 4　　　　　◊ A 8 5
　　♣ 10 6　　　　　♣ A K 6 3 2

The holder of hand No. 1 opens with one spade. His partner responds one no-trump, and he passes. The one no-trump response was the lowest response possible over one spade; it was the next step higher. It warned of a possible minimum.

The holder of hand No. 2 opens with one club. His partner responds one no-trump and *he raises to two no-trump*. The one no-trump response to one club skips three steps; the responder would not have wasted those steps with a minimum hand. In fact, the principle of saving steps is so well established that the response of one no-trump to an opening one-club bid has virtually ceased to exist, or has become conventionally an encouraging bid, since nearly every hand provides a possible response one or more steps lower. When a response of one no-trump to one club is made, it is usually on such a hand as this:

♠ A Q 6   ♡ 6 5 4 2   ◇ K J 3   ♣ 9 5 4

Even with this hand, most experts would prefer to respond one diamond.

OTHER APPLICATIONS OF THE STEP SYSTEM

In some cases the "book" definition of a bid is definitely altered in the light of the step system.

SOUTH	WEST	NORTH	EAST
1 ♣	1 ♠	2 ◇	Pass
2 ♡			

South's two-heart rebid may be a "reverse" bid, but it is not necessarily a strength-showing one. South may hold:

♠ 9 6   ♡ A J 6 5   ◇ 8 3   ♣ A K 7 5 3

The two-heart rebid is the next step above two diamonds; it is the lowest bid South can make. Since North's bid was forcing and South is not permitted to pass, South cannot intelligently refuse to show his heart suit when so cheap an opportunity is offered him. Any bidding theory that dictates another course must be unsound.

The availability of so many different bidding steps may be exploited to achieve economy and safety, and expert bidding may be fully understood only when the implications of the step system are apparent.

South	West	North	East
1 ♠	Pass	3 ♠	Pass
4 ♣	Pass	4 ♡	

In this bidding sequence, North may be expected to hold the heart but not the diamond ace. If North had held the diamond ace there would have been no reason for him to pass over the "step" at which it could be shown most economically.

In other cases an apparently strong bid may rather, by reason of the step system, show weakness:

South	West	North	East
1 ♡	Pass	3 ♣	Pass
3 ◇	Pass	3 ♠	Pass
3 N.T.	Pass	4 ♣	Pass
4 ◇			

South's last bid purports to show a five-card diamond suit—otherwise the suit should not be rebid, under the standard requirements. It is equally likely, however, that South has a weak hand and wants to "get out from under." South may hope that North will next bid four hearts, which he may pass. It must be observed that South has not skipped a step in his rebids, and he *may* have a very weak hand.

Thus the step system is an independent principle in bidding, acting to influence the choice of alternative bids and to modify the meaning of almost any bid, however strict its conventional definition.

10

ACCRETION OF INFORMATION

EVERY BID made in bridge is modified by every bid or failure to bid made previously by the same player. The conspicuous example is a bid by a "passed hand."

SOUTH	WEST	NORTH	EAST
Pass	Pass	1 ◊	Pass
2 ♡			

If South had not passed originally, his jump response would show unlimited strength and require a game contract. Since South passed originally, his bid shows the best hand he could have, less than an opening bid. Published systems make South's bid forcing for one round, but North can still pass, relying on the principle that no limited bid can logically be forcing.

Since a player pieces together partner's hand from his bids and passes, and considers every bid in the light of the limitations established by previous bids and passes, it is almost impossible for a player to recover from a previous mistake.

FOURTH-SUIT FORCING

Many Europeans have embraced a principle called "fourth-suit forcing." When a partnership has previously bid three of the suits, a bid in the fourth suit forces a response (as it does in American bidding) but does not necessarily show strength in the fourth suit (as it most often would in American bidding). It is no more than a device to have the bidding kept open.

In *Blueprint for Bidding,* by Terence Reese and Albert Dormer, the following example is given:

South	West	North	East
1 ♡	Pass	1 ♠	Pass
2 ♣	Pass	2 ◇	

North holds:

♠ A K 8 7 5   ♡ 10 7   ◇ 9 5 3   ♣ A Q 2

North cannot bid no-trump without a diamond stopper but does not wish to have the bidding stop short of game. The fourth-suit bid in diamonds keeps the bidding low, promises nothing, and assures North another chance. In American bidding two diamonds would be equally forcing but would show some control in diamonds.

Even in fourth-suit forcing, however, a limiting bid such as a no-trump or preference bid breaks the chain and the fourth suit thereafter loses its forcing effect.

In the following situation the fourth suit, far from being forcing, virtually demands a pass:

South	West	North	East
1 ◇	Pass	1 ♠	Pass
2 ♣	Pass	2 ◇	Pass
2 N.T.	Pass	3 ♡	

North was too weak to bid two hearts over two clubs. Instead North bid two diamonds, a simple preference bid that invited a pass by South. How can North, who has revealed such weakness, now make a forcing bid that would inevitably result in a game contract? He cannot. North holds:

♠ Q 8 7 5 3   ♡ K J 8 4   ◇ 9 4 3   ♣ 7

Having discovered from South's two no-trump bid that South has some strength in hearts, and a generally strong hand, North fixes the contract at what is likely to be the best combined trump suit. North might also have held:

♠ K J 7 5 2   ♡ 9 7 6 4 3   ◇ 10 7   ♣ 5

The former hand was what North actually held, and the deal occurred in a pair tournament so that it was better to play in a major suit than a minor, but with either North hand and at rubber bridge as well as at duplicate the best contract was three hearts. South held.

$$\spadesuit~64 \quad \heartsuit~A\,105 \quad \diamondsuit~A\,K\,86 \quad \clubsuit~K\,Q\,J\,3$$

and considered his hand too weak for a jump to two no-trump over one spade but good enough to make another try for game over two diamonds. Perhaps North should simply have passed two no-trump with the hand he actually held, and the contract might have been as good as any, but since he managed to make three hearts for 140 points he got a top. With the second, hypothetical, North hand, three hearts was the ideal contract, considering the fact that the bidding system made a two-heart contract impossible. If North had bid two hearts it would have been forcing and a losing game contract would have become inescapable.

The new suit by responder is far from forcing in the following auction.

SOUTH	WEST	NORTH	EAST
1 ♡	Pass	2 ♡	Pass
2 ♠	Pass	3 ♣	

North was not strong enough to bid two clubs originally, so he has limited his hand. South's rebid was a game try, but was not nearly so strong as it would have been if North's response had been one no-trump, for South knew from North's raise that there was a safe landing place in hearts. South rebid to find out if North had a good raise and could jump to four hearts or if North had a weak raise and would have to sign off at three hearts. North replied with the information that his hand was like this:

$$\spadesuit~7 \quad \heartsuit~Q\,75 \quad \diamondsuit~10\,43 \quad \clubsuit~A\,10\,8\,7\,5\,4$$

Players using one no-trump as a forcing response might respond one no-trump on this hand but might find themselves no better off on the second round because they would have to guess between raising hearts and bidding clubs. For players using

Standard American the obvious first response is a raise to two hearts, because the hand is too weak in high cards for two clubs, the wrong distribution for a no-trump response that might be passed, and safe at hearts if the opener passes the raise.

This rebid in clubs (or in any other suit in the same circumstances) nearly always shows a six-card suit and the opener should usually pass it if he has two-card trump support, especially if he opened on a four-card suit. South would pass with

♠ K 10 6 3   ♡ A K 9 6 3   ◇ A 5   ♣ J 3

—which is about what he would need to bid over two hearts.

THE ETHICAL PROBLEM IN FINE-DRAWN INFERENCES

A question of ethics can arise when the negative inferences to be drawn from bids are familiar to an expert partnership and not to their opponents. The following situation used to be exploited by expert pairs in run-of-the-mill duplicate games.

SOUTH	WEST	NORTH	EAST
1 ♡	Pass	1 N.T.	Pass
2 ◇	Pass	2 ♠	

North-South being an expert pair, South knows that North does not have a genuine spade suit. One does not respond one no-trump if he has a spade suit. Therefore North is showing ability to bid no-trump again and *en passant* is seeking to discourage an opening spade lead. I have seen North bid two spades on such a hand as this:

♠ 10 4 3   ♡ 8 6   ◇ K 7 3   ♣ A Q 9 8 2

South knows he must not pass or raise spades. The opponents do not know this. The logic of the situation is clear but when it has been used a few times it assumes the nature of a private understanding. Is it ethical? Apparently it is considered a legitimate exercise of bridge skill, for to my knowledge the ethics of it has never been questioned except by the experts who use it themselves, when they are very conscientious.

There is a similar situation in bridge ethics:

SOUTH	WEST	NORTH	EAST
1 ♠	2 ♡	3 ♠	Double
Pass			

West must not pass. North's raise was forcing, so South must bid again. Why should East double three spades when he can wait one round and double four spades? East apparently has heart support but wishes to discourage his opponents from bidding four spades. When West bids four hearts, North-South may assume that the spades are stacked in the East hand, that West is void of spades and cannot stand the double, and that they had better bow out. Against inept players the stratagem usually succeeds. The double is a brilliant and admirable device the first time it is used, but thereafter its use by the same partnership may almost be considered a convention. I remember one case when West did not catch the hidden meaning of the double the first time it was used, so he passed and South made three spades doubled with an overtrick. The East-West partnership continued to play together and West never made the same mistake again. He even adopted premature doubles as a device of his own, confident that East would never fail to get the message.

11

PERCENTAGE TABLES

TABLE 1

The chances that the opponents' cards in a suit will be divided in a given way:

Your Combined Holding in Suit	Opponents Hold	Opponent's Cards Will Break		
11 cards	2 cards	1-1	52	%
		2-0	48	%
10 cards	3 cards	2-1	78	%
		3-0	22	%
9 cards	4 cards	3-1	49.7	%
		2-2	40.7	%
		4-0	9.6	%
8 cards	5 cards	3-2	68	%
		4-1	28	%
		5-0	4	%
7 cards	6 cards	4-2	48.4	%
		3-3	35.5	%
		5-1	14.5	%
		6-0	1.5	%
6 cards	7 cards	4-3	62	%
		5-2	30.5	%
		6-1	6.8	%
		7-0	0.5	%
5 cards	8 cards	5-3	47	%
		4-4	32.8	%
		6-2	17	%
		7-1	2.9	%
		8-0	0.2	%
4 cards	9 cards	5-4	59	%
		6-3	31.4	%
		7-2	8.6	%
		8-1	1	%
		9-0	0.04	%

TABLE 2

The chance that an opponent's honor will be guarded:

ONE OUTSTANDING HONOR WILL BE

YOUR COMBINED HOLDING	UNGUARDED	GUARDED ONCE ONLY	GUARDED ONLY TWICE	GUARDED THREE TIMES OR MORE
11 cards	52.0%	48%		
10 cards	26.0%	52%	22%	
9 cards	12.0%	41%	37%	10%
8 cards	5.0%	27%	41%	27%
7 cards	2.0%	16%	36%	46%
6 cards	1.0%	9%	27%	64%
5 cards	0.4%	4%	18%	78%
4 cards	0.1%	2%	10%	87%

TABLE 3

Distributions of the cards of a suit among the hands of the four players (or of the four suits in one player's hands):

DISTRIBUTION (of Hand or Suit)	%	APPROXIMATE ODDS AGAINST
4-4-3-2	21.6	4 to 1
5-3-3-2	15.5	6 to 1
5-4-3-1	13.0	7 to 1
5-4-2-2	10.6	9 to 1
4-3-3-3	10.5	9 to 1
6-3-2-2	5.6	17 to 1
6-4-2-1	4.7	20 to 1
6-3-3-1	3.5	27 to 1
5-5-2-1	3.2	30 to 1
4-4-4-1	3.0	33 to 1
7-3-2-1	1.9	50 to 1
6-4-3-0	1.3	75 to 1
5-4-4-0	1.2	80 to 1
5-5-3-0	0.9	100 to 1
6-5-1-1	0.7	140 to 1
6-5-2-0	0.65	150 to 1
7-2-2-2	0.5	199 to 1

DISTRIBUTION (of Hand or Suit)	%	APPROXIMATE ODDS AGAINST
7-4-1-1	0.4	249 to 1
7-4-2-0	0.35	275 to 1
7-3-3-0	0.25	399 to 1
8-2-2-1	0.2	499 to 1
8-3-1-1	0.12	850 to 1
7-5-1-0	0.11	900 to 1
8-3-2-0	0.11	900 to 1
6-6-1-0	0.07	1,400 to 1
8-4-1-0	0.04	2,499 to 1
9-2-1-1	0.02	4,999 to 1
9-3-1-0	0.01	9,999 to 1
9-2-2-0	0.008	12,500 to 1
7-6-0-0	0.006	16,666 to 1
8-5-0-0	0.003	33,332 to 1
10-2-1-0	0.001	99,999 to 1
9-4-0-0	0.001	99,999 to 1
10-1-1-1	0.0003	333,332 to 1
10-3-0-0	0.0002	499,999 to 1
11-1-1-0	0.00002	4,999,999 to 1
11-2-0-0	0.00001	9,999,999 to 1
12-1-0-0	0.0000003	333,333,332 to 1
13-0-0-0	0.0000000006	158,755,357,992 to 1

12

FOUR-DEAL BRIDGE

[As prepared for the American Contract Bridge League]

IN ALMOST all clubs, and in many home games, Four Deal Bridge (Chicago) has superseded the usual form of rubber bridge. "Chicago," so called because it was first regularly played in the Chicago Athletic Club, offers many advantages:

Since four deals complete each rubber or "wheel" (a term derived from the fact that a wheel is completed when the numerals from 1 to 4 have been filled in on the X at the top of the score), the endless rubber is eliminated. Thus games can be played within fixed periods, such as lunch hours, and players can quit within a reasonable approximation of the time they have planned to spend.

Since all rubbers are of approximately the same duration in time, each consisting of exactly four deals, the player who is cut out in a five-hand or six-hand game gets back into action reasonably soon.

No player is "stuck" with the weakest partner for a prolonged rubber, nor can the two best players deliberately prolong the rubber in which they are partners.

The entire game is faster. In one hour it is easily possible to complete a round or "pivot" so that each partnership has a turn.

The scoring is much as in rubber bridge, but it is sufficiently like duplicate that it serves as an excellent preparation for that form of the game—which is becoming increasingly popular everywhere.   R.L.F.

A. *Basic rules*

The Laws of Contract Bridge are followed, except as modified by the following rules.

B. *The Rubber*

A rubber consists of a series of four deals that have been bid and played. If a deal is passed out, the same player deals again and the deal passed out does not count as one of the four deals.

A fifth deal is void if attention is drawn to it at any time before there has been a new cut for partners or the game has terminated; if the error is not discovered in time for correction, the score stands as recorded. A sixth or subsequent deal is unconditionally void and no score for such a deal is ever permissible.

In case fewer than four deals are played, the score shall stand for the incomplete series unless attention is drawn to the error before there has been a new cut for partners or the game has terminated.

When the players are pivoting,* the fact that the players have taken their proper seats for the next rubber shall be considered a cut for partners.

C. *Vulnerability*

Vulnerability is not determined by previous scores but by the following schedule:

First deal: Neither side vulnerable.

Second and Third deals: Dealer's side vulnerable, the other side not vulnerable.

Fourth deal: Both sides vulnerable.

D. *Premiums*

For making or completing a game (100 or more trick points) a side receives a premium of 300 points if on that deal it is not vulnerable or 500 points if on that deal it is vulnerable. There is no additional premium for winning two or more games, each game premium being scored separately.

* In a pivot game, partnerships for each rubber follow a fixed rotation.

E. *The score*

As a reminder of vulnerability in Four-Deal Bridge, two inter-secting diagonal lines should be drawn near the top of the score pad, as follows:

The numeral "1" should be inserted in that one of the four angles thus formed that faces the first dealer. After play of the first deal is completed, "2" is inserted in the next angle in clock-wise rotation, facing the dealer of the second deal. The numerals "3" and "4" are subsequently inserted at the start of the third and fourth deals respectively, each in the angle facing the current dealer.

A correctly numbered diagram is conclusive as to vulnerability. There is no redress for a bid influenced by the scorer's failure to draw the diagram or for an error or omission in inserting a numeral or numerals in the diagram. Such error or omission should, upon discovery, be immediately corrected and the deal or deals should be scored or rescored as though the diagram and the number or numbers thereon had been properly inserted.

F. *Part-scores*

A part-score or -scores made previously may be combined with a part-score made in the current deal to complete a game of 100 or more trick points. The game premium is determined by the vulnerability, on that deal, of the side that completes the game. When a side makes or completes a game, no previous part-score of either side may thereafter be counted toward game.

A side that makes a part-score in the fourth deal, if the part-score is not sufficient to complete a game, receives a premium of 100 points. This premium is scored whether or not the same side or the other side has an uncompleted part-score. There is no separate premium for making a part-score in any other circum-stances.

G. *Deal out of turn*

When a player deals out of turn, and there is no right to a redeal, the player who should have dealt retains his right to call first, but such right is lost if it is not claimed before the actual dealer calls. If the actual dealer calls before attention is drawn to the deal out of turn, each player thereafter calls in rotation. Vulnerability and scoring values are determined by the position of the player who should have dealt, regardless of which player actually dealt or called first. Neither the rotation of the deal nor the scoring is affected by a deal out of turn. The next dealer is the player who would have dealt next if the deal had been in turn.

H.   *Optional rules and customs*

The following practices, not required, have proved acceptable in some clubs and games.

i] Since the essence of the game is speed, if a deal is passed out, the pack that has been shuffled for the next deal should be used by the same dealer.

ii] The net score of a rubber should be translated into even hundreds (according to American custom) by crediting as 100 points any fraction thereof amounting to 50 or more points: e.g., 750 points count as 800; 740 points count as 700 points.

iii] No two players may play a second consecutive rubber as partners at the same table. If two players draw each other again, the player who has drawn the highest card should play with the player who has drawn the third-highest, against the other two players.

iv] Any player may announce, prior to the auction and before he has looked at his hand, which deal it is and who is vulnerable; or may, for his own information, inquire as to these facts when it is his turn to call. There is no redress if no announcement is made or if incorrect information is given.

v] To avoid confusion as to how many deals have been played: Each deal should be scored, even if there is no net advantage to either side (for example, when one side is entitled to 100 points for undertrick penalties and the other side is entitled to 100 points for honors). In a result that completes a game, premiums for overtricks, game, slam, or making a doubled contract should be combined with the trick score to produce one total, which is entered below the line (for example, if a side makes two spades doubled and vulnerable with an overtrick, 870 should be scored below the line, not 120 below the line and 50, 500 and 200 above the line).

GLOSSARY

TERMS LISTED in the Contents and defined in the text are not necessarily included in this Glossary.

ABOVE THE LINE: (in scoring) not counting toward game.

A-B, Y-Z: letters formerly used to designate the players in a whist game, supplanted by compass designations, N-S, E-W.

ACE: the one-spot in a pack of cards.

ACOL: a bidding system, similar to Standard American, popular especially in England.

ADEQUATE TRUMP SUPPORT: sufficient strength in a suit one's partner has bid to justify raising it, usually Q-x-x, J-10-x, or x-x-x-x.

ADJUSTED SCORE: an arbitrary score assigned by the tournament director, when regular play is not feasible (Duplicate Bridge).

ADVANCED SCORE: = part-score.

ADVERSARY: any opposing player; an opponent of declarer.

ADVERSE: pertaining to an adversary, as *adverse lead,* one made by an opponent. (*Note:* this term usually carries no implication of ill-fortune.)

AMERICAN BRIDGE ASSOCIATION: a national organization of bridge players, chiefly blacks, in the U.S., founded 1932.

AMERICAN BRIDGE LEAGUE: a national association of bridge players in the U.S., founded 1927 and originally called *American Auction Bridge League,* in 1937 merged with United States Bridge Association to form the American Contract Bridge League.

AMERICAN CONTRACT BRIDGE LEAGUE: a national organization of bridge players in the U.S., founded 1937.

ANCHOR SUIT: a suit shown inferentially through the use of an artificial bid such as a transfer bid or an Astro bid.

APPROACH BID: a suit-bid made at a lower level than the strength of the hand warrants, for the purpose of exchanging information with partner before deciding on a contract.

APPROACH-FORCING SYSTEM: Culbertson bidding system.

ARTIFICIAL: (of a bid) giving information as to cards or distribution not necessarily related to the denomination named in the bid.

ASKING BID: a bid that systematically asks partner to make a control-showing response.

ASSIST: increase partner's bid; raise.

AUCTION: the period or process of bidding.

AUCTION BRIDGE: the form of bridge prevalent *c.* 1907-29, identical with contract bridge except in scoring.

AX: double (Slang).

BACK IN: come into the bidding after having passed.

BACK SCORE: a record of the number of points (usually in hundreds) that each player has won or lost.

BALANCE: reopen the bidding, relying on the strength assumed to be in partner's hand because the opponents have stopped at a low contract.

BALANCED HAND: a hand that contains no void or singleton.

BARE: 1, to discard the last guard of (a high card). 2, unguarded; alone.

BARON SYSTEM: a bidding system used in England, requiring four-card trump support for a raise.

BARRED: required to pass, in consequence of a penalty.

BASE VALUE: value of an odd trick.

BATH COUP: the play of the low card from A-J-x when an opponent leads the K.

BELOW THE LINE: (in scoring) counting toward game.

BERMUDA BOWL: a trophy awarded annually, except in Olympiad years, to winners of the world team championship, put in play in 1950.

— -BEST: ranking in the ordinal position specified, from the top of the suit, as *third-best*.

BEST CARD: highest card of a suit remaining unplayed; master card.

BID: an offer to contract to win a minimum number of tricks, for the privilege of naming the trump suit; to make a bid.

BIDDABLE SUIT: a holding that meets the systematic requirements for a suit-bid.

BIDDER: any player who bids.

BIDDING: the auction; the period in which bids are made; competing in the auction.

BIRITCH: a card game, precursor of bridge, introduced (1883) in England with the subtitle "Russian Whist."

BLACKWOOD CONVENTION: a bidding method in which bids of 4 and 5 N.T., and prescribed responses, are used to locate aces and kings.

BLANK: 1, unguarded; singleton. 2, = blank suit.

BLANK A SUIT: discard all cards of that suit from one's hand.

BLANK SUIT: a suit of which one holds no cards; a void.

BLIND LEAD: the opening lead.

BLOCK: to hold a high card [in a suit] that prevents partner from running the suit.

BLOCK A SUIT: play high cards in such a way that partner, with a longer holding, cannot keep or regain the lead.

BLUE PETER: a high-low signal asking partner to lead trumps (Whist).

BOARD: 1, = dummy. 2, duplicate board. 3, a deal at duplicate.

BOARD-A-MATCH: a scoring method whereby a team having the higher score on a deal receives 1 point, a tie counting ½ point for each team.

BODY: strength in intermediate cards.

BOLAND CLUB: a variation of the Vanderbilt club system; a two-club rebid denies the high-card values that might have been promised by a previous one-club bid.

BONUS: a score that does not count toward game; premium.

BOOBY PRIZE: a prize given at bridge parties for the poorest score; consolation prize.

BOOK: the tricks that a side must win before it can score for additional tricks; for declarer, six tricks.

BOOST: impel (the opponents) to bid one or more tricks more.

BORDERLINE: barely meeting the systemic minimum requirements.

BRACKET: in a knockout tournament, a group of two, four, eight, etc., contestants scheduled together for a series of elimination matches.

BRIDGE: any form of whist including the exposed dummy, no-trump play, declaring or bidding to designate a trump suit, doubles, and redoubles; especially bridge-whist, auction bridge or contract bridge.

BRIDGE BLOCK: a scorepad (British).

BRIDGE IT: pass the make to partner (Bridge-Whist).

BRIDGE-WHIST: a name now used by historians for the earliest (c. 1896) form of bridge.

BRIDGE WORLD: a monthly magazine founded October, 1929, in New York.

BRING IN (A SUIT): establish or cash (a suit), especially after taking out adverse trumps.

BRITISH BRIDGE LEAGUE: national organization of bridge players in Great Britain.

BUMBLEPUPPY: inferior play, especially in defiance of partnership systems (Whist).

BUSINESS DOUBLE: a double made for the purpose of collecting an increased penalty.

BUST: a very poor hand.

BY CARDS: won in tricks.

BYE: a round of a tournament in which a contestant is not scheduled to play.

BY ME: declaration meaning "I pass."

CALL: declare; bid, pass, double or redouble.

CANAPÉ: bid a short suit before a long suit.

CAPTURE: win a trick by playing a card higher in rank than (an opponent's card).

CASH: lead and win a trick with (an established card).

CAVENDISH: a London club whose name was adopted as a pseudonym by Henry Jones (q.v.) and by several later bridge clubs, especially that in New York where leading bridge experts play.

CHALLENGE: a call proposed (by Sidney Lenz) to be substituted for "double" when the intent is informatory; never incorporated in the laws.

CHICAGO: four-deal bridge, often so called because it originated at the Standard Club in Chicago.

CHICANE: a void in trumps.

CLEAR: establish (a card or suit) by forcing out adverse higher cards or stoppers.

CLOSED HAND: declarer's hand.

CLUB BRIDGE: = four-deal bridge.

CLUB CONVENTION: a bidding system created by Harold S. Vanderbilt, and much copied, in which an artificial opening bid of one club shows a strong hand and an artificial response of one diamond denies strength.

COFFEEHOUSING: talking and acting so as to mislead opponents as to one's cards.

COLD: (of a contract) sure to be fulfilled (Slang).

COLOR: suit.

COLUMN: on a scoresheet, either the area that gives the score of one side or (formerly) reserved for trick scores or premium scores.

COME-ON: signal to partner to lead or continue a suit; echo.

COMMAND: 1, best card of a suit; control a suit with the best card. 2, forcing.

COMPLETED TRICK: a trick to which every hand has played a card.

CONDONE: waive penalty for, or validate, an illegal call or play.

CONTENT: a statement equivalent to "Pass," formerly often used after an opponent's double but never sanctioned by the laws.

CONTESTANT: any player in a game, whether or not active at the moment; any group entered in a contest as a partnership or team.

CONTRACT: the obligation to win a minimum number of tricks.

CONTRACTOR: declarer or dummy.

CONTRACT WHIST: a game in which there is bidding as in contract bridge but play as in whist, with no dummy.

CONVENTION: a call or play whose full meaning is known only by prior agreement.

CONVENTIONAL: systemic; in accordance with an agreed system.

CONVENTIONS: common practices in bidding and play; advance agreements between partners on systemic procedures.

COUNT: 1, a method of hand-valuation. 2, a mental record of the number of cards that have been played (in a given suit). 3, an estimate of the number of cards of each suit originally dealt to, or still held by, another player.

COUP: an end-play, usually one in which declarer (after deliberately reducing his own trump length) captures an opposing trump for which he cannot finesse; a trump pick-up.

COURTENAY, F. DUDLEY (1890-   ):   a bridge authority who was prime mover in the promulgation of the Official System of Contract Bridge and later of the Losing Trick Count.

COVER: play a higher card of the same suit than any previously played to the trick.

CRACK: double (Slang).

CRISSCROSS SQUEEZE: a squeeze in which the entry to each hand is the blank master card of a suit.

CROCKFORD'S: an early London club and gaming rooms; several later bridge clubs have adopted the name.

CROSS-RUFF: alternate trumping of each other's leads by two partners.

CUE: make a cue-bid in (a suit).

CUE-BID: a bid that systemically shows control of a suit, usually by possession of the ace or a void.

CULBERTSON: 1, Ely Culbertson (1891–1955), authority on contract bridge. 2, Josephine Culbertson (1899–1956), his wife, contract bridge authority. 3, Culbertson System, the bidding system once used by the majority of contract bridge players; also *approach-forcing system.*

CUMULATIVE SCORING: method of scoring by determining the net total of the plus and minus scores made on all boards played by a partnership; called also *total-point scoring* (Duplicate Bridge).

CURSE OF SCOTLAND: the diamond nine.

CUT: 1, divide the pack into two parts in completion of the shuffling; such division. 2, draw cards from a spread pack to determine dealer, etc.

CUT IN: gain entry to a table, as by drawing cards for precedence.

CUTTHROAT BRIDGE: 1, a form of contract bridge in which partnerships are established in the process of bidding. 2, three-hand bridge.

DEAL: 1, distribute cards to the players; such distribution; the turn to deal. 2, the period from one distribution of cards to the next, including all such sub-periods as the auction, play, and scoring.

DEALER: the player who distributes the cards.

DECK: pack (of cards).

DECLARANT: = declarer.

DECLARATION: 1, a bid. 2, the contract or denomination (trump or no-trump) at which a deal is played.

DECLARE: bid; make the trump.

DECLARER: the player who for his side first bid the denomination named in the contract, and who thereupon plays both hands of the partnership.

DEFEND: 1, make a sacrifice bid. 2, bid or play as a defender.

DEFENDER: an opponent of declarer or of the first bidder.

DEFENSE: the opponents of declarer.

DEFENSIVE: 1, being a bid or play of a defender. 2, made as a sacrifice bid. 3, constituting defensive strength.

DEFENSIVE BID: 1, a bid made by an opponent of the opening bidder. 2, a sacrifice bid.

DEFENSIVE STRENGTH: cards expected to win tricks against an adverse contract.

DEMAND BID: a bid that systemically requires partner to keep the bidding open; forcing bid.

DENIAL: a bid showing lack of support for partner's declaration.

DENOMINATION: 1, the suit or no-trump named in a bid, 2, rank (of a card).

DESCHAPELLES COUP: the lead of a high card to force out an opponent's high card and thereby create an entry to partner's hand.

DEVIL'S BEDPOSTS: the club four.

DISCARD: play a plain-suit card not of the same suit as the lead to a trick; a card so played.

DISCOURAGING CARD: a card played by a defender to signify no desire to have partner lead or continue that suit.

DISTRIBUTION: division of cards among the hands, especially as to the number of cards of each suit dealt to each hand.

DISTRIBUTIONAL: pertaining to tricks that may be won because of relative suit-lengths rather than by high cards.

DORMITZER: a kibitzer of low intelligence or limited privilege (Jocular). Also, *dorbitzer*, *daubitzer*.

DOUBLE: 1, a call that increases certain scoring items in case the last preceding bid becomes the contract. 2, to make this call.

DOUBLE-DUMMY PROBLEM: a problem of analysis in which all four hands are shown to the solver.

DOUBLE JUMP: a bid of two tricks more than would be necessary for a sufficient overcall, as 3 ♡ over 1 ◇ .

DOUBLE RAISE: a raise to a level two tricks higher than partner's bid or one trick higher than is necessary to overcall an intervening bid.

DOUBLETON: a holding of exactly two cards in a suit.

DOUBLE VALUATION: a valuation method, advocated by Wilbur C. Whitehead, whereby the estimated trick-winning power of a hand was twice its quick tricks (Auction Bridge).

DOWN: 1, in descending order of rank. 2, exposed.

DOWN AND OUT: the play of two cards, higher first, to show no more of the suit.

DRAW: pull cards from a spread pack, to determine dealer, etc.

DRAW BRIDGE: a two-hand bridge game in which a player draws one of the undealt cards after playing to each trick.

DRIVE BRIDGE, DRIVE WHIST: obsolete names for progressive bridge, progressive whist.

DROP: cause (an opponent's high card) to be played futilely, by leading or playing a higher card of the same suit.

DUCK: play a low card rather than try to win the trick.

DUMMY: 1, declarer's partner, or the hand he lays on the table. 2, any form of whist played with one hand exposed.

DUMMY REVERSAL: use by declarer of his own, longer, trump suit for ruffing and of dummy's shorter trump suit to draw trumps.

DUPLICATE or DUPLICATE BRIDGE: a form of whist or bridge play in which all contestants play the same series of hands.

DUPLICATE BOARD: a device for keeping separate the four hands of a deal, for duplicate play.

EAGLE: the symbol on a fifth suit, green in color, at one time added to the standard pack.

EAST: conventional designation of one of the players in a four-hand game.

EASY ACES: two-two division of the aces between the two sides, with no honor score for the deal (Auction Bridge).

ECHO: a signal, the play of a higher and then a lower card of the same suit, made to request a lead or continuation of that suit (Bridge) or to request a trump lead (Whist); to signal in this way.

ELDER: the player at declarer's left, who makes the opening lead.

ELECTIVE CONTRACT: a form of bridge in which the bidding determines the partnership for the play of each deal.

ELEVEN RULE: = rule of eleven.

ELIMINATION: a process in play whereby declarer removes from the hand of an opponent all cards that can safely be led or played against him.

ENCOURAGING CARD: a card played to show a desire to have the suit led or continued by partner, or to show strength in the suit.

ENDPLAY: any of several stratagems (especially, *throw-in*) that can usually be executed only in the last phase of play.

ENTRY: a card with which a hand can win a trick and so gain the lead.

EQUALS: cards in sequence or which have become sequential by the play of all cards intervening in rank.

ESTABLISH: make (certain cards) winners by forcing out adverse higher cards; clear.

ESTABLISHED SUIT: a suit that can be cashed in its entirety without loss of a trick.

EUROPEAN BRIDGE LEAGUE: federation of national bridge organizations of the western European countries, plus Egypt and Lebanon, founded 1934.

EUROPEAN MATCH-POINTS: earliest form of international match-points, usually abbreviated EMP.

EXCESS PENALTY: points scored in excess of an established limit (such as 300 points if the limit is 1,000 and the actual score 1,300), counted only to break a tie.

EXIT: get out of the lead; compel another hand to win a trick.

EXPOSED CARD: a card shown inadvertently, especially in partnership play, and therefore subject to penalty for giving information illegally.

EXPOSED HAND: the dummy hand.

EXTRA TRICK: = overtrick.

FACE: to expose (a card) face up.

FACED HAND: the dummy hand.

FALSE-CARD: 1, a card played with the intention of misleading an opponent. 2, to play such a card.

FILLER: = intermediate card.

FINESSE: 1, a deliberate omission to play one's highest card in the suit led, in the hope or assurance that a lower card played from one's own hand, or a card led from partner's hand, will serve as equivalent in rank to a higher card held by a player who has already played to the trick. 2, to play (a card) as a finesse.

FIT: 1, distribution of cards in two partners' hands so that each can help the other to win tricks. 2, have support for (partner's, or each other's, cards).

FIVE-SUIT PACK: a pack of 65 cards at one time made by adding a fifth suit, crowns or eagles, to the regular 52-card pack; used to play five-suit bridge, a variant of contract bridge.

FLAG-FLYING: bidding for more tricks than can be won, to prevent the opponents from assuming the contract.

FLINT CONVENTION: a method of responding to an opening two no-trump bid so as to stop at three of a suit.

FOLLOW SUIT: play a card of the suit led.

FORCE: 1, compel (a player) to trump if he wishes to win a trick. 2, make a bid that systemically compels (partner) to respond.

FORCED: 1, legally compulsory. 2, imperative for strategical reasons.

FORCING BID: a bid that systemically requires partner to respond or to assure that the auction will be kept open.

FORCING PASS: a pass that requires partner to overcall or to double on adverse bid.

FORCING SYSTEM: = Culbertson System.

FORK: = tenace. Also, *fourchette*.

FOSTER, R. F.:   author of many books on intellectual games; died 1945.

FOSTER ECHO: the play of one's second-highest card when partner opens a king against a no-trump contract.

FOUR ACES: a contract bridge team (1934-c. 1940) composed of Oswald Jacoby, Howard Schenken, Michael T. Gottlieb, David Burnstine, Richard L. Frey; later M. D. Maier, B. Jay Becker, Sherman Stearns, and others.

FOUR-DEAL BRIDGE: a form of contract bridge in which four deals

bid and played constitute a rubber, after which inactive players may enter the game and there is a new cut for partners.

FOUR HORSEMEN: a contract bridge team (*c.* 1932) composed of
P. Hal Sims, Oswald Jacoby, David Burnstine, Willard Karn.

FOURTH-BEST: the fourth-highest card of a suit of four or more
cards in a player's hand.

FOURTH HAND: the last player in turn to call on the first round,
or to play to a trick.

FREAK HAND: a hand of unusual pattern or content; one that
contains eleven or more cards in two suits, or one suit longer
than seven cards.

FREE BID: a bid made voluntarily, not under any systemic compulsion.

FREE DOUBLE: a double of an adverse bid that would be sufficient for game if made undoubled.

GAME: the number of trick points needed to win a game, in
contract bridge 100.

GAME-FORCING: forcing until game is reached.

GET OFF TO: make the opening lead in (a specified suit).

GHOULIES: a game in which only goulash hands are played.

GO DOWN: 1, fail to fulfill the contract. 2, be legally exposed, as
the dummy hand.

GOREN, CHARLES H. (1901–   ):   American authority on contract bridge.

GOULASH: a method of dealing, without shuffling, from cards
sorted by suits, to produce freak hands. Called also *mayonnaise*
or *hollandaise.*

GRAND COUP: the trumping of partner's winning card, to shorten
one's trump length.

GRAND SLAM: the winning of thirteen tricks by one side.

GUARD: a low card accompanying a high card.

GUIDE CARD: a printed card or slip to direct a player to the table
at which he must play in each round (Duplicate Bridge).

GULPIC: a shaded opening bid (Slang).

HAND: 1, the cards originally dealt to a player, or any portion
thereof remaining unplayed. 2, = deal (sense 2), 3, a player
(holder of a hand).

HELP: raise; assist.

HERBERT CONVENTION: a method of responding to a forcing bid or a takeout double, etc., with the next-higher suit to show a weak hand.

HIGH-LOW: the play of a relatively high card followed by a lower card of the same suit, on tricks he is not attempting to win, as a defender's signaling device.

HOLDING, HOLDINGS: the hand or any part thereof.

HOLD UP: refrain from playing (a high card).

HOLLANDAISE: = goulash.

HONEYMOON BRIDGE: any of several forms of bridge for two players.

HONOR POINTS, HONOR SCORE: = premium score, points scored above the line.

HONORS: the five highest trumps, or the four aces at no-trump.

HONOR-TRICK: a card or combination of cards that can be expected to win a trick the first or second time its suit is led.

HOOK: = finesse (Slang).

HOWELL MOVEMENT: a method of progression in a duplicate bridge pair contest.

HOYLE, EDMOND (1679–1769):   English writer whose *Short Treatise on Whist* (1742) stimulated wide interest in intellectual games.

HUDDLE: a long pause for thought by a player before he bids or plays (Slang).

ICY: = cold (Slang). Also, *on ice*.

IMP: = international match-point.

INCORRECT PACK: a pack from which cards are missing or that contains duplicates of any card.

INDEX: the number or letter printed in the corner of a playing card, so that it may be read when held in a fan.

INDIFFERENT CARDS: cards whose rank need not be specified in posing a problem; equals.

INDIVIDUAL: a type of duplicate bridge contest in which partnerships change and score is kept for individuals instead of pairs.

INFORMATORY DOUBLE: a systemic double made primarily to give information to partner.

INITIAL BID: 1, first bid made by a side. 2, first bid of a deal; opening bid.

INSUFFICIENT BID: a bid that is not high enough to supersede the last previous bid.

INSURANCE BID: a sacrifice bid over a very high-scoring contract of the opponents, despite some expectation of defeating that contract.

INTERMEDIATE CARDS: cards middling in rank between the highest and lowest, as tens and nines.

INTERNATIONAL MATCH-POINTS: scoring units used in team and occasionally pair tournaments, designed to modify big swings Duplicate Bridge).

INVERTED MINOR RAISES: a method in which a single raise of a minor suit is forcing, while a jump raise is preëmptive.

INVITATION: a bid that invites but does not command partner to make a response.

IRREGULARITY: any departure from a rule of correct procedure (always in the sense of inadvertent error, not intentional misdeed).

JACOBY, OSWALD (1902–):   American expert on contract bridge and other games.

JONES, HENRY (1831–99):   English authority on the rules of games who wrote under the pseudonym "Cavendish."

JUMP BID: a bid naming more tricks than legally necessary for a sufficient bid.

JUMP TRUMP REBID: a convention in the Culbertson System whereby an unnecessary jump rebid in one's original suit, over a game-forcing bid by partner, shows a solid suit.

JUNIOR: partner of the leader, or senior.

KARPIN POINT COUNT: a valuation method employing the 4,3,2,1 count for high cards and adding distributional points for long suits rather than short suits, introduced by Fred L. Karpin.

KIBITZER: a non-playing spectator, especially one who criticizes.

KNAVE: jack (playing card).

KNOCKOUT TOURNAMENT: a series of matches between two contestants at a time, the loser being eliminated.

LAYDOWN: a contract so easy to fulfill that declarer does or might expose his hand and claim it.

LEAD: play the first card to a trick; the card so played.

LEAD BACK: lead (a suit or card of a suit that partner led originally).

LEAD INTO: lead so as to permit the last play to be made from (a specified hand or combination of cards).

LEAD THROUGH: lead so that (a specified player or card) cannot be last to play.

LEAD UP TO, LEAD TOWARD: lead so as to force an opponent to play before (a specified player or card).

LEAVE IN: pass (a specified bid or double made by one's partner).

LEDGER SCORE: = back score.

LEG: one game won toward the rubber.

LENGTH: 1, the number of cards held in a given suit. 2, a holding of four or more cards in a suit, 3, one's longest suit.

LENZ, SIDNEY S. (1873–1960): noted whist and bridge player and author.

LENZ ECHO: the play of one's second-highest trump to show four or five cards; trump echo.

LEVEL: the number of odd tricks named in a bid.

L. H. O.: left-hand opponent.

LIFE MASTER: a player of the highest rank in tournament bridge.

LIGHT: made on scant or minimal values, as a bid.

LILIES: spades, when declared for trumps at an increased value (Bridge-Whist).

LIMITED JUMP RAISE: a non-forcing double raise of opener's suit.

LINE: the horizontal line on a score sheet, below which trick scores and above which premium scores are posted.

LITTLE SLAM: = small slam.

LOCK: a situation in which a player can surely win a certain number of tricks against any defense (Slang).

LONG CARD: a card left in a hand after all opponents are exhausted of the suit.

LONG SUIT: a holding of four or more cards of a suit; the longest holding in any suit in a hand.

LOSER ON LOSER: an entry-killing play in which declarer discards a losing card on a losing card from the other hand, to place the lead with a particular opponent.

LOSING CARD, LOSER: a card that cannot be expected to win a trick or to fall on a trick won by partner.

LOVE: score of zero.

LOVE-ALL: neither side vulnerable (British).

LOW: 1, being one's lowest card. 2, being a relatively low card, especially when played in ducking.

MAJOR SUIT, MAJOR: spades or hearts.

MAJOR TENACE: the A-Q of a suit, or equivalent combination when some of the high cards have been played.

MAKE: 1, the contract; the denomination or game named in the contract. 2, name the trump suit or game. 3, fulfill (the contract). 4, win a trick with (a specified card).

MAKE THE PACK, MAKE UP: gather and shuffle the pack for the next deal.

MASTER CARD: the highest card of a suit still in play; best card.

MASTER POINT: a unit used in ranking tournament players, awarded in quantities depending on the importance of the tournament and how high the player's score is.

MATCH POINT: a unit used in tournament scoring, 1 match point being awarded for each pair or team defeated on a deal, and ½ match point for each pair or team tied.

MAYONNAISE: = goulash.

MINNIE: a hand that barely meets the accepted requirements for an opening bid (Slang).

MINOR SUIT, MINOR: diamonds or clubs.

MINOR TENACE: the K-J of a suit, or equivalent combination when some of the high cards have been played.

MISDEAL: any irregularity in dealing that requires a new shuffle and deal.

MISNOMER: in early bridge laws, a slip of the tongue in calling, subject to correction without penalty.

MITCHELL MOVEMENT: a schedule used in duplicate pair games, producing two winning pairs, one North-South and one East-West.

MIXED PAIR: in tournament play, a partnership of a man and a woman.

MOVEMENT: a schedule by which players and boards move from table to table in duplicate bridge.

NATIONAL LAWS COMMISSION: the committee of the American Contract Bridge League that prepares contract bridge laws.

NEGATIVE: 1, denying strength, as a response. 2, informatory, as a double.

NEUTRAL SCORE: an arbitrary score assigned by the director, when regular play is not feasible (Duplicate Bridge).

NEW SUIT: a suit that has not previously been bid in the current auction.

NO-TRUMP: a bid to play without a trump suit. Also, *notrump, no trump.*

NO-TRUMPER: a hand of the proper strength and distribution for a no-trump bid.

N-S, E-W: compass points, used to designate the four players.

NUMERICAL BIDDING: determination of the sufficiency of a bid by its scoring value, not the number of odd tricks or rank of suits, so that four spades (120 points) would overcall five clubs (100 points).

ODD TRICK: a trick won by declarer in excess of six.

OFF, OFFSIDE: (of a card) in such position that finesse against it will lose.

OFFENSIVE STRENGTH: cards that are expected to win tricks at one's own declaration.

OFFICIAL SYSTEM: a contract bridge bidding system introduced in 1931 by Work, Lenz, and others.

OLYMPIAD: four-yearly; applied to certain team, pair and par-point contests conducted by the World Bridge Federation.

ON: destined to be won, as a finesse.

150 ACES: all four aces in one hand.

ONE-OVER-ONE: a bid of one in a suit in response to partner's bid of one in a suit, especially when treated as a forcing bid.

ONSIDE: of a card, in such position that a finesse against it will succeed.

OPEN: 1, make the first bid. 2, make the first lead of a suit. 3, face-up on the table.

OPENER: the player who makes the first bid. Also, *opening hand.*

OPENING BID: the first bid of a deal; a hand strong enough for such a bid.

OPENING LEAD: the first lead of a deal.

OPPONENT: 1, a player of the other side. 2, an adversary of declarer.

ORIGINAL BID: = opening bid.

OVER: 1, to the left of; next to bid or play after. 2, higher than. 3, immediately following.

OVERBID: a bid for more than the player can expect to win.

OVERCALL: 1, a bid or declaration legally sufficient to supersede the last previous bid. 2, such a bid when made by a defender. 3, to make such a bid.

OVER-RUFF, OVERTRUMP: play a trump higher than one previously played to the trick.

OVERTAKE: play a card higher than (a card of partner's that would have won the trick).

OVERTRICK: a trick won by declarer in excess of his contract.

PACK: deck; the 52 cards used in the game.

PAR-POINT: designating a contest in which the hands are pre-arranged and points are awarded for achieving results considered to be correct.

PARTIAL: = part-score. Also, *partial score*.

PARTNER: the player with whom one shares a common score.

PARTNERSHIP: the two players who are partners; a side.

PART-SCORE: a trick score less than is necessary for game.

PASS: a call signifying that the player at that turn does not bid, double, or redouble.

PASS OUT A DEAL: abandon the deal after all players pass.

PATTERN: the division of one hand into four suits, expressed by four numbers, as 4-4-3-2.

PENALTY: 1, points scored for defeating an opponent's contract. 2, a disability imposed on a player or side for a breach of law.

PENALTY CARD: an exposed card that must be played at first legal opportunity.

PENALTY DOUBLE: a double made with the expectation of defeating the adverse bid. Also, *business double*.

PETER: a high-low signal or echo.

PIANOLA: = laydown (Slang).

PICK-UP: the capture of an adverse trump that would otherwise win a trick, by plain-suit leads through the adverse hand; commonly called *coup* or *grand coup*.

PIP: any of the suit symbols on a playing card; ♠, ♡, ◇, ♣.

PITCH COUNT: the 4,3,2,1 point count.

PIVOT: a player who retains his seat while the others move to change partners.

PLAFOND: a precursor of contract bridge, played chiefly in France.

PLAIN SUIT: any suit that is not trumps.

PLAY: 1, contribute a card to a trick. 2, the card played. 3, the period during which the hands are depleted by plays to tricks.

PLAYED CARD: a card legally construed to be played, and so non-retractable.

PLAYING TRICK: a card, not necessarily high or a trump, expected to win a trick in actual play. Also, *winner*.

PLUS VALUES: elements of strength in a hand not directly countable under the system of hand valuation being used.

POINT: a unit of scoring or of hand valuation.

POINT-A-BOARD: (Brit.) board-a-match.

POINT COUNT: a method of valuing a bridge hand by assigning relative numerical values to the high cards.

PORTLAND CLUB: a London club that promulgates contract bridge laws in British countries.

POSITION: the relative seating of the players, a factor of tactical importance.

POSITIVE DOUBLE: = penalty double.

POST-MORTEM: discussion of the merits of the bidding and play of a past deal.

POWERHOUSE: a very strong hand.

PRECISION CLUB SYSTEM: a popular new method employing an artificial opening forcing bid of one club to show a minimum of 16 high-card points. Invented by C. C. Wei and adopted in 1972 by the Italian Blue Team.

PREËMPTIVE BID: a high opening bid, made to shut out adverse competition. Also, *preëmpt.*

PREFER: bid or pass so as to select (one of two suits partner has bid).

PREFERENCE, PREFERENCE BID: a bid by which a player indicates which of his partner's bid suits he prefers.

PREMIUMS: all scores other than for odd tricks.

PREPARED BID: a bid made after ascertain that one can rebid safely over any response by partner.

PROGRESSION: the movement of players or boards from table to table in a duplicate or progressive tournament.

PROGRESSIVE BRIDGE: a form of tournament in which players progress according to their scores, the cards being shuffled and dealt at every table.

PROTECTION: a bid made to reopen the bidding, in the belief that partner has passed a strong hand.

PSYCH: make a psychic bid. Also, *psyche, sike.*

PSYCHIC BID: a bid made without cards to support it, for the purpose of misleading the opponents.

PUPPYFOOT: the club ace; any club.

PUSH: bid for the purpose of inducing (the opponents) to bid higher.

QUICK TRICK: the unit in a system of valuation of high cards.

QUINTRACT: a name given to five-suit bridge.

QUITTED TRICK: a trick that has been turned face down.

RAG: a low or worthless card.

RAISE: bid higher in a denomination previously bid by partner; such a bid.

RANK: the ordinal position of a card in its suit, determining what card wins or beats another; the precedence of suits in bidding.

REBID: any bid by a player who has previously bid; make such a bid.

REBIDDABLE: (of a suit or hand) strong eonugh to bid more than once.

REDEAL: a new deal by the same player, after an irregularity in dealing.

REDOUBLE: a call that has the effect of further increasing certain scoring quantities in case the redoubled bid, previously doubled, becomes the contract.

REËNTRY: a card with which a hand can gain the lead after having lost it.

RENEGE, RENIG: = revoke.

RENOUNCE: fail to follow suit because void of the suit led.

REPLAY DUPLICATE: a form of duplicate bridge for two pairs, on the second play the North-South and East-West pairs exchanging positions. Called also *mnemonic bridge*.

REQUIREMENTS: the minimum holdings deemed systemically necessary for a bid.

RESCUE: take out partner's bid (especially when it is doubled) through fear that he will be defeated.

RESPONDER: the partner of the opening bidder.

RESPONSE: a bid made in reply to a bid or double by partner.

REVERSE: a rebid in a suit higher-ranking than the suit one bid originally.

REVIEW: a restating of all previous calls in the current auction.

REVOKE: play a card of another suit when able to follow suit.

ROCKCRUSHER: a very strong hand.

ROTATION: the order (clockwise) in which cards are dealt and turns to deal, call and play progress from player to player.

ROUND: 1, one series of consecutive turns, one turn to each player, in receiving cards during the deal, bidding, playing, or duty of dealing. 2, each period in a tournament during which there is no movement of players and boards.

ROYALS: 1, = lilies. 2, English name of the fifth suit at one time added to the standard pack.

RUBBER: 1, a series of deals that ends when one side has won two games. 2, a series of four valid deals in four-deal bridge.

RUBBER BRIDGE: the form of bridge in which rubbers are played, as distinguished (usually) from progressive and duplicate bridge.

RUFF: play a trump on a plain-suit lead.

RULE OF EIGHT: a method of valuation, in the Culbertson System, based on the assumption that there are 8 honor-tricks in the four hands.

RULE OF ELEVEN: the fact that when a player leads the fourth-best of a suit the difference of its rank from 11 is the number of higher cards of the suit in the other three hands.

RULE OF TWO AND THREE: the doctrine, in preëmptive bidding or overcalling, that a bidder should not risk going down more than two tricks if vulnerable or three tricks if not vulnerable.

RUN: successively cash all one's winning cards in (a suit).

RUSINOW LEADS: a method, in making the opening lead, whereby the lower of touching honors is led: K from A-K, Q from K-Q, J from Q-J, 10 from J-10; introduced by Sydney Rusinow.

SACRIFICE BID: a bid made without expectation of fulfilling the contract, to prevent the opponents from assuming the contract.

SAFETY PLAY: a play that unnecessarily surrenders or risks a possible winning trick because by such play the number of tricks to be lost can be limited.

SANDBAG: = trap.

SCISSORS COUP: a loser-on-loser play.

SCORE: 1, the accumulated total of points won by each player. 2, scoresheet. 3, mark or record the score.

SCOREPAD: a tablet of sheets of paper printed for convenience in scoring.

SCORESHEET: a printed sheet for keeping score.

SCORING TABLE: a summary, in tabular form, of the laws governing scoring.

SCRAMBLED MITCHELL: a Mitchell movement in which the original North-South and East-West pairs exchange compass positions midway of the game, producing a single winner.

SECOND HAND: the second player in turn to call or play.

SECTION: in a tournament, a group of tables playing as a unit.

SEEDING: in a tournament, the placement of the strongest players in different sections or brackets.

SEMI-TWO-SUITER: a hand with one suit of four cards and another, longer suit.

SENIOR: the adversary who leads to the first trick.

SEQUENCE: two or more cards of adjacent rank, as 8-7.

SET: defeat the contract; defeated.

SET MATCH: rubber bridge play with unchanging partnerships. Also *match game*.

SEWED IN: unable to exit.

SHADE: reduce (the requirements) prescribed for a bid or double.

SHAPE: distribution (of a hand); pattern. (Chiefly British.)

SHIFT: = takeout.

SHORT CLUB: the bidding of a two- or three-card club suit to avoid opening a four-card major or to avoid a difficult rebidding problem.

SHORT SUIT: a suit of two or fewer cards.

SHOW: indicate (a certain holding) to partner, by means of a bid or double.

SHUT-OUT: a high bid made to prevent the opponents from bidding cheaply.

SIDE: a partnership.

SIDE SUIT: a suit, especially a long suit, other than trump.

SIGNAL: any convention of play whereby defenders properly give each other information.

SIGN-OFF: a bid that asks partner to pass or to close the auction as soon as possible.

SIMPLE HONORS: the score of 30 for three trump honors held by one side (Auction Bridge).

SIMS, P. HAL (1884–1949):   a leading card player and writer on contract bridge.

SINGLETON: an original holding of one card in a suit.

SKIP BID: 1, = jump bid. 2, = preëmptive bid.

SLAM: the winning of all or all but one of the tricks by one player or side: grand slam, thirteen tricks; little slam, or small slam, twelve tricks.

SLOW PASS: a pass following a marked hesitation, considered unethical if done intentionally because partner may infer values almost justifying a bid.

SLUFF, SLOUGH: = discard.

SMOTHER PLAY: the pick-up of a guarded high trump by an unguarded master trump.

SNEAK: the lead of a plain-suit singleton.

SOLID SUIT: 1, a suit holding composed all of winning cards. 2, a suit that can be established by straight leads, as Q-J-10-9-8.

SOS REDOUBLE: a redouble, made when one's bid has been doubled, to ask partner to take out in his best suit.

SPLIT: play, second hand, one of (equal honors), as K-Q or Q-J.

SPREAD: 1, expose (one's hand) as in putting down the dummy or making a claim. 2, = laydown.

SQUEEZE: lead a suit that compels (adverse hands) to discard; an endplay based on this principle.

STIFF: unguarded; alone (Slang).

STILL PACK: the pack temporarily out of use, when two packs are used alternately.

STOPPER: a holding with which a hand can eventually win a trick against adverse leads of the suit.

STRIP: exhaust the cards of a suit in one or more hands, in preparation for an endplay.

SUFFICIENT BID: a bid that is high enough legally to supersede the last previous bid.

SUIT: 1, any of the four sets of thirteen cards each in the standard pack: spades, hearts, diamonds, clubs. 2, = biddable suit.

SUIT-PREFERENCE SIGNAL: a defenders' signal in play, devised by Hy Lavinthal, whereby the relative rank of a card played or discarded calls for the higher or lower of the available suits other than trumps.

SUPPORT: 1, raise. 2, cards that may be of assistance to partner.

SWINGS: 1, cards in unbroken sequence from the top of the suit down. 2, differences of scores on the same board played at various tables (Duplicate Bridge).

SWISS CONVENTION: a method of responding to a major-suit one-bid with 4 ♣ to show two aces and 4 ◇ to show three aces, plus trump support.

SWITCH: lead a different suit from the one led by oneself or one's partner at the last opportunity.

SYSTEM: a series of agreements between partners as to tactical procedure in various bidding situations.

TABLE: 1, the group of players who compete together, including both active and inactive. 2, = dummy.

TAKEOUT: the bid of a different denomination from that bid by partner.

TAKEOUT DOUBLE: = informatory double.

TEAM: in tournament bridge, four or more players competing as a unit.

TENACE: a combination of high cards, not in sequence.

THIRD HAND: the player third in turn to call on the first round or to play to a trick.

THREAT CARD: a card that may be established by a squeeze.

THREE-NO-TRUMP FORCING RESPONSE: a bid that replaces the forcing double raise by responder. Used by players employing limit double raises.

THROW-IN: an endplay in which an opponent is forced into the lead, to compel him to lead to his disadvantage.

TOP: 1, be the highest card of (a suit or holding). 2, = cover.

TOP OF NOTHING: an opening lead of the highest of three low cards, as the eight from 8-5-2.

TOTAL-POINT SCORING: a method of scoring in duplicate bridge in which the net scores of each pair on each board are totaled and the pair or team having the highest net score is the winner.

TOUCHING: in sequence, as K-Q (touching cards) or ♠-♡ (touching suits).

TOURNAMENT: a contest among a large number of entrants to determine a winner, often with the element of luck eliminated so far as possible.

TOWIE: a form of contract bridge with three active players and one or more other players who participate in the scoring of every deal.

TRANCE: = huddle. (British Slang.)

TRAP: withhold action on a good hand, to lure an opponent into an overbid.

TRAY: = duplicate board.

TREY: any three-spot.

TRICK: a batch of cards formed during the play by the contribution of one card from each hand.

TRICK SCORE: points earned by declarer for odd tricks. Also, *trick points*.

TRUMP: 1, a privileged card or suit, the privilege being that in the current deal every such card ranks higher than any plain (= nontrump) card. 2, play a trump on the lead of a plain suit.

TRUMP ECHO, TRUMP SIGNAL: a high-low with trumps, indicating possession of at least one more trump and (usually) some prospect of ruffing with it.

TRUMP SQUEEZE: a crisscross squeeze in which a trump functions as the master card of one of the suits.

TURN: a player's opportunity, in due rotation, to deal, bid, play, etc.

TWO-BID: an opening bid of two in a suit, when used as a game-forcing bid.

TWO-CLUB SYSTEM: 1, use of an opening two-club bid as an artificial (and the only) game-forcing opening bid. 2, = Stayman convention.

TWO-DEMAND, TWO-COMMAND: the forcing two-bid.

TWO NO-TRUMP AS LIMIT RAISE: a bid employed over a takeout double announcing a strong limit raise, where an immediate jump in partner's suit would be preëmptive and weaker in high card strength.

TWO-SUITER: a hand containing two five-card or longer suits.

TWO-WAY: (of a bid) showing sometimes a strong and sometimes a weak hand.

UNBALANCED HAND: a hand that contains a singleton or void.

UNBLOCK: avoid a block, by unnecessarily cashing high cards, by overtaking, or by discarding cards that block the suit.

UNDER: 1, to the right of; required to bid, play or be played next before. 2, lower than.

UNDERBID: a bid of fewer tricks than one can most profitably bid for.

UNDERPLAY: lead or follow suit with a lower card when holding a higher card; hold up; refuse to cover.

UNDERRUFF: play a lower trump on a trick to which another player has played a higher trump.

UNDERTRICK: a trick by which declarer falls short of his contract.

UNDERTRUMP: = underruff.

UNITED STATES BRIDGE ASSOCIATION: a national association of bridge players in the U.S., founded 1933, in 1937 merged with the American Bridge League to form the American Contract Bridge League.

UP: exposed; face up.

UPPERCUT: ruff with an unnecessarily high trump, to force out an opponent's higher trump.

VANDERBILT, HAROLD S. (1884–   ): bridge authority who introduced contract bridge.

VANDERBILT CLUB: a bidding system employing an opening artificial one-club bid to show a strong hand, with an artificial one-diamond response to show weakness.

VANDERBILT CUP: 1, a trophy donated by Harold S. Vanderbilt, 1928, for the U. S. open knockout team championship, played for annually. 2, a trophy given by the same donor in 1960 for the world team championship, played for each four years.

VIENNA COUP: a squeeze in which a high card must be cashed, temporarily establishing an opponent's card that the opponent will later lose by being squeezed.

VIENNA SYSTEM: a bidding system employing an artificial one-club bid as a weak opening bid.

VINT: a Russian game similar to bridge.

VOID: a holding of no cards in a suit.

VULNERABLE: said of a side having won a game toward rubber.

WEI, C. C. Chinese-born American oil tanker owner and operator; inventor of the Precision Club system.

WHIST: the basic game of the family of card games that includes bridge.

WHIST CLUB OF NEW YORK: a men's club that from 1909 to 1948 promulgated laws of auction and contract bridge in the United States.

WHITEHEAD, WILBUR C.: author of books on auction bridge, died 1931.

WINNER: 1, a card that wins a trick. 2, = playing trick.

WITHOUT: no-trump.

WORK, MILTON C. (1864–1934): the principle authority on auction bridge.

WORK COUNT: the 4,3,2,1 point count.

X: a symbol representing an indifferent low card, as ♡ K x, meaning the heart king accompanied by any card lower than the ten.

YARBOROUGH: a hand containing no card higher than a nine.

YOUNGER: the leader's partner.

CONTRACT BRIDGE SCORING TABLE

TRICK SCORE

Scored below the line by declarer's side, if the contract is fulfilled:

IF TRUMPS ARE	♣	♦	♥	♠
For each trick over six bid and made				
Undoubled	20	20	30	30
Doubled	40	40	60	60
Redoubled	80	80	120	120

AT A NO-TRUMP CONTRACT	UNDOUBLED	DOUBLED	REDOUBLED
For the first trick over six, bid and made	40	80	160
For each additional trick over six, bid and made	30	60	120

The first side to score 100 points below the line, in one or more deals, wins a GAME. When a game is won, both sides start without trick score toward the next game. The first side to win two games wins the RUBBER.

PREMIUM SCORE

Scored above the line by declarer's side:

RUBBER, GAME, PART-SCORE, CONTRACT FULFILLED

For winning the RUBBER, if opponents have won no game	700
For winning the RUBBER, if opponents have won one game	500
UNFINISHED RUBBER—for having won one game	300
—for having the only part-score (or scores)	50
For making any DOUBLED or REDOUBLED CONTRACT	50

SLAMS

For making a SLAM	NOT VULNERABLE	VULNERABLE
Small Slam (12 tricks) bid and made	500	750
Grand Slam (all 13 tricks) bid and made	1000	1500

OVERTRICKS

For each OVERTRICK (tricks made in excess of contract)	NOT VULNERABLE	VULNERABLE
Undoubled	Trick value	Trick value
Doubled	100	200
Redoubled	200	400

HONORS

Scored above the line by either side:

For holding four of the five trump HONORS (A, K, Q, J, 10) in one hand	100
For holding all five trump HONORS (A, K, Q, J, 10) in one hand	150
For holding all four ACES in one hand at a no-trump contract	150

UNDERTRICK PENALTIES

For tricks by which declarer fails to fulfill the contract; scored above the line by declarer's opponents if contract is not fulfilled:

NOT VULNERABLE	UNDOUBLED	DOUBLED	REDOUBLED
For first undertrick	50	100	200
For each additional undertrick	50	200	400

VULNERABLE	UNDOUBLED	DOUBLED	REDOUBLED
For first undertrick	100	200	400
For each additional undertrick	100	300	600